CHRISTIAN NATIONALISM VS GLOBAL JESUS

ANDREW FRASER

CHRISTIAN NATIONALISM vs GLOBAL JESUS

PROJECTS OF PEOPLEHOOD FROM BIBLICAL ISRAEL TO THE COLLAPSE OF BRITISH PATRIOTISM

ARKTOS
LONDON 2025

ARKTOS

🌐 Arktos.com   fb.com/Arktos   arktosmedia   arktosjournal

Copyright © 2025 by Arktos Media Ltd.

All rights reserved. No part of this book may be reproduced or utilised in any form or by any means (whether electronic or mechanical), including photocopying, recording or by any information storage and retrieval system, without permission in writing from the publisher.

ISBN
978-1-917646-14-7 (Paperback)
978-1-917646-15-4 (Hardback)
978-1-917646-16-1 (Ebook)

Editing
Constantin von Hoffmeister

Cover & Layout
Tor Westman

CONTENTS

Preface ix

❧

INTRODUCTION
Our Own Worst Enemy? Anglo-Protestant Theology, British Race
Patriotism, and the European Civil War 1

> In the nineteenth century British/Anglo-Saxon race patriotism was a commonplace feature of Anglo-Protestant culture. We begin by examining why and how the twentieth century "European civil war" led contemporary Anglo-Protestant churches to dismiss the English ancestry and white British ethnicity of most of their communicants as a merely implicit and contingent (if not downright unmentionable) circumstance of no theological significance.

PART ONE
Creedal Christianity: Theological Origins of the Present Crisis

1. Sweet Dreams of Christian Nationalism (But What About the Protestant Deformation, Globalist Churches, and Jewish Political Theology?) 67

> This review essay discusses *The Case for Christian Nationalism* (Canon Press, 2022) by Stephen Wolfe. The author identifies real problems with post-Christian societies. One wonders, however, why Wolfe takes such pains to deny that he is a "kinist," much less a "racist." Indeed, he seems to find it extraordinarily difficult to distinguish between "Christian nations" and "Christian states."

2. Religion, Race, and Ethnicity in Greco-Roman Antiquity:New Perspectives on The Lordship of Jesus, Judaism, and the "Truthiness" of Christianity 101

> We take a deeper, historical dive into the fundamental presuppositions of Wolfe's Christian nationalism. He asserts that "Jesus is Lord" and "Christianity is the true

religion." In what sense, are those statements "true"? Were Jesus and Paul really the founders of a new religion? Was the "resurrection" of Jesus Christ a unique historical event or a mimetic manifestation of a common Greco-Roman literary trope?

3. Metanarrative Collapse: Has the Christian Cosmology Invented by Augustine of Hippo Stood the Test of Time?. 161

Augustine of Hippo rewrote a biblical narrative originally conceived as a Hebrew ethnonational epic. This chapter examines how Augustine's Hellenistic hermeneutic laid the cosmological foundation for Western Christendom. We also consider the efforts of contemporary, neo-Augustinian Radical Orthodoxy to restore that crumbling edifice.

4. Global Jesus Versus National Jesus: The Political Hermeneutics of Resurrection. 183

The ongoing quest for the "true" meaning of Christ's crucifixion and resurrection cannot be separated from the central political conflict of our time: globalism versus nationalism. Were Jesus and Paul wrong in their expectation that the "resurrection of the body" would occur in the lifetime of their followers, at the "end of the age"? How did they conceive the nature of that resurrected "body"? Was it to appear as the holy spirit breathing life into the dry bones of Old Testament Israel, as lamented in Ezekiel 37:4–7? Or did they envisage individual, physical ("glorified"?) bodies emerging from their graves in the far distant future everywhere in the world?

PART TWO

Did Anglo-Saxon Christendom Replicate the "Project of Peoplehood" Posited by the Hebrew Bible?

5. Adam and Eve in Torah: The Lost World of Covenantal Ethnotheology 211

Despite their differences modern biblical literalists and scholarly literary critics alike abstract Adam and Eve from their place in the particularistic ethnotheology of national Israel according to the flesh. Both camps view Adam and Eve, whether biologically or mythically, literally or figuratively, as ancestors or representatives of Everyman and Everywoman. A better interpretation of Genesis 1-3 conceives the pair as characters in the foundation myth of Old Covenant Israel.

6. Exodus 34: Covenantal Ethnotheology and the (Re-)Birth of the First Holy Nation 223

In Exodus 34 God enters into the everyday life of Israel according to the flesh via the channel of grace embodied in Mosaic authority. Having received the Mosaic law, national Israel is thereby empowered to serve as the spiritual womb of the living God, the one to come in an as-yet far-distant future. The modern functionalist interpretation of Exodus 34 holds that covenantal ethnotheology merely reflects the primitive, particularistic, and narrowly ethnocentric character of ancient Israelite religion. This approach downplays the problem in practical theology posed by the story: the national religion lacked a secure cultic foundation. This has been no less a problem for early medieval Angelcynns and contemporary Anglo-Protestants. How can we preserve a Christian nation if the Presence of the Lord is no longer with *us*?

7. Making *Angelcynns*: How Alfred the Great Responded to the Viking Invasions of Wessex. 237
   This essay highlights the theopolitical significance of the Anglo-Saxon king, Alfred the Great. His reign (871–899) brought to fruition the project to establish an Anglo-Saxon Christendom begun by the Venerable Bede in the eighth century. The British-descended peoples of the modern Anglosphere would do well to reclaim Alfred's legacy.

8. Sanctifying the Norman Yoke: William the Conqueror, the *Angelcynn* Church and the Papal Revolution 247
   The Norman Conquest brought Anglo-Saxon Christendom to an end. William the Conqueror was a fellow traveller of the Papal Revolution of the late eleventh century. Earth-hugging Saxon churches gave way to the spires of Gothic cathedrals pointing to an empty sky. The "Romanization" of Alfred's *Angelcynn* church signalled an Age of Disincarnation, thus splitting the secular from the spiritual realm.

9. A Choice Not an Echo: Biblical Israel as Mythic Model for Early Anglo-Saxon Christendom. 259
   It seems that the Old English church of the Anglo-Saxon era reflected what scholars describe as "the Germanization of early medieval Christianity." It has also been said that the Hebrew Bible was the product of a "project of peoplehood." This chapter considers whether the Hebrew Bible served as a model for the creation of the Anglo-Saxon Christendom.

PART THREE

Beyond Creedal Christianity: Neo-Angelcynn Political Theology versus Globalist Churches and the Transnational Corporate State

10. Who are We? Restoring the Ethnoreligious Dimensions of WASP Identity in the Spiritual Wastelands of the Anglosphere 305
    The world-rejecting cosmology of the church in the Mediterranean world of the late Roman Empire stood in opposition to the world-accepting character of Germanic Christianity. Nevertheless, both traditions presupposed the universal reign of Lord Jesus. Christian nationalism therefore remains, for us, something of an oxymoron. Accordingly, in the Anglosphere at least, the postmodern restoration of Christian nationhood should be inspired by a neo-*Angelcynn* theopolitics best organized around four "orienting concepts": process theism, preterism, kinism, and royalism.

11. Was Early New South Wales (1788–1850) a "Christian Community"? . .341
    Anglo-Protestant churches in England (both the established Church of England and its dissenting offshoots) aimed to perpetuate themselves by reinforcing cultural ties between the mother country and the British settler colonies in Australia and elsewhere. Unfortunately, those cultural ties were not always conducive to the creation of a Christian community, either "at home" or in early New South Wales.

12. The White Australia Policy in Retrospect: Racism or Realism? 351
   The White Australia Policy was inaugurated in 1901 at the high-water mark of British race patriotism. This review essay discusses two books, one on the adoption of the WAP, the other on its repeal. Both works view the policy from the perspective of a racial egalitarianism that flies in the face of the intractable reality of racial differences presupposed by the founding fathers of Federation in Australia.

13. Puritans in Babylon: The Impact of Global Christianity on Sydney Anglicans 383
   In the brave new world of "global Christianity," the largest Christian communities are now to be found in the overwhelmingly non-white realm of the so-called "global south." This chapter deals with the response of the evangelical, low-church Anglican diocese of Sydney to the movements that demand conformity to the manifold manifestations of the progressive Cult of the Other.

14. Anglo-Republicanism and the Rebirth of British History: Why Virtuous WASPs Must Challenge the Corrupt Globalist Plutocracy Misgoverning the Anglosphere. 403
   The rise of a globalist system, presided over by the managerial elites of transnational corporate capitalism, has transformed the British-descended citizenry of once-proudly "Anglo-Saxon countries" into random collections of stateless people. This chapter explores the relevance of the Anglo-American republican tradition to a neo-Angelcynn reformation of civil society, outside and apart from the state, throughout the Anglosphere

15. Monarchs and Miracles: Australia's Need for a Patriot King 465
   The eighteenth-century Country Party politician, Viscount Bolingbroke, maintained that only the influence of a Patriot King ("the most uncommon of all phenomena in the physical or moral world") could draw despotic governments and their corrupted peoples back to the original principles of liberty that had their origins in the ancient British constitution. The issue here is whether (and how) Bolingbroke's idea of a Patriot King can be transposed into our own age of woke capital and mass migration to rescue stateless Anglos, now stranded in the (residually) British dominions of the Crown throughout the Anglosphere.

Preface

THIS BOOK sheds much-needed light on contemporary controversies surrounding the seemingly oxymoronic phenomenon of "Christian nationalism," past, present, and future, as problem and as solution.

Part One explores the ostensibly biblical foundations of Christian nationalism, the first-century Jesus movement, and the early Christian church in Greco-Roman antiquity. Part Two examines the extent to which the rise and fall of early medieval Anglo-Saxon Christendom was influenced by the "project of peoplehood" reflected in the Hebrew Bible. In Part Three, the focus shifts to a modern history culminating in the post-Christian collapse of British race patriotism.

Does the contemporary crisis of Anglo-Protestant political theology stem from a failure to recognize in the historical Jesus the mythic model for the miraculous appearance of a Patriot King? The religious, political, and civil institutions of the Anglosphere now oversee the deliberate degeneration of historic Anglo cultures into mere economic zones, populated by rootless, shifting masses of morally debased monads.

Faithful Anglo-Protestants could spark the reformation of the entire Anglosphere by labouring to bring the sweet dream of a Patriot King down to earth. Anglo-American evangelical Protestants are, therefore, a primary target for this book's message. The spiritual reformation of the Anglosphere is a matter of geopolitical theology. Anglo-American Protestants need to understand themselves as a people standing outside and apart from the state apparatus of the global

American empire. In other words, they must mentally nullify the 1776 Declaration of Independence, embracing instead their ancestral British race patriotism in solidarity with their co-ethnics in the United Kingdom, Australia, Canada, and New Zealand still owing allegiance to the Crown.

I was born a British subject before the creation of Australian or Canadian citizenship, at a time when Anglo-Saxons still counted as one of Canada's two "founding races." My intellectual development has been much influenced by what historian C. P. Champion describes as *The Strange Demise of British Canada*. This theme figured largely in my earlier work.

Accordingly, this book was written from an Anglo-Identitarian perspective. My hope is that the flickering flame of pan-British race patriotism will be rekindled by a reformed, neo-*Angelcynn* (Old English for "kin of the Angles") church. Such a reformation would provide a desperately needed theopolitical alternative to the hegemonic, universalist model of creedal Christianity. Nowadays, even American Christian nationalism routinely invokes the deracinated, disembodied Lordship of global Jesus as its heavenly warrant.

For centuries, Anglo-Protestant churches have been famous for sterile struggles between doctrinal orthodoxy and damnable heresy. For all practical purposes, however, mainline Anglo-Protestantism has become indistinguishable from the revolutionary humanism driving the globalist regimes misgoverning the Anglosphere.

From its origins in Greco-Roman antiquity, Christianity was beset by a persistent tension between universalism and particularism. This was manifested first in an opposition between the Neo-platonic image of the cosmic Christ who died on the Cross to atone for the sins of all mankind and the Jewish origins story of a national Messiah come to save "the lost sheep of Israel."

The deeply rooted pull of particularistic ethnic identities was not easy to escape. Even the early Christian church of the ancient Mediterranean world found it difficult to resist the impulse to identify themselves as a particular "third race," neither Greek nor Jew.

Even so, the orthodox Augustinian worldview eventually achieved doctrinal hegemony. This dualistic vision posited the existence of an eternal City of God, above and beyond the temporal world inhabited by the mortal City of Man. That other-worldly cosmology met serious resistance once Christian missionaries encountered the stubborn ethnic particularism of the Germanic tribes in northwestern Europe.

There, the world-rejecting *orthodoxy* of creedal Christianity was often replaced by *orthopraxy* (*i.e.*, the adoption of Christian rituals and practices by pagan converts). Roman Catholic theology's other-worldly doctrines were a tougher sell among Germans and Anglo-Saxons. By and large, they accepted their world as it was, valuing the warrior virtues of heroism far above Christian humility.

Fast-forward to our own postwar world. Following the crushing defeat of German ethnonationalism in 1945, the global Jesus of Anglo-Protestant theology achieved virtually uncontested hegemony. Today, almost all mainstream Anglo-Protestants reject even the mildest manifestations of ethnic particularism as tantamount to racism. Indeed, the advocacy of "Christian nationalism" is denounced regularly from the pulpits of mainline Anglo-Protestant churches in the United States.

One might imagine that the established Church of England would accept Christian nationalism as a matter of course. But the non-negotiable commitment of the English church to global Anglicanism makes that impossible. As for the Anglican leadership in the former British dominions such as Australia, Canada, and New Zealand, they, too, want nothing more than to escape from their traditional but deplorable "Anglo-Saxon captivity."

Even much-reviled Christian nationalists in the USA are held hostage by global Jesus, most obviously in the otherwise groundbreaking work of Stephen Wolfe. Wolfe's book on *The Case for Christian Nationalism* (Canon Press, 2022) recently unleashed a widespread, heated debate on the topic. But, true to form, Wolfe's brand of Christian nationalism affirms that the telos of human history will be realized only when the primary allegiance of all nations is to King Jesus.

Still, it remains to be seen how a distinctively white Anglo-Saxon Protestant ethnoreligious identity can be squared with the ahistorical, universalist reign of Lord Jesus. Wolfe continues to downplay, when not outright denying, the intractably biocultural dimension of Anglo-Saxon identity. He suggests, for example, that even black men such as Booker T. Washington and Justice Clarence Thomas (who happens to be a devout Catholic) have been assimilated into the Anglo-Protestant ethnonation.

By contrast, my thesis is that an exclusive ecclesiastical allegiance to a generic cosmic Christ reduces the distinctive character of every earthly ethnoreligious identity to mere *adiaphora* (*i.e.*, things inessential in the eyes of the church). The rebirth of Anglo-Protestantism requires an ethnoreligious foundation.

The theological refusal to reflect on the ethnonational identity of the historical Jesus must be recognized as the outdated product of historically *Romanised* ecclesiastical establishments, Protestant and Catholic alike. My argument, therefore, is that Anglo-Saxon Christianity should be re-Germanized by re-imagining the *Angelcynn* church of Alfred the Great to fit the needs of our own age.

The primary constituency for such a re-Germanized Christian nationalism is to be found among Anglo-Protestants. Unfortunately, the straightforward narrative of a national Jesus come to save the "lost sheep" of biblical Israel is glossed over in most Anglo-Protestant churches. Instead, the still-future Second Coming of global Jesus remains the bedrock presupposition of Anglo-Protestant theology, however well-grounded "national Jesus," may be in biblical exegesis or historical reality.

Most likely created between the fifth and second centuries BC, the Hebrew Bible presented a poignant and powerful *national* narrative. Conceived by Judean scribes as a pedagogic tool, that biblical narrative inspired the "project of peoplehood" presupposed by the Jesus movement of the first century AD.

Jesus was received by many of his co-ethnics as the Jewish Messiah. But he also became the Hellenic Christ. Jesus Christ was the King of a resurrected Israel for Jews such as Paul and, as such, founded a "third race" of early Christians.

That was then; this is now.

Anglo-Protestants desperately need to develop folkish variants of the Christian tradition. I suggest that the focus of Anglo-Protestantism should be shifted away from its historic preoccupation with personal salvation in the world to come. Anglos now require a sense of rootedness in networks of ethnoreligious communities in which shared ancestry matters as much if not more than doctrinal purity. Colonial and antebellum New England provided many useful examples of churches as godly little republics as well as clear warnings pointing to the dangers of doctrinaire religion. But Jewish synagogues and Islamic mosques offer countless other non-Christian examples of ethnoreligious communities far more productive of in-group solidarity (aka social capital).

An Anglo ethno-religion is both the institutional precondition and moral foundation for the creation of socially cohesive communities. Anglo-Protestant churches must become the ethnoreligious heart of breakaway parallel societies capable of producing healthy, happy, and morally upright families, together with British-descended counter-elites set in opposition to the irresponsible corporate plutocracy now misgoverning the Anglosphere.

It may be that Anglo-Protestants will someday receive as King a Christ of their own. But, as Don K. Preston remarks, he is unlikely to return as a 5'5" Jewish man whose name is Jesus. My book concludes, therefore, with a discussion of what might produce the miraculous appearance of a such a Patriot King, were he to become incarnate in Australia and the other British dominions.

In short, my book offers a sympathetic but penetrating critique of the hitherto unchallenged hegemony of global Jesus within the Anglo-Protestant epicentre of the emergent Christian nationalist movement.

My hope is to persuade Christian nationalists that their predominantly Anglo-Protestant movement, like the first-century Jesus movement, can and should embrace, explicitly, its ethnoreligious character outside and apart from the state.

At the same time, a Christian nationalism grounded in *orthopraxis* rather than strait-laced *orthodoxy* may attract secular, culturally Christian traditionalists. While maintaining their resistance to unconditional *belief* in the established Christian creeds and confessions, such people are more likely to be receptive to a "modernized" folk religion in which the church serves, first and foremost, as a teacher of morality.

In effect, therefore, the book advocates a return to the nineteenth century Broad Church movement in the Church of England pioneered by men such as Sir John Robert Seeley. Younger Anglo-Protestants in particular, along with their agnostic contemporaries, are having their future stolen from them by a corporatist regime destroying every institution that could provide access to stable, prosperous, middle-class family lives of purpose and meaning.

Their rising discontent could find an outlet in an Anglo-Identitarian Christian movement challenging those who currently manage and control evangelical Protestantism in the USA: the power centre that Christian nationalists call "Big Eva." This book aims to provide such an oppositional movement with intellectual ammunition as well as insight into the weaknesses of a Christian nationalism that places the mythology of global Jesus over loyalty to co-ethnics.

In the genesis of this book, I incurred a great debt of gratitude to both Kevin Lamb and Kevin MacDonald, the two editors of *The Occidental Quarterly* who first enabled most of the essays appearing herein to see the light of day. I am also grateful to a friend (who prefers to remain anonymous) who persuaded the editors of *Anglican Tradition* to accept three of the short pieces republished here. The Introduction, and Chapters 9 and 10, were written for this volume.

INTRODUCTION

Our Own Worst Enemy? Anglo-Protestant Theology, British Race Patriotism, and the European Civil War

Anglophobia and the WASP Question

Anglophobia: The Unrecognised Hatred is a short book published in 2022, written by two Anglo-Australians, Harry Richardson, and Frank Salter (President, and former President, respectively, of the British Australian Community). The authors use the term "Anglo" to denote "people descended from the indigenous population of the British Isles in Australia and overseas as well as those who have assimilated into those populations" from kindred ethnicities, particularly those originating from northwestern Europe. They define "Anglophobia" as a form of hateful discrimination analogous to homophobia, Islamophobia, transphobia, and so on. Specifically, they identify Anglophobia as "hostility towards, aversion to, or discrimination against Anglo people" "by non-Anglos, other white ethnicities, and by Anglos themselves."[1]

According to Richardson and Salter, Anglophobia is a major driving force behind the sprawling legal apparatus designed by the corporate welfare state to prevent and/or penalize instances of discrimination against people on grounds of race, colour, sex, social status, age, or

---

[1] Harry Richardson and Frank Salter, *Anglophobia: The Unrecognised Hatred* (Sydney: Social Technologies, 2022), 5.

sexual preference. Such discrimination allegedly arises out of "unjust or prejudicial distinctions." The primary meaning of discrimination, according to the OED, denotes nothing more controversial than "the action, or an act of discriminating or distinguishing; the fact or condition of being discriminated or distinguished; a distinction made." Indeed, the first example of "perfect Discrimination" given in the OED is that "between the Good and Bad." To treat as unlawful the act of distinguishing between persons or groups on the grounds of race, sex, age, and so on necessarily, therefore, overrode, *inter alia*, the common law freedom of association. The current regime holds that invidious distinctions drawn between members of different races, sexes, or other social groups are inherently illegitimate in a multicultural society. All individuals and groups are, by legislative or administrative fiat, presumed to be equal; thus, observable differences (*e.g.*, in behaviour, temperament, or intelligence) between them must be the result, either of irrational prejudice, on the one hand, or unjust privilege on the other.

Not surprisingly, therefore, Anglos are routinely vilified as the beneficiaries of the "white privilege" rooted in the "structural racism [which] disadvantages non-whites socially and economically in Anglo or white societies." In addition, Anglos are "considered guilty of holding 'white supremacist' beliefs" or harbouring other equally irrational prejudices even when they simply express or advocate "on behalf of white or Anglo identity." Anglos, in short, are typically perceived and treated as perpetrators and never as victims of unlawful hostile discrimination. Yet the fact is that they are subject not just to vilification and hostile discrimination but also to "physical attacks against individuals motivated by hostility towards their Anglo identity."[2]

All people, not just Anglos, routinely observe and distinguish between what they deem to be good and bad patterns of behaviour, desirable as against undesirable personality traits, or high versus low

---

2   *Ibid.*, 7–9.

intelligence among members of our own and other groups. Why, then, should one attribute the vilification, hostile discrimination, and violence experienced by Anglos to an irrational "phobia" analogous to supposed "mental disorders" such as Islamophobia, homophobia, and the like invented by woke propagandists? A "phobia," according to the OED, is "an abnormal fear or dread aroused by a particular object or circumstance." Anti-racists, of course, recklessly diagnose every manifestation of Anglo resistance (even such feeble opposition as there has been) to mass immigration as the product either of a "phobia" triggered by migrant groups such as Muslims, or the generalized xenophobia, racism, as well the other irrational prejudices to which white Europeans are supposedly prone. It matters not that a perfectly rational case can and has been made historically for the restriction of immigration into the Anglosphere to people of European descent.[3] Similarly, it is simply slanderous to label as irrational "homophobia" any principled opposition to ongoing efforts by homosexual lobbies to legalize, first, sodomy and pride marches, then same-sex marriage, followed by drag queen story hours, the current trans-sexual revolution, and who knows what other forms of sexual deviancy in the future.

Nor is there any need to invoke an allegedly analogous Anglo*phobia* to explain the vilification, hostile discrimination, or violence suffered by Anglos at the hands of other ethnic groups. Jews, Muslims, Chinese, Indians, sub-Saharan Africans, and Pacific Islanders are not driven to contest Anglo hegemony everywhere in the Anglosphere by irrational fears or a superstitious dread before the mythic bogeyman of "white supremacism." Each of those groups is much more proudly and publicly ethnocentric than atomized Anglos reared in a highly individualistic culture. All these migrant groups compete with majority WASP cultures for space, status, power, and resources. At times, such ethnic rivalry may be relatively friendly. But, once inter-ethnic competition

---

3   See chapter 12.

reaches a certain pitch, mere rivalry readily becomes (open or concealed) enmity towards WASPs.

Indeed, as Richardson and Salter themselves demonstrate, the multiculturalist regime incentivizes vilification of and hostile discrimination against Anglos while excusing or minimizing penalties for physical attacks on Anglo persons and property. Therefore, it is perfectly normal for ethnic groups hostile to Anglos to use any means, fair or foul, to promote their own identitarian interests. Calculated anti-white propaganda and legalized harassment represent tactical manoeuvres by a ruling class seeking to reinforce its political domination. Atop the social pyramid, globalist elites mobilize aggrieved, low-status minorities against Anglo middle-classes. Already intense displays of enmity towards Anglos sometimes escalate into open-source, low-level ethnic warfare. As the Great Replacement accelerates, Anglos around the world can expect ever-increasing levels of welfare parasitism, crime, and violence from alien newcomers, leading to "white flight" in search of ever-scarcer diversity-free "safe spaces." Echoing South African experience, episodes of organized "Anglocide" may lie in the medium-term future of the Anglosphere.

When analyzing the behaviour of minority racial, ethnic, and religious groups in multicultural mass societies, the concept of Anglophobia is of limited utility. The language of abnormal psychology presupposes the existence of civilized norms of behaviour in a homogeneous, high-trust Anglo-Saxon social order. In racially diverse, low-trust societies, conflict and antagonism are the norm. In such a context, to understand the animus towards Anglos found among many racial, ethnic, or lifestyle minorities, we probably need a neologism such as *Anglodium* (i.e., Anglo + odium; Latin suffix denoting hatred, ill-will, enmity).[4] Far from being averse to contact with

---

4 Admittedly, "Anglodium" may sound a bit strange at first. But if one applies its suffix to the various Woke phobias, it takes on a certain catchy, perhaps even rhythmic character, *viz.*, Islamodium, homodium, transodium, and so on. The adjectival/adverbial form is even easier on the ear, as with Anglodius,

Anglos, hundreds of millions of non-whites now regard free access to British-descended (and, more broadly, white) societies as an inalienable human right. They are also aware that historic Anglo hegemony is now a paper tiger. Indeed, in the upper reaches of the social hierarchy, WASP elites are facilitating their own demographic displacement by high IQ minorities such as Jews, Chinese, and Indians.

For that very reason, however, the social psychology of Anglophobia remains relevant to the present crisis. While Jewish, Muslim, Negro, or Chinese Anglophobias are little more than verbal phantoms, *Anglo-Saxon* Anglophobia is a very real and debilitating spiritual disorder among members of what I have called "the invisible race" of WASPs.[5] As a matter of ethnography, the British-descended peoples of the Anglosphere should be described as WASPs rather than Anglos. Strictly speaking, "Anglos" are not always an ethnic or racial group. In Canada, for example, the term "Anglo" has acquired a one-dimensional, predominantly linguistic meaning. This is largely because the several hundred thousand English-speakers ethnically cleansed from Quebec over the decades since the so-called quiet revolution of the 1960s are typically labelled "Anglos."[6] It would be misleading to describe those Anglos as a race, and not just because there were a good many Jews among them. The concept of race is three-dimensional. It just so happens that the acronym "WASP," standing as it does for "white Anglo-Saxon Protestant," perfectly captures each of the three dimensions.

Islamodious (Islodius?), homodius, or transodious. Certainly, no-one could mistake Jewodius propaganda for hate speech directed at Arab Semites.

5   Andrew Fraser, *The WASP Question: An Essay on the Biocultural Evolution, Present Predicament, and Future Prospects of the Invisible Race* (London: Arktos Media, 2011), 15–18, 171–174; C.T. Champion discusses the intra-WASP conflict between Anglophiles and Anglophobes in Canada, especially during the Sixties, throughout his *The Strange Demise of British Canada: The Liberals and Canadian Nationalism, 1964–1968* (Montreal: McGill-Queen's University Press, 2010).

6   James Fulford, https://vdare.com/posts/tucker-carlson-on-anglo-cleansing-in-montreal-and-the-great-replacement, January 30, 2024.

"White" designates the *biological* or *genetic* dimension of race, while "Anglo-Saxon" has to do with its *ethnocultural* dimension. The third, *theological* dimension of racial identity has to do with the historically "Protestant" WASP religious identity. Symbolically speaking, the cryptic character of the WASP acronym captures the fading power and prestige of today's anaemic epigones, mere shadows of the bold Britons on whose empire the sun never set.[7] No longer honoured as the founding race of every British dominion, Anglos are now scattered amidst the denizens of multiracial mass societies, serving as reminders of the evils of white colonialism. Left high and dry, but with the rising tide of colour lapping at the altars of their churches, Anglo-Protestants perform a theological disappearing act every Sunday, insisting that Christianity has nothing to do with any particularistic racial or ethnic identity. As generic Christians, they claim citizenship in a cosmopolitan heavenly city open to the whole of humanity. Meanwhile, of course, in the secular realm as well, their hard-wired *ethnic* identity as Anglo-Saxons remains bereft of any explicit corporate or collective expression. Should the thorny issue of *biological* race come up, WASPs may, reluctantly, self-identify as "whites." But mostly, they regard themselves as "plain vanilla" American, Australian, Canadian, New Zealand, or British citizens.

Whether secular or religious, WASPs disapprove of ethnonationalism most vehemently when it rears its ugly head among their own kith and kin. WASPs are their own worst enemy. Cartoonist Walt Kelly was clearly kidding on the square when he had Pogo, his cute possum character, announce: "We have met the enemy, and he is us!" Dreading above all else the atavistic pull of their inner Briton, highly placed WASPs seem driven by a compulsive need to sacrifice the interests of their co-ethnics for the benefit of other, supposedly disadvantaged,

---

7 Linda Colley, *Britons: Forging the Nation 1707–1837* (London: Pimlico, 1992). Nigel Biggar provides a powerful defense for the now-controversial proposition that Britons were entitled to take a certain pride in their empire in *Colonialism: A Moral Reckoning* (London: William Collins, 2023).

groups. Such indifference to the needs of their own kith and kin has become endemic among "educated" Anglos in the upper reaches of the managerial-professional classes. In pursuit of power, prestige, and wealth, ambitious, WASPs scramble to engage in ritual displays of pathological altruism.[8]

This is a relatively recent phenomenon, related to the shift in the dominant character type among Anglo-Saxon Protestants. According to sociologist David Riesman, the *inner-directed* Protestant individualism of the nineteenth century was well-adapted to the world of small-scale entrepreneurial capitalism in which initiative and self-reliance were valuable character traits. Then, it was as if every individual was guided by a sort of internal gyroscope. Following the rise of large-scale, transnational corporate capitalism, individuals within the burgeoning managerial-professional classes developed a more *other-directed* character type more receptive to rapidly fluctuating signals emanating from within highly organized, interlocking institutions. Under those circumstances, a sort of psychic radar set is more functional than a gyroscope stabilizing an individual's course over time.[9]

The individualism characteristic of British-descended peoples has undergone a metamorphosis during that organizational revolution. According to evolutionary psychologist Kevin MacDonald, despite the great changes over the past two centuries, Western cultures remain what they were in the days of the Puritan revolution: moral communities. The difference is that moral communities within the transnational corporate welfare state are now defined by cultural elites in the media and academia. The "rugged individualism" prized in the moral communities of a highly decentralized, virtually stateless frontier society

---

8   Cf., Barbara Oakley, *et. al.*, *Pathological Altruism* (Oxford: Oxford University Press, 2012).

9   David Riesman, with Nathan Glazer and Reuel Denney, *The Lonely Crowd: A Study of the Changing American Character*. Abridged and Revised Edition with a Foreword by Todd Gitlin (New Haven: Yale University Press [original edition 1961], 2001); see also, Fraser, *WASP Question, passim*.

has been replaced by mass mediated moral communities exposed to rapid shifts in social, sexual, and racial mores, reinforced by fear of social ostracism that might result in job loss. WASPs, especially college-educated, feminist, single women working outside the home, are particularly sensitive to such enforcement mechanisms.[10]

MacDonald notes that "a fundamental aspect of individualism is that group cohesion is based not on kinship but on reputation — most importantly in recent centuries, a moral reputation as capable, honest, trustworthy and fair." Other-directed cultural elites in the media and academia have become "tribal moral communities" in which moral reputations are grounded upon the values of diversity, equity, and inclusivity. Accordingly, individuals expressing opinions or displaying attitudes "that conflict with racial egalitarianism or promote the interests of European-derived peoples" over those of non-white groups face peremptory cancellation.[11] In a highly charged, all-pervasive media environment, personal reputations can be exalted or ruined overnight. No-one should be surprised, therefore, that virtue-signaling WASP elites are highly vulnerable to cynical manipulation by hard-nosed ethnic rivals. This becomes painfully evident when WASPs accused of wrong think are confronted by aggressively *ethnonarcissistic* Jewish journalists and politicians supremely skilled in the art of playing the victim card on behalf of protected groups (including themselves, of course). Quick as a flash, typically *ethnomasochistic* WASPs check their white privilege.[12]

---

10   Kevin MacDonald, *Individualism and the Western Liberal Tradition: Evolutionary Origins, History, and Prospects for the Future* (Kindle Direct Publishing, 2019), 374.

11   Ibid., 373–375.

12   In a richly ironic twist of fate, however, the ruthless Israeli assault on Gaza (and the West Bank) following the Hamas surprise attack on October 7, 2023 has forced most of those same Jewish journalists and politicians onto the defensive, becoming mere apologists for their own brand of "white settler colonialism."

Unfortunately, therefore, the collective well-being of ordinary British-descended people now depends upon the very limited willingness of morally compromised WASPs in positions of power to recognize and act upon the moral imperatives of in-group solidarity. Deracinated Anglos stand in desperate need of leaders ready, willing, and able to resurrect ancestral forms of British race patriotism. But only a sweeping, post-Christian religious reformation can be expected to induce shame among Anglophobic WASP "cloud people" for their failure to act in defense of their co-ethnics. For the foreseeable future, they remain in service instead to a remote and irresponsible globalist plutocracy ready to run roughshod over the biocultural interests and ethnoreligious needs of British-descended "dirt people."

Every so often however, there comes along the one white Anglo-Saxon Protestant man duty-bound (in theory, if not always in practice) to honour the bloodlines of his fellow Anglo-Saxon Protestants. That man is he who wears the British Crown. According to traditionalists such as Julius Evola and Joseph de Maistre, "the most important foundation of the authority and of the right (*ius*) of kings and chiefs, and the reason they were obeyed, feared, and venerated, was essentially their transcendent and nonhuman quality." The "royal race" of kings appears unto their subjects crowned with a glory and honour derived from God. They take their place "without violence on their part," in a sort of "magnificent tranquility." The ascension of a British king can be described as a "legitimate usurpation...which time hastens to consecrate."[13]

Paradoxically, such traditionalism turns every male heir to the throne into a constitutional wild card. No doubt young princes are carefully cosseted and groomed to behave in accordance with the conventional norms of woke propriety. But the occasional appearance of loose cannons such as Edward VIII or, more recently, Prince Harry indicates that royals sometimes do retain a mind of their own. Perhaps

---

13   Julius Evola, *Revolt Against the Modern World* (Rochester, VT: Inner Traditions International, 1995), 7–15.

a reformed Church of England could school princes more fully in the metaphysical character of royal power. Evola emphasized that in traditional societies the "root of every temporal power was spiritual authority," which — vested in a king — acquires a "divine nature disguised in human form." The "traditional idea of real and legitimate kingship" is necessarily connected to a "supernatural power, manifested through a victory or through a thaumaturgical [i.e., magical] virtue."[14] In other words, young princes should be steeped in the ancestral spirit of British race patriotism as embodied in Alfred the Great's *Angelcynn* (meaning "kin of the Angles") model of Christian kingship. Certainly, only God knows whether or when the pitiful plight of his Anglo subjects at home and in the old white dominions might inspire a revivified Patriot King to save us from both ourselves and our Anglophobic elites. And, of course, one must wonder as well whether Anglos are (or could providentially become) worthy of such a miraculous royal appearance?

The unpleasant reality now is that most WASP managers and professionals are, at best, wedded to a shallow secular humanism, often viewing veneration of the sacred as little more than primitive superstition. Anglo-Protestants, for whom religion is about personal salvation, almost always fit comfortably within the secularist consensus. In the now-looming worst-case scenario, the venal materialism that underpins the political economy of the transnational corporate state reigns supreme. Having severed the ancestral fusion of blood, history, and religion from civic belonging, the lost souls of the invisible race are condemned to a collective life sentence of spiritual degradation.

One might think that the Church of England and its Anglican offshoots in the old white Commonwealth would work to relieve such psychic poverty. But one would be wrong to imagine any such thing. Global Anglicanism has abandoned its historic role as the sacramental conduit for British race patriotism around the world. Instead, Anglican churches throughout the Anglosphere pander to the politically correct

---

14   *Ibid.*

pieties which permit cosmopolitan (implicitly Anglophobic) WASPs to pass, imperceptibly, from provincial, pariah status into the woke domain of polite society. The historical development of Anglicanism in Australia provides but one sorry example of the decline and fall of Anglo-Saxon Christendom.

In his book *Anglicans in Australia*, Bishop Tom Frame provides a valuable analysis of the historical context from which the Anglican Church of Australia emerged as well as a critical evaluation of its present place in Australian society. In broad outline, the story he tells is like the experience of Anglicans "at home" and in the other British dominions. Few would dispute the historic accuracy of Frame's principal thesis; namely, that "the Anglican Church has fashioned its identity primarily on English Anglicanism, which relies heavily on Establishment for both its governance and intellectual coherence". He points out, of course, that it was only in the first few decades of British settlement that the Church of England in Australia formally enjoyed the privileges of an established church. By the 1820s, Anglicans were but one of many Christian denominations in the Australian colonies. Their congregations, parishes, and dioceses were private, voluntary religious associations but Anglicans were notably over-represented among colonial elites. Nowadays, of course, aspirations towards an Anglican establishment can never achieve more than an implicit form. The Australian Constitution explicitly prohibits the establishment of a national church such as the Church of England. Nevertheless, Frame contends that the "Australian Church has frequently thought and acted like an Established Church," thanks to the English inheritance that colonial Anglicans carried in their baggage and adapted to their new environment.[15]

---

15 Tom Frame, *Anglicans in Australia* (Sydney: University of New South Wales Press, 2007), 18.

Squandering the British Legacy

The Anglican Church of Australia now claims to be "genuinely national" solely by virtue of its "distinctly Australian" identity.[16] Before 1962, Australian Anglicans mostly identified themselves as independent Australian Britons. Long gone are the days when Anglican leaders in Australia proudly and publicly proclaimed that God has "called our British race to the lead among the nations in fulfilling his purposes".[17] But Australian Anglicans no longer believe that the God of Israel blesses blood as the biocultural basis of belonging to a holy people—not even in their own purportedly "national" church. Instead, the Anglican Church of Australia has adopted the secular State's explicitly non-ethnic definition of Australian nationality.[18]

Anglo-Protestant churches, generally, are now bound to treat the English ancestry and white British ethnicity of most of their communicants as a merely implicit (if not downright unmentionable) and contingent circumstance of no theological significance. Especially within the institutional structures of the Anglican Church, Australians of white Anglo-Saxon Protestant ancestry are now a lost nation, a people that no longer dares speak their name. They have been orphaned by a State and a Church that no longer incorporate their history and destiny as a distinctive people sharing the blood-faith of their Anglo-Saxon ancestors. The idea of Australia as a new Britannia set in

---

16 Frame, *Anglicans*, 86.
17 *Goulburn Monthly Paper* (1 August 1900), quoted in Frame, *Anglicans*, 68.
18 Note, however, that the Commonwealth of Australia did not introduce the status of Australian citizenship until 1948. Even then, "Australian citizens" remained "British subjects" until 1984. According to David Wishart, the *Australian Citizenship Amendment Act 1984* removed "the status of British subject from the law of Australia. That status [had] been accorded to Australian citizens since 1948 and, before then, there was no such thing as Australian citizenship, only British subjection". David Wishart, "Allegiance and Citizenship as Concepts in Constitutional Law," (1986) 15 *Melbourne Law Review* 662.

the southern seas is now dead and buried.[19] To its eternal shame, the Anglican Church of Australia was one of its principal grave diggers.

Before 1962, the British loyalties of the Church of England in Australia were never in doubt. By contrast, the 1962 Constitution of the Church, however, merely confessed to "being derived from the Church of England". The Australian Church also retained and approved the Book of Common Prayer and the Thirty-nine Articles until such time as the doctrine and principles therein might be altered and revised in accordance with the rules set out in the Constitution. Accordingly, the Anglican Church of Australia is now a loose confederation of autonomous dioceses under the nominal supervision of a Primate elected in accordance with a procedure determined by the General Synod representing the lay communicants and clergy of the Australian church.[20] One little-noticed corollary of the legal independence of the Australian Church is that it lost its historic connection with the British monarchy. A tradition of Christian kingship stretching back to the priest-kings of Anglo-Saxon times has been severed.

This is no small matter since Anglicans in both England and Australia traditionally regarded the monarchy as "a symbol of divine authority". The doctrine of the Divine Right of Kings had long since passed into history "but Anglicans believed that the monarchy possessed divine attributes". Frame remarks that they "took pride in the fact that at the apex of government stood one of their own faith — a claim no other denomination could make". From Federation in 1901 until 1962, therefore, the Anglican Church helped keep alive in Australia cultural and other values that derived from Britain. Indeed,

---

19 Alan James, *New Britannia: The Rise and Decline of Anglo-Australia* (Melbourne: Renewal Publications, 2013).

20 See, the Ruling Principles, *The Constitution of the Anglican Church of Australia*, section 4, available on-line at: http://www.anglican.org.au/docs/Constitution%20Canons%20BOOK%20FINALrevclient_indexed.pdf.

"it endowed empire, monarchy, and race with a religious sanction."[21] Even the notoriously progressive Red Bishop of Goulburn, Ernest Burgmann (1885–1967), prized kingship as a guarantor of "personal freedom, social unity, and stability and the just administration of law and order". For that reason, "the monarchy...had played a crucial role in the history of the church".[22] Indeed, until the creation of the Diocese of Goulburn in 1863, the appointment of bishops in colonial Australia had been made by the Archbishop of Canterbury by means of Letters Patent issued by the Crown. Thereafter bishops were elected by autonomous diocesan synods.[23]

In the Federation era, "Australian nationalists did not choose British origins for their nation; that was an inescapable fact of history. They did choose to emphasise British ethnicity as a keystone of national cohesion". According to Russell McGregor, they promoted an "essentialised, ethnicised" form of nationalism.[24] That is to say, the same blood that "congealed the Australian people into a single nation... also connected them to the British parent". The Premier of Victoria insisted in 1899 that the Australasian colonies "were all cradled by the great Mother of the British Race". At the turn of the twentieth century, references to "the crimson thread of kinship" binding Australians to the mother country were a staple of political rhetoric.[25] But Australian ethnicity "was more than a matter of blood: Britishness was the source of the heritage, history, culture and symbols that made Australia heir to a glorious past". McGregor shows that the "myths and symbols that resonated most deeply and meaningfully among the Australian people were Britannic myths and memories. These enabled Australians to

---

21 Brian H Fletcher, "Anglicanism and Nationalism in Australia, 1901–1962," (1999) 23(2) *Journal of Religious History* 215, at 226.

22 Ibid., 222–223.

23 Frame, *Anglicans*, 32, 74.

24 Russell McGregor, "The Necessity of Britishness: Ethno-cultural Roots of Australian Nationalism," (2006) 12(3) *Nations and Nationalism* 493, at 500.

25 Douglas Cole, "The Crimson Thread of Kinship: Ethnic Ideas in Australia, 1870–1914," (1971) 14 *Historical Studies* 511.

transcend local or parochial loyalties, to conceive themselves as a national community with deep temporal roots."[26]

It is indisputable, therefore, that the Britannic heritage was "an essential source of sustenance and strength to Australian nationalism." Not surprisingly, therefore, the so-called White Australia Policy laid down in the very first Act of the Commonwealth parliament "was founded on the assumption that ethnic unity provided the foundation-stone of both national cohesion and political democracy." And, as more than one Member of Parliament observed, White Australia "really means a British Australia." Of course, non-British whites were admitted but only "on the understanding that they would readily assimilate, biologically as well as culturally, into the British-Australian nation."[27]

But it was only in a formal legal sense that the reigning monarch remained the sole, anointed, and living icon of divine majesty within the Church of England in Australia for much of the twentieth century. The Church Constitution of 1962 enacted by the Commonwealth Parliament set the Australian Church on the road to becoming a thoroughly deracinated "little republic" bereft of any corporate connection to the blood royal of the Christian kingship schooled by the Church of England. Ironically, from 1962 until 1973, it was only by virtue of the short-lived Commonwealth *Royal Style and Titles Act 1953* that the Queen retained her constitutional role as the defender of the ancestral faith confessed by Anglicans in Australia.[28]

In 1982, Australian Anglicans further distanced themselves from the genetic legitimacy of their English origins when they renamed their church the Anglican Church of Australia. Earlier in the twentieth century, Australian national feeling did not stand in contradiction to a deep sense of spiritual kinship with England and its Empire. In fact, Anglican loyalists played a significant role in the federation of

---

26 McGregor, "Necessity of Britishness," 501–502.

27 *Ibid.*, 502, 507.

28 The Whitlam Labor government removed all reference to the Queen's role as "defender of the faith" in the amended *Royal Style and Titles Act 1973*.

the Australian colonies in 1901. Accordingly, the Church of England in Australia (as it then was) aspired to become a "church for the nation" when the Commonwealth was created. Frame blames that persistent "mindset" for muting the "prophetic witness" of the Anglican Church of Australia down to the present day. He suggests that the desire to become "the national church" has corrupted Anglicans who court popularity "without requiring the nation to be Christian".[29] The difficulty here is that Frame does not seem to notice the fundamental shift in the meaning of nationhood between 1901 and 1962 associated with the decline in British race patriotism. He simply assumes that the "nation" can be defined solely by reference to the citizenship laws of the Commonwealth of Australia. But, given that legalistic context, the Anglo-Australian people cannot possibly be recognized as an ethno-nation in their own right. Indeed, it is all too obvious that the Anglican Church has no desire to become a church for *that* nation. It is passing strange, then, that Anglicans now rush to recognize the collective identity and ethnic interests of the Aboriginal "nation" and other ethnic minorities in Australia that stand outside and apart from the state.[30]

In its English origins, a church for the nation was necessarily also a church for the state. Clearly, national identity has become problematic socially, and theologically, because the "state" in both England and Australia has detached itself from the "nation". Before the Second World War, membership in the large, partly inbred, extended family of Anglo-Saxon peoples that created the British Empire was seen by Australian Anglicans as the essence of national identity. In response to effort by Bishop Burgmann and others to make the Church more truly Australian, one bishop wrote: "I am inclined to think it is our duty rather to emphasize the solidarity of the British race and the contribution which the British people as a whole can make to the world". But

---

29 Frame, *Anglicans*, 18.
30 Ibid., 141.

the Anglican Church of Australia no longer even pretends to endow "empire, monarchy, and race with a religious sanction."[31]

In tandem with the Church of England, the Anglican Church in Australia (along with its namesakes in Canada, New Zealand, and the USA) has disowned its ancestral and still implicitly WASP heritage. It has sworn allegiance instead to the very transnational corporate state that is committed to the demographic transformation of England, Australia, and every other white European nation. When Frame calls for "a sense of national solidarity" among Australian Anglicans, he is not invoking the "British race patriotism" that gave birth to the Australian nation-state.[32] Instead, the currently dominant vision of Anglicanism strives "to present the Christian gospel in a manner that transcends ethnicity, gender and social status and which reduces the number and extent of human obstacles to Church membership."[33]

No matter how hard Anglicans try to shed their implicitly WASP image, their critics continue to insist that the "Anglican ethos is that of the English middle class".[34] Faced with such rampant Anglophobia, the Anglican Church of Australia no longer viewed the survival of British-Australia as a vital theological issue. Consequently, the social, cultural, and spiritual capital bequeathed to it by the Church and people of England was soon squandered. In any event, after two destructive world wars, both Catholics and mainline Protestants began to view the forces of nationalism as a blight on Christian civilization. Adrian Hastings observes, however, that "a false universalism" has become "an even greater threat, a succumbing to the globalization, economic,

---

31 Fletcher, "Anglicans and National Identity, 1901–1962," 229, 226.
32 Frame, *Anglicans*, 14; see generally, McGregor, "The Necessity of Britishness".
33 Frame, *Anglicans*, 18.
34 Caroline Miley, *The Suicidal Church: Can the Anglican Church be Saved?* (Sydney: Pluto Press, 2002), 58.

cultural, and political, sweeping the world under the pressure of capitalism and American military dominance".[35]

By the Eighties, Anglican leaders were determined to avoid the perceived "dangers of remaining tied too exclusively to their heritage". Accordingly, in 1983 Bishop Reid of Sydney was fearful that "in another generation Anglicans will be seen as an Anglo-Saxon sect". In light of the perceived danger that it might become an ethnoreligious ghetto for "White Australian Anglo-Saxon Anglicans," the Anglican church chose to fashion "a new and dynamic national church" open to people of any and all races and ethnicities.[36] Thus, having embraced multiculturalism, the "Anglican Church of Australia maintains very few links with the Church of England and has little interest in complying with any English practice or in remaining ethnically British".[37]

The Political Theology of the Church of England in War and Peace

Arguably, these changes came about because of the wars waged against Germany by the British Empire in the first half of the twentieth century. Despite the colossal cost in blood and treasure associated with both wars, Anglo-Protestant subjects of the British Crown generally interpret that history from the self-satisfied standpoint of righteous victors. Sadly, such triumphalism soon undercut the British race patriotism that had inspired the foundation of nationhood in Australia, Canada, and New Zealand. Having spent decades demonizing the evils of both Prusso-German militarism in the first war and the "pagan" racialism of the Nazis during the second, Anglican leaders throughout the old

---

35 *Ibid.*, 259; Adrian Hastings, , "Christianity and Nationhood: Congruity or Antipathy?" (2001) 25(3) *Journal of Religious History* 247, at 259.

36 Brian H. Fletcher, "Anglicanism and National Identity in Australia Since 1962," (2001) 25(3) *Journal of Religious History* 324, at 335.

37 Frame, *Anglicans*, 208.

white Commonwealth were programmed to expunge every trace of ethnonationalism among their own British-descended parishioners.

Ironically, the race patriotism which reigned supreme in the British Empire prior to 1914 owed a substantial debt of gratitude to Prusso-German militarism, thanks to the timely intervention of the Prussian army under Marshall Blücher during the Battle of Waterloo, which saved the Duke of Wellington's bacon. Indeed, throughout much of the nineteenth century the English looked upon Germans, not as an existential threat to their imperial interests, but somewhat fondly as a race of *Dichter und Denker*; poets and thinkers inhabiting a romantic landscape ruled by rival duchies, kingdoms, and city-states. British complacency received a shock in 1871when the Franco-Prussian war ended with the proclamation of a unified, victorious, and newly industrialized German Reich.

Benjamin Disraeli, the first and only Jewish Prime Minister (then in opposition), gave voice to the resulting apprehension among the British political class when he rose in the Commons to declare that:

> This war represents the German revolution, a greater political event than the French revolution of last century. I don't say a greater, or as great a social event. What its social consequences may be are in the future. Not a single principle in the management of our foreign affairs, accepted by all statesmen for guidance up to six months ago, any longer exists. There is not a diplomatic tradition which has not been swept away. You have a new world, new influences at work, new and unknown objects and dangers with which to cope, at present involved in that obscurity incident to novelty in such affairs. We used to have discussions in this House about the balance of power. Lord Palmerston, eminently a practical man, trimmed the ship of State and shaped its policy with a view to preserve an equilibrium in Europe....But what has really come to pass? The balance of power has been entirely destroyed, and the country which suffers most, and feels the effects of this great change most, is England.[38]

---

38 Hansard, Parliamentary Debates, series III, vol. 204, February–March 1871, speech of February 9, 1871, pp. 81–82. Available online at: https://hansard.parliament.uk/Commons/1871-02-09. Original English text reprinted in William

After the immediate shock had passed, Kaiser Wilhelm II eventually dropped his master diplomatic strategist and great power politics found a new normal in which the states representing the various European "races" continued to jockey for position. In those days, it was not ideology which divided rival power blocs on the international scene. Rather, the racial patriotism of the British had to contend with rival German, French, Russian, or, fatefully, even Serbian racial patriotisms. Eventually, much to everyone's surprise, European leaders sleepwalked their way into the catastrophic Great War. Both the Church of England and its colonial offshoots awoke to find themselves called away from a sheltered life of comfort and indulgence by "the stern hand of Fate... to an elevation where we can see the everlasting things that matter for a nation—the high peaks we had forgotten, of Honour, Duty, Patriotism, and, clad in glittering white, the great pinnacle of Sacrifice, pointing like a rugged figure to Heaven."[39]

Wilkinson argues that, given the "fact that many of the leading clergy were drawn from the same social groups as many of the leading politicians and military leaders," it is not surprising that "support for the war was virtually unanimous." It turned out, however, that Christians, both "individually and corporately...were ethically ill-prepared to meet the subtlety and complexity of many wartime moral problems." Clergymen often helped to stir up "intense anti-German feeling, accompanied by bitterness towards any suspected of less than wholehearted support for the war effort." In June 1915, for example, the Bishop of London declared that the Church must "help the nation to realise that it is engaged in a Holy War." He called for "a great crusade—we cannot deny it—to kill Germans: to kill them, not for

---

Flavelle Moneypenny and George Earle Buckle, The Life of Benjamin Disraeli, Earl of Beaconsfield, new rev. ed. in 2 vols., vol. 2, 1860–1881. London: John Murray, 1929, pp. 473–74.

39 Alan Wilkinson, *The Church of England and the First World War* (London: SPCK, 1978), 29. On the descent into war, see Christopher Clark, *The Sleepwalkers: How Europe Went to War in 1914* (London: Penguin, 2013).

the sake of killing, but to save the world."[40] Indeed, popular animosity towards Germany and Germans reached such a pitch by 1917 that even King Edward VII was compelled to renounce his ancestral ties to the German House of Saxe-Cobourg-Gotha and adopt Windsor as a family surname.

Such was the "sense of moral certainty implicit in the idea of crusade, the absolute vision of guilt and innocence," that the Church, initially at least, also supported the punitive provisions of the Versailles treaty of 1919. Before long, however, the "simplicity of this easy, crusading rhetoric was a painful memory for post-war churchmen." Feeling partially responsible for the horrors and brutality of the First World War, "the post-war Church was seized with the spirit of ecumenism," committed itself "to a co-operative international future, both in religious and political terms." Seeking "the fellowship of many communions," the Church promoted co-operation and intellectual exchange "chiefly centred around a relationship between English and Northern European Protestants."[41]

George Bell, Bishop of Chichester, was particularly active in fostering ecumenical relationships with German Protestants. He was moved by "a rich, vivid vision of the universal church, in which all Christians could find each other and labor for justice, not merely as members of different confessions but together, as brothers and sisters." He took a keen interest in the German church struggle or *Kirchenkampf* between German Protestants who favoured the creation of a single state church (the *Deutsche Christen* movement) and their opponents in the *Bekennende Kirche* (the Confessing Church, hereafter *BK*). Bell was one of many English churchmen who saw this conflict as a scandalous battle pitting Christianity itself against the iniquitous power of a pagan dictatorship. They greatly admired Martin Niemöller, a charismatic leader of the *BK* who was imprisoned in 1938. Bell also established

---

40 Ibid., 36, 46, 97, 215, 217.
41 Tom Lawson, *The Church of England and the Holocaust: Christianity, Memory, and Nazism* (Woodbridge: Boydell Press, 2006), 56–57.

a deep personal rapport with the young German pastor, Dietrich Bonhoeffer, who worked in London for a time and was later executed for his role in the assassination plot against Hitler.[42]

For most of the interwar period, the Church of England "actually believed that the primary danger to the civilized world came from war. But, when Britain declared war on Germany in September 1939, the Church joined "with the majority of the wider nation" to welcome "that conflict as righteous; Nazi totalitarianism had by then replaced war as the greatest threat to Christian civilization." Significantly, the persecution of the Jews by the National Socialist regime was understood as "simply a manifestation of a much greater problem." Nazi antisemitism "was seen as both illustrative of nefarious Nazi ambitions and as the device which the Nazis used to usher in more general injustice." According to Tom Lawson, in the eyes of the Church, the Jews may have been the first to suffer persecution; they would not be the last. "If any group was painted as the primary victims of Nazism, it was the Christian churches and not the Jews…Christians in Germany, and elsewhere in Europe, were constructed as the eternal opponents of the Nazi menace, necessarily oppressed, and silently opposed to Nazi crimes." Any group or institution within Germany "perceived as being linked to a traditional Christian past" could be held up as standing "apart from the alien Nazi dominators." George Bell, for example, through his relationship with Dietrich Bonhoeffer "had held intimate knowledge of the *Wehrmacht* conspiracy which ultimately ended in the failed attempt to assassinate Hitler on 20 July 1944. Even before the failure of the plot, Bell "deliberately attempted to distinguish between the army and the state in order to bolster the image of an honourable Christian, anti-Nazi, *Wehrmacht*." The ecclesiastical press in England

---

42 Andrew Chandler, *George Bell, Bishop of Chichester: Church, State, and Resistance in the Age of Dictatorship* (Grand Rapids, MI: William B. Eerdmans, 2016), *xi*, 49; Lawson, *Church of England and the Holocaust*, 31–54.

shared Bell's faith in the *Wehrmacht* and the cultural continuity between its "leadership and the traditions of Christendom."[43]

By the end of the war, this transnational ecumenical faith was eroding the once-organic connection between British racial patriotism and English Christianity. William Ralph Inge, a former Dean of St. Paul's, came to believe that racialism is simply "a superstitious variety of nationalism." To his mind, the ecumenical logic of "essential Christianity" implied that "[w]e are all mongrels, and the better for being so." A nation, therefore, is nothing more than "a society united by a delusion about its ancestry and a common hatred of its neighbours." Accordingly, Inge dismissed German racialism as merely "the latest form of collective arrogance and egotism," no less "scientifically indefensible" than any other form of "statist" nationalism.[44] In support of such a sweeping judgement, Inge could call upon an impressive body of German Protestant theology.

The German Protestant Deformation of Christian Nationhood

The rise of Adolf Hitler and his National Socialist movement certainly produced a moral and theological crisis within Germany's Protestant majority. Germans belonging to the Evangelical (i.e., Calvinist or Reformed) and Lutheran churches were sharply but not evenly divided between supporters and opponents of the NS regime. According to Dietrich Bonhoeffer (soon to become the martyred "hero" of the resistance), those who refused to accept the newly triumphant *Führer* as "the God-given executor of historical justice" were only a seemingly "small remnant". Swimming against the tide as Hitler grew ever-more popular, Bonhoeffer insisted that Hitler was really "Satan in the form

---

43 Lawson, *Church of England and the Holocaust*, 90–96.
44 W.R. Inge, *The End of an Age and Other Essays* (London: Putnam, 1948), 127.

of an angel of light".⁴⁵ More moderate dissenters from the religious policies pursued by the government wanted merely to secure the spiritual autonomy of Protestant churches while upholding the legitimacy of the National Socialist Revolution in other areas of life. There were also a great many Germans, organized as the German Christian faith movement (*Glaubensbewegung Deutsche Christen*), who advocated the formal *Gleichschaltung* (synchronisation) of church and state.

Mainstream historical writing on the *Kirchenkampf* typically rests upon one unshakeable premise; namely, that—even before the war—the Nazi regime generally and Adolf Hitler personally were culpably criminal and irredeemably evil. Klaus Scholder, for example, asserts unequivocally that "after Nuremberg one can no longer argue about the criminal character of National Socialism".⁴⁶ Similarly, Robert P. Eriksen, the author of a major study of several prominent German theologians sympathetic to the regime, introduces the subject with this confident claim: "In a century of horrors, Adolf Hitler remains the chief symbol of evil in the twentieth century". Thus, according to the conventional wisdom of the historical profession in and out of Germany, the utter defeat of Nazi Germany made WWII unambiguously the "good war". Why, then, did so few German Christians join the resistance? The decisive factor for most patriotic Germans must have been the war with Poland, Britain and France which placed the church struggle on the back burner. Scholder notes that Hitler offered a "truce" in which "the need for national solidarity seemed to open up a new possibility of a positive relationship between state and church."⁴⁷

---

45 Ferdinand Schlingensiepen, *Dietrich Bonhoeffer 1906–1945 Martyr, Thinker, Man of Resistance* tr. Isabel Best (New York: T&T Clark, 2010), 242.

46 Klaus Scholder, *A Requiem for Hitler and Other Perspectives on the German Church Struggle* (London: SCM Press, 1989), 16. An interesting online counterpoint to Scholder's uncritical assessment of the Nuremberg Tribunal can be found at: Ehud Would, "The Nuremberg Trials: Theonomy Condemned," http://faithandheritage.com/2016/08/the-nuremberg-trials-theonomy-condemned.

47 Robert P. Eriksen, *Theologians Under Hitler* (New Haven, CN: Yale University Press, 1985), 1; Scholder, *Requiem*, 116–117.

Point 24 of the Nationalist Socialist program promised to uphold a "positive Christianity."⁴⁸ For better or worse, however, Germany's catastrophic defeat put an end to any hope that the *Volkskirchen* would be fused with the *Volksstaat*.

Scholder embraces the guilt-tripping narrative then imposed by the victorious Allied powers. The only good Germans were those who worked actively to defeat Hitlerism. He writes that "it was the war in particular which made the claim of the National Socialist regime and its criminal character so clear that opposition and resistance grew" within the churches.⁴⁹ But it was too little and too late. With 20–20 hindsight, mainstream historians find it "difficult to understand how the German people could have supported the Nazi Party with their votes or accepted the leadership of Hitler after he assumed power".⁵⁰ Even more incomprehensible were the attitudes of Germans who viewed steadfast opposition to the *Führer* as treason to the *Volk*. Dietrich Bonhoeffer's biographer, Ferdinand Schlingensiepen, indignantly denies that "the men of the Resistance…betrayed their fatherland". Taking the high moral ground, he simply wonders "how the German elite…could share in the guilt by continuing their unconditional obedience, for so long, to a regime which committed such crimes".⁵¹

For Schlingensiepen, Hitler's evil nature was evident long before the invasion of Poland in 1939. He asserts baldly that in 1933 Hitler "was already planning for war". According to the dominant narrative, the identity of Hitler's chief enemy was clear from the beginning of his political career: "he was filled above all with an out-and-out hatred of Jews. He saw 'worldwide Jewry' as the embodiment of evil".⁵² Scholder opines that "the basis of this world-view was a pronounced

---

48 D. Cajus Fabricius, *Positive Christianity in the Third Reich* (Dresden: Hermann Puschel, 1937), 4.
49 Scholder, *Requiem*, 116–117.
50 Eriksen, *Theologians*, 1.
51 Schlingensiepen, *Dietrich Bonhoeffer*, 241.
52 *Ibid.*, 115.

Manichaeism. It posited a dualism in the world between a higher and a lower race, the Aryans, and the Jews". With unconscious irony, he adds that "[t]he fate of the world was decided in the struggle between the good principle and the evil principle".[53]

Scholder's own thoroughly conventional account of the *Kirchenkampf* is equally beholden to that same simplistic schema. Here, too, the good guys are pitted against the bad guys, with Hitler, the Nazi party, and the *Deutsche Christen* cast as the villains of the piece. The German people are limited, at best. to a supporting role, willing dupes of a criminal mastermind. The mystery at the heart of the dominant narrative is why, in the face of overwhelming force, so many German Christians demonstrated such dogged loyalty to the *Führer* for so long.

Perhaps the solution to that mystery has been obscured by the premise taken as a given by the historiographical establishment. What if the struggle within German churches was not simply a clash between good and evil? Perhaps the conflict was about the theological and moral significance of one particular ethnoreligious identity? What does or should it meant to be a "German Christian"? Is the concept of a uniquely *German* Christianity a theological oxymoron or, worse still, a damnable heresy? If not, then perhaps in the circumstances prevailing in the early and mid-twentieth century Evangelical and Lutheran churches in Germany were morally bound to defend the interests of *das deutsche Volk* against all its enemies. Certainly, Germany had more than its fair share of enemies, foreign and domestic. That being so, it may be that the *Kirchenkampf* marked the first major battle in the ongoing conflict between what we may call globalism and nationalism in Christian ethics.

From the inter-war period to the present, the Church of England has invoked the Neo-platonic myth of global Jesus in promoting the cult of the Other at the expense of British-descended peoples throughout

---

53 Scholder, 97.

the Anglosphere. Accordingly, contemporary Anglo-Protestants are under pressure to be nice to deviant and alien minorities. Church leaders ceaselessly call upon Christians to be "inclusive" and "compassionate" when dealing with "the Other." Introductory texts in theology teach that the "church is always threatened by a false unity that does not allow for the inclusion of strangers and outcasts." Among white Anglo-Saxon Protestants the compulsory embrace of humanity's "rich diversity" is the prescribed antidote to "the ominous coupling of a shadowy religiosity with a militant nationalism or racism in such slogans as 'God and Fatherland' or 'God, family, and country.'"[54]

According to Princeton theology professor Daniel L Migliore, such "vague but uniformly comforting references to God and religious values" shaped "the ideology of too many German Christians during the Third Reich and are still invoked by "chauvinistic movements in the United States and other countries."[55] The association of nationalism with social pathologies owes much of its all-pervasive influence to Karl Barth (1882–1968), a Swiss Protestant theologian who achieved fame and more than a little notoriety in the 1930s through uncompromising opposition to the National Socialist takeover of both church and state in Germany. The fact is, however, that both Barth and Migliore seriously misrepresent the relationship between Christian communities of faith and the blood bonds of national identity.

The Bible provides ample warrant to designate "nations" and "peoples" as essential building blocks in the constitution of the holy, catholic, and apostolic church of Christ. Indeed, Christ directed his disciples to "make disciples of all the nations" (Matthew 28:19). The Old Testament people of Israel thus became the prototype for the Christian peoples of God in the New Covenant creation. Accordingly, the Russian Orthodox Church affirms that all peoples have the "right to national identity and national self-expressions" *within* the Body of

---

54 Daniel L Migliore, *Faith Seeking Understanding: An Introduction to Christian Theology* Second Edition (Grand Rapids, MI: William Eerdmans, 2004), 13, 31.

55 Ibid., 31–32.

Christ. In the nineteenth century, even an Anglican theologian such as FD Maurice saw in the Old Testament the history of a "peculiar nation" whose destiny is fulfilled and completed when the New Testament reveals "a universal Church unfolding itself out of that nation," taking "root in other nations and peoples throughout the ancient world." But, during the twentieth century, ethno-nationalism lost its religious aura of sanctity. In erstwhile "Anglo-Saxon countries" few Protestants any longer believe that it is part of God's plan to form the character of each nation by means of the "spiritual body" within it — the institution known in German as the *Volkskirche*.[56] Even Anglicans reject the idea that the Church of England was and should be again the Church *for* England and the English people, at home and in the diaspora. That decisive break with the past is in large part due to the theological crisis that afflicted the German church during the 1930s.

In Germany, the international movement that American writer James Kurth dubbed Protestant Deformation was part of the collateral damage inflicted on Christian nationhood by the "ideological civil war of the twentieth century." During that conflict, "the universalist extremism of Bolshevism provoke[d] the extremism of the particular in Nazism." Ernst Nolte portrays the role of German National Socialism in the *europäische Burgerkrieg* between 1917 and 1945 as an "excessive" reaction to Bolshevism. In his view, an "excess in what is justified at the outset leads to the unjustifiable."[57] The same dynamic operated in the theological crisis which engulfed Protestant churches in Germany

---

56 Russian Orthodox Church, Patriarchate of Moscow, *Bases of the Social Concept of the Russian Orthodox Church*, II. Church and nation, available online at: http://3saints.com/ustav_mp_russ_english.html#2; Jeremy Morris, *FD Maurice and the Crisis of Christian Authority* (Oxford: Oxford University Press, 2008), 4, 93, 103–105.

57 James Kurth, "The Protestant Deformation and American Foreign Policy," *Orbis* 42, no. 2, 225; François Furet and Ernst Nolte, *Fascism and Communism* (Lincoln, NB: University of Nebraska Press, 2001), 4, 11, 29. See also, Ernst Nolte, *Der europäische Burgerkrieg, 1917–1945: Nationalsozialismus und Bolschewismus* (Frankfurt am Main: Propyläen, 1987).

as growing numbers of academic theologians, pastors, and parishioners eschewed neutrality and took opposing sides in the ideological conflicts dividing society at large. Soon after the *Machtergreifung* (the Nazi seizure of power) in 1933 which endowed Hitler with dictatorial powers, open ideological warfare broke out between the breakaway *Bekennende Kirche* under the intellectual leadership of Karl Barth and the *Deutsche Christen* (*DC*) movement in mainstream Lutheran and Evangelical churches. The latter were soon united under a *Reichsbischof* sworn to serve the *Führer*.[58] Barth rapidly assumed leadership in the creation of the *BK*, drafting much of the *Barmen Declaration* of 1934 which formalized the split within the German church.

Emanuel Hirsch (1888–1972) was just one of many prominent theologians whose loyalty to the NS regime placed them at daggers drawn with Barth and the *BK*. Very early in the ideological civil war tearing Germany and Europe apart, Hirsch aligned himself openly with the right.[59] Meanwhile, on the left, Barth, began his life-long journey as a fellow-traveller, a radical anti-Nazi widely suspected to be soft on Communism. Early in his career, he was known "as the notorious 'red pastor' of Safenwil." Later, during the Cold War, he excused "his peculiar attitude towards aggressive Communism in Hungary" by reference to the "good intentions" that inspired leftist totalitarianism. Barth's ideological allegiances account for his "excessive" reaction to the rise of the *DC* movement. Even "Barth's 'friends' in the Confessing Church thought him too difficult and not diplomatic enough." In fact, he was seen as the "greatest danger" to the church "because he picked too many specific battles with National Socialism."[60] Still, few called

---

58 Steffen Recknagel, *Evangelische Kirche im Dritten Reich-Deutsche Christen und Bekennende Kirche im Zwiespalt zwischen Anpassung und Widerstand* (Norderstedt: GRIN Verlag, 2005), 5–6.

59 Robert P Ericksen, *Theologians under Hitler: Gerhard Kittel, Paul Althaus, and Emanuel Hirsch* (New Haven, CN: Yale University Press, 1985).

60 Frank Jehle, *Ever Against the Stream: The Politics of Karl Barth, 1906–1968* (Grand Rapids, MI: William B Eerdmans, 2002), 2, 89, 54–55.

Barth's "rationality" into question. Barth was not, however, always so generous to his *DC* opponents, whose teachings he dismissed contemptuously as a "blatantly nonsensical" and "irresponsible pseudo theology."[61]

As an intellectual leftist, Barth was predisposed to what has since emerged as globalist neo-communism. As a Christian humanist, he already leaned towards philo-semitism, thus sharing in the cosmopolitan universalism inherent in the messianic traditions of both historical and contemporary Judaism. For Barth, Jews, far from being an especially evil race, were God's ever-present reminder to Christians of the essential sinfulness of mankind at large. Barth broke "radically with those more traditional Christian thinkers who see in Israel's refusal to receive Christ a purely *human* refusal, a merely human blindness to the messiahship of Christ". For Barth, according to John Johnson, "the Jews do not receive Christ because God has ordained their rejection of him." Israel's disobedience, whether in killing Christ two thousand years ago, or in siding with the Bolsheviks in their ideological civil war against bourgeois Christians in modern Europe, "is really a sign of *humanity's* rebellion against God."[62] Barth's frankly irrational faith in the divinely ordained, messianic role of the Jews inevitably provoked counter-excesses among Christians sympathetic to the cause of German national revival.

After the bloody denouement of Europe's ideological civil war left Germany lying prostrate *in Schutt und Asche*, Barth emerged as the clear victor over *völkische* rivals such as Emanuel Hirsch who received what amounted to an immediate dishonourable discharge from the Göttingen theological faculty. Earlier in 1935, Barth had lost his position as "the most highly regarded professor of law in Germany"

---

61 Karl Barth, *Church Dogmatics: The Doctrine of Creation* III 4 (London: T&T Clark, 2009), 309.

62 John J Johnson, "A New Testament Understanding of the Jewish Rejection of Jesus: Four Theologians on the Salvation of Israel," (2000) 43(2) *Journal of the Evangelical Theological Society* 229, at 237.

when he refused to swear an oath of loyalty to the *Führer*.⁶³ But, back in Switzerland, he continued his campaign against Hitler's Germany while working on his *magnum opus*, the twelve volumes of *Church Dogmatics*—which remained unfinished at his death. By the Sixties, he was a world-renowned religious thinker, even appearing on the cover of *Time* magazine. His massive body of work is not, however, without its critics. Barth's "excessive" reaction against the ideal of the *Volkskirche* led him not just to deny that the "*ordo* of nation and nationality" is "immanent in human nature" but to "dichotomize" Christ, as the *head* of the Church, from the ecclesiastical *body* which is the earthly-historical form of his existence.⁶⁴

In other words, Barth denied that the Church can "be regarded as a human production." It does not owe its existence to this world; rather the being of the Church is "secured, unthreatened, and incontestable only from above, only from God, not from below, not from the side of its human members". What Barth "finds important about the church is not its empirical or historical dimensions, but rather its essential identity with Jesus Christ." By contrast, many of Barth's critics identify "the Spirit's work with persistent, enduring social forms" and advocate "a critical historicism focused on the practices, structures, and traditions of historic Christianity." But few, if any, of Barth's academic critics dare to redeem the ideal of the *Volkskirche* from the shame and ridicule heaped upon it by the victors in the ideological civil war of the twentieth century. Theologians critical of Barth's "reluctance to see God's revelation 'captured' in human time" nonetheless join with him to deny that "in the national determination of man we have an order of creation no less than in the relationship of man and woman

---

63 Jehle, *Ever Against the Stream*, 13.
64 Barth, CD III 4, 305; Ian A McFarland, "The Body of Christ: Rethinking a Classic Ecclesiological Model," (2005) 7(3) *International Journal of Systematic Theology* 225, at 226.

and parents and children."⁶⁵ In his struggle to overturn the orthodox Christian doctrine of nations, Barth's ideological triumph was complete. But that victory exacted a steep price.

The Revolutionary Excesses of Christian Humanism

Throughout the Western world, both State and Church have adopted Barth's doctrine of "near and distant neighbours." This doctrine posits that when we encounter "foreigners" or "strangers" — whether as citizens or Christians — we must not allow "being in one's own people" to become "a prison and stronghold". Every man must instead obey God's command "to move out from his beginning and therefore seek a wider field". The result has been that neither the State nor the Church works any longer to preserve and protect what even Barth conceded is our "divine disposition" to love kith and kin over both neighbours and strangers. On the contrary, political and religious leaders alike now act as if "our only impulse" should "be so to strengthen the inner forces of our own land and people that we can not only tolerate many foreign countries and many foreigners who find a second home among us but make them our own". Barth denied that the church can "legitimate its own division along racial lines 'because the community owes to the world a witness...to the mutual fellowship of human beings.'"⁶⁶

In the years since his death, the "inner forces" pushing both State and Church to embrace the neo-communist program of open borders and mass Third World immigration have become so powerful that

---

65 McFarland, "Rethinking," 227; Karl Barth, *God Here and Now* (London: Routledge, 2003), 83; Joseph L Mangina, "Bearing the Marks of Jesus: The Church in the Economy of Salvation in Barth and Hauerwas," (1999) 52(3) *Scottish Journal of Theology* 269, at 278, 302; Karl Barth, CD III 4, 291, 305; Joseph L Mangina, "The Stranger as Sacrament: Karl Barth and the Ethics of Ecclesial Practice," (1999) 1(3) *International Journal of Systematic Theology* 322, at 333.

66 *Ibid.*, 291-294; Mangina, "Stranger as Sacrament," 331.

the historic identity of every Anglo-Saxon Protestant (and European Christian) nation has been thrown into doubt. The universalist humanism invoked to justify the globalist program is based not upon reason but upon an "existential leap of faith" entailing a host of unknown and potentially dangerous consequences. Unless and until Protestant theology recognizes the ecclesiastical legitimacy of the *Volkskirche*, it may be impossible to avoid "excessive" reactions from the forces of ethnoreligious particularism demonized by Barth. Christian ethnopatriotism is down but not out.

Barth acknowledged, of course, that loyalty to one's own people "does not exclude the recognition and respecting of other nationalities or the will to experience fellowship with them." He also knew that it was "not wholly impossible to speak in rational and Christian terms with at least some" defenders of folk-centred, national churches. The need for many such conversations has become much more urgent since the abstract humanism of Barth's theology has transgressed the boundaries within which he sought to confine it. Barth denied that the nation was an order of creation, but he affirmed that there were at least "two distinct circles of natural fellow-humanity." Unlike national identity which is inherently fluid and contingent, Barth maintained that the relationships between man and woman and parent and children are posited "irreversibly, inflexibly, and indestructibly" by the God-given nature of mankind.[67]

Unfortunately, the ideological civil wars of the twentieth century did not come to an end in 1945. By the Sixties, the forces of cosmopolitan universalism had launched an ongoing cultural revolution which seems set to dissolve the last two orders of creation recognized by Barth. Relationships between men and women, parents and children are becoming as fluid, reversible, and removable as national identity now that both the State and many ostensibly Christian churches "tolerate" feminism, homosexuality, gender fluidity, same-sex marriage,

---

67 Barth CD III 4, 308, 288.

abortion-on-demand, artificial insemination, illegitimacy, and single-parent "families" slavishly dependent upon the corporate welfare state. An incremental, creeping, toleration of incest, polygamy, and paedophilia is following not far behind. Already, Muslim colonies in the West have normalized cousin marriages; feminist journalists suggest that all things considered, polygamy offers the best balance between autonomy and intimacy for today's emancipated career woman; and who knows what happens when fashionably "transgressive" same-sex couples invite "their" children into the privacy of Frankenfamily bedrooms?

In these circumstances, a critical re-assessment of Barth's theology of the anti-nation is long overdue. The tortured trajectory of Barth's long campaign against the ideal of the *Volkskirche* is highly instructive. Barth asserted that no place or people can be holy: "God alone is holy."[68] Nonetheless he acknowledged that God had willed Old Israel to become a holy nation. To minimize the normative force of that concession, Barth contended that the covenant between God and Israel was only a provisional arrangement. It was finally brought to fruition by the advent of Christ and his suffering on the Cross. In other words, the central role in the economy of salvation is filled by Christ. Ironically, Barth's Christocentrism left him open to charges of supersessionism; i.e. the belief that Old Covenant Israel was superseded by the New Israel incarnate in the church.[69]

Struggling to resist the supersessionist logic of his Christology, Barth denied that the unbelief of Jews excludes them from "the community of God" because their "election…exists according to God's eternal decree as the people of Israel (in the whole range of its history in past and future, *ante* and *post Christum natum.*)."[70] In effect, Barth provides theological support for the claim that the Jewish ethno-nation

---

68   Ibid., 292.

69   R Kendall Soulen, *The God of Israel and Christian Theology* (Minneapolis, MN: Fortress Press, 1996), 85–94.

70   Barth, *CD* III 4, 292, 310, 197–200.

is a unique order of creation — even though Jews still flatly deny that the coming of Christ changed everything. Of course, Barth does not want to promote the "direct or indirect renewal of Jewish nationalism (which is the prototype of all bad nationalisms)."[71] He does, however, situate contemporary Jews (and the modern State of Israel) in a direct line of descent from Old Israel. As a holy nation elected by God, Israel remains — despite its continued disobedience — the chosen people, an ontological status not available to Gentile nations.

According to Barth, neither in "the sphere of creation" nor "in the *eschaton*, in the light of the final revelation," does Scripture advert to "the problem of nations." He asserted that "we can read...the whole context of Genesis 1–9...without finding a single reference to the presence of individual peoples."[72] A better view is that Genesis 1–9 represents a creation myth; it presupposes the existence of other peoples, such as the Egyptians and the Babylonians; it also provides the Israelites, emerging from exile and ignorant of their own identity with a narrative which distinguishes the covenantal creation of their holy nation from the mythological origins of those other peoples.[73] Throughout Scripture, the sea and the land serve as recurrent metaphors for Gentiles and Jews, respectively. Some say that, as God created his cosmic temple in Genesis One, the Israelites were set apart from the Gentiles on the third day; it was then that "the waters under the heavens" were "gathered together into one place" called the "Seas," thereby allowing "the dry land" to appear (Genesis 1:9).[74] On that reading, contrary to Barth's claim, therefore, the relationship between "nations" and "humanity" was foreshadowed in the sphere of creation.

---

71 Barth, *CD* II 2, 280–281.

72 Barth, *CD* III 4, 310.

73 Ibid., 310; cf John H Walton, *The Lost World of Genesis One: Ancient Cosmology and the Origins Debate* (Downers Grove, IL: IVP Academic, 2009).

74 Norman Voss, "The Six Days of Creation," Covenant Creation Conference, 2010, lecture available online at: http://preteristhosting.com/ad7onet/audio/CCC2010/CCC2010_Lecture_02_Norm_Voss_2.mp3.

Barth believed that a final solution to the naggingly persistent problem of national identity will come with the *eschaton* (i.e. the last days). Only by appealing to an abstract, ahistorical, and passively futurist eschatology could Barth paper over the tension between his doctrine of Israel and his teaching on near and distant neighbours. As we have seen, Barth casually dissolved primordial biocultural distinctions between strangers and neighbours, out-groups, and in-groups, into the lowest common denominator of "humanity." He then declared grandly that an allegedly divine commandment of xenophilia is mandatory for every Christian people.

Barth also licensed — in perpetuity — an obdurate, self-assertive, Jewish ethno-nation whose identity is grounded firmly in the collective rejection of Christ as the Son of God. Accordingly, Barth was no more interested than were the *Deutsche Christen* in continuing the Christian mission to convert individual Jews to the faith. His utopian vision of the *collective* conversion of Jews in the last days left him indifferent to "the role of *personal choice* in the matter of Jewish salvation."[75] Only through the mysterious work of God, he believed, will Jews come to recognize the Lordship of Jesus Christ. Until the apocalypse, however, Jews remain their own Messiah with a self-proclaimed mission "to heal the world." Barth insisted that "the church" must "not dispute... the eternal election of Israel." While expressing sorrow over "the nationalist legalistic Messiah-dream of the Synagogue," Barth affirmed that "the bow of the one covenant" still arches over both unbelieving Jews and faithful Christians. In Barth's humanist ecclesiology, such contradictions and double standards — like the "possibility of unbelief, false belief, and superstition, of ignorance, indifference, hate, and doubt" forever dividing the visible from the invisible church — "all lie close at hand and will continue so to lie as long as time lasts, as long as

---

75 Johnson, "Jewish Rejection of Jesus," 238.

the final revelation of the victory of Jesus Christ has not yet dispersed these shadows."[76]

Barth, along with leading English churchmen such as George Bell and W.R. Inge, believed that Adolf Hitler and the *Deutsche Christen* were, at bottom, engaged in a war on Christianity. In stark contrast, therefore, genuinely faithful German Christians, individually and collectively, were victims of, not participants in, the crimes of the Nazi regime. Barth and Bell were insisted that the *DC* movement, despite its specious claims to orthodoxy, was as anti-Christian as openly pagan Nazis. Unsurprisingly, therefore, Bell was outraged when the British government, during post-war denazification proceedings, "decided, in the summer of 1947, to recognize former *DC* groups as members of the German Evangelical community." Naturally, Bell "welcomed the building of bridges with German Protestantism. But, in failing to distinguish the *DC* from mainstream German Evangelicals, the British government challenged the Anglican interpretation of the past which, as noted, presented Nazism as entirely anti-Christian." In response, Bell angrily berated the occupation authorities for tolerating "Nazis in disguise." He simply refused to recognize former members of the *DC* movement as a legitimate element of the postwar Evangelical church.[77]

The Verdict of German Historiography: A Hung Jury

In 1952, English historian Alan Bullock echoed the essence of the Anglican interpretation of the National Socialist regime in his mammoth biography, *Hitler: A Study in Tyranny*.[78] On the Anglican view, "the idea of denazification was flawed." Anglicans held that there was

---

76 Karl Barth, *CD*, II 2, 204–205; Gerhard Sauter, "Why is Karl Barth's Church Dogmatics not a 'Theology of Hope'? Some Observations on Barth's Understanding of Eschatology," (1999) 52(4) *Scottish Journal of Theology* 407; Barth, *God Here and Now*, 84.

77 Lawson, *Church of England and the Holocaust*, 128–129.

78 Alan Bullock, *Hitler: A Study in Tyranny* (London: Odhams Press, 1952).

no need to denazify anyone apart from the top-tier Nazis elites "who were being dealt with by the International Military Tribunal (IMT) and war-crimes trials." It was "contrary to all Christian principles" to suggest "that the wider population needed to be denazified."[79] But, of course, the Allied Powers operated on the presumption that Germany alone bore the guilt for the Thirty Years War of the twentieth century. The conventional wisdom held that the allies had waged two just wars, the first against the evils of "Prusso-German" nationalism, and the second against Hitler's tyrannical regime. Even today, almost eighty years after the end of the war, legislators in Australia and Canada are still waging a cultural war against the spiritual contagion of "evil and tyranny" emanating from the German past. In Australia, the latest fashion in political virtue-signalling has produced a spate of laws threatening anyone who publicly displays "a Nazi symbol" (even a Roman salute) with imprisonment or a large fine.

Having surrendered unconditionally and suffered occupation for years thereafter by the Allied Powers, Germans themselves have been expected, indeed compelled, to accept the verdict of history as written by the winners. Still, the received narrative is meeting increasing resistance. In the English-speaking world, Bullock's contemptuous portrait of Hitler as a power-hungry and unprincipled opportunist still reigns in the popular imagination. In academic circles, however, it has been challenged, *inter alia*, by R. H. S. Stolfi who was, before his death in 2012, a professor at the US Naval Postgraduate School in Monterey, California, and a Colonel in the US Marine Corps Reserve. Stolfi flatly denies that Hitler can be characterized fairly or accurately as an evil tyrant. His interpretative essay, *Hitler: Beyond Evil and Tyranny*, portrays the *Führer* as a great man, indeed, "as one of Hegel's impossibly rare world-historical personalities."[80]

---

79 Lawson, *Church of England and the Holocaust*, 122.
80 R.H.S. Stolfi, *Hitler: Beyond Evil and Tyranny* (Amherst, N.Y.: Prometheus, 2011), 219–222.

Even a few German historians have dared to push back against the standard narrative of the Third Reich as a criminal regime led by a ruthless dictator bent on world conquest. Given the growing debate among Germans regarding the origins and conduct of both world wars, Anglo-Protestants around the world may soon be asking themselves whether our historical enmity towards Germany was ever justified. Could we have mistaken friend for foe and vice-versa? A reformed Anglican political theology grounded in the recent rethinking of modern German history could be an important step towards the resurrection of the British and German provinces of European Christendom as a family of nations, struggling together to recover their ethnoreligious roots as kindred peoples of God.

Such a vision, it should be obvious, is anathema to contemporary Anglican theologians such as Oliver O'Donovan. O'Donovan makes his disdain for the notion that Christendom might be resurrected more than obvious. The idea of Christendom, he declares, has no claim on our interest now. Certainly, not the claim of resurrection "which is the claim of Israel and Christ. Not even the claim of tradition since tradition is continuity" and we "now have little continuity with Christendom; it is not our tradition anymore; its assumptions are alien to us."[81] But perhaps that is because, in the aftermath of the Second World War, the church in both Germany and the British dominions became an unofficial arm of the transnational corporate welfare state.

The idea that the churches of Germany and England should be of, by, and for the founding stock of Germany and the scattered, British-descended peoples of the Anglosphere is even more alien to Anglican political theologians than the vanished traditions of Christendom. But, before Anglican political theology could, in good conscience, abandon the hope of a restored Anglo-Saxon Christendom, it was bound to anathematize the Germanic provinces of European Christendom as enemies led by a Kaiser and a Führer both of whom allegedly

---

81 Oliver O'Donovan, *The Desire of the Nations: Rediscovering the Roots of Political Theology* (Cambridge: Cambridge University Press, 1996), 194.

committed heinous crimes against humanity in the name of a "pagan" ethno-nationalism.

Faced with the fact of their crushing defeat in both wars, the German people and their leaders were under enormous pressure to plead guilty as charged. In the spirit of Christian charity, perhaps it is time for us to listen to those presenting the long-overdue case for the defense. This is especially so with the crimes alleged against the German nation with respect to the Holocaust. After all, the Canadian government has recently decided that not even Canadians will be allowed to "deny" or "downplay" that pre-eminently Jewish mythos.

The *Historikerstreit* (historians controversy) of the mid-1980s emerged as a conflict between liberals insisting that Germany must atone for its Nazi past by committing itself unreservedly to the West and conservative historians seeking to defend the honour of the German nation, either by comparing the alleged crimes of the National Socialist regime to other similar historical events (*e.g.*, Ernst Nolte) or by attaching sole responsibility for those alleged crimes to depraved ideological fanatics in leadership positions while defending the honour of the *Wehrmacht* (*e.g.*, Andreas Hillgruber).[82] The literature on the *Historikerstreit* is enormous; it also reveals the depth of the divisions within the West German intellectual community, fissures extending well beyond the ranks of the historical profession. The ongoing dispute in the late Eighties first captured international attention when Jürgen Habermas, a prominent leftist political philosopher, issued his famously sharp critique of the "apologetic tendencies" in the work of

---

82 Nolte, *europäische Bürgerkrieg*; and, "Between Myth and Revisionism," in H.W. Koch, ed., *Aspects of the Third Reich* (New York: St. Martins Press, 1987), 17–38. Andreas Hillgruber, *Zweierlei Untergang: Die Zerschlagung des Deutschen Reiches und das Ende das Ende des europäische Judentums* (Berlin: Corso bei Siedler, 1986).

historians such as Nolte, Hillgruber, and several of their professional colleagues.[83]

More recently, the *Historikerstreit* has been reignited by two historians whose work is worthy of special mention. First, a retired *Bundeswehr* general, Gerd Schultze-Rhonhof, has analyzed, at length, the origins of what he calls the war with many fathers. The English translation of his book has captured considerable attention outside Germany.[84] Then there is the work of a very prolific independent historian and publicist, Dr. Stefan Scheil.[85] In his many books, he presents what he describes as a "realist" perspective on diplomatic history. His corpus deals, *inter alia*, with the origins of both the First and Second World Wars. The rest of his work has been devoted to the diplomacy surrounding the escalation of WWII, its conduct, and its aftermath in post-war Germany.

Together, Scheil and Schultze-Rhonhof make a powerful case for the proposition that neither the origins nor the escalation of the war in Europe can be understood by examining the role of Hitler's Germany in isolation as mainstream historians are wont to do. They contend

---

[83] The most notable contributions to the debate in German are collected in *"Historikerstreit": Die Dokumentation der Kontroverse um die Enzigartigkeit der nationalsozialistischen Judenvernichtung* (München: Piper, 1987). A useful book-length discussion in English of the *Historikerstreit* is Charles S. Maier, *The Unmasterable Past: History, Holocaust, and German National Identity* (Cambridge, MA: Harvard University Press, 1997).

[84] Gerd Schultze-Rhonhof, *1939. Der Krieg, der viele Väter hatte: Der lange Anlauf zum Zweiten Weltkrieg* (München: Olzog Verlag, 2003). [English edition. *1939, The War that had Many Fathers: The Long Run-Up to the Second World War* (Lulu, 2011)]. A video of a talk (with subtitles) given by the author on the subject of this book is available at: https://archive.org/details/SchultzeRhonhofManyFathersWPermanentSubtitles.

[85] A complete list of Dr. Scheil's many publications can be found at: http://stefan-scheil.de/veranstaltungen/. Here are the publication details of but one: *Churchill, Hitler und der Antisemitismus: die deutsche Diktatur, ihre politischen Gegner und die europäische Krise der Jahre 1938/39* (Berlin: Duncker & Humblot, 2008 [2. Aufl. 2009]).

that the war with Poland, for example, cannot be understood apart from the aggressive foreign policy driven by the delusions of grandeur which affected the newly independent Polish government in the interwar period (and which were encouraged by Britain and the USA).[86] Similarly, Scheil's interpretation of Operation Barbarossa as a preventive war receives powerful support from the Russian military historian Viktor Suvorov in his book identifying Stalin as *The Chief Culprit* in the origins of the Second World War.[87]

Outside Germany, both Schultze-Rhonhof and Dr. Scheil could be described, uncontroversially, as "revisionist historians". Both challenge the conventional view that Germany alone bears responsibility for the outbreak of the Second World War. Scheil is also critical of the received interpretation of the war's end as a liberation. In Germany, however, both the government and the guild of professional historians deny that such "revisionist" history is a legitimate, good faith effort to arrive at a better understanding of the past. One prominent historian, Wolfgang Benz, spoke for many of his colleagues when he condemned "revisionism" of Dr. Scheil and other "New Right" historians as a deliberate attack on the professional consensus defining *historische Wahrheit* (historical truth). Benz charges that Scheil is merely a politically motivated right-wing activist who seeks to wipe away (or "relativize") the stain of what all decent people recognize as the greatest crime in human history.[88] The question here is whether such a charge can be supported by a fair-minded reading of the historiographical literature on the Holocaust. In my view, the answer is not at all obvious.

---

86   Stefan Scheil, *Polens Zwischenkrieg: Der Weg der Zweiten Republik von Versailles nach Gleiwitz* (Pour le Merité, 2022).

87   Stefan Scheil, *Präventivkrieg Barbarossa: Fragen, Fakten, Antworten* (Schnellroda: Verlag Antaios, 2011); Viktor Suvorov, *The Chief Culprit: Stalin's Grand Design to Start World War II* (Annapolis, MD: Naval Institute Press, 2013).

88   Wolfgang Benz, Geschichtspolitik der „Neuen Rechten": Revisionismus contra historische Wahrheit, Anmerkungen aus aktuellem Anlass, 62(10) 2014 *Zeitschrift für Geschichtswissenschaft*, 785–801.

The Protean Nature of Holocaust Myth

One of the curious features of the *Historikerstreit* was the fact that, although many of the leading actors were historians, prior to the clash between historian Ernst Nolte and the sociologist Jürgen Habermas few German historians had systematically investigated the alleged crimes against the Jews of the National Socialist regime. Indeed, those alleged crimes had only recently become known to Germans and the world-at-large as "the Holocaust." As we have seen, English churchmen before and during the war portrayed Christians, not Jews, as the primary targets of Nazi persecution. Even after the war, in his book *The End of an Age* published in 1948, W.R. Inge barely mentions the Jews when discussing the "curse of war" or Nazi racialism. On the contrary, he asserts that "there is no doubt that the main preoccupation of Germany in *both* [emphasis added] wars was to settle the old quarrel between Teuton and Slav...A duel to the death between Teuton and Slav was inevitable."[89]

The Holocaust Mythos was, in large part, a product of the 1979 TV series which appeared in German as: *Holocaust: Die Geschichte der Familie Weiss*.[90] Writing in the Eighties, Nolte himself seems to have accepted uncritically the popular, mass-mediated narrative revolving around gas chambers and six million dead Jews. He famously suggested that the only difference between the mass murders in the Soviet gulag archipelago and the German KZs (*i.e.*, concentration camps) was the technical innovation of the gas chambers.[91]

Similarly, Holocaust "revisionism" (or "denial" as it is also pejoratively described) only came out of the closet in the late 1970s (and

---

89 Inge, *End of an Age*, 208–209.
90 "Revisiting the TV Series 'Holocaust' Thirty Years On," https://www.cultures-of-history.uni-jena.de/focus/remembering-the-shoah/revisiting-the-tv-series-holocaust-thirty-years-on.
91 Ernst Nolte, "Vergangenheit, die nicht vergehen will: Eine Rede, die geschrieben, aber nicht gehalten werden konnte," in „*Historikerstreit*," 45.

several of the best-known revisionists were not themselves German). Such work was subject to prosecution under the German criminal code for insults to the memory of the Jewish victims of Nazi persecution or for incitement to racial hatred (*Volksverhetzung*). No doubt, that legal environment had a chilling effect on historical investigation of "the Holocaust" as such. Consequently, most of the conflicts between Holocaust revisionists and their mainstream rivals occurred *after* the *Historikerstreit* proper.

At first, Holocaust revisionists such as Fred Leuchter, Jürgen Graf, and Germar Rudolf focused on documentary evidence (or the lack thereof) and forensic examinations of the sites (most famously, Auschwitz) that were said to have been "extermination factories."[92] Some mainstream investigators such as Robert Jan van Pelt have countered the revisionists with their own empirical investigations to build "the case *for* Auschwitz."[93] But, even the thoroughly respectable former editor of *Der Spiegel*, Fritjof Meyer — who rejects the "revisionist" label — gave aid and comfort to revisionists, willy-nilly, by undermining the canonical figure of six million Jewish deaths. He calculated that the Birkenau crematoria, even working at close to maximum capacity, could not have processed more than 400,000 bodies.[94]

Here one should bear in mind that the Soviets originally charged that some four million people were murdered at Auschwitz. The official claim was later reduced to just over a million deaths. Hence, Meyer's work represents another sharp reduction in the number

---

92 See, *e.g.*, Germar Rudolf, *Lectures on the Holocaust: Controversial Issues Cross-Examined* Third, Expanded Edition (Uckfield, TN: Castle Hill, 2017); Samuel Crowell, *The Gas Chamber of Sherlock Holmes and Other Writings on the Holocaust, Revisionism, and Historical Understanding* (Charleston, WV: Nine-Banded Books, 2011).

93 Robert Jan van Pelt, *The Case for Auschwitz: Evidence from the Irving Trial* (Bloomington: Indiana University Press, 2002).

94 Fritjof Meyer, "Die Zahl der Opfer von Auschwitz: Neue Erkenntnisse durch Archivfunde (Number of Auschwitz Victims: New Insights from Recent Archival Discoveries)" (2002) 52(5) *Osteuropa* 631–641.

alleged to have been victims of a murderous Nazi regime at Auschwitz-Birkenau. Even then, he fails to establish that 400,000 murders were *in fact* committed there; his number is simply the upper limit of bodies which it was technically *possible* to cremate. Meyer simply assumes that the great majority of deaths at Auschwitz were victims of gassing rather than typhus or other diseases which raged through the camp. In fact, the objective he sets for himself in this study is a rather modest one. He claims to have brought the dimensions of the civilizational collapse at long last within the realm of the imaginable (*in den Bereich des Vorstellbaren*), thereby conceding that previous accounts of the Auschwitz "extermination factory" stretched the limits of credibility. But the ability to "imagine" 400,000 victims of gassing at Auschwitz does not meet the traditional Anglo-Saxon standard of criminal guilt: proof beyond a reasonable doubt.

In stark contrast to Meyer's body count, the Arolsen Archives of the International Red Cross, suggest that no more than 30,000 Jews died at Auschwitz, out of a total of less than 300,000 deaths in fifteen camps. Nor did the Red Cross report the presence of homicidal gas chambers in the camps. Holocaust sceptics are thus able to point to the lack of compelling documentary and physical evidence for the existence of "extermination factories."[95] But those who put the revisionist case to the German public require, not just material evidence, but also moral courage. More than a few, including Ursula Haverbeck, an indomitable grandmother in her nineties, suffered imprisonment; in her case, for insisting publicly that Auschwitz was a labour camp in which Zyklon B was used a delousing agent, not as a weapon of mass extermination.

Facing such resistance, one suspects that the academic Holocaust industry is ever-more reluctant to stake its credibility on survivor testimony set in Auschwitz as "the capital of the Holocaust". But it is not just the empirical difficulties involved in establishing an accurate and unimpeachable body count, combined with the debate over the actual

---

95 Nicholas Kollerstrom, *Breaking the Spell: The Holocaust, Myth and Reality* (Uckfield, TN: Castle Hill, 2014, 85–90.

causes of inmate deaths, which have encouraged historians to move beyond "the Auschwitz Syndrome."[96] For the most part, historians now writing about the Holocaust follow the methodological advice of Hayden White to not enter into debates focused on facts and forensic analyses but to secure control of the narrative. In pursuit of that objective, a well-known textbook entitled *Debates on the Holocaust* declined to engage with the ghettoized "deniers."[97] Instead, mainstream historians implicitly "downplay" the gas chamber narrative, shifting the centre of gravity in the Holocaust narrative to a multitude of stories set in the "black earth" of the so-called "bloodlands" in Eastern Europe.[98]

Nowadays the Holocaust is presented as a process having more in common with colonial massacres than with the iconic image of the death camp. The result, however, is a remarkable loss of narrative focus. For example, Dan Stone maintains there was not one Holocaust; rather than "a monolithic micro-managed project," there was "a series of 'Holocausts.'" He attributes this to "the shocking collaboration and antisemitic initiative in occupied Europe," a circumstance that suggests that the Holocaust was a European as well as a specifically German project. Indeed, responsibility for the Holocaust is said to have extended beyond Europe. Jews have long complained that they were refused refuge in Canada prior to the war, so that even Canadians contributed to the Holocaust — hence the presumptive need nowadays

---

96 Dan Stone, "Beyond 'the Auschwitz Syndrome': Holocaust Historiography after the Cold War," (2010) 42(5) *Patterns of Prejudice* 454.

97 Hayden White, "The Public Relevance of Historical Studies: A Reply to Dirk Moses," (2005) 44(3) *History and Theory* 333–338; Tom Lawson, *Debates on the Holocaust* (Manchester: Manchester University Press, 2010). *Cf.* the similarly titled book by the revisionist Thomas Dalton, *Debating the Holocaust: A New Look at Both Sides* (Uckfield, TN: Castle Hill, 2020).

98 See, two books by Timothy Snyder, *Black Earth: The Holocaust as History and Warning* (New York: Vintage, 2016); and *Bloodlands: Europe Between Hitler and Stalin* (New York: Basic Books, 2022).

to suppress all those who would deny or downplay the magnitude of the crimes committed against the Jewish people.[99]

Even before the war, Stone suggests, fascistic movements throughout Europe were the precursors to genocide. It may be that Ernst Nolte's study of the long European civil war between Bolshevism and National Socialism does, indeed, provide the most appropriate context for finding what (or whether a) common thread underlies the current historiographical flood of local narratives about the many "indigenous Holocausts" in collaborationist regimes outside Germany. Indeed, it is not just the spatial boundaries of the Holocaust that have been expanded but the temporal frame of reference as well. The Germans are now being called to account for "colonial genocides," not just outside Germany but even before the First World war in German Southwest Africa (now Namibia). Jürgen Zimmerer, for example, draws a straight line between the "Herero and Nama Genocide" and the crimes of the Third Reich. There has been pushback against the "colonial genocide" thesis, however. Dissident scholar Professor Bruce Gilley argues that German colonialism was a positive experience for the indigenous populations. He also rejects postcolonial accusations that German counter-insurgency campaigns in Southwest Africa were "genocidal."[100]

The histories describing the "Holocaust" as "a myriad of events in a myriad of places," relying upon "myriad pieces of data that converge on one conclusion," generally portray Jews as victims.[101] But ethnic con-

---

99 Dan Stone, *Histories of the Holocaust* (Oxford: Oxford University Press, 2010); Irving Abella and Harold Troper, *None is Too Many: Canada and the Jews of Europe, 1933–1948* (Toronto: Lester & Orpen Dennys, 1986).

100 Jürgen Zimmerer, *From Windhoek to Auschwitz? Reflections on the Relationship Between Colonialism and National Socialism* (De Gruyter Oldenbourg, 2023); Bruce Gilley, *In Defense of German Colonialism: And How its Critics Empowered Nazis, Communists, and the Enemies of the West* (Regnery, 2022).

101 Michael Shermer and Alex Grobman, *Denying History: Who Says the Holocaust Never Happened and Why Do They Say It* Updated and Expanded (Berkeley: University of California Press, 2000).

flicts between the Jews of Eastern Europe and host populations were not the novel product of the wars between Germany and, first, Poland and then the Soviet Union. Instead, ethnic conflict between Jews and other national groups, including Poles and Russians, was endemic to the Russian-Polish borderlands. By the end of the nineteenth century, the compact, culturally distinct Jewish population in that region exceeded five million. For the Russian government, the conditions of Jewish life there created a set of problems that the Czarist regime sought to resolve through a program of targeted reforms. According to John Doyle Klier and Andrew Joyce, the reform program foundered on the widespread perception that the Jews were characterized by "religious fanaticism" as well as their reputation for unrestrained "economic exploitation" of non-Jews. Resentment against the Jews eventually boiled over into a series of pogroms throughout the nineteenth century. Both scholars challenge the persistent Jewish "legend" that these pogroms were perpetrated by an antisemitic Russian state bent not on reform but on persecuting passive Jewish victims.[102]

Before or during WWII, there is good reason to question whether Jews were blameless victims devoid of agency. Many Jews and Jewish organizations (ranging from Judeo-Bolsheviks in the USSR to leading politicians, bankers, lawyers, and judges in Britain and the USA) were active participants, first in campaigns encouraging, and then supporting, war against Germany. Nor can we ignore the role of Jews as active belligerents during the war, whether in partisan groups, allied military forces, or civilian agencies deployed against the Germans and their own allies.[103]

---

102 John Doyle Klier, *Russians, Jews, and the Pogroms of 1881–1882* (Cambridge: Cambridge University Press, 2011); Andrew Joyce, "Revisiting the 19th Century Russian Pogroms," (2012) 12(2) *The Occidental Quarterly* 61.

103 Johannes Rogalla von Bieberstein, *Jüdischer Bolschewismus: Mythos und Realität* (Schnellroda: Edition Antaios, 2003); Scheil, *Churchill, Hitler, und der Antisemitismus*; Benjamin Ginsberg, *How the Jews Defeated Hitler: Exploding the Myth of Jewish Passivity in the Face of Nazism* (London: Rowand & Littlefield, 2016).

The field of Holocaust studies has thus become a contest between two, mutually hostile, camps; the one (typically inside academia) devoted to story-telling[104] (featuring heart-wrenching survivor testimony, heartless perpetrators, and callous bystanders); the other, the much-reviled revisionists excluded from academia (*e.g.*, Thomas Dalton, Germar Rudolf, Samuel Crowell and Nicholas Kollerstrom). The latter pursue empirical studies to portray the past *wie es eigentlich gewesen ist* (once thought to be the point and purpose of historical studies). More recently, however, mainstream narratives have been challenged by revisionists with stories of their own to tell. E. Michael Jones and Charles Sanford, for example, have presented Traditional Catholic ripostes to the Holocaust Mythos.[105]

It turns out that in the realm of Holocaust studies, the boundary between history as such and the "memory culture" constructed by public authorities has all but dissolved. Indeed, the Holocaust memory culture has become the official foundation for German national identity after reunification: a state religion or political theology in all but name. The growth of the Holocaust memory culture in both Germany and Western culture more broadly was facilitated through an ecumenical theology invoking the image of a "Global Jesus" anchored in a traditional Augustinian cosmology.[106] Global Jesus is generally conceived as the archetypical, universal "victim" whose resurrected body ascended into the city of God, from which he will return to recreate the cosmos at some indeterminate time in our future. In contrast, the story of the historical "national" Jesus pits his "friends" against his "enemies" in Israel according to the flesh. When read according to the

---

104 Norbert Frei and Wulf Kansteiner, *Den Holocaust erzählen: Historiographie zwischen wissenschaftlicher Empirie und narrative Kreativität* (Jena: Wallstein Verlag, 2013).

105 E. Michael Jones, *The Holocaust Narrative* (South Bend, IN: Fidelity Press, 2023); Charles Sandford, "The Denial of Holocaust Denial: Robert Faurisson's Case for Revisionism," (2021) 41(1) *Culture Wars* 6–37.

106 See chapters 3 and 4.

Hebrew hermeneutic employed by preterist scholars, the biblical narrative ends with the return of Christ in the Parousia that accompanied the destruction of Jerusalem in AD 70.

Could it be that much of the contemporary power of the Holocaust Mythos (in comparison to the abstract and fading hope of the Second Coming) is derived from the setting of the former in the recent past? Those first and second century Christians still sensitive to the Hebrew hermeneutic of the biblical narrative must have been deeply impressed as they saw the hope of the resurrection fulfilled in the emergence of a new Jerusalem in their own lifetime. The enemies of Christ had become his footstool before their eyes. Similarly, the crushing defeat of their German enemies (with a little help from their own powerful friends) enabled Jews to infuse the subsequent resurrection of Israel with enormous rhetorical force as "agents," not "victims."

Unfortunately, post-war Protestant and Catholic churches became increasingly uncomfortable with the language of "friends" and "enemies". After all, such language is rooted in the political theology of war associated with the "colonialist" legacy of the now-defunct *jus publicum Europaeum*.[107] Post-war churches prefer to preach a universalist, humanist faith which underwrites the campaign to create "tolerant," "multicultural" societies in every Western nation. The German church struggle of the 1930s was an early battle in the ongoing cultural war between globalism and nationalism. The battle resumed in the post-war era. All residues of the National Socialist campaign to infuse a distinctively German *Volksgeist* into (especially) Protestant churches were ruthlessly suppressed by the re-education and de-Nazification programs imposed by Allied occupation authorities. The result has been the memorialization of the Holocaust, on the one hand, and, on the other, the pathologization of the autochthonous, "biodeutsche," or "Prusso-German" culture. Over the past seven decades, the Holocaust Mythos has penetrated deeply into other Western cultures. Universalist

---

107 Carl Schmitt, *The Nomos of the Earth: The International Law of Jus Publicum Europaeum* (New York: Telos Press, 2006).

humanism under the aegis of global Jesus was weaponized to wage the ongoing cultural/psychological war on both German and British ethno-national identities.

History, the Holocaust, and the Memory Industry

The official memory industry has not been an unambiguous success story, however. It has had unintended and unwelcome consequences. Some of these were explored in a four-day conference on "Hijacking Memory: The Holocaust and the New Right" hosted by the *Haus der Kulturen der Welt* in Potsdam in early June 2022.[108] Many conference participants criticized the established Holocaust memory culture for its exclusionary impact on non-white German citizens unable to identify with the *biodeutsch* "perpetrators" of the Holocaust. Paradoxically, sharing in a hereditary guilt for the crimes of one's ancestors has become a badge of honour among Germans who laboured for decades to establish the Holocaust memory culture as the foundation of national identity. On the other hand, official insistence on the "singularity" and "uniqueness" of the Holocaust has tended not just to discourage comparative studies of other genocides but also to stigmatize as anti-Semites anyone — even leftist Jews — who criticize the treatment of Palestinians by the Israeli state.

Even so, both those who defend the official Holocaust memory culture, as well as those who press for a more inclusive approach, promote a de-politicized and cosmopolitan theology of genocide. The academic project of Holocaust and genocide studies replaces the existential political distinction between "friends" and "enemies" with a globalized, juridical process that distinguishes among "perpetrators," "victims," and "bystanders." Universalist humanism serves as the religious foundation for this cosmopolitan theology of genocide. Historically,

---

108 Videos of conference presentations — in English and German — are available at https://mediathek.hkw.de/en/search?q=hijacking+memory.

however, among the nations of European Christendom, the necessarily ethnoreligious foundation of the political theology of war had a much more particularistic flavour. It was only *after* the Second World War that the newly coined concept of genocide was incorporated into international law. In effect, German ethnic nationalism was criminalized *ex post facto* as a militarized threat to world peace. The allegedly "barbaric" violence perpetrated by the Third Reich was presented as the product of racial or ethnic hatred to be shunned henceforth by a "civilized" liberal international order marked by the attributes of tolerance and diversity.

Accordingly, the ethnoreligious or ethno-patriotic advocacy of the "New Right" in Germany and elsewhere in the West is certain to "rustle the jimmies" of cosmopolitan individuals such as those speaking at the "Hijacking Memory" conference. Through cosmopolitan eyes, the sponsorship of anti-BDS legislation by the "far-right" *Alternative für Deutschland* party, for example, appeared as little more than a cynical attempt to instrumentalize the memory of the Holocaust in pursuit of a sinister neo-fascist agenda. No less suspect, for cosmopolitans, are those German historians on the dissident right, from Ernst Nolte to Stefan Scheil, who openly defend the honour of the German people and its *Wehrmacht*. Those writers reject the burden of guilt forever imposed upon Germans through the official sanctification of the Holocaust Mythos. For such German patriots, the post-war Nuremburg trials were a sham. Those judged as "perpetrators" of "wars of aggression" and "crimes against humanity" were exclusively drawn from those who lost the Second World War. It mattered not that the "winners" committed multiple acts of "industrialized" mass killing of civilians (*e.g.*, Dresden, Hamburg, Hiroshima, and Nagasaki) far more spectacular than any alleged to have been committed by German forces.

Hence, the Nuremburg process did not deliver justice, either to "victims" or to "perpetrators." Instead, it provided juridical cover for the narrative attributing war guilt solely to the German "Scourge of the

Swastika."[109] Originally, "the final solution of the Jewish question" was but one of the "war crimes" or "crimes against humanity" said to have been committed by the Third Reich. It was only later that the judgement at Nuremburg was invoked to license the creation and steady growth of the Holocaust memory industry as a specifically Jewish franchise, a transnational public-private partnership whose foundation mythos is grounded in the newly minted cosmopolitan theology of genocide. It is an open question, however, whether a putatively de-politicized theology of genocide is in any way superior to a "political theology of war" grounded in a realist recognition of intractable, existential conflicts between friend and enemy.

Moses' on Political Theology and the German Question

Having examined the process of *Vergangenheitsbewältigung* (coming to terms with the past) in Germany as well as the efforts of revisionist historians, in Germany and elsewhere, to mitigate the burden of guilt placed on Germans for the war and the Holocaust, it will be instructive to examine the work of two Australian historians, father and son, who present what amounts to a rebuttal case from expert witnesses in support of the case for the prosecution.

John Moses (currently Professorial Associate at St. Mark's National Theological Centre in Canberra) has played a significant role in producing an Australian version of Anglican political theology which, in effect, demonizes Prusso-German militarism as a long-standing aggressive threat to British liberal democracy, resulting in two world wars. Moses has long been interested in the question of German war guilt which came to prominence in the post-war "Fischer Controversy" (relating to historian Fritz Fischer's claim that it was Germany's insatiable drive for world power that caused WWI). More recently, John

---

109 See, *e.g.*, Lord Russell of Liverpool, *The Scourge of the Swastika: A Short History of Nazi War Crimes* (London: Cassell, 1954).

Moses has re-discovered the vanquished spirit of Prusso-German militarism in "the national spirit whipped up by [another] warlord demagogue," Vladimir Putin.[110]

Moses believes that Putin "has launched Russia on a seemingly inexplicable campaign for massive territorial expansion". His own explanation views the modern world as one locked in a perennial struggle between authoritarian nationalist militarism (Prusso-Germany then; now, Russia) and the cosmopolitan liberal democracies of the Anglosphere. By contrast, the speeches delivered by President Putin and the Defence Minister Sergei Shoigu to the Moscow International Security Conference in August 2022 present a very different and far more convincing picture of the major fault line in contemporary geopolitics. In Putin's view, the dominant conflict is not one between "democracy" and "autocracy" but, rather, between the aggressive militarism of globalist elites and the desire of Russia and other nations to preserve and protect their own sovereignty. In short, the conflict is one between globalism and nationalism. Globalist plutocrats are not thinking about how to improve the lives of their citizens in Western countries. Instead, they are obsessed with their own self-interest and super-profits.

It is little wonder that John Moses opposes Putin's "special military operation" in the Ukraine. As a life-long champion of cosmopolitan humanism, Moses naturally sides with globalist elites in their cultural and demographic wars on ethno-nationalism throughout the West. Moses' career in academe and the church has influenced mainstream Anglican political theology in Australia, providing a fertile seedbed for the intellectual formation of his son Dirk's important influence on

---

110 John Moses, "Making Australia Home, or Who Do You Think You Are? A Personal Footnote," (2022) 24(12) *Queensland History Journal* 1136; and "The Prusso-German Idea of War: The Values of a Virtual Rogue State," (2012) 10/12 *History Compass* 901; and "The Machiavellian Motivations of Vladimir Putin" (2022) 46(5) *Quadrant*, 21–23; available online at: https://quadrant.org.au/magazine/2022/05/the-machiavellian-motivations-of-vladimir-putin.

the field of Holocaust and genocide studies. Dirk Moses completed a doctoral dissertation under Martin Jay which was published in 2007 as *German Intellectuals and the Nazi Past*.[111] His more recent work criticizing what he calls "The German Catechism" puts a secularized veneer on the cosmopolitan, Anglican brand of political theology espoused by his father.[112] As set out by the younger Moses, the German Catechism (in effect, the official political theology of a reunified Germany) takes the following form:

The German Catechism

1. The Holocaust is unique because it was the unlimited *Vernichtung der Juden um der Vernichtung willen* (exterminating the Jews for the sake of extermination itself) distinguished from the limited and pragmatic aims of other genocides. It is the first time in history that a state had set out to destroy a people solely on ideological grounds.

2. It was thus a *Zivilisationsbruch* (civilizational rupture) and the moral foundation of the nation.

3. Germany has a special responsibility to Jews in Germany, and a special loyalty to Israel: "*Die Sicherheit Israels ist Teil der Staatsräson unseres Landes*" (Israel's security is part of Germany's reason of state)

4. Antisemitism is a distinct prejudice — and was a distinctly German one. It should not be confused with racism.

---

[111] A. Dirk Moses, *German Intellectuals and the Nazi Past* (Cambridge: Cambridge University Press, 2007); For those who read German, Moses' book can be compared with Stefan Scheil, *Transatlantische Wechselwirkungen: Der Elitenwechsel in Deutschland nach 1945* [Effects of the Transatlantic Transformation: The Changing of the Elites in Germany after 1945] (Duncker & Humblot, 2012).

[112] A. Dirk Moses, "The German Catechism," *Geschichte der Gegenwart*, 23 March 2021, available online at: https://geschichtedergegenwart.ch/the-german-catechism.

5. Antizionism is antisemitism.

Moses is sharply critical of the assumptions underlying this catechism. To be sure, the catechism served an important function in denazifying the country. Moreover, Moses certainly approves of the Holocaust memorial in Berlin. But he maintains that Germany and Germans have changed. Not only has the catechism outlived its usefulness; it imperils the very freedom that Germans ostensibly prize. Its *völkisch* assumptions and fetishization of European civilization versus the Asiatic barbarians who created the gulag archipelago are reminiscent of Nolte's historical apologetics. In short, the catechism is riddled with a multitude of contradictions revealed by the emergence of new multicultural Germany with its *Passdeutsch* (passport German) citizens, together with a host of non-German voices. Moses insists that the time has come to set that superseded civil religion aside and to renegotiate the demands of historical justice in a way that respects all victims of the German state and Germans of all kinds.

Moses, like his father, is an anti-racist. He therefore opposes the juridical concept of genocide for its fixation on racial and ethnic differences. He acknowledges, of course, that the Holocaust became the ideal typical form of genocide, "the crime of crimes," because Germans allegedly sought to annihilate the Jewish people simply because of "who they were". At the same time, he rejects the German catechism because it inadvertently accentuates the visibility of race and ethnicity in the public realm, even among those who deny the biological reality of race. In effect, the catechism privileges the *Biodeutschen*, the descendants of those who perpetrated the Holocaust. "New" Germans cannot participate on equal terms in the national cult of guilt. Moreover, because the meaning of genocide in general is restricted to racially motivated violence, many other mass killings of civilians will not fit within the category of genocide. An obvious example is those counted as collateral damage and excused as military necessity (*e.g.*, those killed and injured in the indiscriminate area bombing of

German cities in WWII); another case concerns those who become targets of state violence for political reasons (*e.g.*, participants in an insurrection).

Moses' critique, therefore, seeks to move beyond "genocide" as the upper threshold of criminality by immunizing "civilians" in general from state violence. This raises an obvious question: how would Moses react if one "civilian," say European or Anglo-Australian, population is faced with a mass influx of other, alien, "civilians"? What should civilians do if globalist state and corporate élites (notionally responsible for the defense of the host population's homeland), far from acting to repel the "enemy" invasion (if need be, by force of arms), actually greet the "rising tide of colour" with open arms?

Just such a scenario was described by the French author, Jean Raspail, in his now-frighteningly realistic, dystopian novel, *The Camp of the Saints*, first published in 1973.[113] The fictional problem identified by Raspail has become a reality for the Anglo-Saxon peoples, now reduced to *de facto* statelessness. As it happens, Dirk Moses has little sympathy for Europeans or Australians who fear that "mass immigration of non-Europeans is overwhelming and will ultimately 'replace' European populations". He dismisses heightened concern that mass Third World immigration is a form of "reverse colonialism" driving "the Great Replacement". Concerns that this process is leading to "white genocide" are, according to Moses, nothing less than "fantastical paranoia based on obdurate blindness to how power works, policy is generated, and processes unfold."[114] It is worth noting that Moses never adverts to the long history of hysteria and overreach among Jews, a paranoia that has led them, for well over a century, to promote mass third world immigration as a means of undermining homogeneous

---

113 Jean Raspail, *The Camp of the Saints* tr. Norman Shapiro (Petoskey, MI: Social Contract Press, 1995)

114 A. Dirk Moses, "'White Genocide' and the Ethics of Public Analysis," (2019) 21(2) *Journal of Genocide Research* 201, at 208–210.

white populations in Europe and the Anglosphere which, they believe, might otherwise target isolated Jewish minorities for persecution.[115]

Moses is adamant that the cultural and demographic transformation of Europe and the Anglosphere is not genocidal; "only coercive measures could be, and then only with the intention to destroy a group." But are not official multicultural policies and the semi-official cancel culture coercive? Diversity, inclusion, and equity (DIE, for short) are promoted and enforced by corporate, church, state, and media elites, as are anti-discrimination laws (protecting only non-whites and non-Christians); hate speech codes; and affirmative action (*aka* anti-white discrimination). With respect to intentionality, at criminal law, one intends the natural and ordinary consequences of one's actions. There can be no doubt that cultural and demographic transformation was an easily foreseeable consequence of mass Third World immigration into Europe and the Anglosphere. Nor could it come as a surprise that the great replacement will effectively destroy (*vernichten*) Anglo-Saxon nations, in whole or in part.

Clearly, the founding stock of the various Anglosphere nations *are* becoming shrinking minorities in their own homelands. Is one not entitled to infer that a transnational and plutocratic corporate ruling class "intends" to bring about that result through, *inter alia*, mass immigration? In the conclusion to their book on *Anglophobia*, Richard Harrison and Frank Salter observe that the Australian state was severed from the nation in the 1960s and 1970s when hostile cultural elites came to power. Those smugly cosmopolitan, "Anglophobic," elites abolished the traditional White Australia Policy which had protected Anglo-white demographic dominance without ever putting the matter to a popular vote. Enjoying bipartisan support, globalist elites were free to avoid a democratic decision-making process. In effect, they became

---

[115] Rockaboatus, "The Jews and Their Long History of Hysteria and Overreach," *The Occidental Observer*, June 17, 2022, available online at: https://www.theoccidentalobserver.net/2022/06/17/171380.

the all-but openly declared, existential enemies of the founding race throughout the Anglosphere.[116]

Implicitly at least, Harrison and Salter agree, declaring that "[d]ispossessing a nation of its protective state is a hostile act." Why cannot the elder and the younger Moses acknowledge that the "democratic" political process was hijacked long ago by arrogant and irresponsible transnational corporate, media, and bureaucratic elites? At the end of WWII, having crushed the "evil and tyrannical" (worse still, fiercely nationalist) fascist menace, the Anglo-American corporate-welfare state launched a coordinated campaign to fundamentally transform the ethno-cultural foundations of every Anglosphere nation, while subverting European civilization more broadly. The fact that almost all churches, courts, and universities collaborated in this nation-destroying project bespeaks a spiritual scandal of epic proportions.

Surely this sorry spectacle, at play for more than seventy years, reeks of coercive intent. Even supposing that an indictment of "white genocide" will not support a count of criminal conspiracy against our "hostile elites," how can they defend themselves against charges of criminal negligence? It appears to be legitimate for professional historians in Germany, such as Martin Broszat, to describe the origins of the Holocaust itself in "functionalist" or "structuralist" terms, rather than as the product of a clearly formulated, "intentional" plan.[117] Why then is the demographic displacement of white Europeans not the functional equivalent of genocide?

The globalist plutocracy has waged relentless psychological and demographic warfare on the British peoples. Utterly without shame, they and their minions remain recklessly indifferent to their wholesale subversion of the pillars of national independence. Every Anglo-Saxon people has been stripped of the right to live in a homeland of their own, behind borders securing their collective identities as free and

---

116 Richardson and Salter, *Anglophobia*, 194–202.

117 Martin Broszat, "The Genesis of the Final Solution," in Koch, (ed.), *Aspects of the Third Reich*, 390–429.

independent ethno-nations. Hence, neo-liberal globalism is responsible for the slow, lingering death of just about every British-derived (or European) nation.

These days weapons of mass migration are an evolving feature of fourth-generation warfare. The cynically manipulative social engineering techniques of fifth-generation warfare are also at play.[118] Where there is war, kinetic or otherwise, one can expect war crimes. Novel forms of warfare will produce novel war crimes, not all of which will be recognized as such by the powers that be. Consequently, the unchecked power of globalist plutocracy is creating an unprecedented moral and spiritual crisis throughout the Anglosphere.

Deliberate demographic displacement must become a central issue in a reformed Anglo-Protestant political theology. But the pressing need for a second Reformation is obvious not just to dissident Anglicans but to at least some German Christians as well. Martin Sellner, in an article discussing Dirk Moses' piece on the German catechism, highlights the deadly dichotomy facing his people; namely, the historical choice facing Germans between "*Vernichtung*," requiring annihilation of racial, religious, and ethnic "enemies," or "*Selbstvernichtung*" through the self-annihilation entailed by an endless influx of "new Germans" from every corner of the world.[119]

It is worth noting the ironic fact that the *Selbstvernichtung* process now seems further advanced among the "invisible race" of WASPs (the "winners" in WWII) than among the *Biodeutschen* (the "losers") in Germany. If one defines an ethnic Australian (more narrowly than Harrison and Salter) as a person of "Anglo, Saxon or Celtic stock, whose

---

118 See, William S. Lind and Lt. Col. Gregory A. Thiele, *4th Generation Warfare Handbook* (Kouvola, Finland: Castalia House, 2015); and, LTG (Ret.) Michael T. Flynn and Boone Cutler, *The Citizen's Guide to Fifth-Generation Warfare* (Boone Cutler Media, 2023).

119 Martin Sellner, "Postkoloniale Angriffe auf den „Auschwitz-Mythos," May 21, 2021; available online at: http://sezession.de/64268/postkoloniale-angriffe-auf-den-auschwitz-mythos.

ancestors arrived pre-WWII," fully-fledged "bio-Australians" are now a minority of the population. Fifty years ago, the founding stock provided the overwhelmingly majority of the twelve million inhabitants of Australia. Since then, the country's population has doubled, mainly through mass immigration. Consequently, just over fifty percent of the Australian population now have first-or second-generation migrant backgrounds.[120] Australia's ruling class took the advice that Bertolt Brecht offered to the East German government as it sought to quell a workers' rebellion; it is literally dissolving "the Australian people" and electing a new one.

Conclusion

The key to understanding the Protestant deformation of Christian nationhood, in both Germany and Australia, lies in Barth's futurist eschatology: the belief that all the earthly divisions of race, class, and gender, between Jew and Gentile, male and female, slave and free, will be overcome in the apocalyptic appearance of a new heaven and a new earth. In the present age, however, all the nations of the earth are separated from God in his heaven by an impassable gulf. Alienated from the incarnate Word of God, humans face the constant temptation to worship instead "the gods of power, wealth, nationality, and race that clamor for our allegiance".[121] In the age to come, the elect will be taken up into the Kingdom of God, into a New Jerusalem where Christ will be seated on his throne with all the saints of Old and New Israel by his side.

Barth's highly refined brand of millennialism contributed to a broader ecumenical movement that led liberal Protestants to embrace mass Third World immigration while pointing conservative evangelicals, especially in the USA, towards Christian Zionism. Christian

---

120 David Hiscox, "Census: Australians are a Minority in Australia," June 29, 2022, available online at: https://xyz.net.au/2022/06/census-australians-are-a-minority-in-australia.

121 Migliore, *Faith Seeking Understanding*, 5.

humanism is not alone in its addiction to millennial teleology. Every revolutionary movement in the modern era has invoked its own secularized version of the apocalyptic myth of the Second Coming. The religion of humanity simply translates the eschatological hopes of Christian believers into secular utopias and myths of human perfectibility. In concurrent campaigns to engineer the salvation of the chimerical abstraction they call "humanity," both Christians and Communists committed countless excesses. In pursuit of the millennium, "progressives" of all stripes brought Christendom to the brink of extinction.

Barth's Christian humanism marks a sharp departure from the orthodoxy of the early church. From that perspective, neither individual Jews nor the modern State of Israel should be set upon a pedestal as avatars of ancient Israel. On the contrary, it was axiomatic that Christians must not rest until they have made disciples of every Jew. For early Christians, old Israel no longer existed. God was no longer bound hand and foot to the Old Covenant. The advent of Christ changed everything; in particular, it changed what it means to be a Jew. Until the New Covenant was consummated in AD 70, while every "jot and tittle" of the Law remained in force, to be a Jew was to be a member of God's holy nation; but, even during Christ's lifetime, as can be seen most clearly in the Gospel of John, the meaning of the word "Jew" was changing, until finally after AD 70 it denoted a people which defined itself mainly in and through the continuing rejection of Christ.

Once the New Covenant creation was inaugurated, the early church was called to exercise and expand Christ's spiritual dominion over a world without end. Barth, of course, explicitly rejected a theology of dominion. "The sign which [the church] is called to erect is a sign other than the sign of dominion. For this reason, it will not conceive its task to be the establishment of a rule of its own. It will not proceed to build a city of God in opposition to the cities of the world, a realm of the pious against the realm of the godless, an island of the righteous and blessed in the midst of the sea of wickedness".[122] Barth designed a defeatist theology to accommodate the church to "post-Christendom". By contrast, the early church set out to make disciples of every nation. Having been rejected by the Jews and driven out of the Middle East by the Muslim conquest several centuries later, Christ found his only secure earthly habitation in the hearts and minds of the European peoples. It was in Old Europe that the first and greatest Christian nations came into being, thereby fulfilling the prophecy of Israel's Messiah that the leaves of the tree of life will be "for the healing of the nations" (Revelation 22:2). Barth's ever-so-nice Christian humanism threatens to undo that glorious achievement.

A reformed neo-*Angelcynn* political theology would resume the task of healing the nations of the Anglosphere. A first step would involve recognition of a shared British responsibility for both world wars. Indeed, there is a real need for an *Angelcynn* apology to Germans for the horrors inflicted upon them by the British during and after both wars.

Closer to home, an Angelcynn political theology would recognize the necessity of Britishness to the ethnoreligious identity (such as it is) of WASP peoples. Following the strange demise of both British Canada and British Australia, the collapse of British identity everywhere in the Anglosphere poses an existential threat to the invisible race.[123] To wage spiritual warfare in their own defence, the British-descended peoples will need a transnational network of *neo-Angelcynn* churches. The resurrection of an ethno-religion capable of reuniting British-descended peoples will provide the spiritual seedbed for the reconstitution of WASP elites. Only then can we hope to see an effective challenge to

---

122 *Cf.*, David Chilton, *Paradise Restored: A Biblical Theology of Dominion* (Horn Lake, MS: Dominion Press, 2007). Karl Barth, *God in Action* (Eugene, OR: Wipf & Stock, 2005), 34:

123 McGregor, "Necessity of Britishness"; Champion, *Strange Demise of British Canada*; Stuart Ward, *Australia and the British Embrace: The Demise of the Imperial Ideal* (Melbourne: Melbourne University Press, 2011).

corrupt misgovernance by an irresponsible and misanthropic globalist plutocracy.

As things stand, the Anglo-Saxon diaspora has been plunged into a condition of permanent insecurity by globalist policies of mass immigration and multiculturalism. Dirk Moses regards the quest for "permanent security" as illegitimate. He declares: "Permanent security is the unobtainable goal of absolute safety that necessarily results in civilian casualties by its paranoid tendency to indiscriminate violence. To solve the problem of genocide concealing permanent security, this book proposes replacing the former with the latter: permanent security should be illegal."[124] If such a rule were to become incorporated into the law of nations, one wonders whether it would apply to *peoples* as well as states.

Are the British-descended *peoples* of the Anglosphere expected to renounce "permanently" the right of collective self-defence? Must Anglos simply submit to the existential threat of permanent insecurity imposed by *states, corporations* and, it must be said, *churches*, all working together to replace them with hordes of non-white migrants drawn indiscriminately from the four corners of the globe? Moses does not address that issue. But in his discussion of "white genocide," he dismisses the desperate desire of many WASPs for permanent security against deliberate demographic displacement as "fantastical paranoia."[125] The fact is however, both pathologically paranoid Anglos as well as their complacent, "normie" co-ethnics have real, powerful, and ruthless enemies. Who knows if or when their inner Saxons will wake up and begin to hate?

---

124 See, A. Dirk Moses, *The Problems of Genocide: Permanent Security and the Language of Transgression* (Cambridge: Cambridge University Press, 2021), 1.
125 Moses, "'White Genocide' and the Ethics of Public Analysis," 209.

PART ONE

Creedal Christianity: Theological Origins of the Present Crisis

1. Sweet Dreams of Christian Nationalism (But What About the Protestant Deformation, Globalist Churches, and Jewish Political Theology?)

Introduction

WEAK-WILLED Anglo-Protestants in Canada meekly acquiesced in official recognition by their federal government of Jewish political theology in the form of the Holocaust mythos. This is hardly surprising in light of their failure a few years earlier to resist repeal of a milquetoast Criminal Code provision prohibiting only the most egregiously vulgar displays of blasphemous libel.[1] Having already surrendered the historical theological hegemony of Protestant Christianity in English Canada, Anglo-Protestants hardly seem likely

---

1   Few people were ever prosecuted for blasphemous libel in Canada, the last in 1935. This was probably a consequence of the giant loophole in s. 296(3) of the Criminal Code: "No person shall be convicted of an offence under this section for expressing in good faith and in decent language, or attempting to establish by argument used in good faith and conveyed in decent language, an opinion on a religious subject." There is a similar exemption [see, s. 319(3)(1)(c)] in the recently enacted law prohibiting denial, downplaying, or condoning of the Holocaust. One might reasonably expect more vigorous efforts to be pursued by organized Jewry in contesting the application of that exemption clause whenever cases of public skepticism or outright denial of the Holocaust are deemed threatening to their theopolitical interests.

to resurrect the ethnoreligious mythos which inspired the Old English church of their medieval ancestors. Such Protestant pusillanimity stands in stark contrast to the aggressively ethnocentric political theology of organized Jewry, not just in Canada, but across the entire Anglosphere. If contemporary WASPs had any self-respect, they would rush to remedy the absence of a spiritually compelling, bioculturally adaptive, Anglican/Anglo-Protestant ethnotheology.

Optimism on that score is probably unwarranted, however. Few WASPs know or care much about their ethnoreligious origins. Even most members of the Anglican church believe that had its origins in the sixteenth-century Protestant Reformation. It was then that Henry VIII formally broke with Rome for reasons of state. Before then, the *ecclesia Anglicana* had been absorbed within the institutional framework of a papal monarchy asserting universal jurisdiction. Allied with a French-speaking, Anglo-Norman ruling class, the Roman Catholic papacy had no reason to preserve the explicitly ethnoreligious character of the Old English Church. Nor did the break with the papacy precipitate an Anglo-Saxon ethnoreligious revival; beyond replacing the Pope with the King as the formal head of the Church of England, the new state religion retained its traditional commitment to the catholicity of the Three Creeds enshrined in the Thirty-Nine Articles. But, whatever the intentions of those who set the Protestant Reformation in motion, over the next few centuries, the combined impact of English and American Protestantism deformed beyond recognition the very idea of Christian nationhood.

As James Kurth writes, the doctrinal base of the Anglo-Protestant Reformation "protested against the idea that the believer *achieves* salvation through a hierarchy or a community, or even the two in combination." Of course, the reformed Church of England "accepted hierarchy and community for certain purposes, such as church governance and collective undertakings [but] they rejected them for the most important of purposes, reaching the state of salvation." Protestant reformers held that "the believer *receives* salvation through an act of grace by

God." It is divine grace that "produces in its recipient the faith in God and salvation that converts him into a believer." Hence, "reformers placed great emphasis on the Word, as revealed in the written words of the Bible." They denied that only a priestly hierarchy could deliver the right interpretation of the Bible to individual believers. Indeed, authoritative hierarchies were more likely to impede the work of divine grace upon individual believers seeking a direct relationship with God through personal study of the Holy Scriptures.[2]

The initial "Protestant rejection of hierarchy and community in regard to salvation spread to their rejection in regard to other domains of life as well." From the beginning, "some Protestant churches rejected hierarchy and community in regard to church governance and local undertakings." Nowhere were such anti-institutional tendencies more pronounced than "in the new United States, where the conjunction of the open frontier and the disestablishment of churches in the several states enabled the flourishing of new unstructured and unconstrained denominations."[3]

Over the past five-hundred years, the Protestant faith gradually lost its spiritual intensity, a process which began when salvation by grace was replaced by the "half-way covenant" in which grace could be evidenced by works.[4] Then, even "the idea of the necessity of grace began to fade." Once "work in the world was no longer seen as a sign of grace but as a good in itself," good works offered the promise of personal salvation. The transformation of religious experience into a personal relationship to God was an early expression of Anglo-Protestant individualism. In our own time, the transformation of religion into a personal and private matter has culminated in the recognition of universal human rights as the sacred birthright of every individual.

---

[2] James Kurth, "The Protestant Deformation and American Foreign Policy," (1998) 42(2) *Orbis* 221, at 225–226.

[3] *Ibid.*, 227.

[4] Perry Miller, "The Half-Way Covenant," (1933) 6(4) *New England Quarterly* 676.

According to Kurth, "this means that human rights are applicable to any individual, anywhere in the world."

Thus, "the *ultima ratio* of the secularization of the Protestant religion" has become an "expressive individualism" in which the imperial self is free to express his/her/its "contempt for and protest against all hierarchies, communities, traditions, and customs." In other words, Kurth writes, "the long declension of the Protestant Reformation has reached its end point in the Protestant Deformation," producing a religion without God, "a reformation against all forms."[5]

Expressive individualism in America was inspired by the romantic-humanistic ethic prevalent among Progressive reformers in the late nineteenth- and early twentieth centuries, most of whom were middle-class WASPs. But it was the massive wave of immigration from southern and central Europe which provided the raw material enabling the WASP clerisy to manufacture the cosmopolitan spirit characteristic of urban America during the Progressive Era.

Confronted with the tightly packed masses of immigrants in New York and Chicago, middle-class reformers learned "to interpret Protestant Christianity in a very peculiar, almost secular way." In adapting "the tenets of egalitarian humanism to their polyglot, culturally charged context," the reform movement established "settlement houses" to assist alien newcomers in adjusting to life in America. Anglo-Protestant reformers such as Jane Addams and John Dewey led the campaign to recognize and accept immigrant cultures "as a 'gift' to the American amalgam." They implored the American nation "to shed its Anglo-Saxon ethnic core and develop a culture of cosmopolitan humanism, a harbinger of impending global solidarity."[6] Other Anglo-Protestant reformers such as William James urged their fellow WASPs to embrace a pragmatic approach to religious experience, choosing whichever "type of religion is going to work better in the long run." It

---

5   Kurth, "Protestant Deformation," 229, 236.
6   Eric P. Kaufmann, *The Rise and Fall of Anglo-America* (Cambridge, MA: Harvard University Press, 2004), 95–98.

did not matter much whether God was dead, so long as "we form at any rate an ethical republic here below."[7]

An American century later, Kurth notes that, by then, almost every nation with a Protestant religious tradition has "by now adopted some version of the human rights ideology."[8] One might add that the many manifestations of Anglo-Protestant humanism in various corners of the Anglosphere do not always maintain logical consistency. In Canada, for example, the offence of blasphemous libel was removed from the Criminal Code in the name of the universal human right to free expression just four years before the decision to criminalize anyone who condones, denies, or downplays the Jewish Holocaust.[9] No-one should be surprised to learn that organized Jewry overwhelmingly approved both pieces of legislation. After all, Jews are now held up as exemplary victims of those who would deny or abuse human rights. At the same time, however, neither measure appears to have encountered any serious opposition from Anglo-Canadian Protestants, even though both (especially taken together) would have been interpreted as deformations of Christian nationhood by earlier generations of Protestants in English Canada. Almost everywhere in the Anglosphere, such Protestant deformations of traditional Christian mores have been consecrated, sooner or later, by globalist churches with the full support of the Holocaust industry.

All too often, either the Church of England or its Anglican successors in Australia, Canada, New Zealand, and the United States have been in the vanguard of that moral declension. We need to understand the

---

7   Eugen McCarraher, *Christian Critics: Religion and the Impasse in Modern American Social Thought* (Ithaca, NY: Cornell University Press, 2000), 15.

8   Kurth, "Protestant Deformation," 237.

9   For the common law background to s.296 of the *Criminal Code* (as it then was) and an illustration of the liberal conventional wisdom successfully calling for its repeal ten years later, see Jeremy Patrick, "Not Dead, Just Sleeping: Canada's Prohibition on Blasphemous Libel as a Case Study in Obsolete Legislation," (2008) 41 *University of British Columbia Law Review* 193.

historical roots of such dysgenic institutional behaviour. Unfortunately, even the recent rise to prominence of "Christian nationalism" in the USA is unlikely to reverse the Protestant Deformation.

Christian Nationalism, American-Style

A recent book by Stephen Wolfe making *The Case for Christian Nationalism* has much to recommend it.[10] An unapologetic paleoconservative, the author blames the postwar Global American Empire (GAE) for undermining Christian nationhood at home in the USA, perhaps terminally. "In the New America," he observes, "the ground of patriotic sentiment is *away* from the Old America. Thus, civic holidays, national heroes, memorials, and patriotic events are all coloured according to the grand narrative of progress." Even mainstream conservatives are committed to the progressivist narrative of US history, so much so that they are the staunchest supporters of the military which, they believe, fights to defend "the American way of life." But, despite his experience as a West Point graduate serving in the U.S. army in the world-wide "fight for democracy," Wolfe now advises young men not to get "blown up in the name of liberal imperialism; shed blood to open up markets for Netflix and Pornhub; [or to] make the world safe for dudes in dresses."[11]

He holds the GAE responsible for undermining the moral and cultural foundations of Christian nationhood. Not only has the imperial regime imposed homosexual marriage upon all the states by judicial fiat, it also steeps young minds in critical race theory and genderbending ideology. Meanwhile, the floodgates have been opened to a tidal wave of non-Western immigration, further eroding the once-dominant Anglo-Protestant character of American national identity. Nevertheless, in opposition to the relentless onslaught of nihilistic

---

10 Stephen Wolfe, *The Case for Christian Nationalism* (Moscow, ID: Canon Press, 2022).

11 Ibid., 435–438.

disenchantment, Wolfe holds out the hope that Christian nationalism could inspire a "true revolt against the modern world." He believes in the possibility of "the pursuit of higher life — both the life to come and a life on earth that images that life to come." Indeed, he insists that Christians can still regard the world as their "inheritance in Christ." With undisguised passion, Wolfe presents Christian nationalism as "a collective will for Christian dominion in the world."[12]

But what prevents Christians from exercising the biblical mandate to exercise dominion over this world? The problem, as Wolfe sees it, is essentially psychological. American Christians "have been so conditioned to affirm what we *feel* to be good that the feeling determines for us what is true. Conversely, we deny any thought that we feel is bad." Some beliefs, notably Christian nationalism, are *psychologically* more difficult for churchgoers to entertain than others.[13]

Most Anglo-American Protestants, for example, have long been conditioned, by both church and state, to regard religion as a private and personal matter. Wolfe's vision of Christian nationalism cuts across the grain of those habits of religious privatism. For example, Wolfe calls upon civil government to protect and preserve the exclusively Christian identity of the nation by penalizing "open blasphemy and irreverence in the interest of public peace and Christian peoplehood." Few mainstream Christians will be "comfortable" with his argument that "Sabbath laws are just, because they remove distractions for holy worship."[14]

Similarly, Wolfe's case for upholding the legitimacy of traditional gender hierarchies has already attracted accusations of "misogyny." On this issue, however, Wolfe pulls no punches. He declares that Americans "live under a gynocracy — a rule of women." He concedes that this "may not be apparent on the surface, since men still run

---

12 Ibid., 443, 447–448.

13 Ibid., 454–455.

14 Ibid., 31.

many things. But the governing virtues of America are feminine vices, associated with certain feminine virtues, such as empathy, fairness, and equality." Any such defence of "toxic masculinity" runs contrary to feminist norms eagerly enforced by the established secularist regime. But Wolfe remains unrepentant, declaring flatly that the "rise of Christian nationalism necessitates the fall of gynocracy."[15]

Inevitably, therefore, the very idea of Christian nationalism represents an existential threat to the Woke liberal regime. Wolfe bluntly characterizes "the secularist ruling class" as "the enemies of the church and, as such, enemies of the human race."[16] At the same time, he recognizes that to resist the moral and political consensus enforced by a godless regime, Christians must summon the hitherto absent strength of will necessary to affirm what is true even when it causes them enormous psychological discomfort.

To his credit, Wolfe admits that many Christian leaders deliberately undermine political action in opposition to the secularist regime. Instead, they "advance a sort of Stockholm syndrome theology" which excludes "Christians from public institutions" but requires them "to affirm the language of universal dignity, tolerance, human rights, anti-nationalism, anti-nativism, multiculturalism, social justice, and equality." Wolfe deplores the fact that any Christian who "deviates from these dogmas" faces exclusion from the ranks of respectable churchgoers.[17] What, then, is to be done? Wolfe turns to Christian political theory in search of an answer. Unfortunately, the result, even for many of his Christian readers, leaves much to be desired.

Nationalism and Christianity

Wolfe's book has attracted wide interest in a multitude of online reviews and podcast discussions. Understood as a political programme,

---

15   Ibid., 448, 454.

16   Ibid., 455–456.

17   Ibid., 4–5.

Wolfe's conception of Christian nationalism is often pronounced DOA, dead on arrival. For example, Neema Parvini, author of *The Populist Delusion*, dismisses Christian Nationalism as a "political fantasy."[18] In fairness, however, Wolfe himself readily agrees that, on the national level at least, the idea has little chance of success. He does not present the book as a viable "action plan."[19] Instead, he sets out the principles that should guide any Christian nation. Wolfe's preferred model of Christian nationalism is grounded in a Reformed Presbyterian version of two kingdoms theology which distinguishes between God's redemptive work of salvation and his providential governance of earthly affairs.

Accordingly, he defines Christian nationalism in the following manner:

> Christian nationalism is a totality of national action, consisting of civil laws and social customs, conducted by a Christian nation as a Christian nation, in order to procure for itself both earthly and heavenly good in Christ.[20]

In other words, "Christian nationalism is nationalism modified by Christianity" which is to say that "the Gospel does not supersede, abrogate, eliminate, or fundamentally alter generic nationalism, it assumes and completes it." Apart from Christianity, therefore:

> Nationalism refers to a totality of national action, consisting of civil laws and social customs, conducted by a nation as a nation, in order to procure for itself both earthly and heavenly good.[21]

According to Wolfe, "the specific difference between generic nationalism and Christian nationalism is that, for the latter, Christ is essential

---

18 Neema Parvini, "Christian Nationalism Is a Political Fantasy" December 1, 2022 https://chroniclesmagazine.org/view/christian-nationalism-is-a-political-fantasy/; see also, *The Populist Delusion* (Perth: Imperium Press, 2022).

19 Wolfe, *Christian Nationalism*, 433.

20 Ibid., 9.

21 Ibid., 11.

to obtaining the complete good." The ordering of people to heavenly life would have been "a natural end for even the generic nation" but for the fall. "Had Adam not fallen, the nations of his progeny would have ordered themselves to heavenly life." Following the advent of Christ as the Redeemer, "the Gospel is now the sole means to heavenly life." If nations are to achieve their "complete good," even "earthly goods ought to be ordered to Christ." Without Christ, pagan and secularist nations may be "true nations but they are incomplete nations. Only the Christian nation is a complete nation."[22]

Wolfe situates all nations and nationalisms, Christian or otherwise, within a Reformed Presbyterian vision of salvation history. Wolfe describes his argument as a "Christian political theory" rather than a "political theology" grounded in his own biblical exegesis. His understanding of Scripture relies instead upon the work of sixteenth- and seventeenth Reformed theologians. That Reformed tradition developed within a metanarrative framework established by Augustine of Hippo (354–430 AD). Augustine and the later Reformed tradition posit a fundamental metaphysical distinction between the City of Man and the City of God. Both interpret Scripture through the lens of a Hellenistic hermeneutic envisioning the creation *ex nihilo* and future destruction of the earthly world as the appearance and foreordained disappearance of corruptible material existence following the Day of Judgement.[23]

Augustine's Neo-platonic cosmology presupposed the absolute dependence of both mankind and the material world itself upon an omnipotent, omniscient, and omnipresent God. Following in Augustine's footsteps, Wolfe believes that modern Americans seduced by the delights of mortal life in Mammon have wandered far from heavenly goods, thereby losing sight of "the invisible things of God." Given the inherent difficulty mortal beings experience in apprehending such

---

22 Ibid., 15.

23 Augustine, *City of God Against the Pagans*, ed. And trans. R.W. Dyson (Cambridge: Cambridge University Press, 1998), bk. XX, ch.1, 965.

invisible divine "objects," Wolfe, too, recognizes our spiritual debt to the revealed Word of God. He holds fast to the Augustinian doctrine that, guided by the light of the Gospel, Christian nations should view their entire existence as a journey towards the unchangeable heavenly life, and their affections should be entirely fixed upon that.[24]

It follows that "politics" in every Christian nation must be understood as "the art of establishing and cultivating necessary conditions for social life for the good of man." The point of a Christian political life comes from God; it must aim to create civil governments capable of shoring up social order "for man's complete good." In other words, the difference between generic nationalism and Christian nationalism is that the latter "expresses a Christian nation's *will* for heavenly good in Christ and that all lesser goods are oriented to the higher good."[25]

Presented in such universalistic, all-encompassing terms, Wolfe's "Christian political theory" transforms "politics" into "public administration." Civil government, he says, must aim to identify the most effective earthly means within any given society to realize a heavenly destiny common to faithful believers in every Christian nation.

Action versus Behaviour in Political Theory

In this context, the "totality of national *action*" is better understood as a socially ordered system of *behaviour* premised upon the existence of one common interest, *i.e.*, the interest of every Christian society not just in its own earthly survival and collective vitality but also in the heavenly salvation of every believer. Public administration, as distinguished from politics, may become detached from natural persons and lodged instead in a social life-process which requires that human behaviour conform to the developmental needs (both spiritual and material) of society. Wolfe seems unaware that "politics," strictly

---

24 *Cf.*, Augustine, *On Christian Doctrine*, (Radford, VA: Wilder Publications, 2013), 12–14, 22.

25 Wolfe, *Christian Nationalism*, 89, 180.

speaking, originally required the institutionalization of a realm of freedom in which civic *action* became possible.

The distinction between "action" and "behaviour" was central to Hannah Arendt's political theory. In her view, "action" enabled the individual to distinguish himself from others in the public realm. For a citizen to leave the private sphere of the household "to devote one's life to the affairs of the city demanded courage" because entry into the "political realm had first to be ready to risk his life, and too great a love for life obstructed freedom, was a sure sign of slavishness." With the administrative victory of society over the public realm, the possibility of individual *action* gives way to the statistical regularities of human *behaviour*, while the equality of men possessed of the acknowledged right to reveal themselves in their own distinctive public persona becomes degraded into conformism to the assumed common interest of society as a whole.[26]

Not only does Wolfe's "Christian political theory" fail to offer an "action plan," it fails even to recognize the existential need for a public realm. It is only in such a *res publica* that individuals, families, tribes, and nations can distinguish themselves, one from the other, through exemplary modes of civic action. Such recognition of the distinctive character of political life has been the exception rather than the rule in human affairs. Arendt may have been concerned primarily with the phenomenology of politics but she well understood that the unique character of a civic mode of action was first discovered in ancient Greece, most famously in the Athenian *polis*.[27] To fully understand the early experience of politics and its decline in the totally administered societies characteristic of the modern transnational corporate welfare state, it is necessary to study, not just its biocultural preconditions

---

26 Hannah Arendt, *The Human Condition* (Chicago: University of Chicago Press, 1958), 36, 40–44; see also, Hanna Fenichel Pitkin, *The Attack of the Blob: Hannah Arendt's Concept of the Social* (Chicago: University of Chicago Press, 1998).

27 Christian Meier, *The Greek Discovery of Politics* trans. David McLintock (Cambridge, MA: Harvard University Press, 1990).

but their historical development and theopolitical subversion. Unfortunately, Wolfe's argument treats Christianity, nationalism, politics, and civil government in generic, free-floating terms altogether detached from the biocultural history and theological presuppositions of any Christian nation.

Christian Meier observes that "ever since the Renaissance it has been possible to use the word *politics* to designate any action of which the state is capable." Wolfe simply assumes that this modern sense of the term effectively delimits its meaning, past, present, and future. In classical Athenian democracy, however, the *polis* became identical with its citizens and "the majority of citizens gained supreme authority (with the help of those nobles who placed themselves in their service)." For Aristotle, the word *political* meant "appropriate to the *polis*." His concept of politics denoted it as "the science of the highest good attainable through human action." Politics presupposed the unity of the citizenry as a whole: "the general civic interest...transcended all particularist interests." Consequently, "there was no way in which anything resembling a state could establish centralized power or state institutions that were divorced from society."[28]

This great experiment in participatory politics rested on the "importance of familial and religious piety in Athenian democracy." Indeed, "those who failed in their familial, religious, or military duties" could be excluded from the *polis*. The civic unity of the *polis* "was founded on family, patriarchy, community, military courage, common ancestry, and an intense patriotism." Indeed, it has been said that Athenian democracy was based upon a prototype of "racial citizenship." In contrast to other Greeks, "Athenians claimed to be racially pure...having supposedly sprung from the Attic soil as true *autochtones*." Bolstered by that myth of autochthony, the direct democratic politics associated with Athenian citizenship "was grounded in strong racial identity and pride in one's lineage." In short, Athens was "a spirited and nativist

---

28 Ibid., 14, 20–21.

democracy" in which even prominent residents not of Athenian blood (such as Aristotle) were excluded from citizenship.[29]

There was also an important geopolitical dimension to the character of the Athenian polity. This can be seen in the contrast between Athens and Sparta. In the eyes of an imperial power such as the mighty, multinational, military monarchy of Persia, Athens and Sparta represented a Greek power which "was that of patriotic, fractious little republics, defined by civic freedom." The forms of civic power in each city-state emerged out of very different geopolitical circumstances. Sparta was a land power characterized by autarchy, hierarchy, community, and a rigorous military discipline organized to guard against the danger of rebellion by an enslaved population of helots. Athens was a sea power in which international trade and a strong navy encouraged a commercial culture, democracy, individualism, and technology.[30]

Guillaume Durocher suggests that "Athens embodied the long-term superiority of dynamic commercial, democratic-individualist, and technologically advanced systems over static, austere, hierarchical-communitarian, and primitive ones." Like the modern, Anglo-Saxon thalassocracies in Great Britain and the United States, Athens was "dynamic and expansive in peacetime" while "able to adopt sufficiently hierarchical-communitarian characteristics in wartime."[31]

At the same time, the high level of social solidarity in both polities and its vital contribution to their respective war-fighting abilities gave the Greeks a sophisticated and distinctive understanding of the friend-enemy distinction. A bright-line distinction was drawn between one's enemies inside the *polis* and outsiders threatening society. The modern German jurist Carl Schmitt identified the difference between friend

---

29 Guillaume Durocher, "Athens: A Spirited and Nativist Democracy," (Fall 2018) 18(3) *The Occidental Quarterly*, 74–75, 78; See also, Susan Lape, *Race and Citizen Identity in the Classical Athenian Democracy* (Cambridge: Cambridge University Press, 2010), *ix*, 59.

30 *Ibid.*, 72.

31 *Ibid.*, 73, 80.

and foe as the existential essence of politics. He took note of the gradations in the Greek understanding of enmity encoded in the *koine* dialect of ancient Greek and later carried over into the New Testament. Unfortunately, the linguistic precision of the Greek original was lost when translated into English or German. As we have seen, Wolfe relies upon English versions of Reform theology for his rare forays into biblical exegesis. He may never have recognized, therefore, that the (mis)translation of Matthew 5:43–44 conceals a fundamental fault line between idealist and realist political theologies.

When Jesus enjoined his followers to "love your enemies," he was not laying the moral foundation of Christian pacifism. Wolfe is no pacifist, however; he vigorously defends the martial virtues "as a necessary feature of masculine excellence."[32] Nevertheless, like most Christians, Wolfe strenuously resists the temptation to build our identities by discriminating between "us" and "them." Having internalized the anti-discrimination ethos of the civil rights revolution, many Christians mistakenly believe that Jesus asked his followers to "love" their persecutors. As a matter of fact, he merely urged them to "pray for them which despitefully use you, and persecute you" (Matt.5:44). Carl Schmitt took a more realistic view of the Sermon on the Mount. He tackled the translation issue, clarifying what Jesus meant when asking his audience to love their "enemies." In the Greek original, Jesus uses the word *echthroi* to denote persons who might be "private" or "personal" enemies of their fellow citizens (or, in this context, fellow Jews engaged alongside him in a spiritual battle to fulfill the law of Old Covenant Israel). He was not talking about the "public" or "alien" enemies (*polemoi*) of the Jewish people.[33]

Unless one keeps that distinction in mind, Christian charity can easily degenerate into a pathological altruism incapable of addressing existential threats to one's nation as such. Christian nationalism

---

32 Wolfe, *Christian Nationalism*, 76.

33 *Cf.* Carl Schmitt, *The Concept of the Political* trans. George Schwab (New Brunswick, NJ: Rutgers University Press, 1976), 28–29.

should be based upon a realist political theology which, in turn, should ground itself in a multi-dimensional understanding of the history and biocultural foundations of every Christian nation.

The Origins and Ends of Mankind in History and Christian Mythology

History can be understood as an intellectual discipline providing narrative or analytical accounts of past events based upon the empirical investigation of reliable sources. It is worth noting that "scientific" history in this sense was the product of two Greeks writing in the fifth century BC. According to R.G. Collingwood, Herodotus and Thucydides "quite clearly recognized both that history is, or can be, a science and that it has to do with human actions." Their histories were not legends; they were research. They were "an attempt to get answers to definite questions about matters of which one recognizes that one is ignorant."[34] Nothing could be further from this methodology than Wolfe's universal, one size fits all, and thoroughly unscientific schema of salvation history.

The study of human biocultures is also a scientific enterprise which relies upon the empirical study of interactions between biological and cultural phenomena as they have evolved within various population groups. By contrast, Wolfe's account of Christian nationalism simply presupposes a neo-Augustinian vision of the divinely-ordained stages of the salvation history of mankind, a generic "Christian narrative of creation, fall, redemption, and glorification."[35] This story presents the past, present, and future of humanity in general as it unfolds in four stages: a state of integrity; a state of sin; a state of grace; and, finally, the state of glory.

---

34   R.G. Collingwood, *The Idea of History* (London: Oxford University Press, 1961), 17–18.

35   Wolfe, *Christian Nationalism*, 41.

Wolfe's speculative account of the prelapsarian state of integrity is truly breathtaking in what one critic describes as its intellectual irresponsibility. He spends an entire chapter describing the sort of "civil fellowship" that Adam's progeny would have arranged but for the fall. As Bob Stevenson observes, Wolfe's vision of the prelapsarian world rests on the biblical account found in

> 61 verses, comprised of 1,253 words describing the world before our first parents saw the goodness of the forbidden fruit, took and ate. If we only include the parts where humanity exists — and thereby human society, sociability, diversity of gifts, normative roles etc. — that number is reduced to 36 verses, consisting of 764 words.[36]

It is impossible to construct an account of what a counter-factual prelapsarian world would look like based on those 764 words. Wolfe's uses his own reason and imagination to reconstruct the structure of the unfallen world that might have been. Wolfe contends that families, tribes, nations, and cultural diversity would all have been natural in the original state of integrity. So, too, would have been hierarchy and the need for the masculine leadership, and the martial virtues essential to self-preservation. Wolfe's portrait of the state of integrity calls to mind the image of the sinless noble savage and is equally devoid of evidence grounded in physical or cultural paleoanthropology. Wolfe appears to be one of those Christians for whom it has long been "standard doctrine that every member of the human race is descended from the biblical Adam." How interesting, therefore, that it was a seventeenth-century "Calvinist of Portuguese Jewish origin from Bordeaux" who challenged Christian orthodoxy with the "beguilingly simple" claim "the human beings existed before the biblical Adam."[37]

---

36 Bob Stevenson, "The Case for Christian Nationalism: A Review (Part Two)." https://bobstevenson.net/the-case-for-christian-nationalism-a-review-part-ii-84384e87eab1.

37 David N. Livingstone, *Adam's Ancestors: Race, Religion, and the Politics of Human Origins* (Baltimore: Johns Hopkins University Press, 2008), 5, 26,33.

The impact of Isaac La Peyrère (1596–1676) on theological hermeneutics was such that many modern Christian scholars now accept that, in Hebrew hermeneutics, Adam need not be, and probably was not conceived as the first human being. On that reading, sin was in the world well before Adam. Adam's story was not about universal human origins but rather about the origins of Israel. Having been created at the exodus and brought to the promised land of Canaan, Israel was bound by a law which it disobeys, suffering exile as a consequence. In this way, "Israel's drama — its struggles over the land and failure to follow God's law — is placed into primordial time."[38] In other words, the biblical Adam is better understood in mythical terms as proto-Israel.

In any case, after the fall, according to Wolfe's rendition of the orthodox Reformed hermeneutic, the world becomes subject for the first time to sin, creating the need to augment the powers of civil government to suppress sin and maintain civil order. With the advent of Christ, however, the redemption of mankind becomes possible and "Christians take up the task of true and complete humanity." Wolfe contends that "restorative grace sets the redeemed apart on earth — constituting a redeemed humanity on earth — and, on that basis, Christians can and ought to exercise dominion in the name of God." In that way, "grace perfects nature." Christians "are perfected for heavenly life but also restored in their perfection for obedience in earthly life."[39] Wolfe never considers the possibility that the mission of the historical Jesus was limited in scope: *i.e.*, the redemption of Old Covenant Israel, not humanity at large.

Nations and Ethnicity

When discussing the meaning of nationhood, Wolfe rejects "the so-called creedal nation concept" according to which a nation is "united

---

38   Peter Enns, *The Evolution of Adam: What the Bible Does and Doesn't Say About Human Origins* (Grand Rapids, MI: Brazos Press, 2012), 65–66.
39   Wolfe, *Christian Nationalism*, 100, 101, 110–111.

around a set of propositions that creedalists consider universally true or at least practically advantageous for all and so readily acceptable by all." His target is the "egalitarian themes and rights-talk" characteristic of mainstream American political discourse." He concedes, however, that his argument "does not preclude political or social creeds that serve to unite a people." He gives as an example of a "universally true statement" the proposition that "Jesus is Lord," claiming that it "certainly serves to unite the people of a Christian nation." Wolfe claims that "Christianity is the true religion" as another example of a universally valid spiritual proposition.[40] One wonders whether and how that spiritual truth was recognized during the religious wars of the seventeenth century in Europe or the American Civil War during the nineteenth century.

Wolfe acknowledges that such Christian propositions cannot and do not serve as the "*foundation* for nations."[41] The question then, of course, becomes: What *is* the foundation or basis for nationhood, Christian or otherwise? Unfortunately, Wolfe never provides a clear answer to that question. The cover of Wolfe's book with the image of a cross, radiating beams of light superimposed upon a map of the lower forty-eight United States, suggests that his project will be focused upon an *American* version of Christian nationalism. But, as one of his critics observes, "the interior of his 478-page tome tells a very different story. Indeed, America hardly comes up in the first nine [of ten] chapters, and much of what he writes could be applied to any Christian (by which he means Protestant) nation."[42]

For Wolfe, it is axiomatic that every "Christian nation acknowledges God as the author of nations in general and as the providential author of their particular nation." But the "universal truths of Christianity do not nullify national particularity. Each Christian nation has a distinct

---

40 Ibid., 119–120, 186.

41 Ibid., 120.

42 Mark David Hall, "The 500-Year-Old Case for Christian Nationalism" https://providencemag.com/2022/11/the-500-year-old-case-for-christian-nationalism.

way of life." It is true, he says, "that fellow Christians, regardless of nationality, are united *spiritually*, as fellow members of the kingdom of God." But this "is chiefly a heavenly or eschatological relation, made possible by grace, not nature." The spiritual brotherhood making man "fit for a *heavenly* kingdom" is not well suited to provide the practical tools (such as a common language) enabling the everyday cooperation between individuals and families necessary "to procure the full range of goods required for living well in this world."[43]

While Wolfe recognizes the particularity of every nation, he locates the sources of that particularity in a "lived experience" shared by everyone, a "sense of familiarity with a particular place and the people in it." This "sense of *we*" is not "rooted…in abstractions or judicial norms (e.g., equal protection) or truth-statements." He appears not to notice that he grounds his own argument in a general "truth," applicable to all nations, tribes, and peoples, before and after the fall. All of us, Christians and non-Christians alike, share "a pre-reflective, pre-propositional love for one's own, generated from intergenerational affections, daily life, and productive activity that link a society of the dead, living, and unborn." Particularity, for Wolfe, is a property attached "to a people *in place*." He describes his concern for the "lived experience" of particular peoples in particular places as a "a sort of phenomenological topography."[44]

He admits that the "idea of a nation is notoriously difficult to define, and identifying true nations is equally challenging." But he is careful to deny that nationhood can or should be identified "on the basis of a modern racialist principle." He disavows any suggestion that his position is "a 'white nationalist' argument." On his view, "the designation 'white,' as it is used today, hinders and distracts people from recognizing and acting for their people-groups." Having rejected the concept of race, Wolfe then uses "the terms *ethnicity* and *nation*

---

43 Wolfe, *Christian Nationalism*, 176, 199.

44 Ibid., 120, 134.

almost synonymously," if not necessarily very consistently. His use of the terms as synonyms is especially confusing when he announces that he will use "*nation*...to emphasize the unity of the whole" since "every people-group has internal differences" (e.g., those based on class) "though no nation (properly speaking) is composed of two or more ethnicities."[45] Most readers, I suspect, would take the latter observation to imply that there can be no American nation. After all, is not the United States today composed of a patchwork of different ethnicities (not to mention "races")?

But Wolfe almost immediately begins to fudge the issue of ethnic and national identity. "Ethnicity, as something *experienced*," he declares, "is familiarity with others based in common language, manners, customs, stories, taboos, rituals, calendars, social expectations, duties, loves, and religion." All of these permit communication and completion of common projects. What about blood ties? According to Wolfe, while a "community of blood" may be "crucial to ethnicity. But this should not lead us to conclude that blood ties are the sole determinant of ethnicity." He prefers to think of ethnicity or nations as a function of "soul" or "spiritual principle."[46]

Accordingly, "the ties of blood do not directly establish the boundaries of one's ethnicity. Rather, one has ethnic ties of affection because one's kin conducted life with other kin in the same place." In other words, if a Southern white man's kin lived in a particular place alongside the extended families of black slaves or sharecroppers, together they would leave "behind a trace of themselves and their cooperation and their great works and sacrifices." Both groups, white and black, could then be said to share a common Southern or even American ethnicity because their collective kinfolk "belonged to *this people* on *this land*," and were bound together by a common *Volksgeist*.[47]

---

45   Ibid., 119, 135.
46   Ibid., 136, 140.
47   Ibid., 139.

Wolfe never specifies his own ethnicity. Instead, he waves the issue away with the commonplace observation that "white Americans" often assign their ethnicity "to some distant European ancestry." The closest he comes to coming out of the closet is when he writes that "I might say that I'm Italian, German, and English" without making it clear whether that is an autobiographical fact or, instead, just a hypothetical example of a typical white American response to the question of personal "ethnic identity."[48] Perhaps Wolfe actually is just some random Euromutt castaway. On the other hand, he could be related somehow to the prominent Anglo-Irish family of the eighteenth-century English Major General James Wolfe.

Once upon a time (not so very long ago), every English-Canadian schoolchild literally sang the praises of General Wolfe as "the dauntless hero" who "planted firm Britannia's flag on Canada's fair domain." Wolfe died on the Plains of Abraham near Quebec City, having defeated the French General Montcalm. British North America was thereby rid (for a time) of a dangerous imperial rival. Ironically, Wolfe's victory smoothed the path of rebellious American colonists ready to break with the British Crown to create a continental empire of their own.

Many English-Canadians, including myself, would be proud to claim General Wolfe as an ancestor. (Indeed, though I can boast no such connection, I have a large print of Benjamin West's famous painting of Wolfe's death hanging on the wall of my library). Wolfe of West Point, however, prefers to believe that one's genetic origins, while "not entirely irrelevant…say little about who you are, at least with regard to your everyday life." At most, they provide little more than "some mildly interesting fact you use in small talk."[49]

Relating ethnicity primarily to the topography of lived experience has the effect of obscuring the intertwined significance of history, biology, and culture. Wolfe has no apparent interest in either in the

---

48 Ibid., 136.
49 Ibid., 136.

historical origins or the "ethnic genetic interests" of his own people, whoever they might be. Indeed, he writes that "Given my friendships and associations with people of different ancestry, I can say that being "white" [much less of British ancestry] is unnecessary both to recognize themselves in what I describe and to cooperate with someone like me in a common national project."[50]

Remarkably, in Wolfe's mind, ethnicity can *cross* racial lines. According to Neil Shenvi, Wolfe has affirmed in a personal conversation that "People of different ancestral origins can be part of the same ethnicity."[51] How else can Wolfe entertain the hope that an *American* Christian nationalism will emerge?[52] Kevin DeYoung remarks that "the all-important concept of 'nation' sometimes operates in Wolfe's thinking more organically like an ethnicity, sometimes more loosely like a culture, sometimes more locally like a love of people and place, and sometimes more traditionally like a nation-state with a recognizable set of laws, a governing magistrate, and the power of the sword."[53]

Wolfe argues that all nations can be Christian nations seeking "their temporal and eternal good through their own civil arrangements." He devotes a chapter to defend the proposition that a Christian nation has "a natural law right to revolution against tyrants to that end." Of course, so long as "a legitimate ruler uses civil power to command what is just and the people disobey this command, they are disobeying God himself…because the law itself, though human, is an ordinance of God." But God does not bestow civil authority "to command what is unjust…for God's ordinances to man are always just." It follows that no

---

50 *Ibid.*, 119.
51 Neil Shenvi, "Of Gods and Men: A Long Review of Wolfe's Case for Christian Nationalism, Part III-Objections" https://shenviapologetics.com/of-gods-and-men-a-long-review-of-wolfes-case-for-christian-nationalism-part-iii-objections.
52 Wolfe, *Christian Nationalism*, 431, 475.
53 Kevin DeYoung, "The Rise of Right-Wing Wokeism" https://www.thegospelcoalition.org/reviews/christian-nationalism-wolfe.

unjust command can bind the conscience. A tyrant, "though he may have the appearance of civil authority, is but a man ordering fellow men to great evil." If necessary, forcible resistance to such commands may be justified. Even a Christian *minority* may "revolt against a tyranny directed against them and, after successfully revolting, establish over *all* the population a Christian commonwealth."[54]

In Wolfe's Christian political theory, it is axiomatic that "although civil administration is fundamentally natural, human, and universal" it "was created to serve Adam's race in a state of integrity, as an outward ordering to God." In our redeemed state of grace, "those who are restored in Christ are the people of God. Thus, civil order and administration is for them." This raises the question of the political status of non-Christians in a Christian commonwealth. Any answer to that question is a matter of prudence, recognizing, of course, that the civil administration "must guarantee equal protection and due process with regard to human things for all people…But this does not entail equal participation, status, and standing in political, social, and cultural institutions." Non-Christians cannot "be expected to take an interest in conserving the explicit Christian character and ends of these institutions and of society."[55]

Wolfe invokes the Anglo-Protestantism practiced in Puritan New England as a source of inspiration in shaping any future Christian commonwealth. There and in the new nation during the founding era, liberty of conscience was to be respected. No one could be compelled to believe or profess the Christian faith. The civil power dealt with heresy or dissent with a view to "practical considerations" relating to the "public harm caused by public error and on the limitation of civic action for spiritual reformation." Accordingly, the civil power acted not to wreak vengeance on the enemies of God but "as a means to safeguard the souls of those under the magistrate's care." Punishment

---

54 Wolfe, *Christian Nationalism*, 329–330, 334, 345.
55 Ibid., 346, 392.

was meted out only to those who publicly sought to promote heresy and unbelief, to subvert the established church, to denounce its ministers, or to instigate rebellion against Christian magistrates. The fundamental Anglo-Protestant view was "that the Gospel and religious belief cannot be coerced; it is a matter of persuasion, and one must decide for oneself."[56]

What went wrong? Why did the American republic not remain as a Christian nation, on the Anglo-Protestant model? Wolfe's answer in a nutshell is: modern R2K theory. That is to say, the mainstream Anglo-Protestant view still rests upon a two kingdoms theology distinguishing church and state. But the radical two kingdoms view is that only pastoral vocations in the church are part of God's kingdom while the state rests on a natural law that applies in a neutral fashion to all men everywhere, Christians and non-Christians alike. This, of course, begs the question: how did the R2K position come to dominance in the church? To answer that question requires a realistic political ethnotheology of Christian nationhood, one willing to confront several highly charged issues that Wolfe is at pains to avoid and obfuscate. What was it about the Anglo-Protestant tradition that led to the erosion of its earlier determination to create and preserve a Christian nation in America?

The Elephant in the Room

One scholar suggests that WASPs were their own worst enemy. According to Eric Kaufmann, the decline of Anglo-America was not due to external factors; in particular, it did not follow an organized campaign by rival ethnic groups seeking to challenge WASP hegemony. He contends that the decisive "forces of dominant-ethnic decline" emerged instead "from *within* Anglo-Protestant America."[57] There is a large element of truth to the Kaufmann thesis. The modern American

---

56 Ibid., 390–392, 414–415.
57 Kaufmann, *Rise and Fall of Anglo-America*, 4.

corporate capitalist society that emerged in the late nineteenth century was the unique product of the interaction between a kind of person, a kind of economy, and a kind of religion.[58]

Brian Gatton suggests that the most significant psychological and spiritual force driving WASPs to commit *hari-kari* was the other-directed nature of the "social self" fabricated by the corporate system.[59] In the early modern period a God of Will was worshipped by the bourgeois individual of the Protestant ethic, whose enterprising ways helped the modern capitalist economy to take off. But while the driven personality of the inner-directed Protestant supplied power on the runway, once in flight the economy relied on technique, not on character, to keep itself aloft. As Donald Meyer put it in his study of the American gospel of positive thinking, "if at the center of nineteenth century social imagination stood a man, in the twentieth he was replaced by a system."[60]

> The dominant ethos of the Anglo-American corporate system depends upon a novel blend of psychology, economics and theology. The economy became an object of religious devotion for the managerial and professional classes. Today, in all sectors of society and culture, economic development has become an occasion for dependency rather than belonging. Our abject subjection to the mysterious movements of the global economy parallels the relationship of Protestant believers to their "hidden God, the God of Will" who can be known "only in His works, not in His nature." In an awful recurrence, we are returning to the situation of the early Protestants as an abyss opens between us and an economy invested with all the attributes

---

58 Donald Meyer, *The Positive Thinkers: A Study of the American Quest for Health, Wealth, and Personal Power from Mary Baker Eddy to Norman Vincent Peale* (Garden City, NY: Anchor, 1966), 177.

59 Brian Gatton, "Hari-Kari of the Anglo Elite," (2006) 25(4) *Journal of American Ethnic History* 181. For more on the distinction between inner-directed and other-directed character types, see David Riesman, *The Lonely Crowd: A Study of the Emerging American Character* (New Haven: Yale University Press, 2001 [original ed. 1961]).

60 Meyer, *Positive Thinkers*, 177.

of divinity. Its inner workings surpass ordinary human understanding. Among our elites and opinion leaders, insight, knowledge, and intelligence can do no more than serve the disembodied forces animating the society of perpetual growth. It is not the courage or the strength of our political and corporate leaders, nor our respect for tradition that sanctifies the system. It is faith alone. Awesome and inscrutable, spectacular and self-propelling, the system invites adoration.[61]

No doubt the emergent other-directed character of the WASP middle-class was a uniquely Anglo-American adaptation to the organizational imperatives of corporate capitalism. But if the home-grown "corporate self" provided the seedbed for the cosmopolitan spirit of the Progressive Era, the WASP clerisy had plenty of help from other ethnic groups, especially Jews, in nurturing a full-blown cult of the Other. Indeed, Kaufmann credits Felix Adler, a leading Jewish intellectual, with a leading role in awakening Progressive reformers to the possibilities inherent in this new pluralist vision of American national identity.[62] In his own recent book, *Whiteshift*, Kaufmann, too, is remarkably sanguine about the demographic, cultural, and political impact of mass third world immigration on the future of the white majority in Anglo-American society.[63]

An interesting comparison can be made between Eric Kaufmann and Stephen Wolfe on the issue of immigration-induced cultural change. In principle, Wolfe advocates limits on immigration from culturally alien sources, even though they might be Christian.[64] Kaufmann, on the other hand, treats "white opposition to mass immigration as a problem to be solved, not as an expression of legitimate ethnic interests or democratic will." Both are confident, however, that, so long as the rate of change is less than alarming, assimilation

---

61 Ibid., 177–178.

62 Kaufmann, *Rise and Fall of Anglo-America*, 91–95.

63 Eric P. Kaufmann, *Whiteshift: Populism, Immigration, and the Future of White Majorities* (London: Penguin, 2018).

64 Wolfe, *Christian Nationalism*, 199–204.

of cultural outsiders will be possible. Kaufmann merely cautions that whites must be allowed "some social space to express their identity."[65]

Both are what Frank Salter describes as "ethnic traditionalists" in the sense that "they support immigration so long as the immigrants assimilate, regardless of the impact on [white] ethnic identity, even if [the white majority] eventually disappears."[66] It may be that the differences between them with respect to the scale of immigration reflect differences in their respective racial and ethnic identities. Whatever the precise weight any given European ethnicity may have contributed to Wolfe's identity, he is unquestionably white. Kaufmann's ancestry is noticeably more exotic: part-Jewish, part-Chinese, and part-Hispanic. Perhaps that explains why Kaufmann promulgates the ideal of a "whiteshift" over the next century or two when he expects (and hopes) most Westerners will become "what we now term 'mixed-race.'"[67]

For his part, Wolfe certainly does not actively promote race-mixing as an end in itself; nor, however, does he accept that a "community in blood" is "the sole determinant of ethnicity." Sensitive to accusations of "racism," he is not opposed to intermarriage in principle.[68] Nor does he approve inter-ethnic or inter-racial marriages merely as particular exceptions to a general rule requiring respect for ethnic and racial boundaries. Hannah Arendt, by contrast, frankly accepts that "every mixed marriage constitutes a challenge to society." While opposing the legal prohibition (but not social disapproval) of interracial marriage, Arendt preferred to treat mixed marriage as a private matter between individuals "who have so far preferred personal happiness to social adjustment that they are willing to bear the burden of discrimination." On Arendt's realist view, such discrimination is a necessary evil. If people (and, presumably, churches) are not free to shun those whose

---

65 Frank Salter, "The Ethnic Predicaments of the Shrinking White Majority," (September 2019) 63(9) *Quadrant* 31, at 34–35.

66 *Ibid.*, 33.

67 Kaufmann, quoted in Salter, "Ethnic Predicaments," 33.

68 Wolfe, *Christian Nationalism*, 139.

private lives, social mores, or ethnic identity they disapprove, "society would simply cease to exist and very important possibilities of free association and group formation would disappear."[69] By contrast, Wolfe treats race-mixing as a positive good which, over time, will create the "bonds of affection" that will enable the formation of "various brotherhoods and tribes and shared or public pastimes." Nationhood, for Wolfe, is a spiritual phenomenon, not a matter of hematology.[70]

Despite their differences, however, neither Wolfe nor Kaufmann examine the role of ethnic rivalry (much less antagonism) between Jews and WASPs as a major contributing factor to the decline of Anglo-Protestant "cultural Christianity." Such reluctance to tackle the Jewish question directly is noteworthy given their joint preoccupation with the immigration issue. After all, Jews led the long campaign to overturn the national origins regime (adopted in 1924), designed to radically restrict the numbers of immigrants to the USA from areas outside northwestern Europe. Elsewhere in the Anglosphere, too, Jews have been active in promoting non-white immigration, especially after the passage of the 1965 Hart-Celler Act in the USA.

A secular, part-Jewish, cosmopolitan such as Kaufmann cannot be expected, perhaps, to highlight the prominent role played by Jews in undermining the institutional supports for Christian nationhood. But, given the prominence that Wolfe gives to his discussion of "the good of cultural Christianity," it seems strange that he completely ignores the issue. Wolfe understands cultural Christianity as "the force that normalizes Christian culture," even for many who neither attend churches readily nor publicly profess Christian beliefs. It is a "social power" which "directs people *to* activities wherein they can procure the things of eternal life, both inside and outside the instituted church."[71]

---

69 Hannah Arendt, "Reflections on Little Rock,"[originally published in 1959] in Peter Baehr, ed. *The Portable Hannah Arendt* (New York: Penguin, 2000), 238–239.

70 Wolfe, *Christian Nationalism*, 139–140.

71 Ibid., 213..

Much to the amusement of cosmopolitan urban sophisticates ("cloud people"), Wolfe holds up the fictional North Carolina town of Mayberry (home to the "dirt people" of the Sixties *Andy Griffith Show*) as the avatar of cultural Christianity. This folksy, small town was "a community of few and small concerns, high social trust, and an ease of life." Wolfe remarks that "any American" watching that show today "cannot but feel nostalgia for an America lost by negligence and malevolence."[72]

Note that Wolfe attributes the destruction of the world of Mayberry, a *place* where everybody went to church and probably "all the kids were above average," to both negligence and malevolence. But, surprisingly, even West Point graduate Wolfe declines to identify the foremost enemy of American cultural Christianity. This reflects the fatal flaw in Anglo-Protestant political theology: the absence of an explicit ethnoreligion anchored in the history and destiny of the Anglo-Saxon peoples. Jews are far more ethnocentric than even the ethnic traditionalist minority among WASPs. The most important difference between Jews and Anglo-Protestants is the propensity of the former community towards a high level of what Salter labels "ethnic nepotism". In other words, Jews are much more likely to exhibit a strong belief "in the unity of family and racial kinship." Jewish parents are much more likely than WASPs to see their children as an essential "contribution to the immortality of their race."[73]

Arguably, Jewish elites believe that it is in their ethnic genetic interest to dismantle the institutional supports for Christian nationhood and have pursued legal, political, and cultural strategies to achieve that end throughout the Anglosphere. In the USA, this campaign included a battery of legal challenges which successfully ended school prayers and bible reading. A famous book entitled *The Authoritarian Personality*, sponsored by the American Jewish Committee, appeared

---

72 Ibid., 226.
73 Salter, "Ethnic Predicaments," 32–33.

in 1950 and inspired a multi-pronged attack on the Christian family which continues down to the present day. Mass third-world immigration, feminism, pornography, contraception and abortion, and, more recently, transgender rights have all been weaponized by Jewish activists waging a concerted war on cultural Christianity.[74]

The reconstitution of Christian nations in the USA and the rest of the Anglosphere will require the emergence of a counter-elite ready, willing, and able to contest the Jewish Ascendancy, not just within the state, but also on the terrain of civil society, in the corporate sector, the media, academia, and the legal profession.[75] Any such counter-elite must be driven by an ethnoreligious spirit if it is to have any chance of success. The greatest weakness of Wolfe's vision of Christian nationhood is that he treats the particularity of each people and place as adiaphorous, a thing indifferent, not affecting the universal spiritual unity of the kingdom of God.

Conclusion

For Wolfe, Christ redeemed humanity as a whole; the constituent elements of mankind's transient life in this world were to be perfected by ordering the various Christian nations/ethnicities to Christ. Wolfe takes it for granted that humanity has a *telos* in common, already known to Christian theology. But what if race is not just a social construct but also possesses an intractably biological dimension? What if the phenomenology of place is ultimately grounded in the

---

74 Simple internet searches for material on "the Jewish role" in each of those movements will yield ample evidence to support this proposition. A more systematic academic introduction to these issues can be found in Kevin Macdonald, *The Culture of Critique: An Evolutionary Analysis of Jewish Involvement in Twentieth-Century Intellectual and Political Movements* (Long Beach, CA: 1st Books, 2002 [originally published by Praeger in 1998]).

75 Andrew Fraser, *Reinventing Aristocracy in the Age of Woke Capital: How Honourable WASP Elites Could Rescue Our Civilisation from Bad Governance by Irresponsible Corporate Plutocrats* (London: Arktos, 2022).

evolutionary history of distinctive biocultures? Race is a trinitarian phenomenon: race-as-biology, race-as-culture, and race-as-theology, all develop together within a complex differentiated historical process. Every "people-group" (the tender-minded synonym for tribes, nations, and races) possesses its own language, culture, patterns of experience, and goals; they cannot all be squeezed together into the simplistic schematic structure of a neo-Augustinian metanarrative.

Anglo-Protestants desperately need to situate themselves within a theologically informed ethnohistory. Such an ethnotheology must come to grips with biocultural science, with genetic similarity theory, and with a consciousness of the importance of ethnic genetic interests to the physical and spiritual well-being of their people.[76] Only in that way can Anglo-Protestants hope to understand the rise, decline, fall, and possible restoration of Anglo-Saxon Christendoms throughout the Anglosphere.

As things stand now, Anglo-Protestant theology bears a large share of responsibility for the deformation of Christian nationhood. Perhaps the most telling symptom of the present crisis is Wolfe's claim that there can never again be a chosen nation or people. No Christian nation today, he writes, can be "a holy nation in the sense that Israel was holy when under the Mosaic Covenant. No nation today is God's nation by some special divine command or by exclusive divine favor." Wolfe acknowledges that a people can only become or maintain themselves as a Christian nation "in an explicit sense, [by] an act of *national will.*"[77] But here, he is intellectually crippled by the idealist, other-worldly character of his historical and political theology. A more realistic

---

76 Good introductions to these fields can be found in Frank Salter, *On Genetic Interests: Family, Ethnicity, and Humanity in an Age of Mass Migration* (London: Routledge, 2006); J. Phillipe Rushton, *Race, Evolution, and Behavior: A Life History Perspective* Third Edition (Port Huron, MI: Charles Darwin Research Institute, 2000); and Andrew Fraser, *The WASP Question: An Essay on the Biocultural Evolution, Present Predicament, and Future Prospects of the Invisible Race* (London: Arktos, 2011).

77 Wolfe, *Christian Nationalism*, 176.

account of the origins of the Mosaic Covenant might understand it as a product of a historical process in which both divine command *and* national will were involved.

As one writer, who goes by the name of Jung-Freud, contends, "if Jews believed in many gods for different peoples as pagan folks did, then there would have been no need for the Covenant." Instead, Jews took a different path. "Out of boldness, imagination, arrogance, megalomania, or whatever," they "came to believe in only one God for themselves." But they also taught their children that no other gods were real and that it was a grave sin to worship them. But why would that one God favour the insignificant small-time people of Israel over all other tribes? That seemingly insoluble puzzle made it *necessary* for the Israelites to come up with the Covenant. Without it, "there was no guarantee that God would stick with the Jews."[78]

Considering the heroic role of Anglo-Protestants in the foundation of the nations of the Anglosphere, why should they, too, not feel in their bones that they can and should enter into a special covenant with God? After all, the process by which a people enter into covenant with the divine must be akin to what has long been known to the Orthodox Christian tradition as the experience of "theosis" or "deification." Perhaps, a "stateless" people, such as the ancient Israelites on their exodus journey to the Promised Land, is more receptive to communion with the divine.

But the Jews are not the only people to experience "statelessness." In our own time, the "nation-states" of the Anglosphere have been subordinated to the hidden hand of globalist plutocracy. Consequently, the Anglo-Saxon peoples, both "at home" and in the diaspora, are now *de facto*, if not yet *de jure*, "stateless." Perhaps providentially, certainly ironically, such political and cultural dispossession may have created

---

78 Jung-Freud, "Why the Euraces (Or European Races) Need Their Own COVENANT(s) in a One-Truth and One-Power World" https://www.unz.com/jfreud/why-the-euracesor-european-races-need-their-own-covenants-in-a-one-truth-and-one-power-world.

the conditions for a spiritual renaissance. WASPs may yet rediscover the ethnoreligious spirit that once moved Alfred the Great to look to Covenant as the essential medium for the collective deification of his embryonic *Angelcynn* nation.[79]

Given that possibility, it is no wonder that organized Jewry does everything in its power to demonize the ethnoreligious spirit of Christian nationalism throughout the Anglosphere.[80] But let us not forget that such cultural subversion also successfully targeted once-great Christian nations such as Germany as well — with the active cooperation of the Anglo-Saxon nations. Anglo-Protestant theology happily sanctified the thirty-year war waged on Germany. Now re-educated, guilt-tripped, and thoroughly demoralized by a systematic process of *Überfremdung*, Germany remains securely under the thumb of the globalist American regime overseeing its proxy war on Orthodox Christian Russia. "Our" phony victories in those wars should be sources of shame rather than pride. Compare the negative, dysgenic, maladaptive impact of Anglo-Protestant Woke political theology with the positive, eugenic, and adaptive success of the Jewish political theology grounded in the Holocaust Mythos. In the one case, blasphemy laws are conceived as a violation of human rights; in the other, "condoning, denying, or downplaying" Jewish suffering is a shocking offence against the laws of God and man, alike.

It is long past time for Anglo-Protestant political theology to identify and clearly distinguish friend from foe in the holy war we are compelled to wage for the earthly survival and spiritual salvation of the Anglo-Saxon race worldwide.

---

79 See chapter 14.
80 See, *e.g.*, Rabbi Deborah Waxman, PhD, "Ethnonationalism is a Grave Threat to Democracy" https://www.reconstructingjudaism.org/news/ethnonationalism-is-a-grave-threat-to-democracy.

2. Religion, Race, and Ethnicity in Greco-Roman Antiquity: New Perspectives on The Lordship of Jesus, Judaism, and the "Truthiness" of Christianity

Introduction

ON THE DISSIDENT right down-under, the intellectual, spiritual, and moral bankruptcy of mainstream Australian "conservatism" is a well-worn topic. Everyone expects conservatives to cuck when the question of white genocide or the great replacement is raised. Should attention shift away from racial politics to the relationship between politics and religion, however, most conservatives and radical rightists reveal a shared loyalty to a secular regime separating church and state.

This became evident to me while listening to a recent podcast discussion between Blair Cottrell (a photogenic, patriotic chad and working class, "tradie," activist) and Joel Davis (an online personality and activist of a more educated and intellectual bent).[1] At first, both stuck to the usual script, agreeing that Anglo-Australian (or white) nationalism will never become a serious contender for state power in Australia so long as the Labor-Liberal duopoly retains its long-established stranglehold on mainstream party politics. But then, the conversation briefly strayed off the beaten path. Frankly clutching at straws, Cottrell

---

1 *The Joel & Blair Show* https://www.youtube.com/watch?v=Y1ZRketjuIY&t=3532s.

wondered whether religion — Christianity, in particular — might offer an alternative medium for fruitful nationalist activism, outside and apart from the state. Davis immediately demurred, advising against mixing religion and politics. While avowing his personal faith in Catholicism (since abandoned) as the "true religion," he worried that making race a religious issue (or vice versa) would undermine the already fragile unity of the embryonic nationalist movement among white Australians.

In a supposedly secular society such as contemporary Australia, such a view passes as the conventional wisdom. Significantly, what goes unmentioned here is the relationship between *ethnicity*, specifically Anglo-Australian, or white Anglo-Saxon Protestant (WASP) ethnicity, in its relationship to both state and church. This is especially remarkable in Australia where WASPs are still a (shrinking) majority of the population. How, then, did religion become separated from Anglo-Australian ethnonationalism? Indeed, how was Anglo-Australian ethnicity itself relegated to the margins of political discourse on the dissident right? Why should an Anglo-Protestant ethnic majority adopt instead a generic "white" or "European" racial identity? Why should they forswear their collective birthright to an ancestral stock of social, cultural, and spiritual capital — the common blood, language, and religion — generated in the course of a unique history played out on a global stage?

After all, not so very long ago, Irish Catholics in Australia and elsewhere routinely employed the church in pursuit of their ethnic interests, in opposition, if need be, to their Anglo-Protestant "fellow whites." Interestingly, the secularization of politics in Ireland has coincided with the accelerating demographic displacement of the Irish people. Apart from the Irish, do Jews not mix religion and politics? Who can deny that Judaism is an ethnoreligion with a distinctive political theology of its own grounded, nowadays, in the Holocaust mythos? Significantly, in Canada, "Holocaust denial" is now a crime under a newly enacted blasphemy law which came hot on the heels of the 2018 repeal of blasphemy laws originally intended to protect the Christian religion.[2] In the rest of the Anglosphere, social conventions alone still enforce public respect for Jewish political theology by governments, the corporate sector, and society at large. Moreover, synagogues have long been a significant vehicle for Jewish ethnopolitical action. What prevents Anglo-Protestants from viewing "their" churches in a similar light?

It is not that either Catholic or Anglo-Protestant churches seek to build a wall between religion and politics (understood as who gets what, when, where, and how). Rather, they refuse to mix religion with *ethnicity* (much less race). Or to be more precise, while countenancing ethnic congregations for non-white minorities, churches expect Anglo-Protestant parishioners to maintain a strict separation between their "ethnicity" and their "religion." Christian clerics, across denominations, turn a blind eye to the enchanted world of Greco-Roman antiquity, where religion, as such, did not actually exist. In fact, in the Roman empire of the first century, not even Jesus (or his apostle Paul) distinguished religion from ethnicity.

For Jews, no less than Samaritans, Greeks, and Romans, one's identity, fate, and destiny derived from kinship with the gods of one's family, tribe, and city. "What modern people think of as 'religion,' ancient people articulated and experienced as family inheritance, [and] 'ancestral custom.'" In such a world, *"ethnic distinctiveness and religious distinctiveness are simple synonyms, and native to all ancient peoples."* Moreover, Paula Fredriksen adds, "ancient peoples, Jews included, did not 'believe' or 'believe in' their ancestral customs. They enacted them; they preserved them; they respected them; they trusted or trusted in them." In pre-Christian antiquity, the two key populations were gods and humans. Ancient societies "could thrive only if gods were happy. Cult was the index of human loyalty, affection, and respect." Just as "cult

---

2   Andrew Fraser, "Friend or Foe? The Holocaust Mythos, Global Jesus, and the Existential Crisis of Anglican Political Theology," (2022) Vol. 22(3) *The Occidental Quarterly* 63.

was an ethnic designation," so too "ethnicity was a cult designation." In other words, "gods ran in the blood. Peoples and their pantheons shared a family connection."[3]

Accordingly, it was only because Jesus of Nazareth was acknowledged as the Son of Israel's God that he could expect to be exalted as King of the Jews. Indeed, he declares explicitly that he "was not sent except to the lost sheep of the house of Israel" (Matt. 15:24). Similarly, the apostle Paul used the widespread diaspora of Hellenized Jews as the base for his outreach to the God-fearing pagans of the Roman Empire. Indeed, Paul saw his mission to the pagans as the medium through which he might reconnect with those "lost Israelite sheep." As we will see, Jesus and Paul shared an ethno-theology in which the history of Israel according to the flesh was the medium through which the spiritual destiny of the Israel of God was to be fulfilled.

What prevents churches throughout the Anglosphere from developing an ethno-theology enabling white Anglo-Saxon Protestants (WASPs) to recover a shared ethnoreligious spirit of meaning, value, and purpose? I believe that Blair Cottrell had some such intuition at the back of his mind during his discussion with Joel Davis. Joel, by contrast, confines (dare I say, dooms) the Anglo-Australian nationalist movement to a secular, explicitly "one-dimensional" strategy of racial politics. Looking back on the Jesus movement of the first century, however, I am convinced that the regeneration of deracinated, spiritually anemic Anglo-Australians will require a multi-pronged and transnational, *three*-dimensional movement. The goal must be to reinvigorate the historic bonds of religion, race, and ethnicity within and between the peoples of the British diaspora. Nothing less than a broad spectrum, deep-seated renaissance of British race patriotism

---

3   Paula Fredriksen, "Divinity, Ethnicity, Identity: 'Religion' as a Political Category in Christian Antiquity," in Armin Lange, *et.al.*, *Comprehending Antisemitism through the Ages: A Historical Perspective* (Open Access: De Gruyter, 2021), 101–120, at 102–103; *idem*, "Judaizing the Nations: The Ritual Demands of Paul's Gospel," 56 *New Testament Studies* 232, at 234–235.

will overcome the soul-destroying, nihilistic materialism of globalist plutocracy. Any such Great Awakening in our time requires a religious reformation reconnecting Anglican (and other Anglo-Protestant) churches to their ancestral roots in the Angelcynn church fostered by Alfred the Great (849–899).

The Problem with Christian Nationalism

Why then, have I criticized the American-style Christian nationalism championed by Stephen Wolfe?[4] Certainly, in many respects, we are on the same side. Not only is Wolfe opposed to the globalist regime headquartered in Washington D.C. and New York, but he is also critical of the evangelical Protestant establishment. Before publication of his best-selling book on Christian nationalism, Wolfe had already written a series of online articles deploring "the sorry state of evangelical rhetoric."[5] There he charged that American evangelicals have become addicted to the use of shopworn rhetorical devices designed to capture the moral high ground from their critics without ever having to take them seriously. Most obviously, virtue-signalling Christians routinely remind those advocating an end to mass third world immigration that we must "love our neighbours." Wolfe rightly complains that serious moral and political discourse, is impossible so long as such rhetorical devices are automatically invoked to short-circuit debates with anyone who could lead evangelicals down the path to ethnonationalism.

Wolfe presents a persuasive critique of "christianizing rhetorical devices." He refers there to the evangelical habit of grounding arguments in what they take to be "an undeniable Christian truism" (*e.g.*, "all of us are made in the image of God"). This rhetorical tactic forces opponents "to contend with an undeniable statement offered for a

---

4   See chapter 1.
5   Stephen Wolfe, *The Case for Christian Nationalism* (Moscow, ID: Canon Press, 2022); *idem*, "The Sorry State of Evangelical Rhetoric," http://sovereignnations.com/2018/06/22/sorry-state-evangelical-rhetoric.

predetermined moral conclusion."[6] For my own part, I first began to push back against the unreflective moral certitude of Anglo-Protestant discourse when, as a bookish teen-ager in small-town Ontario, I discovered the English philosopher Bertrand Russell.

A callow youth with an embryonic goatee, I relished my newfound vocation as the village atheist. I was amazed by the ease with which I could confound church-going classmates with talking points I lifted from Russell's treasure trove of skeptical essays.[7] Still, I was no more a militant atheist than Russell himself, being much more taken by his skeptical agnosticism. After high school, as I studied history through to an honours degree and graduate school, I simply lost interest in the milk-and-water sermonizing style of Anglo-Protestantism, Canadian-style.[8]

Not until my early thirties was my childhood Sunday School receptivity to Christianity fortuitously rekindled. Having, at long last, graduated from law school in Canada in the mid-seventies, I seized the opportunity to avoid the grind of legal practice by teaching law in Australia. Fortunately, I soon landed a job in a new law school in Sydney where I developed and convened a first-year, foundation course on the history and philosophy of law. That course was based on the premise that the common law tradition grew out of a Greco-Roman civilization reshaped by the triumph of Christianity. So, while remaining an unchurched agnostic, I gradually absorbed the sort of cultural Christianity now stoutly defended by Stephen Wolfe.

Not long afterwards, while working on a master's degree at Harvard Law School, I discovered the fascinating interplay between Anglo-American Protestantism and the classical republican traditions shaping the federal constitution of what seemed, by comparison with European absolutism, the almost stateless character of American civil

---

6   Ibid.

7   Bertrand Russell, *Sceptical Essays* (London: Unwin Books, 1960).

8   Pierre Berton *The Comfortable Pew: A Critical Look at Christianity and the Religious Establishment in the New Age* (Philadelphia: J.B. Lippincott, 1965).

society. Although it has attracted accusations of authoritarian statism, Wolfe's Christian nationalism owes a lot to the Anglo-Protestant evangelical tradition of anti-institutional populism. Long story short: American constitutional history has been shaped by the political theology of evangelical Protestantism which exalted the double majesty of the Divine Economy and good King Demos. Over the years, I have written good deal on that subject.[9]

Decades later, after leaving legal education behind (let us say, involuntarily) I began to wonder, as Blair Cottrell did above, whether Christianity, particularly the Anglican church, could ever develop an effective response to the spiritual, moral, and intellectual crisis of WASP managerial, professional, and political elites. I persuaded myself that I should at least get some skin in the game by getting baptized in a local Anglican church. Having lamented the collapse of English Canadian nationalism as a young man, I am now deeply disturbed by the disastrous decline of WASP hegemony everywhere in the Anglosphere.[10] Embarking on a search for the spiritual roots of that crisis, I decided to earn a degree in theology.

I therefore possess personal, political, and professional interests in the prospects for an ethnoreligious solution to the existential crisis now facing the Anglo-Saxon peoples. Unfortunately, Wolfe rests his own case for Christian nationalism upon an *a priori* faith in a pair of "undeniable Christian truisms." Hoping to establish the legitimacy of a Christian nation ruled by a Christian prince, he simply asserts the truth value of two "mixed syllogisms" which combine natural law

---

[9] See, Andrew Fraser, *The Spirit of the Laws: Republicanism and the Unfinished Project of Modernity* (Toronto: University of Toronto Press, 1990), esp. 31–40, 129, 216; *The WASP Question: An Essay on the Biocultural Evolution, Present Predicament, and Future Prospects of the Invisible Race* (London: Arktos, 2011), 241; and *Reinventing Aristocracy in the Age of Woke Capital: How Honourable WASP Elites Could Rescue Our Civilisation from Bad Governance by Irresponsible Corporate Plutocrats* (London: Arktos, 2022) 16.

[10] Cf. George Grant, *Lament for a Nation: The Defeat of Canadian Nationalism* (Ottawa: Carleton University Press, 1988 [orig. ed. 1965]).

with certain "supernatural truths," or theological presuppositions revealed by grace. He claims, for example, that the catchphrase "Jesus is Lord" is a "universally true statement." Likewise, the proposition that "Christianity is the true religion," grounded as it is in revelation rather than reason, requires no argument.[11] But surely, even if one accepts the presupposition that those statements are "true," one is entitled to ask: "In what sense are they true?" What if the most that can expect to find in such "undeniable Christian truisms" is some sort of "truthiness"?[12]

Wolfe's political theory of Christian nationalism aims to secure the Lordship of Jesus by resurrecting blasphemy and Sabbatarian laws designed to drive atheism and heresy from the public sphere. In principle, this political program knows no borders. If Christianity is the true religion, it must be "a universal religion — a religion for *all* nations." But, Wolfe concedes, "it does not eliminate nations." Rather, Christianity completes, indeed, it *perfects* nations as well as individual recipients of divine grace.[13] A non-Christian nation (or person) is, therefore, an *imperfect* nation (or person).

So long as America retained its identity as a Christian nation, Wolfe contends, it was entitled to defend itself against advocates of atheism and immorality. And so, it did. For example, even in secular and cosmopolitan New York City and, as late as 1940, concerned citizens successfully campaigned to prevent Bertrand Russell from taking up a teaching position at the City College in the fields of logic, mathematical theory, and the philosophy of science. The justification for this violation of academic freedom: As the author of notorious (but, to many, high-minded, measured, and persuasive) essays such as those collected in my broken-backed copy of *Why I Am Not a Christian*, Russell was allegedly an unrepentant advocate of atheism,

---

11 Wolfe, *Christian Nationalism*, 120, 183.

12 Defined by the Merriam-Webster Dictionary as: *a truthful or seemingly truthful quality that is claimed for something not because of supporting facts or evidence but because of a feeling that it is true or a desire for it to be true.*

13 Wolfe, *Christian Nationalism*, 26.

public nudity, and free love.[14] Clearly, at that time, American Anglo-Protestants had few qualms about using state power to enforce creedal conformity. The churches then were still a force to be reckoned with and Wolfe clearly hankers after those days.

But that was then; this is now. In the past fifty years or so, Protestant churches and their denominational theological colleges have offered little resistance, and more than a little support and encouragement to the rise of Woke America. Wolfe, of course, recognizes that the ascension of an evangelical "Christian Prince" to state power is unlikely to occur anytime soon. Nor does he expect "really existing," mainstream Protestant churches to enter the political arena themselves, fighting to reverse the browning of America, overturn the gynocracy, or dismantle the Global American Empire (GAE). At most, churches might be third-party beneficiaries of a lay, pan-Protestant, nationalist movement combating demonic powers and principalities on their behalf. A more counter-intuitive threat to Globohomo is hard to imagine.

Nevertheless, Wolfe has become a prominent figure on social media, regularly sniping at an evangelical establishment on board with the globalist agenda of the transnational corporate welfare state. In his view, the globalist regime threatens both his religion and his nation. As a Reformed Presbyterian political theorist, however, Wolfe rides two unruly horses — ethnicity and religion — simultaneously. Only by keeping both his ethnic identity and his religious faith on a steady diet of blood thinners can he keep his seat. But any Christian nationalism worthy of the name must recognize, sooner or later, that strong gods demand the unapologetic fusion of race, ethnicity, and religion.

Religion and Ethnicity: Then and Now

On Wolfe's political theory, ethnicity is, by nature, a particularistic phenomenon situated within earthly kingdoms governed by civil

---

14 Bertrand Russell, *Why I Am Not a Christian*, Edited with an Appendix on the "Bertrand Russell Case" by Paul Edwards (New York: Simon and Schuster, 1957).

magistrates, the realm Augustine of Hippo described as the City of Man. Reformed theology and Protestant churches, on the other hand, are oriented by grace towards a heavenly kingdom, the eternal City of God, where the Lord Jesus reigns, sitting at the right hand of the Father. Civil magistrates must accommodate the ethnic identities, needs, and interests of his subjects, but the triune God of Reformed theology is colour-blind. Many New Testament scholars now contend, however, that this presupposition contradicts an undeniable *historical* truism fundamental to the cosmology shared even by Jesus of Nazareth and Paul, his apostle to the Gentiles. In the enchanted realm of Greco-Roman antiquity, religion and ethnicity were indistinguishable; they were literally *syngeneic*, originally a Greek word signifying both kinship and citizenship.

In those days, every member of the same *genos* shared a family connection extending "not only horizontally, between citizens of the Hellenistic polis; it also extended vertically between heaven and earth." In short, Greco-Roman cities "were not secular spaces. They were family-run religious institutions."[15] That enchanted world was saturated with gods; every forest and river, every family, tribe, and city had its own gods who must not be offended lest they visited retribution on those subject to their supernatural powers. For Jews, Greeks, and Romans, one's religion was not about beliefs, creeds, and confessions of faith. In the world we have lost, religion was synonymous with the ritual rites and obligations prescribed by one's mythological ethnic identity and ancestral allegiances.[16]

Wolfe, however, is loath to ground Christian nations in a syngeneic fusion of religion and ethnicity. Instead, he thinks of ethnicity as the "phenomenological topography" of a "people in place." Rather grudgingly, Wolfe acknowledges that ethnicity may run in the blood.[17] But

---

15 Paula Fredriksen, "How Jewish is God? Divine Ethnicity in Paul's Theology," (2018) 137(1) *Journal of Biblical Literature* 193, at 194–195.

16 Fredriksen, "Divinity, Ethnicity, Identity," 106.

17 Wolfe, *Christian Nationalism*, 134–137.

Christian identity, he believes, transcends primitive notions of kinship with the ancestral gods of family, tribe, or nation. Like Wolfe, Anglo-Protestants generally remain stubbornly resistant to the notion that spirit is fused together with blood, indissolubly, in holy communion with the water of life (1 John 5:8).

At the same time, Wolfe's Christian political theory remains resolutely old-fashioned in its respect for ecclesiastical authority. Anglo-Protestantism may be a bloodless religion, but it still adheres to ancestral creeds formulated in late antiquity by the Church Fathers. Notably, in preparation for his book, Wolfe immersed himself in the works of seventeenth-century Reformed theologians largely unknown to more than a few of his fellow Anglo-Protestants. Even more anachronistic is his reliance upon the Thomist tradition of natural law dating back to the Middle Ages. Biblical exegesis, on the other hand, is conspicuously absent from his work. Like most Anglo-Protestants, he is content to leave that task to the pastors and theologians who stand behind the Westminster Confession of Faith. Nor has he engaged with the growing body of contemporary New Testament scholarship ready, willing, and able to challenge the foundational "supernatural truths" of Wolfe's old-time religion.

Wolfe's brand of Christian nationalism will need more than recycled theological truisms dredged up from dusty Calvinist tracts to gain traction outside the echo chambers of pious evangelicalism. Mindlessly repeating that "Jesus is Lord" carries little weight outside that charmed circle. Similarly, after four centuries of experience with Anglo-Protestantism, it will be a hard sell to persuade Moslems, Jews, and nihilistic atheists, much less millions of marginalized white men, that "Christianity is the true religion" destined to "perfect" the already perfectly fictional "American nation." As Wolfe recognizes himself, the conventional attachment to a non-creedal, unchurched, cultural Christianity reaches its vanishing point when one's nation turns into a gay disco.

Indeed, already in 1940, it was evident that Bertrand Russell was far from being a lone skeptic in opposition to the merely voluntary Protestant establishment. At home, religious diversity was an established fact: Catholics, Jews, and Mormons had secure beachheads in America. Abroad, the country would soon join godless Soviet communists in its war on Germany. Hardly surprisingly then that, within a few decades after the war, the USA was to be utterly transformed by a civil rights revolution and its corollary, mass third world immigration. Mainline Protestant churches put up only token resistance before they obediently fell in line with the entire progressive agenda.

Nowadays, secular humanists, rationalist skeptics, mythicists, historicists, and atheists aplenty have found influential platforms in the religious studies departments of major American universities. Offering challenging new perspectives on once undeniable Christian truisms, they present a solid *prima facie* case for free thought in religious matters. Their claim that the "supernatural truths" asserted by Christian churches rest less on reason and revelation than on myth and fable cannot easily be swept under the carpet.

Pushed beyond the pale by both evangelical theological seminaries and mainstream Protestant churches, independent preterist scholars and dissident churches question the creedal promise that some time in our future the Lord Jesus "will come again in glory to judge the living and the dead." Conservative evangelicals insist that Jesus will return physically ("as a 5⊠ 5⊠ Jewish man," in Don K. Preston's wry phrase) riding on clouds of glory, at the end of the Christian age, to usher in a new heaven and a new earth. By contrast, preterists employ a Hebrew hermeneutic in defending their persuasively biblical covenantal eschatology. They hold that the *Parousia* (*i.e.*, the Second Coming of Jesus Christ, occurred, as prophesied in the Old and New Testaments, with the destruction of the Jerusalem Temple in AD 70. Hence, many New Testament scholars, skeptics and preterists alike, can agree that, *for those of us in the present*, the futurist eschatological hope, as preached in the creedal churches (though differing as to its pre-millennial, post-millennial, or amillennial timing) is little more than a chimera.

Do bible-believing preterists and skeptical scholars deserve a respectful hearing from creedal Christian nationalists? In principle, Stephen Wolfe approves the restoration of Sabbatarian and blasphemy laws to exclude political atheism and public heresy "from acceptable opinion and action."[18] Wolfe publicly affirms creedal orthodoxy on eschatology; he "looks to the future coming of Christ (Tit. 2:13)" and hopes "for the glorification of the body promised to us in Christ (Phil. 3:21)."[19] One cannot but wonder whether he would vote to convict preterists such as Don K. Preston were he to sit on a jury in a prosecution for public heresy.

Wolfe certainly believes that "public heresy has the potential to harm other's souls by causing doubt or distraction or by disrupting public peace." According to his Christian political theory, therefore, the civil "magistrate, who must care for the souls of his people, may act to suppress that heresy." Note as well that Wolfe agrees in principle with Francis Turretin, his favourite seventeenth-century theologian, that arch-heretics "publicly persistent in their damnable error…can be justly put to death."[20] Having endorsed Don K. Preston's views on fulfilled eschatology, repeatedly and in public, I fear that a "Christian prince" would convict me of arch-heresy. I can only hope that he might find it imprudent to condemn me to death.

Anglo-Protestant "nationalists" proposing to outlaw atheism and heresy could ease the minds of those who might be accused of public atheism by explaining just how the historical Jesus became the eternal Lord of the Anglo-Saxon, British-descended peoples. WASP agnostics will ask why only a bloodlessly cosmic "Christianity" can be their "true religion." Looking further afield for potential defendants,

---

18 *Ibid.*, 384–387.
19 Stephen Wolfe, "The Church Among Nations," August 1, 2023, *American Reformer* http://americanreformer.org/2023/08/the-church-among-the-nations.
20 Wolfe, *Christian Nationalism*, 387–388, 391.

Wolfe's Pan-Protestant program to enshrine the "supernatural truths" of creedal Christianity into public and criminal law is sure to generate powerful pushback from a multitude of other groups. Massive resistance will come, not just from mild-mannered academics and pious preterists, but from marginalized Muslims, deeply entrenched Jewish elites, miscellaneous unbelievers, and moral degenerates, not to mention businesses, large and small, which profit from the abolition of Sunday blue laws and the concomitant licencing of atheistic, materialist nihilism seven days a week.

Note as well that the heretical theological voices discussed below have found mass audiences on, *inter alia*, YouTube channels such as MythVision Podcast.[21] Many Christian nationalists such as Stephen Wolfe (as well as white nationalists who happen to be Christian, such as Joel Davis in Australia) are themselves adept in the use of social media. But, wedded as they are to the "supernatural truths" enshrined in traditional church creeds, they are certain to be pushed onto the political and intellectual defensive. Indeed, as we have seen, Davis prudently prefers not to mix Catholic religion with his ethnopolitics. And for good reason, since what churchgoers take to be the most self-evident of theological truisms — the notion that Jesus and the apostle Paul were Christians — is now up for debate. Certainly, among contemporary New Testament scholars, no consensus supports the proposition that Jesus was sent or that Paul was called to found a new religion, especially one cleansed of his own ethnic identity.

Jews, Judaism, and the Idea of Israel in the First Century AD

My argument is an ethno-theological interpretation of the origins and outcome of the Jesus movement in the first-century world of Greco-Roman antiquity. In a nutshell, Jesus and Paul inspired a dissident ethnoreligious movement "within Judaism"; neither presented

---

21 https://www.youtube.com/@MythVisionPodcast.

himself as the Founder of Christianity. The movement first emerged in Judea after the death and reported resurrection of Jesus. By the time Jerusalem was destroyed by Roman armies in AD 70, the gospel had been carried to the ends of the known world through the social networks and synagogues established within the far-flung diaspora of Hellenistic Jews.

Not all Jews, either in Judea or in the diaspora were supporters of the Jesus movement. The Jesus movement was at odds with ethnonationalist Judeans involved in a long-simmering rebellion against Rome, leading to the Jewish wars in 66AD. Those Judean nationalists followed in the footsteps of the Maccabean rebellion against Hellenistic influence in the second century B.C. During his ministry, Jesus also came into conflict with the leaders of the Temple cult centred on Jerusalem. The Jesus movement stood for an ethno-theology with two central features. First, its aims were explicitly geopolitical in scope, extending beyond Judea to the entire known world (*oikumene*); and, secondly, the movement was driven by the sense of urgency inherent in its apocalyptic eschatology. Both Jesus and Paul taught that the "end of the age" was nigh. They and their followers looked forward to the long-promised but now imminent restoration of "all Israel" in a new heaven and new earth.

The suggestion made in the previous paragraph that the Jesus movement developed "within Judaism" is a deceptively simple claim. To the modern mind, the term "Judaism" connotes a "religion" which itself is misleading. Moderns associate "religion" with a set of doctrines pertaining to the nature of the divine or supernatural realm. Even the term "Judean" is anachronistic when used to signify an "ethnicity" as distinct from the modern category of "religion" supposedly implicit in the word "Jew." But, as we have already seen, the very attempt to distinguish religion and ethnicity in the ancient world is itself anachronistic.[22] In particular, it makes no sense to distinguish the ethnic

---

22 See also, Jason A. Staples, *The Idea of Israel in Second Temple Judaism* (Cambridge: Cambridge University Press, 2021), 17–18.

and religious aspects of Jewishness in this period. In translations of ancient texts, however, the English word "Judaism" is often supplied in place of phrases literally denoting "the ancestral traditions, laws, and customs of the Jews." This suggests that the "various elements that constitute our religion" were "inextricably bound up with other aspects of their life." In the Greco-Roman world, generally, there were "a variety of modes in which people could think about and interact with the divine world," including ritual and myth. These aspect of ancient life "overlapped and interacted in various ways" without forming the sort of "integrated system" or "unified understanding of the divine" that we call "religion."[23]

Certainly, there were no ancient Hebrew or Aramaic words which correspond to our "Judaism." There were Greek and Latin words that appear to do so (namely, Ἰουδαϊσμός and *Iudaismus*) but, before the period 200–500 AD, they are used only a very few times, in Greek, most during the Maccabean period of the second century, BC. The very restricted usage of that Greek word for Judaism usually occurs "*in explicit or implicit contrast with some other potential affiliation, movement, or inclination.*" This brings us to Hellenism and its cognate verb, Hellenize. The basic meaning of Hellenize was "to express oneself in Greek," occurring "chiefly in contexts where there are doubts about the speaker's ability because he is a foreigner or uneducated."[24]

Significantly, the first attestation of the word Hellenism is in the same second-century BC text that hosts the first occurrences of the word Judaism. The latter word "appears to have been coined in reaction to cultural Ἑλληνισμός" (Hellenism). In that context, "Judaism" signified "a certain kind of *activity* over against a pull in another, foreign direction," specifically Hellenism which "introduced foreign ways — Greek cultural institutions, education, sports, and dress — into Jerusalem." It therefore refers to "a *defection* that threatens the heart

---

23 Steve Mason, "Jews, Judeans, Judaizing, Judaism: Problems of Categorization in Ancient History," (2007) 38 *Journal for the Study of Judaism* 457, at 480, 482.

24 Ibid., 463–464.

and soul of Judean tradition." The Maccabean revolt "was a countermovement, a bringing back of those who had gone over to foreign ways: a "Judaizing" or Judaization, which the author of 2 Maccabees programmatically labels Ἰουδαϊσμός (Judaism)."[25]

The term "Judaism," therefore, has a double meaning corresponding to the difference between what anthropologist call an *etic* meaning, derived from an external or observer's point of view and the *emic* or insider's view that a first-century Jew would have as a participant in his own collective way of life. From that emic point of view, it makes no sense to distinguish between ethnicity and religion.[26] A further source of confusion over terms such as Jew and Jewishness has to do with the difference between modern and ancient understandings of the relationship between Jews, Judeans and the idea of Israel. Jason Staples points out that moderns usually presume that, after the Babylonian Exile, the term 'Israel' is synonymous with ethnic Jews.[27] In fact, historically speaking, "Israel is an entity larger than (but including) the body of ethnic Jews." Here, "Jew" or "Judean" "refers to persons descended from the southern kingdom of Judah [whether they live outside Judea or not], *which is only a part of the larger historical entity called Israel.*" By contrast, "Israel" is a polyvalent term with at least four distinct references in the Hebrew Bible: (1) the patriarch Jacob/Israel; (2) "the nation composed of his descendants, that is, all twelve tribes of 'Israel,' including Judah"; (3) the northern kingdom, the ten tribes of the "house of Israel," excluding the southern kingdom, the "house of Judah"; and (4) the returnees from Judah after the Babylonian Exile.[28] The *Ioudaioi* (Judeans) were the only Israelites who returned from Babylon. According to the late first-century Jewish historian, Josephus,

---

25   Ibid., 464–467.
26   Ibid., 458–460.
27   Staples, *Idea of Israel*, 25.
28   Jason A. Staples, "What Do the Gentiles Have to Do with 'All Israel'? A Fresh Look at Romans 11:25–27," (2011) 130(2) *Journal of Biblical Literature* 371, at 373–375.

the other ten tribes were scattered "beyond Euphrates till now and are a boundless multitude, not to be estimated by numbers."[29]

Keep in mind that the Hebrew Bible came into being after the disappearance of those ten lost tribes. This fact is crucial to an understanding of the Jesus movement in the first century. Staples emphasizes that "*the Hebrew Bible is scripture collected and edited by Jews, for Jews, about Israel.*" He observes that "interpreters have been too quick to assume that the (actual) Jewish audience of these texts is the same as the Israel to which the texts are rhetorically addressed." Instead, most of Israel existed only in the historical imagination after the Babylonian Exile. Accordingly, "through the collection and redaction of the prophetic literature and authoritative historical narratives that ultimately comprised the Hebrew Bible, exilic and post-exilic Jews established a continual reminder of the broken circumstances of the present, constructing an Israel *not* realized in the present." These early Jews, in other words, located "themselves in a liminal space between the memory of a past 'biblical' Israel and the hope for a future restored Israel." They created a "restoration eschatology" which looked forward, not to "the end of the *world*, but rather the end of the present *age* and the dawn of a new one." In that new creation "all Israel" was to be restored by the in-gathering of all twelve tribes of the Dispersion into Zion.[30] The Lordship of Jesus the Christ was closely associated with the longed-for restoration of "all Israel."

Although the ten lost tribes remained but a ghostly presence during the first century, a highly visible Jewish diaspora had been a well-established historical presence in major centres of the Greco-Roman world for hundreds of years. In fact, the Hellenized Jews of the diaspora greatly outnumbered those living in Judea. Rodney Stark estimates that while there were about one million Jews in Palestine, there were somewhere between four and six million to be found in wealthy

---

29 Quoted in Staples, *Idea of Israel*, 49.
30 Ibid., 89, 94–95.

and populous urban communities throughout the Roman empire. Indeed, "Jews had adjusted to life in the diaspora in ways that made them very marginal vis-à-vis the Judaism of Jerusalem." Because the Hebrew language skills of most Hellenized Jews "had decayed to the point that the Torah had to be translated into Greek." The Septuagint itself, therefore, became another medium through which Hellenistic perspectives found expression. Jews of the diaspora were Hellenized to the point that they needed the sort of cultural compromise allowing a Jew to remain a Jew while claiming full entry into "the elect society of the Greeks." As for the other side of the ethno-cultural divide, many so-called God-Fearers, or Gentile "fellow-travellers," were attracted to Hellenized Jewish traditions and customs, especially their moral teachings and monotheism, without being willing to "take the final step of fulfilling the Law" by giving up their own cultic gods and undergoing circumcision.[31]

Stark suggests that, when Jewish authorities decided not to require god-fearing Gentiles to observe the Law in full, they went some way towards the creation of a "religion" free of ethnicity.[32] This claim is seriously misleading. Paula Fredriksen observes that it was "a normal aspect of ancient Mediterranean life" to show respect for gods not one's own, for Jews no less than pagans. To forge "an *exclusive* commitment to a foreign god, however — an act unique to Judaism in the pre-Christian era — was tantamount to changing ethnicity" and, hence, would have been perceived as an act of disrespect to the gods of the host city. At the same time, however, majority cultures were "religiously commodious." Interested Gentiles "were free to frequent Jewish gatherings," assuming "whatever Jewish practices, traditions,

---

31 Rodney Stark, *The Rise of Christianity: How the Obscure, Marginal Jesus Movement Became the Dominant Religious Force in the Western World in a Few Centuries* (New York: Harper One, 1996), 57–58.

32 Ibid., 59.

and customs they wished, while continuing unimpeded in their own cults as well."[33]

The Jesus movement therefore found receptive audiences throughout the Hellenized Jewish diaspora among both Jews and Gentiles. Even so, Stark contends, the movement "offered twice as much cultural continuity to the Hellenized Jews as to Gentiles."[34] On this point, Stark's interpretation gains added force if one takes the view, *contra* Stark, that the first century Jesus movement developed "within Judaism" and, hence, pre-dated the "parting of the ways" which marked the historical beginning of Christianity proper in the second century.[35] Given "the marginality of the Hellenized Jews, torn between two cultures," the Jesus movement "offered to retain much of the religious content of both cultures and to resolve the contradictions between them." Not only were diasporan Jews "*accustomed to receiving teachers from Jerusalem*," but movement missionaries (such as Paul) "were likely to have family and friendship connections with at least some of the diasporan communities." The Jesus movement, in short, built a distinctly Hellenized religion on Jewish foundations, injecting "an exceedingly vigorous other-worldly faith" into the abstract universalism of Platonic philosophy.[36] It was in that cross-cultural context that Jesus became God.

---

33 Paula Fredriksen, *Paul: The Pagan's Apostle* (New Haven, CN: Yale University Press, 2017), 54, 60.

34 Stark, *Rise of Christianity*, 59.

35 See, generally, James D.G. Dunn, *The Partings of the Ways: Between Christianity and Judaism and their Significance for the Character of Christianity* (London: SCM Press, 1991); *cf.* Paula Fredriksen, "What 'Parting of the Ways'? Jews, Gentiles, and the Ancient Mediterranean City," in Adam H. Becker and Annette Yoshiko Reed, *The Ways that Never Parted: Jews and Christians in Late Antiquity and the Early Middle Ages* (Mohr Siebeck, 2003), 35–63.

36 Stark, *Rise of Christianity*, 59–62.

What Do We Know About Jesus and His Movement?

For Christians such as Stephen Wolfe, the declaration that "Jesus is Lord" signifies that Jesus is God. It is, however, not at all obvious that the historical Jesus considered himself to be a divine being, on a par with the ruler of all creation, the Lord of lords and King of kings. Nor did his disciples. James Dunn contends, however, that the "earliest forms of the Jesus tradition were the inevitable expression of their faith in Jesus." The first forms of that disciple faith were not yet the "Easter faith, not yet of the gospel as it came to be expounded by Paul and the other first apostles." They were nonetheless "born of, imbued with, expressive of [a] faith" produced by "the impact Jesus had made severally upon them." Dunn insists that there is no point in scholarly efforts to distinguish the "historical Jesus" from the Christ of faith. There is only one Jesus available to us; namely, "*Jesus as he was seen and heard by those who first formulated the traditions we have.*" According to him, "we really do not have any other sources that provide an alternative view of Jesus or that command the same respect as the Synoptic Gospels in providing testimony of the initial impact made by Jesus."[37]

But, of course, the earliest written versions of the pre- and post-Easter disciple faith did not appear until twenty or so years after the death and reported resurrection of Jesus. Dunn appeals to a process of oral transmission to bridge the gap between the death of Jesus in 30 AD and the earliest manifestation of a written tradition of faith in the Lordship of Jesus Christ. He assumes that "the great majority of Jesus' first disciples would have been functionally illiterate." So, too, would most of the earliest followers of the Jesus movement. Accordingly, we cannot assume that Jesus himself was literate. That being so, "it remains "*overwhelmingly probable that the earliest transmission of the Jesus tradition was by word of mouth*." Inevitably, therefore, oral faith tradition

---

37 James D.G. Dunn, *A New Perspective on Jesus: What the Quest for the Historical Jesus Missed* (Grand Rapids, MI: Baker Academic, 2005), 25, 31.

was a *group* tradition "used by the first churches and [was] presumably at least in some degree formative of their beliefs and identity."[38]

Having grown accustomed to the written forms of the Jesus tradition, we naturally prefer such literary explanations. While Dunn presents a case for confidence in the oral histories lying behind the written gospels, he acknowledges the "brutal fact...that we simply cannot escape from a *presumption of orality* for the first stage of the transmission of the Jesus tradition." As a "living tradition" of oral *performances*, the early Jesus tradition must have been both stable and variable, fixed and flexible. Dunn maintains, however, that the variability of the oral tradition "is not a sign of degeneration or corruption. Rather, it puts us in touch with the tradition in its living character, as it was heard in the earliest Christian groups and churches, and can still be heard and responded to today."[39]

Dunn's thesis begs at least two important questions. One such issue, whether the earliest *ekklesia* of the Jesus movement can properly be described as "Christian," will be dealt with below. The other is whether the gospels really were histories or biographies. In other words, did they transmit a true and historical witness to the characteristic features of the Jesus tradition, thereby reflecting "the original impact made by Jesus' teaching and actions on several at least of his first disciples?"[40] On this issue, Dunn reflects the conventional approach to the Synoptic gospels. Ever since the nineteenth century, most scholars have characterized the gospel authors as literate spokespersons for their religious communities.

Robyn Faith Walsh, however, doubts that the gospel writers were engaged in "documenting intragroup 'oral traditions' or preserving the collective perspectives of their fellow Christ-followers (e.g., the Markan, Matthean, or Lukan 'churches')." Instead, she argues, "that

---

38   Ibid., 41, 36, 43.

39   Ibid., 53, 125.

40   Ibid., 69–70.

the Synoptic gospels were written by elite cultural producers working within a dynamic cadre of literate specialists — including persons who may or may not have had an understanding of being 'in Christ.'" Her recent work on early Christian literature compares "a range of ancient *bioi* (lives), histories, and novels" to the gospels, concluding that the latter works "are creative literature produced by educated elites interested in Judean teachings, practices, and paradoxographical subjects in the aftermath of the Jewish War" (66-73 AD).[41]

Walsh contends that the gospel writers were not "strictly concerned...with writing histories." Nor, however, should their works be treated "principally as religious texts." New Testament scholars, she believes, "muddle" the social context in which the gospel writers worked by presuming antecedent "oral traditions, Christian communities, and their literate spokesmen." Like Dunn, they "continually look for evidence of socially marginal, preliterate Christian groups...treating the gospel writers not as rational actors but as something more akin to Romantic Poets speaking for their *Volk*."[42]

In contrast, Walsh approaches the gospels as a classical scholar "would any other kind of Greco-Roman literature." She observes that "Greek and Roman authors routinely describe themselves writing within (and for) literary networks of fellow *writers* — a competitive field of educated peers and associated literate specialists who engaged in discussion, interpretation, and the circulation of their works." Given "such a historical context, the gospel writers are not the 'founding fathers' of a religious tradition." Rather, they are better understood as "rational agents producing literature about a Judean teacher, son of God, and wonder-worker named Jesus." The gospels, therefore,

---

41 Robyn Faith Walsh, *The Origins of Early Christian Literature: Contextualizing the New Testament within Greco-Roman Literary Culture* (Cambridge: Cambridge University Press, 2021), *xiii–xiv*.

42 *Ibid.*, 3–6.

"represent the strategic choices of educated Greco-Roman writers working within a circumscribed field of literary production."[43]

Walsh calls into question Christianity's own myth of origins, treating it as an example of the "invention of tradition."[44] Unlike Dunn, she rejects the "limiting perspective that accepts the first-century Jesus movement as a recognizable and coherent social formation." It is only the "uncritical acceptance of Christianity's myth of origins" that authorizes the assumption that "Christianity" emerged in the first century as a "spontaneous, cohesive, diverse, and multiple" movement. She does acknowledge that "it is possible that the authors of the Synoptic gospels were associated in some measure with a group of persons either interested in or actively participating in practices pertaining to the Jesus or Christ movement." But "ultimately," she says, that "remains conjecture."[45]

Speaking of conjecture, it is significant that Walsh blithely asserts that the Synoptic gospels were produced in the "aftermath of the Jewish War" while, in the next paragraph, remarking that her study does "not scrutinize dates for these writings."[46] The cognitive dissonance created by the juxtaposition of those two statements immediately called to my mind the vivid impression left by the professor in my first-year honours history class as he repeatedly and forcefully emphasized the importance of accuracy in the dating of historical documents and events. This is a perennial issue in New Testament scholarship. Despite the existence of several solid studies dating, not just the Synoptic gospels, but the New Testament, as a whole, to the period prior to the destruction of the Jerusalem Temple in AD 70, it is commonplace for scholars

---

43   Ibid., 5–6.
44   Eric Hobsbawm and Terence Ranger, (eds.), *The Invention of Tradition* (Cambridge: Cambridge University Press, 1984).
45   Walsh, *Origins of Early Christian Literature*, 32–33, 35.
46   Ibid., *xiii–xiv*.

to assign later dates to the book or books under discussion.⁴⁷ Studies of the Book of Revelation are particularly prone to this practice since a post-70 date allows scholars to ignore the destruction of Jerusalem and instead to treat the book as a prophecy of the doom awaiting the Roman empire, the papacy, or modern-day America. Agnostics and atheists who, by definition, deny the credibility of biblical prophecies of a providential divine judgement on Old Covenant Israel also have an obvious incentive to assume late dates for the New Testament writings as do theologians committed to a futurist eschatology.

Walsh clearly prefers a late date for the Synoptic gospels. On her account, their authors were independent of oral tradition, producing creative literature by employing the conventional tools of their trade. The stories they crafted were "beholden to the dictates of genre, citation, and allusion" arising from within a circle of peers. No mere reflection of oral tradition, their literary choices presented "an idealized view of Jesus and his life using details more strategic than historical." Consequently, their work now presents scholars seeking to reconstruct the past based on such creative literary artefacts with a problem: "how can we meaningfully distinguish between fiction and history?" But is it necessary to choose between "oral tradition" emanating from functionally illiterate, religious "communities" and the "creative literature" produced by gospel authors who "were similarly trained and positioned, working within cadres of fellow, cultural elites?"⁴⁸

Walsh doubts that whatever faith might have been engendered by Jesus among his disciples and those who heard their stories was sufficiently powerful to inspire a spontaneous, cohesive, and autonomous ethnoreligious movement operating in his name before the Jewish War. Given such skepticism, Walsh's assumption of a late date for the gospels makes sense. By the late first century, if Hellenistic writers had

---

47 *Cf.* John A.T. Robinson, *Redating the New Testament* (Eugene, OR: Wipf and Stock, 1976) and Jonathan Bernier, *Rethinking the Dates of the New Testament: The Evidence for Early Compostion* (Grand Rapids, MI: Baker Academic, 2022).

48 Walsh, *Origins of Early Christian Literature*, 4–6.

little more than Paul's letters to work with, they clearly would have been on their own in fleshing out the story of a Judean Christ.

But there *is* a strong case for an early date for each of the Synoptic gospels. Moreover, something like Walsh's literary community of educated Hellenized Jews was certainly present in both Judea and the diaspora well before AD 70. Members of a Hellenistic Jewish intelligentsia already steeped in the Septuagint version of the Hebrew Bible must have been influenced by a widespread sense of impending doom spreading among first-century Jews of all social classes. Writers steeped in such an apocalyptic interpretation of restoration theology would have been well-placed to serve as "organic intellectuals" and publicists for the embryonic Jesus movement in major urban centres throughout the empire.[49] Such an ethnoreligious movement had little need for well-researched and fully documented biographies of the historical Jesus. Instead, the authors of the Synoptic gospels competed with other writers (and each other) to generate idealized mythic portrayals of a god-like messiah come to usher in the kingdom of God.

Jesus as Lord

In Mark, probably the first, and shortest, of the Synoptic gospels, the very first verse identifies Jesus as the Son of God. For Christians, ever since the Council of Nicaea in the early fourth century, "Son of God has been *the* key title for Christ." As such, it "has all the overtones of the full-blown Trinitarian formula— 'Son of God' means second person of the Trinity, 'true God from true God, begotten not made,' etc." But, as James Dunn points out, this was not the case in Jesus' lifetime. In the Hebrew Bible "it could be used collectively of Israel...

---

49 The term "organic intellectuals" was coined by the Italian Marxist, Antonio Gramsci (1891–1937), but it is not at all anachronistic when transposed into the context of an ethnoreligious movement with geopolitical ambitions in the first century. See, Quintin Hoare and Geoffrey Nowell Smith, (eds. and trans.) *Selections from the Prison Notebooks of Antonio Gramsci* (New York: International Publishers, 1971), 5–23.

or in the plural in reference to angels, the heavenly council...or in the singular of the king." Indeed, more generally still, the title could be used to characterize anyone *"who was thought to be commissioned by God or highly favoured by God."* Even in relation to Jesus, *"initially at least, 'son of God' did not necessarily imply any overtones of divinity."*[50] In time, of course, the title, as applied to Jesus, did suggest that he was divine *in some sense*. But even though first-century Jews "believed that there was only one God Almighty," as Bart Ehrman reminds us, "it was widely held that there were other divine beings—angels, cherubim, seraphim, principalities, powers, hypostases." Moreover, there was no impassable gulf between the human and the divine. "Angels were divine, and could be worshipped, but they could also come in human guise." Conversely, it was possible for humans to become angels or demi-gods.[51]

What about Jesus? In all three Synoptic gospels, when (1) Jesus is baptized by John; (2) the heavens were torn asunder; (3) a voice from heaven was heard; (4) the voice declared Jesus to be his Son; and (5) the Spirit descended. Similarly, the temptation narratives which follow agree that (1) the Spirit led Jesus into the wilderness; (2) Jesus' sojourn there lasted forty days; and (3) he was tempted by Satan. Whether Matthew and Luke predate the gospel of Mark or expand upon it, their temptation stories provide essential insight into how Satan tempted Jesus in the desert. They reveal the psychic fault line within Jesus' messianic consciousness. The Son of God is bound by filial loyalty to the Father; yet Jesus is also by right the uncrowned king of the Jews, and presumably of a restored Israel as well. Hence, he is bound by religious obligations rooted in blood, law, and tradition to share and respect the worldly ambitions of his tribe and people. In Mark's mythic image of Paradise Restored, Jesus remains curiously passive while Satan actively

---

50   Dunn, *Partings of the Ways*, 170–171.
51   Bart D. Ehrman, *How Jesus Became God: The Exaltation of a Jewish Preacher from Galilee* (New York: Harper One, 2015), 83.

works his wiles. By contrast, in Matthew and Luke, Jesus resolutely resists three powerful temptations.[52]

Knowing that Jesus has fasted for forty days and nights and is bound to be famished, Satan challenges him to demonstrate that he really is the Son of God by commanding that the stones at his feet be made bread (Matt. 4:2). Satan's first temptation calls to mind John the Baptist's rebuke to the Pharisees and Sadducees several verses earlier in the text. There, John warns them "not to say within yourselves, We have Abraham to our father: for I say unto you, that God is able of these stones to raise up children unto Abraham (Matt. 3:9). John expects the carnal pride displayed by these representatives of the Jewish religious establishment to be followed by a fall. Anticipating Paul's mission to the Gentiles (Rom. 11:11), John is certain that the ethnoreligious movement soon to be launched by Jesus will produce so many children of Abraham (according to the spirit) that Abraham's seed (according to the flesh) will be provoked to jealousy. In effect, when tempting Jesus to flaunt his miraculous powers as the Son of God, Satan serves as a stand-in for the Pharisees and Sadducees.

Having failed in his first attempt, the tempter holds out another enticement calculated to fire the imagination of first-century Jewish Zealots keen to restore Israel to her former imperial glory. Satan takes Jesus to the top of the highest mountain, pitching the prospect of dominion over all the kingdoms of the world if only he will "fall down and worship me (Matt. 4:9; Lk. 4:7). Jesus rejects this temptation as well. Nor is he moved to weaken his determination not to tempt God when Satan sets him upon a pinnacle of the Jerusalem temple, inviting Jesus to prove that he is the Son of God by jumping off the edge, trusting in angels to save him from certain death (Matt. 4:5–7; Lk 4:9–12).

Matthew 4:1–11 and Luke 4:1–13 help us to see that Satan's three temptations reflect the irrepressible conflict between the two *personae* incarnate in Jesus' messianic consciousness, the exalted Son of God,

---

52 Andrew Fraser, *Dissident Dispatches: An Anglo-Identitarian Guide to Christian Theology* (London: Arktos, 2017), 424–446.

and the historical king of the Jews. During those forty days in the desert, Jesus struggled to reconcile those potentially contradictory roles. In both gospel narratives, Jesus resolves his messianic identity crisis. In doing so, he learns how to preach the Word to his people — the lost sheep of Israel (Matt. 10:6) — in accordance with the will of the Father. He also learns that Satan will dog his footsteps to the cross and beyond. Clearly, the temptation narratives in the Synoptic gospels encapsulate the world-historical conflict between the spiritual Israel of God and Old Covenant Israel according to the flesh. In fact, the seismic shift in the foundations of the cosmic temple during the first century drove the entire cast of characters in the gospels towards the creation of a new heaven and a new earth.[53]

It is a mistake to read the temptation stories as an account of the sort of existential crisis that might face any human being in any time and any place.[54] Jesus faced those temptations, not because he was a human being but as a remarkably gifted and devout Jewish holy man descended through the royal line of David from the seed of Abraham. Scot McKnight demonstrates that "Jesus' God is the national God of Israel, not some abstract universal deity. He is the God of Abraham, Isaac, and Jacob; he is the God of David and of the prophet; he is the God of the Maccabees and of John the Baptist." Jesus' vision of the kingdom of God was animated not "by an abstract religious feeling but [by] a concrete realistic vision for God's chosen nation." It "concerned Israel as a nation and not a new religion". Accordingly, "[w]hen Jesus taught his disciples to pray for the kingdom to come (Matt 6:10), he surely had in mind more than an existential encounter with the living God that would give his followers an authentic experience".

---

53 On the Old Testament account of the creation of the cosmic temple, see John H. Walton, *The Lost World of Genesis One: Ancient Cosmology and the Origins Debate* (Dover Grove, IL: IVP Academic, 2009).

54 See, *e.g.*, Helmut Thielicke, *Between God and Satan: The Temptation of Jesus and the Temptability of Man* [orig. ed., 1938] (Farmington Hills, MI: Oil Lamp Books, 2010).

For McKnight, it follows that "[t]he most important context in which modern interpreters should situate Jesus is that of ancient Jewish nationalism."[55]

Both John and Jesus "had one vision for their contemporary Israel, and that was for Israel to become what God had called it to be."[56] For Jesus, God was not a universal deity. Israel stood in a covenantal relationship with the Father known to no other nation. Throughout the narrative of the Hebrew Scriptures, "God never destroys his offspring... but rather pursues them in order to bring them to perfection."[57] The *telos* of that covenantal history was to be perfected in the Lord Jesus and the righteous remnant of Old Covenant Israel; they alone were the true Israelites, forever separated from the false Israelites when the nation faced its final judgement (Matt 13:41–43). Jesus' messianic mission was "to lead Israel away from a national disaster and towards a redemption that would bring about the glorious kingdom." From the time of his confrontation with Satan in the wilderness it became clear to him that he would have "to offer himself consciously and intentionally to God as a vicarious sacrifice for Israel in order to avert the national disaster."[58]

But there was more than one vision of Israel's destiny in the popular imagination of first-century Judaism. Steeped in a tradition of chauvinistic religious rhetoric dating back to the Maccabean revolt in the second century BC, most first-century Judeans scoffed at the notion that "true Israelites" were not "destined to be part of God's eschatological people...on the basis of heredity." They rejected the charge made by John the Baptist and Jesus that Israel according to the flesh had "forfeited their enjoyment of covenant blessings and was in exile "because

---

55 Scot McKnight, *A New Vision for Israel: The Teachings of Jesus in National Context* (Grand Rapids, MI: William B. Eerdmans, 1999), 69, 83, 6, 10.

56 Ibid., 6.

57 Anthony D. Baker, *Diagonal Advance: Perfection in Christian Theology* (Eugene, OR: Cascade Books, 2011), 77.

58 McKnight, *New Vision*, 147, 13.

of unfaithfulness and sinfulness." Certainly, they did not believe that "God was forming a new people" based solely on repentance, righteous obedience, and covenant faithfulness."⁵⁹

Most first-century Jews were confident that the God of Israel would rest forever in a temple made by hands in Jerusalem. Few took seriously Jesus' warning that in their lifetime a newly inaugurated kingdom of God would pronounce final judgement on Old Covenant Israel and throw the "false Israelites" into the flames of hell. (Matthew 13:40–43). Jesus knew his fellow Jews longed instead for the restoration of national Israel according to the flesh. Indeed, inspired as he was by his own national vision for Israel, he shared the messianic longing resonating within the blood faith of his people. In his heart of hearts, Jesus could not properly deny the satanic spirit of the Maccabees and the zealots a fair hearing.⁶⁰ Indeed, Jesus saw that spirit at work even in his disciples, most notably on the occasion in Mark 8:31–33 when he administered the sternest possible rebuke to Peter: "Get thee behind me, Satan; for thou savourest not the things that be of God, but the things that be of men."⁶¹

To put the matter plainly, it was not his generic humanity tempting Jesus with bread, universal dominion, and independence from the Father. Rather, it was his inner Jew. The historical Satan emerged within the breast of the historical Jesus Christ. As a charismatic personality, at ease in crowds, recognized in childhood as the king of the Jews, and by the Father as his Son, Jesus could hardly fail to empathize with all but the most grandiose aspirations of his own once-holy people.

---

59   Ibid., 62, 110–115.

60   Ibid., 136–137, 146–147, 96.

61   Mark does not identify Satan's three temptations in 1:13, but in 14:30 (just before standing trial before the Sanhedrin) Jesus predicts, accurately, that a satanic impulse will cause Peter to "disown me *three* times" before the cock crows twice. Shortly afterward, the disciples fall asleep *three* times while on guard duty, revealing the tempter within at work again with a suite of counter-Trinitarian snares likely to entrap Jesus' closest followers (Mark 14:37–41).

Did Jesus Think He Was God?

In the New Testament, Jesus is often given the title "Christ," a Greek translation of the Hebrew word for messiah, meaning "one who is anointed." As with a "Son of God," to be *anointed* was to be "chosen and specially honoured by God...in order to fulfill God's purposes and mediate his will on earth." Both titles could be "used to refer not to a divine angelic being, but to a human being." Some Jews "deeply committed to the ritual laws given in the Torah" had the idea that the messiah would appear as a great and powerful priest who would serve as a future ruler of Israel, interpreting and enforcing the law of God. More commonly, first-century Jews looked forward to the appearance of a messiah as a mighty warrior who would overthrow the oppressors who had taken over the promised land, thereby restoring both the Davidic monarchy and the nation of Israel. Others held to a more apocalyptic vision in which the coming of the messiah would bring a new creation, not just a political revolution, but "the Kingdom of God, a utopian state in which there would be no evil, pain, or suffering of any kind."[62]

According to Bart Ehrman, it seems likely "that Jesus's followers, during his lifetime, believed that he might be this coming anointed one." But they certainly did not expect him to die and rise from the dead. Nor did Jesus. But he did think of himself as the messiah. He did expect to become the king of Israel, not by means of political struggle or military victory, but when God intervened in history to destroy the forces of evil and to make Israel a kingdom once again ruled through his messiah. He prophesied, publicly and privately, that the kingdom would arrive when the Son of Man came in judgement against everyone, and everything opposed to God. In fact, Ehrman observes, "Jesus told his disciples — Judas Iscariot included — that they would be seated on twelve thrones ruling the twelve tribes of Israel in the future kingdom." Ehrman is convinced that "Jesus must have thought that he

---

62   Ehrman, *How Jesus Became God*, 113–115.

would be the king of the kingdom of God soon to be brought by the Son of Man." Everyone knew that the future king of Israel would be the anointed of God, the Messiah. "It is in this sense that Jesus must have taught his disciples that he was the messiah."[63]

Both Jesus and his disciples expected that the messiah was destined to defeat the enemy; instead, the putative messiah was "arrested, tortured, and crucified, the most painful and publicly humiliating form of death known to the Romans." Such an outcome "was just the *opposite* of what Jews expected a messiah to be." But then "they came to believe that Jesus had been raised from the dead, and this reconfirmed what had earlier been disconfirmed." Their faith was restored: "He really is the messiah. But not in the way we thought!"[64]

Ehrman hastens to add that, while the historical Jesus did think of himself as "a prophet predicting the end of the current evil age and the future king of Israel in the age to come," he never — not in the Synoptic gospels at least — called himself God. Of course, in the gospel of John, "Jesus does make remarkable claims about himself." For example, in John 8:58, "Jesus appears to be claiming not only to have existed before Abraham, but to have been given the name of God himself." Ehrman argues that not only was the gospel of John produced later than the Synoptics, but verses, such as Jesus' proclamation that "I and the Father are one" (John 10:30), "simply cannot be ascribed to the historical Jesus." Instead, Ehrman tells us, "What we can know with relative certainty about Jesus in that his public ministry and proclamation were not focused on his divinity; in fact, they were not about his divinity at all." Rather, they were about "the kingdom that God was going to bring. And about the Son of Man who was soon to bring judgement upon the earth."[65]

---

63 Ibid., 115–119.
64 Ibid., 116–118.
65 Ibid., 124–128.

But, if the historical Jesus never claimed to be God, how did this messianic Judean prophet become a Hellenized cosmic Christ? That story, Ehrman explains, begins with the crucifixion and death of Jesus. "It was only afterward, once the disciples believed that their crucified master had been raised from the dead, that they began to think that he must, in some sense, be God."[66] Before his death, the followers of Jesus believed that he was the messiah, the king of the future kingdom. After the discovery of the empty tomb, they were convinced that he had been exalted to the heavenly realm. It was then that they *knew* he was the future king and fully expected him to come from heaven to reign as the Son of Man. In his role as the Son of Man, Jesus would have been understood to be a divine figure. Indeed, in one sense or other, in all four of his exalted roles — as messiah, as Son of God, as Son of Man, and as Lord — Jesus was divine. But, in no sense did his followers understand Jesus to be God the Father. Ehrman emphasizes that:

> whenever someone claims that Jesus is God, it is important to ask: God *in what sense*? It took a long time indeed for Jesus to be God in the complete, full, and perfect sense, the second member of the Trinity, equal with God from eternity, and "of the same essence" as the Father.[67]

How Did Jesus Become God?

Even if Jesus did not become fully God until the fourth century, his divine status was assured at the resurrection. As a historian, however, Ehrman does not think "we can show — historically — that Jesus was in fact raised from the dead." When "it comes to miracles such as the resurrection," he declares, "historical sciences simply are of no help in establishing exactly what happened." In other words, Ehrman is not saying "that the *resurrection* is what made Jesus God." Rather, "it was

---

66 *Ibid.*, 128.
67 *Ibid.*, 208–209.

the *belief* in the resurrection that led some of his followers to *claim* he was God." In short, Ehrman denies the historicity of the resurrection. As far as he is concerned it never happened. As for the empty tomb, it too is no more than legend. Victims of crucifixion were not given proper burials. Indeed, he claims there is good reason to accept "the rather infamous suggestion," made by John Dominic Crossman, "that Jesus's body was not raised from the dead but was eaten by dogs."[68]

Other historians make the similarly unorthodox suggestion that the facticity of the empty tomb and resurrection narrative may not have mattered, as such, to those who constructed it. Richard C. Miller, for example, contends that the gospel resurrection narratives were never intended to *demonstrate* historical truth through research and evidence. Sometime around 150 AD Justin Martyr admitted as much in his *1 Apology*. As summarized by Miller, the burden of Justin's Christian apologia was as follows: "We, O Romans, have produced myths and fables with our Jesus as you have done with your own heroes and emperors; so why are you killing us?" This appears to be an admission "that the earliest Christians had composed Jesus' divine birth, dramatically tragic death, resurrection, and ascension within the earliest Christian Gospel tradition as fictive embellishments following the stock structural conventions of Greek and Roman mythology."[69] In other words, the gospel accounts of the risen Jesus differ in detail but not in kind from fables surrounding antique Mediterranean demigods such as Hermes, Dionysus, and Heracles, as well as emperors such as Caesar Augustus.

Indeed, Miller observes, Justin's argument does "not even qualify as an 'admission' per se but merely arose as a statement in passing, as though commonly acknowledged both within and without Christian society." Justin's point, however, was not just that there was "nothing unique" or *sui generis* about the "dominant framing contours of the

---

68 Ibid., 132, 157.

69 Richard C. Miller, *Resurrection and Reception in Early Christianity* (New York: Routledge, 2015), 2.

Jesus narrative." His apology also "asserted that the classical pantheon was, in truth, a cast of demons." Nor was this assertion the product of a reasoned line of argument. Rather, Justin flatly declared "that the gods were to be understood as wicked and impious. Only out of ignorance did the classical world regard such demons as deities." It might seem that the Greeks were saying the same things as the Christians but, Justin affirms, the Greek legends "arose by the inspiration of 'evil demons' through the 'myth-making of the poets'" By contrast, Justin simply pronounces the Christian narratives to be "true" without providing any further evidence or reasoned argument to support his claim.[70]

This was a rhetorical rather than philosophical or historical strategy. Justin was attempting "to assign archaic precedence to Judeo-Christian tradition." He simply proposed "that demons inspired the classical writers to produce lies or fictions that proleptically mimicked the Christian Gospel narratives." Miller suggests that Justin's apology marked a step beyond the task facing the gospel writers in the first century. That is to say that, at first, the gospel "stories succeeded inasmuch as they were capable of appropriating, riffing on, and engaging the conventions of the classical literary tradition" in ways which appealed to an audience comprising both Hellenistic Jews and Gentile God-fearers in diaspora synagogues. By the middle of the second century, however, "early Christian had their sights on a higher prize: a comprehensive cultural revolution of the Hellenistic Roman world." In this strategic context, it was no longer "enough that Jesus should join the classical array of demigods...he must obtain a *sui generis* stature, while condemning all prior Mediterranean iconic figures." Such ambitions placed new demands on the rhetorical style of Christian apologetics, requiring "an underlying shift in the proposed modality of the Gospel narratives, moving along the continuum from fictive mythography towards historical fact."[71]

---

70 *Ibid.*, 1–3.
71 *Ibid.*, 4–5.

At their appearance in the first century, however, the gospels, the letters of Paul, and the Acts of the Apostles already reflected a "fundamental metanarrative or theme" which amounted to "the systematic abrogation of nearly every isolationist, separatist practice of early Judaism." According to Miller, "the *forms* of these urban early Christian constructions were, more often than not, at their core lifted from the structures of classical antique culture, often with a mere outward Judaistic decor." The resurrection narratives of the New Testament were "first composed, signified, and sacralized in the Hellenistic urban world of Roman Syria, Anatolia, Macedonia, and Greece, these works typically reflected and played on crudely stereotypical myths of Jewish Palestine." Their syncretic language reflected the adaptation by early Judeo-Christian theology of antique Greco-Roman forms such as "Zeus-Jupiter, with his own storied demigod son born of a mortal woman."[72]

So outlined in the neutral scholarly language of "comparative analysis," it is easy to miss the explosive significance of Miller's thesis. But, simply by refusing to apply the definite article in reference to the allegedly "unimaginable miracle" which is collectively supposed to be "the singular impetus for the birth of Christianity," Miller challenges the fundamental presuppositions of contemporary Christian apologetics. He denies that one can speak, in the context of Greco-Roman antiquity, of *the* Resurrection, *the* Empty Tomb, *the* Event, *the* Mystery. He condemns the tacit agreement according to which classicists designate and relinquish to New Testament scholars a uniquely partitioned and sacralized discursive space surrounding "the question of the historicity of Jesus' narrated resurrection." His own study identifies "a detailed, shared conventional system between the Gospel *resurrection* narratives" and what are known to classicists as "the extant *translation* narratives of Hellenistic and Roman literature."[73]

---

72 Ibid., 12–13.

73 Ibid., 15–16 (emphasis added).

Miller subsumes the "resurrection" language of the Gospels under the broader "translation topos" found in Hellenistic and Roman cultures. He demonstrates how the latter "tradition functioned in an honorific capacity." In other words, "the convention had become a protocol for honoring numerous heroes, kings, and philosophers, those whose bodies were not recovered at death." He points to "the translation of Romulus…as the quintessential, archetypical account for a pronounced 'apotheosis' tradition in the funerary consecration of the *principes Romani.*" The Romulus fable relates how the

> legendary founding king of Rome, while mustering troops on Campus Martius, was caught up to heaven when clouds suddenly descended and enveloped him. When the clouds had departed, he was seen no more. In the fearsome spectacle, most of his troops had fled, but the remaining nobles instructed the people that Romulus had been translated to the gods. An alternate account arose that perhaps the nobles had slain the king and invented the tale to cover up their treachery. Later, however, Julius Proculus stepped forward to testify before all the people that he had been eyewitness to the translated Romulus, having met him travelling on the Via Appia. Romulus, according to this tale, offered his nation a final great commission and again vanished.[74]

Miller provides a lengthy catalogue of similar translation fables and contends that such tales "provide a mimetic background for the Gospel narratives." Like Robyn Faith Walsh, Miller finds that Greek, Roman, and first century Hellenistic Jewish writers competed, not just with each other, but with older authors such as Homer to mimic, improve upon, and embellish existing examples of the translation *topos,* or genre. He argues, very persuasively, "that the textualized Romulus indeed figured prominently within early Christian resurrection narrative construction." He then discusses what such mimetic, rhetorical performances "achieved within the cultural milieu of a Romano-Greek East, that is, in the primitive centuries of the rise of Christianity." In

---

74 *Ibid.*, 16.

a distinctly understated fashion, Miller remarks that his "book also tacitly delivers a rather forceful critique of standing theories regarding the likely antecedents of the early Christian 'resurrection' accounts." In particular, he takes careful aim at modern Christian apologetics which deny *any* antecedents. He attributes such efforts to endow *the Resurrection of Jesus Christ* with a *sui generis* status to "a perspective typically arising out of 'faith-based discourse.'"⁷⁵

Miller "sets forth a more satisfying thesis, a model that more comprehensively explains the available data, namely that such narratives fundamentally relied upon and adapted the broadly applied cultural-linguistic conventions and structures of antique Mediterranean society." In this cultural context, the early Christian resurrection tale functioned "as an ideology and not as an argued event of history." Early Christian writers, Miller writes, "did not attempt a case for the historicity of the resurrection of their founding figure." Instead, Jesus was deployed in the gospel resurrection narratives as "a mythic literary vehicle." Miller defines "myth" as "a sacred narrative or account" that served to frame the present for the Jesus movement. The resurrection myth functioned, like the Greco-Roman translation fable, "to undo tragic loss, reclaiming the hero in a modal reverie of heroic *exaltatio*."⁷⁶

Miller argues that the innovation of the Gospel postmortem accounts did not reside in the employment of the translation fable convention per se, but in the scandal of the application of the embellishment to a controversial Jewish peasant, an indigent Cynic, otherwise marginal and obscure on the grand stage of classical antiquity." Jesus emerges as a mythic literary figure in the gospels rather than as a historical actor. As Miller puts it, the risen Jesus became the iconic "image of a counter-cultural ideology" through the conscious appropriation by the gospel writers of the literary protocols of the ancient Hellenistic

---

75 *Ibid.*, 16.
76 *Ibid.*, 16–17, 158, 162.

Roman world.⁷⁷ In accordance with such protocols, Paul and the gospel writers presented Jesus as unique, not because he was exalted as a god following his death, but because he was *better* than the other gods of the classical world.

The "Truthiness" of Christianity

In short, Miller "challenges the classic conception of what many regard as the most sacred narrative of Western civilization, namely, that the New Testament stories of Jesus' resurrection provided alleged histories variously achieving credibility among their earliest readers." Instead, he provides "the first truly coherent case that the earliest Christians comprehended the resurrection narratives of the New Testament as instances within a larger conventional rubric commonly recognized as fictive in modality." Modern scholarship, by contrast, mistakenly assumes that these texts were intended to present "a credible, albeit extraordinary account of an historical miracle." On that assumption, one may then approach the question "from one of two polarized *loci*: (1) with a faith-based interest in honoring (defending) the most sacred tenet of Christianity; (2) with an atheistic interest to disprove the claims of orthodox Christian doctrine." Both positions are unsound. The first thesis mistakenly supposes that gospel writers proposed the resurrection of Jesus as a historical reality; the second, antithetical, possibility is that the narrative was peddled as an early Christian hoax. In dialectical terms, Miller advances an "authentic synthesis (*tertium quid*): the early Christians exalted the leader of their movement through the standard literary protocols of their day, namely, through the fictive, narrative embellishment of divine translation."⁷⁸

It should be obvious that a sincere, honest response to Miller's investigation by Christian nationalists such as Stephen Wolfe will demand "a fearless, rational, unwavering commitment to the pursuit

---

77 *Ibid.*, 180.
78 *Ibid.*, 180–182.

of truth."⁷⁹ Unfortunately, Christians, generally, appear ill-equipped to meet this intellectual challenge. Faith-driven presentations of the gospel resurrection tales seem historically plausible only so long as one's audience knows nothing of their classical literary provenance. The quarantine protecting the New Testament resurrection stories from exposure to their ancient cultural analogues is unlikely to be lifted anytime soon.

Given Wolfe's personal preference for the work of older theologians, he has been isolated from critical currents in contemporary New Testament scholarship. On social media, Wolfe has expressed admiration for the work of the early twentieth-century Orthodox Presbyterian scholar, J. Gresham Machen (1881–1937). My guess is that Machen has influenced Wolfe's understanding of the twin "supernatural truths" which upon which his case for Christian nationalism is grounded: "Jesus is Lord" and "Christianity is the true religion." In 1921 Machen published a study entitled *The Origins of Paul's Religion*. There, he argued that the truth of Christianity was to be found in a study of its origins. Machen acknowledged Jesus as the Founder of Christianity but, because He Himself wrote nothing and "the record of his words and deeds is the work of others," Machen turned to the testimony of Paul as "a fixed starting point in all controversy." As Paul was such a central figure in the early history of the Jesus movement, Machen was confident that if one could "explain the religion of Paul… you have solved the problem of the origin of Christianity."⁸⁰

According to Machen, the religion of Paul "was something new." His mission to the Gentiles "was not merely one manifestation of the progress of oriental religion, and it was not merely a continuation of the pre-Christian mission of the Jews." Certainly, "the possession of an ancient and authoritative Book" was "one of the chief attractions

---

79 Ibid., 182.
80 J. Graham Machen, *The Origins of Paul's Religion; The James Sprunt Lectures Delivered at Union Theological Seminary in Virginia*, Leopold Classical Library, [Original publication, 1921], 4–5.

of Judaism to the world of that day." Authority in religion was in short supply. Paradoxically, however, "if the privileges of the Old Testament were to be secured...the authority of the Book had to be set aside. The character of a national religion was...too indelibly stamped upon the religion of Israel." At best, Gentile converts could "only be admitted into the outer circle around the true household of God." For Paul, Machen declares, Gentile freedom (*i.e.*, from the law) "was a matter of principle." This principle had, of course, been "anticipated by the Founder of Christianity, by Jesus Himself." But, if so, the doctrine of Gentile freedom was based "upon what Jesus had done, not upon what Jesus, at least during His earthly life, had said." It was unclear what He intended with respect to the universality of the gospel. The "instances in which He extended His ministry to Gentiles are expressly designated in the Gospels as exceptional." Certainly, as far as his disciples were concerned, "Gentile freedom, and the abolition of special Jewish privileges, had not been clearly established by the words of the Master." This meant that there was "still need for the epoch-making work of Paul."[81]

Machen contends that Paul's distinctive achievement was not the geographical expansion of the Church. Seas or mountains were not "really standing in the way of the Gentile mission." Instead, it was "the great barrier of religious principle." Paul "overcame the principle of Jewish particularism in the only way in which it could be overcome; he overcame principle by principle." The real apostle to the Gentiles, Machen believed, was Paul the theologian, not Paul the practical missionary. It was his achievement to exhibit "the temporary character of the Old Testament" by enriching the historical, logical, and intellectual understanding of the death and resurrection of Jesus. Consequently, "Gentile freedom, and the freedom of the entire Christian Church for all time, was assured."[82]

---

81   *Ibid.*, 12–15.
82   *Ibid.*, 17, 19.

Machen declares that, by convincing others, Jews, and Gentiles alike, that Jesus is Lord, Paul compelled the religion of Israel to go forth "with a really good conscience to the spiritual conquest of the world." Henceforth, "when Christian missionaries used the word 'Lord' of Jesus, their hearers knew at once what they meant. They knew at once that Jesus occupied a place which is occupied only by God." In the final chapter of his book, Machen defends "the historical character of the Pauline message." The religion of Paul, he concludes, "was rooted in an event…the redemptive work of Christ in his death and resurrection." It was based on "an account of something that had happened…only a few years previously." The facts of that event, the death and resurrection of Jesus, "could be established by adequate testimony," Machen writes. Moreover, "the eyewitnesses could be questioned, and Paul appeals to the eyewitnesses in detail" (*cf.*, 1 Cor. 15:3–8). He staked everything on the truth of what he said about Jesus' crucifixion, death, and resurrection. Machen poses the issue in uncompromising terms: If Paul's account of that event "was true, the origin of Paulinism is explained; if it was not true, the Church is based upon an inexplicable error."[83]

Richard C. Miller's mimetic criticism of the gospel resurrection narratives presents defenders of Machen's Christian apologetic, such as Stephen Wolfe, with a stark choice. If *the* Resurrection of Jesus was, as a matter of fact, just one among many classical fictive narratives of divine translation, in what sense (if at all) can one still proclaim that "Jesus is Lord" and that "Christianity is the true religion?" Neither Paul's nor Machen's appeal to "eyewitness" testimony will be sufficient to close the case. That possibility has been foreclosed by Miller's detailed examination of the "eyewitness" tradition that became "the political protocol in the consecration of those most supremely honored in Roman government" during the Julio-Claudian dynasty.[84]

---

83   *Ibid.*, 13, 316.
84   Miller, *Resurrection and Reception*, 75.

The legendary example of Julius Proculus, the alleged "eyewitness" to the post-mortem appearance of Romulus, contributed to the "senatorial tradition of the eyewitness to the apotheosis of the Roman emperors" between 27 BC and 284 AD. The chief historians of the period typically devoted considerable space to the tale. The "senators (as an act of *consecration*), plebes, and successors assigned glory and deification to a deceased emperor through the process of formal "eyewitness" testimony to the monarch's translation." For example, following the death of Caesar Augustus, "the Roman senators carried an effigy of his body in grand procession to the Campus Martius, the location where Romulus achieved apotheosis." In accordance with the structured requirements of the translation fable, this "public funeral did not involve the actual corpse of the emperor, but a substituted wax effigy." According to tradition, "the witnesses must not find any charred bones, once the pyric flames have gone their course." The scenario also provided for a prominent eyewitness "who took oath that he had seen the form of the Emperor on its way to heaven, after he had been reduced to ashes."[85]

One suspects, however, that Anglo-Protestant evangelicals are unlikely to be impressed by such scholarly skepticism as to the historicity of the Resurrection of Christ Jesus. Faith-based conservative evangelicals still condemn as a "heretic" any supposed Christian questioning — what Stephen Wolfe might call the "supernatural truth" of — the futurist eschatology outlined in various creeds. Accordingly, Pastor Douglas Wilson (whose Canon Press publishes Wolfe's book on Christian nationalism) recently joined many other religious leaders in signing an open letter which calls upon Gary DeMar (head of the American Vision ministry) to recant his alleged refusal to affirm "the future, bodily, and glorious return of Christ, a future, physical, and general resurrection of the dead, the final judgement of all men, "and the tactile reality of the eternal state." DeMar was accused of denying

---

85   Ibid., 66–75.

"critical elements of the Christian faith" by declining to label full preterism as "heretical"[86] (preterists hold that all of God's promises to Old Covenant were fulfilled at the time of the destruction of the Jerusalem temple in 70 AD).[87]

But what is "truth?" A *correspondence* theory of truth holds that a statement "is true if it corresponds to the facts; and, conversely, if it corresponds to the facts, it is true." It would be difficult to maintain that any of the propositions put to Gary DeMar by his critics satisfies a correspondence theory of truth. On the other hand, the scholarly field of "mimetic criticism" lends credibility to a *coherence* theory of truth. Here, truth is defined "as a relation not between statement and fact, but between one statement and another." On this view, "no actual statement…is made in isolation: they all depend upon certain presuppositions or conditions and are made against a background of these."[88] A practitioner of mimetic criticism such as Richard C. Miller might agree, therefore, that is true that Romulus, Caesar Augustus, and Jesus Christ were all resurrected (or translated) from the dead through exaltation to divine status. But would Wolfe or Pastor Wilson concede that Jesus' resurrection, along with the Second Coming of Christ, are truths anchored, not in history as it happened, but in the realm of myth, legend, or fiction? If not, creedal Christianity is characterized, at best, less by its demonstrable "truth" than by its "truthiness."

Was Paul a Jew, an Israelite, or a Christian?

It may still be, however, that the religion of Jesus and Paul was true in another, pragmatic, sense. Miller hints at this issue when he observes that "the mythic dimensions of cultural stories, rather than being the

---

86 "An Open Letter to Gary DeMar of American Vision," https://reformation.substack.com/p/an-open-letter-to-gary-demar.

87 See, *e.g.*, Don K. Preston, *Who is this Babylon?* (Ardmore, OK: JaDon, 2011) and https://bibleprophecy.com.

88 W.H. Walsh, *Philosophy of History: An Introduction* (New York: Harper Torchbooks, 1960), 73, 76.

mere arbitrary product of a supposed whimsical human imagination, arise out of the innate anthropological, psychic disposition of the peoples who produce and value them." In other words, myths "arise out of the subconsciously discerned survival and adaptive needs" of individuals and groups in relation to their "social and physical environment.[89] Robyn Faith Walsh more pointedly observes that Paul was "constructing a myth of origins for his audience." Many of his rhetorical strategies were "constituent of Paul's larger project of religious and ethnopolitical group-making." She characterizes Paul as "a religious and ethnopolitical entrepreneur" for whom "ethnicity is not a blunt instrument; it is an authoritative frame for achieving cohesion among participants, and one that calls for a sense of shared mind and practice." Accordingly, Paul "proposes that God's *pneuma* is intrinsically shared among his addressees, binding them together."[90] On a purely pragmatic view, Paul's ethnotheology became true or false depending upon whether it *worked*. Of course, any assessment of the degree of practical success achieved by Paul and the Jesus movement turns on our understanding of the goals they pursued.

Practitioners of mimetic criticism, such as Walsh, Miller, and Dennis R. MacDonald, locate New Testament writers within the discursive realm of Greco-Roman literature.[91] They show that the work of Paul and the gospel writers functioned as a strategy for constructing new, or resurrecting old, social identities, aiming in the first instance at Hellenized Jews and God-fearing Gentiles in both Judea and, more broadly, throughout the Dispersion. Other scholars have moved beyond literary analysis to examine the geopolitical breadth of the movement's

---

[89] Miller, *Resurrection and Reception*, 104.
[90] Walsh, *Origins of Early Christian Literature*, 37–39.
[91] Dennis R. MacDonald, *Synopses of Epic, Tragedy, and the Gospels* (Claremont, CA: Mimesis Press, 2022). This reference work based on MacDonald's mimetic criticism provides a comprehensive collection of parallels between New Testament writers and classical Greco-Roman literature. There is no space here to discuss those examples.

aims as well as the deep historical roots of its ethno-religious identity. Together, both approaches effectively undermine J. Gresham Machen's claim the "universalism of the gospel" was incarnate in both Jesus, whose redemptive work made possible the Gentile mission, and Paul, who discovered the true, theological significance of Gentile freedom.[92]

Certainly, Machen found it difficult to deny that Jesus attached an ethnic identity to the God of Israel. He conceded that Jesus' disciples would not have been "obviously unfaithful to the teachings of Jesus if after He had been taken from them they continued to minister only to the lost sheep of the house of Israel."[93] Closer to our own day, another prominent Pauline scholar, James Dunn acknowledged that Jesus recognized the covenantal boundary around Judaism by "his choice of twelve to be his closest group of associates, with its obvious symbolism (12 = the twelve tribes)" and in "the picture of the final judgement in terms of the twelve judging the tribes of Israel (Matt. 19:28/Luke 22:30)." But, like Machen, Dunn gives Paul credit for making clear the importance of "Gentile freedom." Paul brought the universal significance of the gospels into the light of day. He taught that "faith in Christ *is* the climax of *Jewish* faith, it is no longer to be perceived as a specifically Jewish faith; *faith should not be made to depend in any degree on the believer living as a Jew (judaizing).*"[94]

But did Paul really refuse to require his Gentile converts to *judaize* as Dunn claims? This raises an even more fundamental question: What were the goals of Paul and the Jesus movement? Were Jesus and Paul on the same page with respect to those goals? Jesus certainly looked forward eagerly to the imminent end of the age and the promised restoration of the twelve tribes of Israel. He was not alone. "Whether in the diaspora or (however defined) in the homeland," restoration theology occupied a prominent place in the Jewish mind in the first

---

92 Machen, *Origin of Paul's Religion*, 13–14.

93 *Ibid.*, 15.

94 Dunn, *Partings of the Ways*, 114, 133.

century. Diaspora Jews may have lived in pleasant and prosperous circumstances but they never "dropped traditional restoration eschatology in favor of a more positive perspective on the dispersion." In fact, educated Hellenistic Jews regularly portrayed diaspora as exile. At the same time, most believed that "the diaspora would ultimately turn out for the best." Staples suggests that "exile and diaspora simultaneously serve[d] as punishment for sin and the means for redemption, the greater good brought out of redemptive chastisement."[95] Amidst such a tense but expectant socio-cultural atmosphere, Jesus' direction to his disciples to serve the lost sheep of Israel launched an apocalyptic, ethno-religious movement aiming to resurrect the twelve tribes of Israel.

But how could Paul's mission to the Gentiles serve the goals of a restorationist theology focused on the idea of Israel? The standard Christian answer turns on a reading of Romans 11:25–26. There, Paul suggests that the salvation of "all Israel" will not happen "until the fulness of the Gentiles be come in." Creedal Christian theologians, such as Manchen and Dunn, interpret such passages as downplaying the specifically, and narrowly, Jewish restoration eschatology in favour of an apocalyptic vision embracing the whole of humanity. Dunn, for example, writes that Paul's "apocalyptic perspective…looked beyond the immediacy of the situation confronting his mission and the Israel of God." In doing so, he "set the local or national crisis of Israel's identity within a cosmic framework." The coming Kingdom of God "had a universal significance." Like Machen, Dunn maintains that Paul was against "Jewish privilege" and in favour of Gentile freedom and equality in the eyes of God. "No national or ethnic status, or we may add, social or gender status (cf.Gal. 3:28), afforded a determinative basis for or decisive assurance of God's favour." That universalist principle applied not just to Israel but to the world at large.[96]

---

95 Staples, *The Idea of Israel*, 204, 208.

96 James D.G. Dunn, *The New Perspective on Paul*, Revised Edition (Grand Rapids, MI: William B.Eerdmans, 2008), 328–329.

Paula Fredriksen takes issue with this interpretation of Paul's mission. She flatly rejects any reading of Paul's letters from which he "emerges as the champion of universalist ('spiritual') Christianity over particularist ('fleshly') Judaism." She sets herself in opposition to scholars such as Machen and Dunn for whom "Paul stands as history's first Christian theologian, urging a new faith that supersedes or subsumes the narrow *Ioudaïsmos* of his former allegiances." In her view, far from superseding his Jewish identity, Paul preached "a Judaizing gospel, *one that would have been readily recognized as such by his own contemporaries.*" His "core message to his gentiles about their behavior was not 'Do not circumcise!' Rather, it was "Worship strictly and only the *Jewish* god." He required Gentile "ex-pagans" to abandon the "lower gods" of their kinfolk. They would retain their native ethnicity but live, in a certain sense, outside and apart from their co-ethnics. Having received the holy spirit, these Gentiles "were to live as *hagioi,* 'holy,' or 'sanctified' or 'separated-out' *ethne,* according to standards of community behavior described precisely in 'the Law.'" But he did not expect, much less require, Gentile males to undergo circumcision. On the other hand, he nowhere "says anything about (much less against) Jews circumcising their own sons...He opposed circumcision for *gentiles,* not for Jews." Israel must remain Israel. God's coming Kingdom "was to contain not only gentiles, but also Israel, defined as that people set apart by God by his Laws (e.g., Lev 20.22–24)."[97]

Paul, according to Fredriksen, "maintains and nowhere erases the distinction between Israel and the nations." At the same time, however, his rhetoric erases "the distinctions between and among 'the nations' themselves." The nations or "*ethnē* function as a mass of undifferentiated 'foreskinned' idol-worshippers (if outside the movement) or of 'foreskinned' ex-idol-worshippers (if within)." The God of Israel is also the god of other nations as well. "*But the nations by and large will know this only at the End.*" And the point to bear in mind here is that "Paul,

---

97 Fredriksen, *Paul,* 108, 111–113.

a member of a radioactively apocalyptic movement, sees time's end pressing upon his generation *now*, mid-first century."[98] Moreover, "for Paul, *the more intense the pitch of apocalyptic expectation, the greater the contrast between Israel and the nations*." It was this "ethnic-theological difference between Israel and the nations, the nation's ignorance of the true god, is what binds all of these other *ethnē* together in one undifferentiated mass of lumpen idolators." At the End, "this sharp dichotomy is resolved *theologically*, but *not ethnically*: Israel remains Israel, the nations remain the nations (cf. Isa 11.10; Rom 15.10)."[99]

According to Paul's "eschatological arithmetic" the world consists of the seventy nations listed in the Table of Nations (Genesis 10) and the twelve tribes of Israel. At the End, all "will, somehow, receive Christ's *pneuma*" (spirit)." Gentiles-in-Christ (who Fredriksen describes as "eschatological Gentiles") will "rejoice *with* saved Israel, but they do not 'become' Israel...Even eschatologically — that is, 'in Christ' — Jews and Gentiles, though now in one 'family' are not 'one.'"[100] Yet, paradoxically, while Paul's *ethnē*-in-Christ are *not*-Israel, they are not only "enjoined to Judaize to the extent that they commit to the worship of Israel's god alone and eschew idol-worship," they "must behave toward each other in such a way that they fulfill the Law." For Paul, "the only good gentile is a Judaizing gentile."[101]

Clearly, there are unbridgeable differences between Fredriksen, a convert to Judaism, on the one hand, and Anglo-Protestants such as Machen, Dunn, and Doug Wilson, on the other. But, on one issue, at least, they all agree: both Jesus and Paul must be considered failed

---

98 Paula Fredriksen, "Paul, Pagans and Eschatological Ethnicities: A Response to Denys McDonald," (2022) 45(1) *Journal for the Study of the New Testament* 51, at 56.

99 Fredriksen, *Paul*, 114–116.

100 *Ibid.*, 88; Matthew Thiessen and Paula Fredriksen, "Paul and Israel," in B. Matlock and M. Novenson (eds.), *The Oxford Handbook of Pauline Studies* 365, at 378.

101 Fredriksen, *Paul*, 117, 125.

prophets. Fredriksen is confident that "the historian and theologian know something that the actors in this [eschatological] drama could not; namely, that Jesus Christ would *not* return to establish the Kingdom within the lifetime of the first (and, according to their convictions, the only) generation of his apostles."[102] Unsurprisingly, atheistic/agnostic scholars such as Bertrand Russell, Bart Ehrman, and Richard C. Miller share that view.

Consequently, few scholars of any stripe, Jewish, Christian, or non-believer, will appeal to a pragmatic theory of truth to uphold the truth of the eschatology of the first century Jesus movement. Fredriksen even expresses surprise that Paul remained convinced even at mid-century that the End would come within his own lifetime: *How, after a quarter-century delay, could he reasonably assert that 'salvation is nearer to us now than when we first believed?*"[103]

Despite Fredriksen's incredulity, Paul's expectations turn out to have been reasonable on the assumption that he looked forward to the end of the Old Covenant *age*, not the end of the *world*. Tom Holland, to cite but one prominent scholar, suggests that both Jesus and Paul framed their eschatological expectations as a New Exodus. Paul insisted "that Israel's experience of Exodus whether from Egypt or Babylon was only a rehearsal of the forthcoming eschatological salvation." Israel was separated from God and "shut up under Sin," refusing to heed the message of the gospel. Israel herself "was now behaving like Pharoah" in opposing the Exodus of the people of God. In the mimetic character of that New Exodus, Paul could hardly be surprised that forty years would elapse before judgement was visited upon Old Covenant Israel and "the holy city, new Jerusalem" came

---

102 Paula Fredriksen, "Judaism, the Circumcision of Gentiles, and Apocalyptic Hope: Another Look at Galatians 1 and 2," (1991) 42(2) *Journal of Theological Studies* 532, at 533.

103 *Ibid.*, 533 n.4.

"down from God out of heaven" (Rev. 21:2).[104] And, remembering the death of Moses, Paul must have known that he might not live to see that day (Deut. 34:1–8). In other words, *prima facie*, a pragmatic case can be made for the credibility of the eschatology foreshadowed in the religion of Paul. Certainly, the covenant eschatology of Don K. Preston and other preterist biblical scholars does just that.[105]

The work of Jason A. Staples on Paul and the resurrection of Israel lends additional support to the biblical truth of both restoration theology and covenant eschatology. It is important here to note the difference between Staples' thesis and Fredriksen's claim that both Jesus and Paul were working "within Judaism." Fredriksen has no doubt that Paul was "an *ancient* Jew, one of any number of whom in the late Second Temple period expected the end of days in their lifetimes." She is no less confident that, in Paul's mind, "whether 'now' (mid-first century) or in the (impending) End time, 'Israel' is *the Jews*."[106] Staples calls both propositions into question. He points out that Paul prefers "to identify himself as 'of the nation of Israel, of the tribe of Benjamin' (Phil 3:5; Rom 11:1; 2 Cor 11:22) rather than using the more generic term 'Jew'. In addition, Paul frames his ministry in 'new covenant' language, suggesting the centrality of the restoration of all Israel to his gospel."[107]

Paul's "new covenant" theology echoes Jeremiah 31:31 but, Staples reminds us, "Jeremiah's prophecy primarily concerns the reconstitution of all Israel — that is, that both Israel and Judah will be restored by means of God's writing the law on their hearts." This implies, however, that "the covenant will be made only with Israel and Judah," given that

---

104 Tom Holland, *Contours of Pauline Theology: A Radical New Survey of the Influences on Paul's Biblical Writings* (Fern, Scotland: Mentor, 2004), 211.

105 Don K. Preston, *"We Shall Meet Him in the Air:" The Wedding of the King of Kings!* (Ardmore, OK: JaDon, 2010).

106 Paula Fredriksen, "What Does it Mean to See Paul 'within Judaism'?" (2022) 141(2) *Journal of Biblical Literature* 359, at 379; Fredriksen, "Reply to McDonald," 60 (emphasis added).

107 Staples, "What Do the Gentiles Have to Do with 'All Israel,'" 378.

gentiles are not mentioned in the prophecy. But it turns out "that faithful gentiles (those with 'the law written on their hearts'; see Rom 2:14–15) *are* the returning remnant of the house of Israel, united with the faithful from the house of Judah (cf. the 'inward Jews' of Rom 2:28–29)." It matters not "whether Paul actually imagines that *all* redeemed gentiles are literal descendants of ancient Israelites." Gentile inclusion was to be the means of Israel's promised restoration because the seed of the northern tribes was mixed "among the gentiles — thus God's promise to restore Israel has opened the door to gentile inclusion in Israel's covenant." Staples cites Hosea 8:8 to sum up the situation: "Israel [the north] is swallowed up; they are now in the nations [gentiles] like a worthless vessel."[108]

As it happened, by scattering the northern tribes among the nations, God provided for the salvation of gentiles as well. In Romans 11:25–26, Paul indicates that when "the fullness of the nations" has come into the new covenant, "all Israel" would be saved. Staples contends that by referring to "the fullness of the nations" Paul echoes "Jacob's use of the same phrase in his blessing of Joseph's sons" (Gen. 48:19) where he promises that the seed of Ephraim [the northern tribes of Israel] "will be the fullness of the nations." Thus, the new covenant also "fulfills the promises to Abraham that all nations would be blessed, not 'through' his seed (i.e., as outsiders) but by inclusion and incorporation *in his seed* (Gal 3:8)." The "blessing of Ephraim therefore serves as an extension of YHWH's promise to Jacob/Israel and Abraham *as it specifically pertains to the nations*." In other words, the "physically uncircumcised peoples displaying the 'work of the Torah written on their hearts,' (Rom 2:14–15) are God's way of resurrecting the house of Israel which must be united with the faithful from the house of Judah." These faithful Gentiles need not, however, "become Jews (that is, *Judah*) in order to become members of Israel — rather they have already become Israelites through the new covenant." In effect, Paul "continues to preach God's

---

108 *Ibid.*, 380–381.

special election of Israel, the lasting value of Israel's covenant, and the restoration and ultimate salvation of Israel; but he extends this election to gentiles without any requirement of circumcision, food laws, or any other external markers of covenantal membership." Paul undoubtedly shocked many of his peers by proposing that "gentile converts are not saved 'as gentiles' but actually become equal members of Israel alongside their law-observant Jewish brothers."[109]

Paul's gospel, therefore, is not exactly "within Judaism" but nor is it "something wholly 'other.'" Staples suggests that Paul's mission was carried out "within Israelism," that was "specifically a restorationist form of Israelism based on the conviction that the new covenant with both Israel and Judah had been inaugurated by the death and resurrection of Israel's messiah, a Jew named Jesus." God resurrects "Israel from the nations by the incorporation of foreskinned gentiles receiving the spirit promised to Israel and Judah in the new covenant." Having "received the spirit of the Messiah," faithful gentiles-in-Christ "become parts of the Messiah's (circumcised) body" and were effectively "transformed into actual descendants of Abraham through something like a DNA transplant." Accordingly, the "*ethical* transformation of Paul's former gentiles is therefore also an *ethnic* transformation, restoring Israel through the process of gentile transformation and adoption into the eschatological people of God."[110]

By contrast "fleshly circumcision amounts to little more than cosmetic surgery" through which the mere appearance of kinship substitutes for an underlying genealogical transformation. For Paul, "membership in new covenant Israel" was "defined by the circumcision of the heart by the spirit" rather than "by circumcision performed by human hands." It was by way of a miraculous spiritual transformation

---

109 Ibid., 382–383; see also, Jason A. Staples, *Paul and the Resurrection of Israel: Jews, Former Gentiles, Israelites* (Cambridge: Cambridge University Press, 2024), 307–312.

110 Staples, "What Do the Gentiles Have to Do with 'All Israel,'" 383; Staples, *Paul and the Resurrection of Israel*, 316, 339.

that faithful gentiles-in Christ and their *seed became the fullness of the nations* Paul in Romans 11:25-27 expected as the fulfillment of Jacob's prophecy. The salvation of "all Israel" could not be limited to Jews alone, however. "Since 'all Israel' includes both houses of Israel and the northern house is indistinct from the nations, 'all Israel' must include both Jews and gentiles." In other words, the scattered, "spiritual," seed of the northern tribes could be reincorporated into Israel "only through the ingathering of the nations." Having been assimilated into the nations following their dispersion, the ten tribes of Israel ceased "*to be Israelites*." As an ethnicity, the whole "house of Israel" had passed away and become the "dry bones" of Ezekiel 37. According to Paul, they "must now be resurrected (37:1-14), being re-adopted from among the nations among which these insensible Israelites had been scattered and assimilated." As "spirit-filled gentiles" they were "not just religiously converted;" they were "in fact *ethnically transformed* into Israelites through the process of adoption by incorporation into the body of the Messiah."[111]

Far from being a failed prophet, therefore, Paul's vision of "the expansion of Israel by restoration and addition" became a reality in the first century. The first century *ekklesia* (comprised of both Jews and former gentiles) were "in direct continuity with ancient Israel. Gentiles coming into the body of Christ indeed become members of Israel, but they are in no way replacements — they are restorations and additions." This was "not a transfer of Israelite status from one group to another. In Paul's vision, Israel's ethnic identity was restored and reunited with Israel's God. Even gentile inclusion itself is in continuity with ancient Israel, since Israel has been ethnically intermingled among the nations, requiring gentile inclusion for Israelite restoration." It must be remembered that in Paul's day "a church led by and primarily composed of Jews was still grappling with the question of gentile inclusion." Within a generation or two, however, the church

---

111 Staples, "What Do the Gentiles Have to Do with 'All Israel,'" 387-388; Staples, *Paul and the Resurrection of Israel*, 339, 346, 316.

was increasingly composed of gentiles. In the period after the Jewish Wars, "the nuance and subtlety of Paul's argument were lost, succeeded by the blunt replacement theology (or 'third race' notion) of the patristic period."[112]

In short, it was not that Paul's (and Jesus') vision had failed; rather, it was derailed by the rebellion against the Roman empire by stiff-necked, neo-Maccabean, Judean chauvinists, together with the synagogue of Satan headquartered in Old Jerusalem (Rev. 2:9). No surprises there! Recall that after the devil finished tempting Jesus in the desert "he departed from Him until an opportune time" (Luke 4:13). Even as Paul's mission neared its objective, there was still time to derail the New Exodus. On the other hand, Paul probably expected the heavenly response to any such satanic schemes to resemble the Days of Vengeance in 70 AD.[113]

Looking on the bright side, Paul knew that "far from rejecting Israel, God has reached out and saved more of Israel than anyone could have imagined." His "faithfulness to Israel is so great that he has provided to save all—even Gentiles—*in* Israel." Prior to the Jewish Wars, God was not moving to a new people but was "gathering, restoring, and reconciling even those who were thought to be irretrievably lost." As it reasonably seemed to Paul, "God's covenant-keeping power extends beyond the grave, capable even of bringing life from the dead (Rom 11:15) of producing Israelites from the Gentiles."[114]

Conclusion

What lessons should crypto-Anglo white or Christian nationalists take away from the first-century Jesus movement? First, notice that this movement emerged among a people in which the diaspora population

---

112 Staples, "What Do the Gentiles Have to Do with 'All Israel,'" 389.

113 David Chilton, *The Days of Vengeance: An Exposition of the Book of Revelation* (Tyler, TX: Dominion Press, 1987).

114 Staples, "What Do the Gentiles Have to Do with 'All Israel,'" 390.

outnumbered their co-ethnics in Judea. In addition, both at home and in the dispersion, Jews were experiencing a spiritual identity crisis. Perhaps Paul's mission to resurrect the lost sheep of Israel has unexpected relevance to those of us who long for the restoration of the lost tribes of Greater Britain.[115]

Paul's push for the resurrection of Israel presupposed a deep-seated, ancestral inseparability of ethnicity and religion. That is to say that the family, the tribe, the nation can, jointly and severally, serve as the syngeneic medium through which the divine, God or the gods, expresses itself in the collective life of a people. For his followers, the messianic myth of Jesus Christ incarnated the perfected telos of national Israel. Today, it is impossible to imagine the renaissance of British race patriotism apart from the reunion of Anglo-Saxon ethnicity with an ancestral religion. Such an ethnoreligious revival must develop both within the Anglo-Saxon diaspora and its ancestral homeland (where the native English and Celtic peoples are undergoing demographic replacement at the hands of a hostile plutocratic elite).

The sacred mythology of Jesus the Christ inspired Paul's ethnoreligious movement. The resurrection of British race patriotism, too, must draw on ancestral traditions of sacral kingship rooted in both Anglo-Saxon history and Anglo-Norman Arthurian legend. A counter-cultural ethnoreligious movement across the Anglosphere

---

[115] The idea of Greater Britain dates from the mid- to late nineteenth century at the peak of British imperialism. Historians now look back upon the Greater Britain project as a failed utopian vision. Could a Greater Britain really rise from the dead, like the first-century idea of Israel, within an Anglo-Saxon diaspora under the thumb of the transnational corporate welfare state? As one might expect, recent scholarship provides ample grounds for pessimism. See, Sir John Robert Seeley, *The Expansion of England: Two Courses of Lectures* (New York: Cosimo Classics, 2005) [Original Edition, 1891]; John Wolffe, *God and Greater Britain: Religion and National Life in Britain and Ireland, 1843–1945* (London: Routledge, 1994); and two books by Duncan Bell, *The Idea of Greater Britain: Empire and the Future of World Order* (Princeton, NJ: Princeton University Press, 2007); and idem., *Dreamworlds of Race: Empire and the Utopian Destiny of Anglo-America* (Princeton, NJ: Princeton University Press, 2020).

could summon into being our own long-awaited messiah, the Patriot King prophesied by Henry St. John, Viscount Bolingbroke during the Financial Revolution of the eighteenth century.[116]

British race patriotism could find legitimate expression once again, not in the godless transnational corporate welfare states now mismanaging the Anglosphere, but through a patriot prince devoted to the spiritual welfare of the British peoples. The modern counterpart of the first-century Jesus movement could emerge in the form of an *Angelcynn* Network of *ekklesia*. Its members would work to secure the independence of the British monarchy in its constitutional role as defender of the faith. The chief aim of the *Angelcynn* movement would be to re-consecrate the Crown as head of reformed Anglican churches throughout the Anglosphere, including the USA. Clearly, King Charles III is unlikely to seek or accept such a role. The goal must therefore be to shame some honourable man among his heirs and successors into defending the ethnoreligious identity and biocultural interests of the Anglo-Saxon peoples outside and apart from the governments of the historic white Commonwealth.

Such a movement would revise and reform, not reject, the Christian heritage of the Anglican church. Rather, Jesus and Paul would recover their rightful place in the *Angelcynn* tradition. As historical figures, Jesus and Paul would be honoured as Israelite ethnoreligious patriots. They must also continue to be exalted for their divine agency in consummating the covenantal history of Israel. Drawing inspiration from both, Anglo-Saxons world-wide could begin the process of exalting gods of our own. It is long past time, for example, to "translate" Alfred the Great, recognizing him, at long last, as an English David, a Son of God in his own right, who modelled his English kingdom on Old Covenant Israel.

As a practical matter, such an ethnoreligious strategy means that "nationalists" such as Joel Davis and Stephen Wolfe (to name but two)

---

116 See, "The Idea of a Patriot King," in David Armitage, (ed.) *Bolingbroke: Political Writings* (Cambridge: Cambridge University Press, 1997), 217–294.

must come out of the WASP closet. In Australia, Joel Davis would no longer conceal his Anglo-Saxon identity under a white skin suit worn within a supposedly secular political space. One might also hope that he would cease to profess a universalist Catholic faith altogether detached from his ethnic identity. Stephen Wolfe, on the other hand, foreswears his ancestral WASP identity in favour of a civic-minded Americanism. His inner faith, however, exalts the supernatural truths of a worn-out Augustinian metanarrative; his Lord Jesus is a cosmic Christ, sitting at the right hand of the Father in the heavenly City of God. Like other members of the invisible race, Wolfe eschews both whiteness and Anglo-Saxondom. Here in the City of Man, he retains "Anglo-Protestantism" only because it is the "true religion" of creedal Christianity. Every other earthly source of ethnoreligious identity is adiaphorous, a matter of indifference in the eyes of God.

As a spiritual diet, this is thin gruel indeed. Looking instead to the original Jesus movement for inspiration, WASPs can and must rise from the dead. We desperately need a messianic new covenant *Angelcynnism*. Come, Patriot King. Come!

3. Metanarrative Collapse: Has the Christian Cosmology Invented by Augustine of Hippo Stood the Test of Time?

Introduction

FROM ITS BEGINNINGS in the first century A.D. Christianity anchored its cosmology in the Bible. But what is the Bible? As a book in hand, of course, it is a collection of ancient texts, the product of the religious history of a remarkably durable and professedly holy ethno-nation in the ancient Near East. One might well ask, therefore, just what spiritual truths or religious guidance could, or should such a book convey to people like me, specifically, white Anglo-Saxon Protestants living in the twenty-first century? Is the Holy Bible just another "social construct," a mere cultural artefact, or is it instead the literal Word of God?

Intellectual heavyweights among mainline Anglo-European Protestants such as Karl Barth concede that the Bible is indeed a "humanly composed and selected" collection of "human words" while professing a neo-orthodox faith that scripture remains "the witness of divine revelation."[1] But how should faithful Christians interpret the testimony of that witness? Or, should we say "witnesses"? After

---

1   Karl Barth, "The Word of God for the Church," in G.W. Bromley & T.F. Torrance (eds.) *Church Dogmatics Study Edition* Vol. 1, Pt. 2 (London: T&T Clark, 2009), 457–473, at 468.

all, Protestants differ with Catholics as to whether this or that ancient Hebrew or Jewish text should be included in the biblical canon. At the end of the day, however, even if all churches somehow settle upon on a single, canonical corpus of antique texts, the theological significance of the biblical metanarrative, from Genesis to Revelation, will remain open to competing interpretations — as it always has been.

The difficulty of distinguishing heresy from orthodoxy forced the early church to master the art of theological hermeneutics. The church fathers expounded the Word of God using a bewildering variety of literal, allegorical, moral, and anagogical (mystical) methods of biblical interpretation. In quick succession, rival camps staked out their respective claims to the true or most useful understanding of the Bible story. First in best dressed were the mostly Hebrew and Jewish authors and participant observers responsible for the original texts of both the Old and New Testaments. Marinated in Scripture, the Mosaic law, and the prophetic tradition, they read and told their stories of the creation, fall, and redemption of Old Covenant Israel through an ethnocentrically thickened, Hebraic hermeneutic lens. Their insider's view of the Hebrew religious culture revolving around the Jerusalem Temple was far removed from the cosmopolitan, Hellenic, or Greco-Roman presuppositions underlying the Christian tale of two cities told several centuries later by Augustine (354–430 AD), the bishop of Hippo in North Africa.

Augustine Rewrites the Bible Story

In effect, Augustine had to re-invent the bible story. According to a Hebraic hermeneutic grounded in the salvation history of Old Covenant Israel, the narrative ends sometime in the first century AD, just before the destruction of "the great city...where also our Lord was crucified" (Rev.11:8). Augustine rewrites the end of the bible story by projecting the end times into the future of his own Christian age. He reads Revelation as a prophecy of the apocalyptic Day of Judgement still in store for the earthly City of Man. He also put his own dramatic spin on the creation stories in Genesis 1–3.

By both precept and example Augustine prescribed authoritative hermeneutic rules and techniques designed to accomplish the twin tasks of understanding the Bible oneself and then teaching others orthodox Christian doctrine.[2] Augustine not only provided a compelling doctrinal foundation for the formal Creeds of the church; he also helped to secure the actual historical triumph of the church. He held out the hope that a novel Christian cosmopolis could bring peace, order, and good government to a chaotic, multicultural mélange of peoples during the dying days of the Roman Empire in the West. Augustine's interpretation of the bible story brought the heavenly City of God down to earth as the *mythomoteur* or constitutive myth for a new race of Christians.[3] He provided his fellow Christians with a coherent sense of who they were as a people, where they came from, and where they were going. Augustine's Hellenistic hermeneutic was an earthly success; it inspired a reverence for ecclesiastical Tradition which still guides Christian interpretations of Sacred Scripture along approved paths.

One example of the importance of Tradition in contemporary theological hermeneutics is the scholarly movement known as Radical Orthodoxy (hereafter, RO). This group of mainly academic writers and thinkers represent an Anglo-Catholic style of "postmodern critical Augustinianism."[4] Like Augustine, writers such as John Milbank and Catherine Pickstock seek to demonstrate their orthodoxy by promoting theology as the restored queen of the sciences to whom philosophy

---

[2] Saint Augustine, *On Christian Doctrine* (Radford, VA: Wilder Publications, 2013), 12.

[3] Denise Kimber Buell, *Why This New Race: Ethnic Reasoning in Early Christianity* (New York: Columbia University Press, 2005).

[4] John Milbank, "'Postmodern Critical Augustinianism': A Short *Summa* in Forty Two Responses to Unasked Questions," (1991) 7:3 *Modern Theology* 226.

must pay obeisance.⁵ Unlike Augustine, however, they are philosophical radicals with scant interest in biblical exegesis. RO much prefers to engage in theological entryism, courting the post-modern heirs of Augustine's Hellenic Neo-platonism. An outspoken Remainer and cosmopolitan xenophile, Milbank is on a mission to wean continental intellectual leftists away from an increasingly satanic secularism. In place of the hegemonic "globohomo" liberalism of the transnational corporate welfare state, Milbank promotes a neo-Augustinian politics of virtue which aims to "immanentize the eschaton" by bringing the heavenly City of God back down to earth.⁶

Not surprisingly, such theological dalliances with the spiritual heirs of Marx and Freud deepens the widespread suspicion among the many neo-pagan thinkers on the dissident or Alt Right that "Christianity was essentially an alien, even subversive, Jewish ideological influence on European civilization, and one which has been, at least in some ways, incompatible with the culture of Europeans."⁷ According to Alain de Benoist's dismissive reading of the Bible, for example, "Judeo-Christian monotheism" posits "universal peace" as "an ideal at the end of history."⁸ As we will see, this simplistic interpretation of the bible story owes more to St. Augustine of Hippo than to the Hebraic hermeneutic through which Jewish Christians viewed the origins, history, and destiny of Old Covenant Israel.

The apostles Peter, Paul, and John, for example, clearly looked forward eagerly to the imminent end — in their own generation — of

---

5 John Milbank and Catherine Pickstock, *et.al., Radical Orthodoxy: A New Theology* (London: Routledge, 1999).

6 John Milbank and Adrian Pabst, *The Politics of Virtue: Post-Liberalism and the Human Future* (London: Rowman & Littlefield, 2016. The phrase "immanentize the eschaton" was coined by Eric Voeglin in his 1952 book, *The New Science of Politics*.

7 Richard Storey, *The Uniqueness of Western Law: A Reactionary Manifesto* (London: Arktos, 2019), 22.

8 Alain de Benoist, *On Being a Pagan* tr. Jon Graham (Atlanta, GA: Ultra, 2004), 142–144.

the Mosaic Age. They expected the story of Old Covenant Israel to reach its apocalyptic conclusion in the first century AD, not at the end of human history. Peter and Paul were Jews, that is true. But they did not invent the millenarian Christian eschatology sanctified by ecclesiastical Tradition. That futurist biblical hermeneutic was pioneered by Augustine of Hippo, himself the product of a Greco-Roman rather than the Hebraic hermeneutical tradition. Richard Storey is one of many scholars who concludes, therefore, that "Christianity is Hellenistic, a rightful successor of the natural law tradition" and "that it lies at the heart of Western civilisation."[9] Such a judgement, of course, begs the question of whether either the Hebraic or the Hellenistic hermeneutic offers a true or useful understanding of Sacred Scripture. To answer such a question, we must first compare the two.

Hebraic Hermeneutics

Ancient Hebrew culture presupposed a cosmology alien to the modern mind. Strange though it seems to us, on a Hebraic reading, the story of creation in Genesis One has nothing to do with the origins of matter. Rather, like other ancient Near Eastern peoples, Israelites "believed that something existed not by virtue of its material properties, *but by virtue of its having a function in an ordered system.*"[10] In other words, "what was most crucial and significant" to the biblical "understanding of existence was the way that the parts of the cosmos functioned, not their material status."[11]

As John Walton observes, Genesis One therefore offers an account "of functional origins rather than...of material origins. Consequently, to create something (cause it to exist) in the ancient world means to give it a function, not material properties." On this view, the cosmos

---

9 Storey, *Uniqueness of Western Law*, 22.
10 John H. Walton, *The Lost World of Genesis One: Ancient Cosmology and the Origins Debate* (Downers Grove, IL: IVP Academic, 2009), 26 (emphasis in original).
11 Ibid., 28.

presupposed by the creation account begins "with no functions rather than no material." The "function of any given thing within the entire cosmos conceived as a divine temple has to do its purpose rather than its material properties." For ancient Hebrews, a temple was a symbol of the cosmos. "This interrelationship makes it possible for the temple to be the center from which order in the cosmos is maintained." Genesis One describes the creation of the cosmic temple with all of its functions and with God dwelling in its midst."[12]

Preoccupied with the function of things rather than their origins, "biblical texts nowhere state or argue for *creatio ex nihilo*." Creation was conceived, instead, as an organizational process intended to bring order out of chaos. James Hubler notes that these "texts are strangely quiet about the material for the cosmos." Down to the first century AD, even Hellenized Jews simply presupposed *creatio ex materia*. To propose creation *ex nihilo* "would have been a unique position and could never have been justified without considerable explanation or argumentation."[13]

For ancient Hebrews and first century Jews alike, a materialist account of creation would have been pointless. They were committed to the function of the temple as the focal point of cosmic order, not just in the here and now but also in the Messianic Kingdom to come. It went without saying that not all cosmic temples in the Near East were created equal. Only the temple of the Hebrews in Jerusalem mattered to them. Hebraic hermeneutics presupposed a self-conscious and explicit ethno-theology. The highly particularistic ethno-religion of Old Covenant Israel remained resistant to the cosmopolitan and universalistic spirit of Greco-Roman culture at the advent of Jesus Christ. Indeed, the previously unknown concept of Judaism was invented only in the second century BC, around the time of the Maccabean revolts,

---

12   Ibid., 35, 50, 81, 84.

13   James Noel Hubler, "Creation ex Nihilo: Matter, Creation, and the Body in Classical and Christian Philosophy Through Aquinas," *Publicly Accessible Dissertations*. 980, 79, 89. http://repository.upenn.edu/edissertations/980.

in order to encourage Judean resistance to the culturally subversive influence of Hellenism.¹⁴

Contemporary WASP theological hermeneutics is far removed from such an unabashedly ethnocentric mindset. Even someone as steeped in ancient Near Eastern cultures as John Walton automatically reads the second creation story in Genesis 2–3 as an account of *human*, as distinct from Israelite, origins.¹⁵ It has long been "standard doctrine" among Christians "that every member of the human race is descended from the biblical Adam." How interesting, therefore, that it was a seventeenth century "Calvinist of Portuguese Jewish origin from Bordeaux" who challenged Christian orthodoxy with the "beguilingly simple" claim "that human beings existed before the biblical Adam."¹⁶

Isaac La Peyrère (1596–1676), who was most likely a Marrano Jew, resurrected ancient Hebraic hermeneutics by tracing "ceremonial Judaism...back beyond Moses to the Garden of Eden and thus to Adam himself."¹⁷ In support of this novel biblical interpretation, La Peyrère offered "a fresh if rather naïve" exegesis of Romans 5:12–14. He aimed to show that sin, and hence other human beings, had been in the world before Adam. "By this neat piece of exegetical reshuffling" La Peyrère effectively conjured "a range of irritating inconsistencies in the Genesis record...out of existence" with "a ready-made explanation for Cain's fear, after his banishment from the Garden of Eden, that he would encounter hostile individuals seeking to kill him; it delivered a

---

14 See, generally, Steve Mason, "Jews, Judeans, Judaizing, Judaism: Problems of Categorization in Ancient History," (2007) 38 *Journal for the Study of Judaism* 457.

15 John H. Walton, *The Lost World of Adam and Eve: Genesis 2–3 and the Human Origins Debate* (Downers Grove IL: IVP Academic, 2015).

16 David N. Livingstone, *Adam's Ancestors: Race, Religion and the Politics of Human Origins* (Baltimore: Johns Hopkins University Press, 2008), 5, 26, 33.

17 Richard H. Popkin, "The Marrano Theology of Isaac La Peyrère," (1973) 5 *Studi Internazionali di Filosofia* 97–126; Livingstone, *Adam's Ancestors*, 33.

population to inhabit the city he built; it provided a possible answer to the question about where his wife came from."[18]

La Peyrère's impact on theological hermeneutics is such that many contemporary Christian scholars now accept that, according to Hebraic hermeneutics, Adam need not be, and probably was not conceived as the first human being. Rather, the biblical Adam is best understood as proto-Israel. Adam's story "is not about universal human origins but Israel's origins."[19] Thus, the story of Adam mirror's Israel's story from exodus to exile. God creates a special person, Adam; places him in a special land, the garden; and gives him law as a stipulation of special communion with God (not to eat of the tree of the knowledge of good and evil). Adam and Eve disobey the command and …their punishment is death and exile from paradise.[20] Similarly, "Israel was 'created' at the exodus…and brought to the good and spacious land of Canaan." Israel was also bound by a law which it continually disobeys with the result that Israelites are exiled from the holy land which God gave them. In this way "Israel's drama — its struggles over the land and failure to follow God's law — is placed into primordial time."[21]

Within that Hebraic hermeneutic, just as the Old Testament begins with the primordial origins of the cosmic temple, the New Testament brings the bible story to a close in the last days of Old Covenant Israel. It was then, in the first century AD, that the Jerusalem temple lost its function as the linchpin of cosmic order in the old heaven and the old earth. The Passion of Christ marked the beginning of a second Exodus, this time with the Sanhedrin playing the role of Pharaoh. The last Adam led his suffering and persecuted people towards a new heaven and new earth. In the Day of the Lord, some forty years later, the Son of Man returned on clouds of glory to destroy the Temple made by

---

18 Livingstone, *Adam's Ancestors*, 33–34.
19 Peter Enns, *The Evolution of Adam: What the Bible Does and Doesn't Say About Human Origins* (Grand Rapids, MI: Brazos Press, 2012), 65.
20 *Ibid.*, 66.
21 *Ibid.*, 66.

hands, replacing it with a heavenly New Jerusalem where God was to dwell forevermore with his people, the spiritual seed of Abraham (Rev 21:2–3).

Clearly, the apostles placed a distinctively Jewish Christian spin on traditional Hebraic hermeneutics. But there can be no doubt that "Paul's expectation of the imminent parousia of the Lord is in general to be explained as being in agreement with Palestinian Judaism, or at least some of it."[22] In its simplest form, Jewish eschatology held that the righteous remnant of Old Covenant Israel would be redeemed from the evils of the world by "the Messianic Kingdom that puts an end to this condition."[23] What finally separated Palestinian Judaism from Jewish Christianity was the fall of Jerusalem. First century "Judaism was a God-ordained religion." Paul and Jesus himself knew well that false Judaizing teachers could continue "to deceive and confuse people as long as the temple existed." Jewish Christians faced an uphill battle when calling "on the Jews to lay aside Judaism which was given by God and at one time acceptable to God." The task of the church was simplified "when Jerusalem fell, the temple was destroyed, and [false teachers] could no longer use [the existence of the temple] as a means to confuse people."[24]

As Don K Preston observes, the "relationship of the temple with the identity of the Israel of God can hardly be overemphasized."[25] No Jewish Christian "could view the catastrophe which befell the Jewish state, with its capital and sanctuary, as anything else than the just punishment of the nation for having crucified the Messiah." Any Jew who accepted that judgement "ceased from that moment to be a Jew;

---

22 E.P.Sanders, *Paul and Palestinian Judaism: A Comparison of Patterns of Religion* (Minneapolis: Fortress Press, 1977), 543.

23 Albert Schweitzer, quoted in *Ibid.*, 476.

24 Franklin Camp, quoted in Don K. Preston, *Like Father, Like Son On Clouds of Glory: A Study of the Time and Nature of Christ's Second Coming* (Ardmore, OK: JaDon Management, 2010), 153.

25 *Ibid.*, 153.

for a Jew who accepted the downfall of his state and temple as a divine dispensation, thereby committed national suicide."[26] The temple was "the symbol of God's relationship with his people." God abandoned the temple when that relationship was broken through the martyrdom of the saints and the prophets. The time set for the vindication of the martyrs and for the saints to receive their reward "is the time of the kingdom, the judgment, and the resurrection." Jesus' emphatic declaration "that the vindication of all the martyrs was to occur *in his generation, in the fall of Jerusalem* is a prophecy of unsurpassed eschatological import"[27] (Matt. 23:32ff; Rev 11:15ff). How remarkable then, that Augustine (and the church following in his footsteps) should all but miss "a moment of such radically important, decisive, redemptive historical significance."[28]

For Augustine, the destruction of the Jerusalem Temple *per se* had no special theological significance. Rather, that event was a providential means to an end; namely, the increase of the Church of Christ throughout the whole world. Most Jews were blind to the prophecies of Christ contained in the Hebrew Scriptures. Augustine believed that it was thanks to the fall of Jerusalem and "for the sake of such testimony, which even against their will, they furnish us by having and preserving such books, that [the Jews] are scattered throughout all the nations, wherever the Christian Church spreads."[29] Augustine, of course, knew that Jesus had predicted "the destruction of the earthly Jerusalem" but he insisted that a careful exegesis of the bible would distinguish a local happening of interest only to the Jews from "the end of the world and...the last and great day of judgement."[30]

---

26 Adolph Harnack, quoted in *ibid.*, 154.

27 *Ibid.*, 154–156 (emphasis in original).

28 R.C. Sproul, quoted in *ibid.*, 154.

29 Augustine, *The City of God Against the Pagans*, R.W.Dyson (ed. & tr.) (Cambridge: Cambridge University Press, 1998), Bk. XVIII, chapters 46–47, 892–894.

30 *Ibid.*, Bk. XX, ch. 5, 973.

Augustine's Hellenistic Hermeneutic

Augustine's interpretation of the biblical metanarrative portrays both the creation and the end of the world as the appearance and disappearance of corruptible material existence. He had no doubt that the New Testament writers were predicting the literal end of the earthly world when, as "[t]he whole Church" expected, Christ would "come down from heaven to judge the living and the dead."[31] Augustine was clear that the Day of Judgement applied not just to the people of Israel but to "the rest of the nations as well."[32] Faithful Christians, those who live according to the spirit, would exchange the perishable goods of mortal existence for the "Supreme Good" of an imperishable "eternal life" in the City of God. Other mortals, those who live according to the flesh, would suffer the "Supreme Evil" of "eternal death," the nothingness inherent in the absolute privation of the Good.[33] It was out of just such nothingness that the world was created on Augustine's understanding of Genesis One. Furthermore, Augustine's understanding of Genesis 2–3 identifies Adam, not as proto-Israel, but as the first human being. Accordingly, it not just Old Covenant Israel but mankind which faces judgement at the end of the world.

Augustine's Neo-platonic cosmology presupposed the absolute dependence of both mankind and the material world itself on an omnipotent, omniscient, and omnipresent God, Seduced by the delights of our mortal life "we have wandered far from God," losing sight of "the invisible things of God."[34] The inherent difficulty mortal beings experience in apprehending such invisible divine "objects" must make us eternally thankful for the revealed Word of God. But a proper understanding of sacred scripture depends upon two things, according to Augustine: "the mode of ascertaining the proper meaning,

---

31 Augustine, *City of God*, Bk. XX, ch. 1, 965.
32 Ibid., Bk. XX, ch. 5, 973.
33 Ibid., Bk.XIX, ch.3, 918.
34 Augustine, *Christian Doctrine*, 14.

and the mode of making known the meaning when it is ascertained." Understanding the world generally requires that we distinguish between things and signs. "All instruction is about things or about signs; but things are learned by means of signs." There are spiritual as well as material things and signs. Higher spiritual things are the true objects of enjoyment and use. A man should view his whole life as "a journey towards the unchangeable life, and his affections [should be] entirely fixed upon that."[35]

The Bible is both a material and a spiritual thing which can be used or enjoyed in order to understand and participate in the imperishable City of God. Augustine reminds his readers, however, that not every spiritual or material thing can be judged by its outer form. On the surface, biblical prophecies of the Day of the Lord may appear to be addressed only to Old Covenant Israel, warning of the impending destruction of Jerusalem. The inner form of such scriptural signs of things to come can sometimes only be understood "by comparing all the similar passages on the subject which occur in the three evangelists Matthew, Mark, and Luke." Augustine points as well to John "who tells us most clearly that the judgement should take place at the resurrection of the dead."[36] Clearly, Augustine conceives the resurrection of the dead as a material and bodily, not a solely spiritual, phenomenon. No such event has taken place; therefore, he expects the fulfillment of that prophecy to occur at some still future time.

Augustine knew, of course, that many "wise men of this world" scoffed at any suggestion "that the earthly bodies of men" can "be carried over into a heavenly habitation." To ward off such skepticism, he drew upon an idea that appeared quite suddenly in the late second century AD to defend the idea of a bodily resurrection. Augustine deployed the doctrine of *creation ex nihilo* to demonstrate that "He Who in making this world...has already accomplished something far more

---

35   Ibid., 12–13, 22.
36   Augustine, *City of God*, Bk. XX, ch. 5, 973–974.

wondrous than the transformation in which our adversaries refuse to believe." If God has already bound "incorporeal souls" to earthly bodies, why should we doubt "that bodies, though earthly, should be raised up to abodes which, though heavenly, are nonetheless corporeal."[37]

During Augustine's lifetime, such metaphysical speculation on the origins of matter had already become commonplace among Neo-platonic philosophers such as Plotinus. Augustine followed Plotinus in contending that "*creatio ex nihilo* was the expression of God's omnipotent ability to create without need of supporting causes." Such a doctrine was nowhere to be found in the New Testament.[38] Neither the New Testament writers nor Plotinus were responsible for the connection made by Augustine between the creation story and the eschatological hope of a still future resurrection of the body.

Augustine taught "that because every created intelligence had its origin *ex nihilo*, it also had to look beyond itself for its end. Every creature lacked God's perfection and was therefore mutable. Because it was mutable it could fall away from that end and become evil."[39] At the same time "the resurrection of our Lord from the dead" added "a great buttress of hope" to our faith. Our bodies, too, after the death we suffer because of sin "shall at the resurrection be changed into a better form…this corruptible shall put on incorruption, and this mortal shall put on immortality." He urged the faithful to believe "that neither the human soul nor the human body suffers complete extinction but that the wicked rise again to endure inconceivable punishment, and the good to receive eternal life."[40]

---

37 Ibid., Bk.XXII, ch. 4, 1111–1112.
38 Hubler, "Creation ex Nihilo," 143, 107.
39 *Ibid.*, 143.
40 Augustine, *Christian Doctrine*, 20–22.

Augustine's Practical Theology

One may well doubt whether Augustine's interpretive techniques offered a true understanding of the biblical metanarrative, especially when compared to a Hebraic hermeneutic solidly grounded in the lived apostolic experience of the church in the first century AD. On the other hand, one might defend Augustine's biblical metanarrative on the ground that it was demonstrably useful to the church in the increasingly chaotic circumstances of the late Roman Empire in the West. Augustine offered much more than abstract metaphysical speculation. The hermeneutical rules and techniques he outlined in *On Christian Doctrine* were clearly conceived as an aid to practical theology:

> It is the duty, then, of the interpreter and teacher of Holy Scripture, the defender of the true faith and the opponent of error, both to teach what is right and to refute what is wrong, and in the performance of this task, to conciliate the hostile, to rouse the careless, and to tell the ignorant both what is occurring at present and what is probable in the future.[41]

The practical tasks of the early church were set largely by the perceived need to help individuals cope with the anomic conditions of the Hellenistic world. Alexander's conquests resulted in extensive social amalgamation and ethnic admixture throughout the Greece and the Near East, destabilizing Hellenic culture and traditional Greek religion. Greeks and other peoples lost their national religions. Alexander's cosmopolitan policies caused citizens "who formerly derived a sense of unity, stability, and even immortality from their common ancestral religion… to feel alone, alienated, and threatened." The decline of traditional social institutions led individuals "to focus more upon their own personal existence and seek membership in nonbiologically related universal cults that provide opportunities for socialization and a promise of individual salvation." The early Christian emphasis idea of salvation "referred primarily to the bodily resurrection of the

---

41 *Ibid.*,112.

individual," an eschatological hope bound to have a certain appeal to deracinated Hellenic man.[42] Everything that "weakened the particularism of cities" encouraged the spread of the universalistic idea of "humanity" and world-rejecting religions that extended their benefits to all mankind.[43]

Augustine insisted that a proper interpretation of the Bible must "tend to build up [the] twofold love of God and our neighbour."[44] As a practical matter, Augustine's reading of the Bible creates a curious paradox: the very process of creating a new Christian society in accordance with Augustine's prescription, dissolves "the human race... into its many individuals." According to Hannah Arendt, the Christian believer relates in love to his neighbor "only insofar as divine grace can be at work in him. I never love my neighbour for his own sake, only for the sake of divine grace…We are commanded to love our neighbour, to practice mutual love, only because in so doing we love Christ."[45] Or, as Augustine put it:

> Whoever, then, loves his neighbour aright, ought to urge upon him that he too should love God with his whole heart, and soul, and mind. For in this way, loving his neighbour as himself, a man turns the whole current of his love both for himself and his neighbour into the channel of the love of God, which suffers no stream to be drawn off from itself by whose diversion its own volume should be diminished.[46]

Every individual was isolated in his relationship to God; he is also a member of the human race. So, too, is our neighbour. As a

---

42 James C. Russell, *The Germanization of Early Medieval Christianity: A Sociohistorical Approach to Religious Transformation* (New York: Oxford University Press, 1994), 63–67, 73.

43 Ibid., 70.

44 Augustine, *Christian Doctrine*, 32.

45 Hannah Arendt, *Love and Saint Augustine* [original dissertation 1929] (Chicago: University of Chicago Press, 1996), 111.

46 Augustine, *Christian Doctrine*, 23.

consequence, the "mere common existence of believers grounded in the self-same God becomes the common faith and community of believers."[47] Paradoxically, it is the very isolation of the individual before God, that allows the collective body of Christian believers to detach itself from human history and project itself forward, beyond the end times, into the heavenly City of God. In the pre-Constantinian era, the church successfully created a Christian *ethnos* (or *natio* in the Latin West).[48] Eusebius of Caesarea (c. AD 260–339), the first great church historian, identified Jesus Christ as the founder "of a people not heard of since time began that now is not hidden in some corner of the earth but is found everywhere under the sun." Equipped "with weapons of faith" the souls of that people "proved stronger than adamant in struggles with their enemies."[49] The fact that Augustine and many of the early church fathers made universalizing claims does not negate this proposition.

On the contrary, according to Denise Kimber Buell, "saying that Christianity is open to all people is not mutually exclusive with defining Christians as members of an ethnoracial group." In the ancient world race or ethnicity "was often deemed to be produced and indicated by religious practices." It was all too easy, therefore, for early Christians to use forms of "ethnic reasoning to legitimize various forms of Christianness as the universal, most authentic manifestation of humanity."[50] Eusebius, for example, famously proclaimed the triumph of Constantine as the foreordained fusion of universal empire with a universal church. And, indeed, Byzantine Caesaropapism did manage to preserve the synthetic unity of church and state for over a thousand years in the Eastern half of the Roman Empire.

---

47 Arendt, *Love and Saint Augustine*, 112.
48 Buell, *New Race*, 41.
49 Eusebius of Caesarea, *The Church History* (Paul L. Maier tr. & commentary) (Grand Rapids, MI: Kregel, 2007), 313.
50 Buell, *New Race*, 61, 2–3.

But, barely a century later, pagans bitterly blamed the church for the sack of Rome by barbarian hordes. Augustine was compelled to recognize that Latin Christian identity could no longer be anchored safely in perishable earthly kingdoms. Amidst the accelerating collapse of the Roman Empire in the West, Augustine's universalistic vision of the eternal City of God provided the embryonic Roman Catholic church with a powerful *raison d'être*. In a material world mired in sin, corruption, and decay, the church became the visible earthly conduit to the heavenly realm. In our own day, however, it no longer seems possible to tie Christian identity to the eschatological destiny of the entire human race.

Augustinian Hermeneutics in the Post-Christian West

So long as the intellectual horizons of late antiquity were bounded by the limits of the Greco-Roman *oikumene*, Augustine's literal or allegorical equation of the biblical metanarrative with the history of the whole human race was at least plausible. On "the faith of Holy Scripture, which not unworthily has marvellous authority throughout the whole world and among all nations," Augustine maintained that "from one man, whom God created as the first, the whole human race took its origin." Christian writers computed "from the sacred writings that six thousand years have not yet passed since the creation of man." To support such claims, Augustine was compelled to reject as "wholly untruthful" Greek and Egyptian "writings which purport to contain the history of many thousands of years of time."[51] To the extent that it rested upon such self-serving assertions, however useful Augustine's biblical hermeneutic may have been to the early church, its truth claims remain highly suspect. The question for those of us living in what is widely acknowledged to be a "post-Christian" world is simply:

---

51 Augustine, *City of God*, Bk. XII, chapters 9 & 10, 511–512.

does an Augustinian understanding of the Bible remain at all useful, even for Christians if not for the church?

Nowadays, few people, not even many Christians, regard the first few chapters of the Book of Genesis as a reliable guide to the origins of mankind. Indeed, as a practical matter, the very idea of "humanity" is itself little more than an abstract concept. More than two centuries ago, the reactionary Catholic monarchist, Joseph de Maistre, issued the following response to the French constitution of 1795 which "like its [revolutionary] predecessors has been drawn up for Man":

> Now, there is no such thing in the world as Man. In the course of my life, I have seen Frenchmen, Italians, Russians, etc.; I am even aware, thanks to Montesquieu, that one can be a Persian. But, as for Man, I declare I have never met him in my life. If he exists, I certainly have no knowledge of him.[52]

De Maistre rejected the idea of "humanity"; he remained nonetheless an orthodox defender of Catholic ecclesiastical Tradition. For him, biblical hermeneutics, the task of revealing the true understanding of Holy Scripture, was a matter best left to the church, not to the laity. Despite his disbelief in the religion of humanity, de Maistre did not deny that Augustine's tale of two cities had been, and perhaps still could be, useful as a matter of practical theology. After all, Christendom arose at a time when the peoples of the Mediterranean basin could imagine themselves to be the entire "human race." Accustomed to ideas of imperial citizenship, they were open to the idea that all the nations of the *oikumene* shared a common "humanity," at least on the spiritual level. Certainly, the Augustinian Tradition did much to transform the warring tribes of Western Europe into a family of Christian nations.

Since Augustine's lifetime, as the boundaries of the "human race" expanded to incorporate a great many previously unknown "sub-races" and ethnic groups differing radically in intelligence, behavior, and

---

52 Joseph de Maistre, *Considerations on France* [originally published 1797] (Cambridge: Cambridge University Press, 1995), 53.

temperament, the idea of Man has become little more than a philosophical abstraction bereft of any necessary or organic connection to Christian identity. Indeed, European-descended Christians steeped in the Augustinian Tradition now comprise but a shrinking minority of "the human race." Strangely, however, it is these people who cling to the most "adamant" and unyielding faith in the idea of Man. It seems not to matter whether a humanist hermeneutic is true, or even useful in helping us understand the Word of God. A faith that was once merely orthodox has become increasingly radical in its stance towards the truths contained in Holy Scripture and their usefulness to the church in a post-Christian society.

Conclusion

Unfortunately, contemporary Radical Orthodoxy (RO) gives more weight to the Augustinian inventions of creation *ex nihilo* and futurist eschatology than to the Hebraic hermeneutic and cosmology of those who wrote and edited the Bible. RO grounds its own theological hermeneutic firmly in Tradition. RO theologians such as John Milbank and like-minded political philosophers such as Jean Bethke Elshtain share the Augustinian presupposition that all nations and peoples share a common ancestor and, therefore, have all been made in the image of God. Despite our common origin, however, Elshtain resists the "bland assertion that we are all alike." Following Augustine, she declares that the further apart we are, the greater the need to shore up our faith in our shared humanity.[53]

Elshtain is convinced that "the importance of plurality, of the many emerging from a unique one, cannot be underestimated in Augustine's work." For her, as for Milbank, human unity hidden within diversity is an *ontological* not merely historical condition, one which obtains whether one speaks of ancient Israel, the western Mediterranean in

---

53 Jean Bethke Elshtain, *Augustine and the Limits of Politics* (Notre Dame, IN: University of Notre Dame Press, 2018), 103.

Augustine's lifetime, or the modern post-Christian West. From this trans-historical perspective, Elshtain argues that "*From one* creates a fragile but real ontology of peace, or relative peacefulness." From the beginning, human beings were tied by bonds of affection. Over time, they became further bound by ties of kinship and affection. The more fragile and attenuated those ties become, however, the more important the ontology of peace is to human beings. As relationships of kinship and affection "are dispersed, finally encompassing the whole globe, and in light of the confusion and confounding of human languages, the more difficult it is to repair to this fundamental kinship or sociality in order to strike a blow for peace and against war." Augustine provided us with "a perfect vision of peace" in the Heavenly City. But, she adds, "there is earthly work to be done in the name of peace." This ontological primacy of peace over war holds true wherever Man is to be found, in Old Covenant Israel, the Mediterranean world of late antiquity, or modern America.[54]

Like Elshtain, Milbank privileges ontology over history in the realm of politics and ecclesiology.[55] He reads the biblical metanarrative as the story of a struggle between the "ontology of violence" and the "ontology of peace." His version of Augustine's Hellenistic hermeneutic presupposes that "the absolute uniqueness of every individual... makes difference ontologically ultimate and worthy of the highest valuation." Out of this world of difference the commandment to love thy neighbour brings forth the highest form of unity in love of God. Augustinian Christianity "denies ontological necessity to sovereign

---

54 *Ibid.*, 102–105.

55 See, the critique of Milbank by Todd Breyfogle, "Is There Room for Political Philosophy in Postmodern Critical Augustinianism," in Wayne J. Hankey & Douglas Hedley, (eds.) *Deconstructing Radical Orthodoxy: Postmodern Theology, Rhetoric, and Truth* (Aldershot: Ashgate, 2005), 48–66, at 53.

rule and absolute ownership," both of which rest upon coercion and violence.[56]

RO, therefore, "seeks to recover the concealed text of an original peaceful creation beneath the palimpsest of the negative distortion of *dominium*." Milbank declares that the "Church, in order to be the Church, must seek to extend the sphere of socially aesthetic harmony." The tradition of Christian charity seeks "something like the 'peaceful transmission of difference', or 'differences in continuous harmony'. Moreover, Milbank believes that "Christianity from the start considered that it could be adequately repeated in very diverse cultural settings, involving very different sets of cultural roles." Like Augustine, Milbank and Elshtain agree that it is only the outer form of the biblical metanarrative that has to do with the history of the ancient Israel of God. Milbank flatly rejects what he calls the "antique ethics of the city." In place of the civic virtues once nurtured within the ancient *polis*, he sets "the ethics of the *ecclesia*" which "is able to accord only a *qualified* value to particular historical formations."[57] The "concealed text" of the bible story from Genesis to Revelation, serves as the template for "the progressive, visible realization in time of the universal community."[58]

Milbank's Augustinian hermeneutic thus presupposes a still-future eschaton which channels the ontology of peace into the course of human history. This presupposition helps Milbank neatly avoid the questions begged by the "metaphors of coercive action by God in the Book of Revelation." Could that story of Christ's eschatological action be taken literally to refer to the first-century destruction of Jerusalem? Can God himself be held responsible for such a catastrophic holocaust? Perhaps the original Hebraic hermeneutic of Holy Scripture offers every nation and people in the post-Christian West an understanding of the biblical metanarrative that is both true and useful.

---

56 John Milbank, *Theology and Social Theory: Beyond Secular Reason* Second Edition (Oxford: Blackwell, 2006), 423.

57 *Ibid.*, 422–423.

58 Breyfogle, "Postmodern Critical Augustinianism," 54.

White Anglo-Saxon Protestants, in particular, might turn to the Bible in somewhat the manner of their Angelcynn ancestors in the time of Alfred the Great.[59] That is to say, the Anglo-Saxon peoples around the globe should still look to the bible stories about the rise and fall of Old Covenant Israel not just for a great store of spiritual wisdom, but also as a divine warrant for the creation of their own holy Christian nation. Finally, the end of the biblical narrative at the bloody fall of Jerusalem sends a clear warning of the terrible divine judgement awaiting the British peoples should we, too, fall under the spell of Satanism. Who knows? Perhaps the modern English nation can emulate ancient Israel by incubating and then, miraculously, giving birth to our very own Patriot King.[60] Lord knows, we stand sorely in need of such a savior!

---

59   Sara Foot, "The Making of *Angelcynn*" (1996) 6 *Transactions of the Royal Historical Society*, 25–49; see also, Judith McClure, "Bede's Old Testament Kings," in Patrick Wormald, *et.al.,*(eds) *Ideal and Reality in Frankish and Anglo-Saxon Society* (Oxford: Basil Blackwell, 1983), 70–90.

60   See, Henry St. John, Viscount Bolingbroke (1678–1751), "The Idea of a Patriot King," in David Armitage (ed.) *Bolingbroke: Political Writings* (Cambridge: Cambridge University Press, 1997). 217–294.

4. Global Jesus versus National Jesus: The Political Hermeneutics of Resurrection

Introduction

BIBLICAL INTERPRETATION IS, if not the only, certainly the core task of theological hermeneutics. Unfortunately, religious conflict and biblical interpretation have always been joined at the hip. Is it therefore the case that theologians engage in "politics" when they offer authoritative interpretations? Is it too much of a stretch to characterize biblical hermeneutics as a branch of political theology? It does seem that biblical interpretation fits comfortably within almost any definition of the "political." Politics is commonly associated with power. And he who controls the interpretation of the Word of God sets boundaries between Christian orthodoxy and heresy; he also shapes and sanctifies the ecclesiastical role in relationships between faithful Christians and their triune God. Indeed, the "political" nature of theological hermeneutics becomes self-evident the moment priests, pastors, and professors try to define what they mean by "politics."

When Christian thinkers in the modern West turn their minds to politics, they generally fall somewhere along a spectrum stretching from those most attracted to cosmopolitan humanism to those characterized by a more parochial or patriotic political realism. The humanists, perhaps typified by the German Reformed theologian Jürgen Moltmann, espouse a future-oriented, eschatological vision of politics. Moltmann portrays politics as "the search for forms of human association and for uses of the powers of nature which foster the realization of full human life."[1] This *global* vision of Christian politics stands in stark contrast to the more *national* focus of another famous German political theologian, the Catholic jurist Carl Schmitt. Highly sceptical of liberal humanism, Schmitt believed that the political has to do with the existential conflict between friend and enemy.[2]

The Resurrection as a Problem in Political Hermeneutics

In effect, Moltmann's political "theology of hope" grounds Christian faith in an ontology of peace set in opposition to the ontology of violence he saw in Schmitt's hard-nosed historical realism.[3] Whether such differences over the definition of the political are ontological or merely historical, the tension between cosmopolitan and parochial perspectives is baked into the cake of biblical hermeneutics. Even scholarly disputations over the resurrection of Jesus Christ are filtered through explicitly political interpretations of biblical texts. Political theology cannot be swept under the rug. The stakes are too high.

The survival of Christianity as we know it depends upon its capacity to maintain the faith in the risen Christ set out, *inter alia*, in the Nicene Creed:

> For our sake [Jesus Christ] was crucified under Pontius Pilate; he suffered death and was buried. On the third day he rose again in accordance with the Scriptures; he ascended into heaven and is seated at the right hand of the

---

1 Daniel L. Migliore, "Biblical Eschatology and Political Hermeneutics," (1969) 26(2) *Theology Today* 116, at 118.
2 Carl Schmitt, *The Concept of the Political* tr. George Schwab (New Brunswick, N.J.: Rutgers University Press, 1976), 26.
3 Jürgen Moltmann, *Theology of Hope* (New York: Harper & Row, 1967); Carl Schmitt, *Political Theology: Four Chapters on the Concept of Sovereignty* tr. George Schwab (Cambridge, MA: MIT Press, 1988).

Father. He will come again in glory to judge the living and the dead, and his kingdom will have no end.

Individual believers, no less than various branches of the church universal, have vital interests, spiritual *and* material, in the perceived truth and/or utility of their version of the resurrection story. Theological hermeneutics is, has been, and forever will be in search of the "proper" interpretation of the "paschal mystery" at the heart of the Easter story.

Certainly, it is becoming painfully obvious that the ongoing quest for the "true" meaning of Christ's crucifixion and resurrection cannot be separated from the central political conflict of our time: globalism versus nationalism. Can it be mere coincidence that interpretations of the Easter story portraying the crucified-and-resurrected Messiah as a "global Jesus" are a staple of mainline Protestant preaching? "Global" Christianity teaches that the bodily resurrection of Jesus Christ represents the hope of a still-future resurrection of the dead for the whole of "humanity". Accordingly, most professing Christians would greet the very idea of a "national Jesus" as an oxymoron at best and a heresy at worst. But just as secular nationalism has arisen in opposition to the process of globalization in the temporal realm of politics, a growing number of Christian scholars, across a range of disciplines, now offer a "national Jesus" as a compelling alternative to the globalized interpretation of the resurrection story.

In the emerging story of "national Jesus," neither the historical Jesus nor his apostle Paul offer a vision of the future extending beyond the then-imminent, spiritual restoration of national Israel. Among historians it is not at all controversial to observe that "Jesus' God was the national God of Israel, not some abstract universal deity".[4] Moreover, Jesus made it clear that his impending death "concerned Israel as a nation". He did not want to create a "new religion. He wanted

---

4   Scot McKnight, *A New Vision for Israel: The Teachings of Jesus in National Context* (Grand Rapids, MI: William B. Eerdmans, 1999), 69.

to consummate God's promises to Israel, and he saw this taking place in the land of Israel."[5]

Outside the historical profession, a dissident band of biblical exegetes reject the traditional church doctrine that the crucifixion-and-resurrection represent the fulfillment of Israel's covenantal history.[6] These "preterist" (from the Latin, *præter*, meaning "past") scholars locate both the Easter story and the subsequent *parousia* (a.k.a. the Second Coming) of Jesus Christ in the first century AD. The story of Jesus, they say, is an epic narrative inextricably bound up with the historical destiny of national Israel. If they are right, the covenantal eschatology inscribed in the biblical metanarrative tells us nothing about the future of "humanity."

The resurrection of Jesus Christ was, as the creeds affirm, a shadow or a type of a second, general resurrection. But preterists contend, the resurrection of the dead of which the apostle Paul spoke was a *spiritual* process occurring there and then in the first century; he was not expecting the physical bodies of dead people to climb out of the grave. Jesus did not appear in bodily form to Saul or his companions on the road to Damascus (Acts 9:3–8). His spiritual presence represented "the firstfruits of them that slept" (1 Cor 15:20); namely, the Old Testament saints together with those in Paul's generation who had "fallen asleep" in Christ. The resurrection body of Christ was transfigured into the fulfilled *telos* of national Israel according to the flesh. On this biblical hermeneutic, the vindication of the martyrs, the spiritual restoration of Israel, was consummated with judgement at the Day of the Lord marking the end of the Mosaic Age. In short, the apocalyptic destruction of the temple in Jerusalem in A.D. 70 inaugurated the new heaven and a new earth.[7]

---

5   Ibid., 6.

6   *Cf.*, Brian D. Robinette, *Grammars of Resurrection: A Christian Theology of Presence and Absence* (New York: Crossroad Publishing, 2009), 294.

7   One of the most prolific preterist scholars is Don K. Preston who has published too many books to list here. One useful introduction to his work is: Don K.

Anyone who reads the Easter story faces a hermeneutic choice: global Jesus or national Jesus. Whether or not we recognize the fact, the hermeneutic judgement we render on that issue has political significance. Historical criticism and covenantal eschatology, separately and together, provide growing support for a hermeneutic of resurrection centred on a national Jesus. Thus far, however, those who challenge the hermeneutical hegemony of "global Jesus" have been, for the most part, blind to the implications that a national Jesus carries into the realm of contemporary political theology. On the other hand, the progressive champions of global Jesus have been much less reticent. Indeed, like Moltmann, the "postmodern critical Augustinians" who now carry the torch for the political theology of hope wear their politics proudly on their sleeves.[8]

Global Jesus as Universal Victim

For Brian Robinette, "the language of resurrection is cosmic in scope," extending in time and space far beyond the *Sitz im Leben* of biblical Israel. He upholds the traditional view that the crucifixion-and-resurrection of Jesus was "the precondition for Israel becoming the 'light unto the nations'". During his ministry, Jesus had demanded righteousness and obedience from his followers. He insisted that Israel's hope for restoration was crucially dependent upon repentance and forgiveness of sin. Flying in the face of such warnings, "Jesus' crucifixion stands as the ultimate expression of human sin and guilt." God's response is utterly astonishing: by raising Jesus from the dead, God extends an "offer of forgiveness to Israel." God made Israel a light unto the nations, first, by raising Jesus from the dead, thereby serving "eschatological justice to an innocent victim whilst unmasking the guilt of his accusers and murderers." At the same time, by resurrecting

---

Preston, *We Shall Meet Him in the Air: The Wedding of the King of Kings!* (Ardmore, OK: JaDon Management, 2009).

8 *Cf.*, John Milbank, "'Postmodern Critical Augustinianism': A Short *Summa* in Forty-Two Responses to Unasked Questions," (1991) 7(3) *Modern Theology* 225.

Jesus from the dead, God acquits "those responsible for this death, using their own ignorance and sin as the very means to save them from self-condemnation" by welcoming the return of the risen victim.[9]

Robinette maintains that this acquittal applies to every human person. All of us who have denied hospitality to the Other now have the opportunity "to participate in a new community, the *ecclesia*, founded upon the *welcome* of the victim." Within the redemptive logic of Israel's own story, therefore, God's offer of forgiveness is "universal in its breadth."[10] The death of the "risen victim...manifests the sin of the world in which *all* are implicated."[11] The Easter story is not just about an historical event long ago and far away for which we carry no responsibility. Both justice and mercy are extended to all human persons when God vindicates "an innocent victim from the dead."[12] The human spirit bears collective guilt for an historical crime even though we were not physically present where and when it was committed. The sin, guilt, and forgiveness of which Robinette writes are ontological, not historical, in nature.

In effect, like Augustine of Hippo long before him, Robinette rewrites the metanarrative of biblical Israel as the as-yet-unfinished story of humanity-at-large. He presents the crucifixion-and-resurrection story as an ahistorical, onto-theological drama. It was not just the disciples who were passively complicit in "Jesus' lynching." *All* of us "are entrenched in the dynamics that led to Jesus' death — including you, dear reader." We may not be "literally contemporaneous with the events that led to Jesus' crucifixion in first-century Jerusalem" but "we *are* contemporaneous insofar as the dynamics involved in his crucifixion are operative in our own lives. Had *we* been there, the text is urging, we would have done the same thing."[13] We, too, would have

---

9   Robinette, *Grammars*, 309, 294–295.

10 Ibid., 293–294.

11 Ibid., 309–310 emphasis in original.

12 Ibid., 309.

13 Ibid., 293–294.

violently expelled Jesus from Israel's midst. Sharing in the ontological guilt of the historic perpetrators of deicide, we, too, must pray for forgiveness.

For Robinette, the bodily resurrection of Jesus was both a demonstration of God's power and a "universal offer of forgiveness to humanity." By raising Jesus from the dead, God "overcomes *death* itself. It transforms death's absolute non-presence into God's self-presence to us in the crucified-and-risen One." God triumphs "over those structural powers, including death itself, that led to the brutal death of God's eschatological prophet; thus, the message of Easter draws our attention to God's solidarity with the victims in our history." Two thousand years after the empty tomb was discovered, Robinette believes, the "eschatological counter-gaze of the forgiving victim" still invites us to perceive just how deeply engrained are the processes by which we obtain our "identity, whether individually or in groups, through the expulsion of the Other." Christian reflection on the resurrection "unseals the collective amnesia that has allowed us to suppress the injustice of our violent exclusions, showing once and for all that the effort to build our identities through the denial of hospitality to the human Other — is in fact a rejection of the divine Other."[14]

Whenever and wherever, Christians welcome "the Gift of the risen victim," the heavenly ontology of peace finds its earthly abode. Historically speaking, the ontology of violence gave way incrementally to an ecclesiastical realm of peace on earth. Robinette holds that the second, general resurrection is a real historical process which began in the first century church and continues today. The already-but-not-yet resurrection of the dead has guided us "into a new story whose truth can set us free for full human flourishing."[15]

---

14 Ibid., 296, 309–310, 301.

15 Ibid., 293.

Global Jesus and the Christian Hermeneutics of Mission

Robinette is convinced that the "human person" becomes a "catholic personality" by allowing "the Spirit of the risen Christ to graciously penetrate our self-enclosed patterns of perception and behaviour, and to disarm those many defences that prevent us from allowing the Other to be welcomed as co-constitutive." Openness to the Other promises an "enrichment of the self" as we become "a personal microcosm of the eschatological new creation." In that way, "we anticipate (or 'analogize') the general resurrection of the dead in which God will be all in all." Human personhood is sanctified through a transition from a life "dominated by sinful existence to genuine freedom," a transition which "comes only by welcoming an Other whose *alterity* is not an obstacle to human flourishing but the condition of possibility for it."[16]

On this interpretation, the cross and resurrection are not mere *signs* of forgiveness. Like Robinette, John Milbank believes that "Jesus' death is efficacious...also as a material reality." This is "because it is the *inauguration* of the 'political' practice of forgiveness; forgiveness as a mode of 'government' and social being." Milbank describes this practice as "*itself* ongoing atonement." In other words, if atonement is "to be materially efficacious it *cannot* be 'once —and for all', like the sign or metaphor of atonement," it "must be continuously renewed."[17]

Both Milbank and Robinette turn to political thought and action as a means of making atonement effective in the real world. Robinette suggests that because "sin replicates itself through interpersonal, social, and cultural relations," the central theme of atonement is the idea of a divine victory over the evil powers of the world. He warns us never to "lose sight of the fact that Jesus was crucified by a political power." Of course, Jesus himself had no interest in obtaining political power but

---

16 *Ibid.*, 309, 305.
17 John Milbank, "The Name of Jesus: Incarnation, Atonement, Ecclesiology," (1991) 7(4) *Modern Theology* 311, at 327.

"his ministry was profoundly political insofar as it sought to reorient our social construction of reality." Indeed, Jesus was put to death "as a political criminal because he represented a thoroughgoing challenge to the way we order interpersonal and social relationships, above all the way we order our world through the production of victims." By participating in God's "alternative Kingdom" we aim to embody the risen victim by means of solidarity "with the victims of our world." It means associating "with those who are deemed the outsiders, the contaminants, the monsters, the prisoners, the dispensable, and the unclean according to the dominant purity maps in any given social-cultural setting."[18]

In today's political climate, Robinette's vision of Christian political practice seems indistinguishable from fashionably progressive purity spirals. He is unlikely to face ostracism from academic colleague when he declares that the "ministry of reconciliation is one that puts the Christian in a mode of service to the Other." All right-thinking people—especially white people—are under constant pressure "to become highly sensitized and responsive to those social mechanism that produce victims." Not even the most enthusiastic globalist or leftist proponent of mass Third World immigration would object to Robinette's claim that "[b]y offering hospitality to those who suffer expulsion or want, we offer hospitality to Christ himself (Matt. 25:34-46)."[19] Indeed, Robinette simply follows in the footsteps of Jürgen Moltmann's footsteps when he offers a "political interpretation of biblical eschatology...indebted to the philosophy of revolution of Hegel, Marx, and Ernst Bloch."[20]

Contrary to popular misconceptions, Marx's attitude towards Christianity was not exhausted by his famous dictum that "religion is the opium of the people." Far from being opposed to religion *per*

---

18 Robinette, *Grammars*, 304, 312–313.
19 *Ibid.*, 307.
20 Migliore, "Biblical Eschatology," 122.

se, Marx sought to make "the living protest garbed in religious myth practically effective." Recognizing the power latent in religious mythology and ritual, Marx aimed to bring about "an historical realization of religion...by translating myth into action."[21] The political hermeneutic utilized by both Moltmann and Robinette parallels radical Marxist protests against oppression. Both proclaim "the liberation of the suffering creation out of real affliction."[22] Both believe that the "proper interpretation of the gospel is its historical realization." Robinette shares Moltmann's conviction that Christian hermeneutics is an inescapably political "hermeneutics of mission."[23]

Biblical interpretation thus becomes a way of promoting revolutionary change in historical time in the name of the risen victim. Moltmann, like Robinette, uses the biblical images of the "needy and the outcast, and foremost of the crucifixion and resurrection of Jesus as clues to the purpose and goal of God's activity and his summons to man." The image of global Jesus as universal victim transforms the gospel into "a power which intensifies and universalizes the quest of man for an all-embracing community of justice and freedom." By arousing the hope of "God's coming universal reign," the gospel of the risen victim "provokes men to resist the institutional stabilization of present conditions."[24]

But it is not just institutional life that will be destabilized by this Christian humanist dialectic of atonement. Human beings no longer "have to try to cling to their identity through constant unity with themselves but will empty themselves into non-identity...into what is other and alien."[25] Robinette insists that Christians must set out to undermine "every tendency to build our identities according to 'us'

---

21 *Ibid.*, 122.

22 Moltmann, quoted in *ibid.*, 123.

23 *Ibid.*, 123.

24 *Ibid.*, 128–129.

25 Moltmann, quoted in Robinette, *Grammars*, 309.

and them.'" Atonement requires "a 'catholic' identity that welcomes the Other in hospitality."

Robinette acknowledges that such a political hermeneutic flatly denies the existential distinction between "friend" and "enemy." In fact, the truly radical character of Christian hospitality towards the Other only "comes into focus when we consider that this Other may be our 'enemy.'" We imitate global Jesus most faithfully "when we engage with love those who persecute us."[26]

Here, however, we should be aware that, as a matter of fact, Jesus did not ask his listeners to "love" their persecutors in the Sermon on the Mount; rather, he urged prayers on their behalf. It is even more important to realize what Jesus meant when asked the audience to love their enemies. In the Greek, he refers specifically and only to "private" enemies (*echthros*) not to "public" or "alien" enemies (*polemoi*).[27] Unless one keeps such distinctions in mind Christian hermeneutics of mission can easily degenerate into pathological altruism.[28] The existential distinction between friend and enemy cannot be dissolved by transforming Christianity into a deracinated, cosmopolitan cult of the Other. National Jesus knew better than to mistake historical choice for ontological essence.

Towards a National Jesus

The postmodern Augustinian account of the paschal mystery imparts an onto-theological character to "global Jesus." By contrast, those who recount the story of "national Jesus" portray him as an historical figure firmly grounded in the ethno-religious culture of his own people. The difference between these two hermeneutic strategies is evident when one examines Robinette's account of Pentecost in light of Acts 2:1–14.

---

26 *Ibid.*, 311.

27 *Cf.*, Schmitt, *Concept of the Political*, 28–29.

28 *Cf.*, Barbara Oakley, *et. al.*, *Pathological Altruism* (New York: Oxford University Press, 2012).

Here, too, Robinette presents the "risen victim" as the foundation of a true community of human persons, in place of the false unity sought by those who had treated Jesus as a scapegoat for their own sinful lives. Now that Jesus, the stone rejected by the builders, has become the cornerstone of a new creation, the "speaking of many languages at Pentecost suggests the reversal of Babel," manifesting a new kind of universality. Even though the apostles were all Galileans, when the Holy Spirit came upon them, the multitude present heard them speaking in the language "of every nation under heaven." According to Robinette, the "catholicity expressed here is not the conforming of all languages into one…but a unity-in-difference that welcomes the otherness of the Other as enrichment."[29]

What Robinette neglects to mention (and what is stated explicitly in Acts) is that the multitude was made up mainly of people belonging to the far-flung Jewish diaspora visiting Jerusalem for the harvest feast day. Familiar, of course, with the languages of their foreign domicile, these Jewish visitors were astonished to hear the apostles speak in their adoptive tongues. Clearly, the Pentecost crowd was not a random agglomeration of humanity-at-large come together for no reason. Instead, this post-resurrection Pentecost, the Festival of the Firstfruits, anticipated the crucial role played by the Jewish diaspora as an instrument of divine Providence destined to spread the light of Israel unto the nations. Historians acknowledge that "the Jews of the diaspora… provided the initial basis for church growth during the first and early second centuries." In fact, Jewish Christianity played a central role in the church well into the fourth century AD.[30]

This Jewish role in the spread of Christianity should surprise no-one. Jewish Christians were not adopting a new religion; they were embracing the long-awaited consummation of their national destiny. It was the Gentile Christians in the early church who transformed the

---

29 Robinette, *Grammars*, 308.

30 Rodney Stark, *The Rise of Christianity* (New York: Harper One, 1997), 49.

Jewish "national Jesus" into a "global Jesus." Historian Scot McKnight shows that Jesus' teaching was not directed to humanity at large. His "vision was not an abstract religious feeling but a concrete realistic vision for God's chosen nation, Israel." He proclaimed that the kingdom of God had come near. This kingdom was "none other than what was anticipated and expected by Jews for millennia; it was the fulfillment of prophetic, and at times apocalyptic, visions."[31] The Jewish hope of salvation was national and corporate not individualistic:

> In particular, this hope meant liberation of Israel from its enemies, including Rome. Jesus was a child of his people, and his people were children of their history. To think of the kingdom apart from national deliverance was an impossibility for Jews of Jesus' day and for Jesus himself.[32]

McKnight maintains that "national Jesus" taught his followers to think of themselves in familial terms as the children of God, their Father, *'abbā'*. For Jesus, "God's Fatherhood is not universal; rather, like the Fatherhood of YHWH in the Hebrew Bible, it is confined to the covenantal relationship with Israel." Jesus had no conception of "the universal Fatherhood of God and the brotherhood of humanity." He clearly thought of God's Fatherhood as a relationship reserved for himself and his followers. Not even all those claiming to be the biological seed of Abraham enjoyed this special relationship with the Father. Only those members of the covenant people who renounce idolatry, sinfulness, and unfaithfulness to God are destined to become part of God's eschatological people. Only this righteous remnant of Old Covenant Israel "are to be brothers and sisters in a new family" which calls God *'abbā'* "because he relates to them as a father does to his children."[33]

The children of this family are called to render unwavering obedience to their Father. Jesus repeatedly warns his followers "that those

---

31 McKnight, *New Vision*, 183, 85.

32 Ibid., 37, 86.

33 Ibid., 58–64.

who fail to obey God will be punished, even to the point of torment."
These warnings had deep roots in both the Deuteronomic and priestly
traditions of the Hebrew Bible. McKnight sees Jesus' prediction of the
destruction of Jerusalem as part of that history: "if God's covenant
people faithlessly abandon his covenant ordinances, God will wreak
havoc on the nation."[34] Unlike Robinette, who locates the fulfillment
of Israel's history in the crucifixion-and-resurrection of the universal
victim, McKnight points out that Jesus himself "prophesied the destruction of Jerusalem as the climactic event in Israel's history that
would end the privilege of Israel in God's plan." The cross did not mark
the end of the law; nor did it vindicate the prophets. Jesus emphasized
early in his ministry that neither the law nor the prophets were to be
fulfilled until the old heaven and the old earth passed away (Matt.
5:17–18). Clearly, the law and the Old Covenant temple cult remained
in place until the fall of Jerusalem, the event which brought the Mosaic
Age to a close.

McKnight sees no reason to believe that Jesus saw any further ahead
than A.D. 70 when he expected that Israel's fate "would be wrapped
up in conjunction with that catastrophic event."[35] Jesus appeared "on
the scene convinced that within a generation God would act climactically to judge Israel." McKnight is convinced that even Jesus' "death,
so central to the Christian understanding of salvation was connected
to his preaching of impending judgement with its attendant woes." He
went to the cross knowing "that he had to offer himself consciously
and intentionally to God as a vicarious sacrifice for Israel to avert the
national disaster." McKnight acknowledges that this may have been an
atoning, substitutionary sacrifice. But Jesus died, not to bear the sins
of Jews and Gentiles alike, but to redeem Israel.[36] As G.B. Caird put

---

34 Ibid., 36–37.

35 Ibid., 138–139.

36 Ibid., 112–113.

it, Jesus was "confident that in him the whole Jewish nation was being nailed to the cross, only to come to life again in a better resurrection."[37]

N.T. Wright on Paul's Resurrection Theology: Global or National?

N.T. Wright, the former Anglican bishop of Durham, is an influential scholar-theologian-priest and the author of many gargantuan studies of the historical Jesus and the apostle Paul. He, too, maintains that the meaning of the cross and resurrection is not to be found in theological abstractions but in "certain very specific and concrete aspects of the history of Israel." Such a forthright challenge to the conventional wisdom has provoked much interest and some consternation. In Alister McGrath's summary of Wright's argument, the "pattern of cross and resurrection, reflecting that of exile and restoration, has determinative significance for Israel rather than a universal significance for all humanity."[38]

In other words, Wright agrees that, linked as it was with the idea of the covenant, the death of Jesus had a "corporate significance" for Israel, rather than an "individual significance" for either sinners or victims in other times and places. The crucified-and-resurrected Jesus should be understood, therefore, "as a redemptive representative of Israel, bearing her specific curse and making it possible for her as a people to achieve her intended national destiny."[39] In *Jesus and the Victory of God*, Wright thus aligns himself with historical critics who have found a "national Jesus" hidden beneath deeply-encrusted

---

37 Caird, quoted in *ibid.*, 113.

38 Alister E. McGrath, "Reality, Symbol, and History: *Theological Reflections on N.T. Wright's Portrayal of Jesus*," in Carey C. Newman, ed., *Jesus and the Restoration of Israel: A Critical Assessment of N.T. Wright's* Jesus and the Victory of God (Downers Grove, IL: InterVarsity Press, 1999), 176.

39 *Ibid.*, 176–177.

ecclesiastical creeds and Tradition.[40] In his more recent, studies on Paul, however, the "global Jesus" literally rises from the grave of "national Jesus."

Wright presents the apostle Paul as a proto-Augustinian, Judaeo-Christian "theologian". On Wright's reading, Paul's "freshly-inaugurated eschatology" projects the second, general resurrection of the dead far beyond the fall of Jerusalem and into our own twenty-first century future.[41] In doing so, Wright credits Paul with the invention of a Christian theology in which "global Jesus" reigns over the whole of humanity. According to Wright, "Paul's expectation of 'the day of the Lord' included the expectation that on the last day, that which was already true would at last be revealed: Jesus is lord, and Caesar is not." On Wright's interpretation of Paul's vision of final eschatology, then, "the creator and covenant God will, at the last, put the whole world to rights."[42]

Wright presents Paul's allegedly rock-solid faith in the *bodily* resurrection of Jesus Christ as the foundation for his eschatological vision of the resurrected bodies of all those who have fallen asleep in Christ. Wright's emphasis upon the physical resurrection of Jesus presupposes that "national Jesus" was a genuinely historical, human person, deeply rooted in the covenantal history of national Israel according to the flesh. The death of "national Jesus," the man, entailed his descent into nothingness. Jesus' resurrection, thanks to his reading of Paul, brings Bishop Wright back within the bounds of credal orthodoxy. As Robinette puts it, the post-Easter narrative shows the creativity of God "in a significantly new light. Creation from nothing is logically coherent with (and in Christian theology historically dependent upon) a view of God who raises to life what has succumbed to the *nihil* of

---

40 N.T.Wright, *Jesus and the Victory of God: Christian Origins and the Question of God*, vol. 2 (Minneapolis: Fortress Press, 1996).

41 N.T. Wright, *Paul and the Faithfulness of God* (Minneapolis: Fortress Press, 2013), 408.

42 *Ibid.*, xvi, 26–31, 1085.

death."[43] Wright and Robinette continue to espouse the Augustinian doctrine that *creatio ex nihilo* underwrites the credal promise of the physical resurrection of the body. Just as the earthly city was created out of nothing, so, too, Augustine expected that at the end of the world Christian believers would rise from the dead, in a newly embodied form, to enter the heavenly city of God.

The resurrection was an unprecedented physical event that set aside the laws of nature. Wright's historical investigation of the crucifixion-and-resurrection aims to explain how Christians came to believe in the reality of such an event. He concludes that early Christians themselves offer the most convincing *historical explanation* for an empty tomb "previously housing a thoroughly dead Jesus" and subsequent reports "that his followers saw and met someone they were convinced was this same Jesus, bodily alive though in a new transformed fashion." He says simply "that something happened, two or three days after Jesus' death, for which the accounts in the four gospels are the least inadequate expression we have". Beyond that point, "the historian alone cannot help."[44]

It was the apostle Paul who went beyond history to provide a *theological* account of a resurrection-event so unexpected that not even the teachings of "national Jesus" had prepared his followers to understand, the world-historical, indeed cosmic, significance of the empty tomb. Wright finds in 1 Corinthians 15 one compelling example of just how Paul transfigures "national Jesus" into "global Jesus." For Wright, "there can be no doubt that Paul intends this entire chapter to be an exposition of the renewal of creation, and the renewal of humankind as its focal point." Paul's resurrection theology presupposes both a God, not only capable of creating the world out of nothing, but a just God determined to defeat the power of death. But if death is to be defeated, then

---

43 Brian D. Robinette, "The Difference Nothing Makes: *Creatio Ex Nihilo*, Resurrection, and Divine Gratuity," (2011) 72 *Theological Studies* 525, at 527.

44 N.T. Wright, "Jesus' Resurrection & Christian Origins," (2008) 16(1) *Stimulus* 41, at 49.

"[a]nything other than some kind of bodily resurrection, therefore, is simply unthinkable."[45]

Wright flatly rejects the suggestion that Paul was concerned with any sort of "non-bodily survival of death." Paul had no need, Wright argues, to argue for the immortality of the soul: many people in Corinth "believed in that anyway." After all, even two thousand years later, no such resurrection has occurred; history has not witnessed millions of Christian believers rising from their graves. Naturally enough, therefore, many in Corinth found it hard to swallow the idea of a physical resurrection of the dead: "everybody knew dead people didn't and couldn't come back to bodily life." Chapter 15, Wright argues, was intended to answer that challenge. According to Wright, Paul's argument ran "as follows: what the creator god did for Jesus is both the *model* and the *means* of what he will do for all Jesus' people." Throughout the chapter, Jesus' resurrection serves as "the prototype and model for the future resurrection."[46] When Paul describes the body into which Christians hope to be resurrected, "the unique, prototypical image-bearing body of Jesus" is identified as "the model for the *new bodies* that Jesus' people will have."[47] Even those presently alive on the last day, when the kingdom finally arrives, Paul promised, "will not lose their bodies, but have them changed from their present state to the one required for God's future."[48]

Paul, according to Wright, portrays the *parousia* of "global Jesus" as the moment when "all those who belong to him are themselves raised bodily from the dead." Wright describes the result as "the establishment of a final, stable 'order' in which the creator and covenant God is over the Messiah, and the Messiah is over the world." In the new creation, humans are destined to play "an intermediate role between

---

45 N.T.Wright, *The Resurrection of the Son of God: Christian Origins and the Question of God* vol. 3 (Minneapolis: Fortress Press, 2003), 313–314.

46 Ibid., 316.

47 Ibid., 54 (emphasis added), 348.

48 Ibid., 357.

creator and creation." The "human task and the messianic task thus dovetail together: the Messiah, the true Human One, will rule the world in obedience to God."[49]

The following questions suggest themselves: If Paul's resurrection theology did indeed take this universalist form, could he have expected the *parousia* to arrive anytime soon? Would he have been likely to identify it with the fall of Jerusalem in the lifetime of his followers? Wright's response is clear. He long ago dismissed the idea of an imment *parousia* as an "old scholarly warhorse" that "can be put out to grass once and for all."[50] So too, Wright rejects "the suggestion that Paul was hoping to bring about…some kind of large-scale last-minute conversion of Jews, and perhaps even the *parousia* itself… Paul did not think the *parousia* would necessarily happen at once, and he certainly was not trying to provoke or hasten it by his missionary work."[51] In Wright's interpretation, Paul's cosmopolitan theology and over-the-horizon perspective were firmly fixed on the transfiguration of the entire cosmos; Paul was definitely not a present-minded apostle of "national Jesus" warning of the apocalyptic judgement soon to fall upon Old Covenant Israel according to the flesh.

Nonetheless, the vision of "global Jesus" attributed to Paul by Wright is a far cry from the mindset of "national Jesus" as he hung upon the cross in *Jesus and the Victory of God*. Jesus and Paul do not seem to be on the same page. Wright is annoyed by those for whom such divergence is cause for concern. He regards it "as illegitimate in principle, and very difficult in practice, to conduct historical Jesus research" as if Paul and Jesus both saw the world in the same light. He asserts that "[p]recisely because the resurrection made such a huge difference to everything" Paul simply must have viewed the world differently from the way that "national Jesus" had viewed it prior to the

---

49 Ibid., 336.

50 N.T. Wright, *The New Testament and the People of God: Christian Origins and the Question of God* (Minneapolis: Fortress Press, 1992), 462.

51 Wright, *Paul*, 1497.

Easter event.[52] This is a plausible position: but is Wright's interpretation of 1 Corinthian 15 really about history at all?

Arguably, Wright's forty-page exegesis of chapter 15 is more a defence of credal orthodoxy than an analysis of the historical context of a biblical text written in first-century Corinth (about which we learn next to nothing). In Wright's interpretation, Paul is portrayed as a Hellenized, Judaeo-Christian preacher-theologian laying the doctrinal foundations for medieval high Christology. Wright describes Paul's message as simplicity itself: *Jesus is lord*. The point of Paul's theology, therefore, "was to name the Messiah, to announce him as lord, in the culture-forming places, the cities to and from which all local or international roads ran."[53]

Anyone looking more deeply into the situation facing Paul in Corinth as he wrote chapter 15 may well doubt whether Paul had enlisted in the service of Wright's "Human One." Just as plausibly, Paul was working to vindicate the Old Testament saints of national Israel. It is just possible that the resurrected Messiah, "the firstfruits of those who have fallen asleep" (1 Cor. 15:20), remained a "national Jesus," still determined to rescue his people from the death-like grip of sin. Perhaps, a more truthful and useful understanding of Paul's account of the resurrection of the dead can be achieved by treating him as a deeply patriotic historical actor actively engaged in the political art of scriptural hermeneutics.

The Resurrection of the Dead in Covenantal Eschatology

The covenantal eschatology of national Israel offers a much more persuasive hermeneutical framework within which to interpret Paul's understanding of the resurrection body. Samuel G. Dawson, an

---

52 N.T. Wright, "In Grateful Dialogue: A Response," in Newman, *Jesus & the Restoration of Israel*, 267.

53 Wright, *Paul*, 1503.

American preterist scholar, has written at even greater length than Bishop Wright (no mean feat!) on 1 Corinthians 15. In doing so, he portrays a "national Paul" very different from the "global Paul" one meets in Wright's work (or in mainstream theology generally). This should not come as a surprise. Paul publicly declared that he "was saying none other things than those which the prophets and Moses did say should come" (Acts 26:22). Dawson points out that "Paul's concept of the resurrection wasn't that fleshly (or even transfigured) bodies would come out of holes in the ground at all, because that's not what Moses and the prophets taught." He taught, instead, "the resurrection of Old Covenant Israel from the death of its fellowship with God."[54]

The problem Paul faced with his "brethren" in Corinth was not that some doubted the resurrection of Christ or that others denied the resurrection of anyone. Rather, some doubted the resurrection of the Old Covenant saints. Paul's concept of the resurrection "depicted the ongoing translation of the body of death headed by Adam (which would, of course, contain Old Covenant Israel) to the body of life headed by Christ." It follows that "[i]f Israel, the rest of the firstfruits, was not being raised when Paul wrote these words, then Christ wasn't raised, for his own resurrection was the first of the firstfruits." As Paul was writing to the Corinthians, those who denied that the Old Testament saints were being raised were, in effect, denying the resurrection of Christ. In other words, Paul taught that "the faithful Old Covenant Jews were going to be the rest of the firstfruits, and the dead in Christ were going to be the rest of the fruit at the harvest." Gentile Christians in Corinth were generating dissension by saying that "Israel's last days had come and gone, because God was through with them since the cross." Paul replied, according to Dawson, that "God's promises to Israel were irrevocable, so that the salvation of Gentile Christians was

---

54 Samuel G. Dawson, *Essays on Eschatology: An Introductory Overview of the Study of Last Things* (Amarillo, TX: SGD Press, 2009), 105, 109.

linked to theirs at the coming of the Lord (which the Corinthians were eagerly awaiting, 1:7)."[55]

Dawson contends that when Paul turns to the nature of the resurrection body, he raises the question as to how the dead ones *are being raised* (*n.b.*, not how *are* the dead raised) and with what manner of body *are they coming* (*n.b.*, not *do they come*). Now, if some Corinthian Christians expected "a resurrection of biological bodies to certain dead persons," such questions would not arise. Dawson attributes a spiritual concept of the resurrection to Paul breaking sharply with Wright's insistence on the transfigured but still bodily nature of the resurrection. Dawson breaks even more dramatically with Wright when he points out that Paul never speaks of resurrected "bodies." Instead, Paul refers only to "the resurrection of one body, the Old Covenant faithful who were being transformed into the body of Christ." Dawson observes that the "prophets [*e.g.* Ezekiel, Daniel, Hosea, and Isaiah] from which Paul preached had foretold the resurrection of a single body." The hermeneutic problem here, Dawson concludes, "comes down to whether the resurrection Paul spoke of was of *one body* in his *present time* or of *billions of bodies* more than *two thousand years* in the future."[56]

A fair-minded person who compares Wright's exegesis of 1 Corinthians 15 with that offered by Dawson could conclude, at the very least, that the strength of the case for "global Paul" has been seriously compromised. Dawson reinforces the strength of that proposition by his discussion of how the politics of hermeneutics manifests itself in the translation of 1 Corinthians 15. His seemingly arcane argument as to the importance of the present passive verb tense in chapter 15 gives rise to the suspicion that translators committed to "global Paul" have (perhaps unconsciously) put a thumb on the hermeneutic scale.[57] It is beyond my linguistic competence to adjudicate on this matter but, if

---

55   Ibid., 144–146.
56   Ibid., 177–178, 184.
57   Ibid., 136.

Dawson is correct, generations of English-speaking bible readers have been nudged ever so subtly to believe in a "global Jesus" as well as a "global Paul" presiding benignly over the church universal until the time of the end. Translation bias is a form of hermeneutical — and thus political and cultural — warfare.

Dawson points out that:

> The *present active* tense shows how the subject of the sentence is acting. An entirely different concept, the *present passive* tense shows how the subject of the sentence is *being acted upon*. Yet [in most translations of 1 Corinthians 15] this present passive tense is often ignored, or completely changed to a future![58]

Although the present passive is used "relatively rarely, it's a precise verb form. Paul meant to use it instead of a future, yet in many cases, Paul's intention has not been honoured. He spoke of the subject (the dead ones) receiving the action (rising) at his present time, not at some future time at least two thousand years later." For example, the New King James Version of the bible renders 1 Corinthians 15:16 as" "For if the dead do not rise, then Christ is not risen." Dawson would translate this passage as: "For if the dead are not [lit., *being*] raised, neither hath Christ been raised."[59]

Translation bias is but one hurdle that a hermeneutic grounded in covenantal eschatology faces. A stubborn adherence to the ecclesiastical traditions that underwrite the futurist eschatology to which mainstream Christianity adheres is another. Such powerful commitments to tradition pose a threat to ecclesiastical integrity in many other ways as well. Preterist scholars have been driven to the fringes of the ecclesiastical and academic world. Don K. Preston, to name but one prominent preterist, has been attacked as a heretic and shunned by

---

58   *Ibid.*, 135.
59   *Ibid.*, 136, 145.

the mainline Protestant churches in his hometown.[60] Theological colleges and seminaries simply ignore covenant eschatology in their bible studies classes despite the obvious sincerity and skill with which the massive contributions made by preterist scholars to biblical exegesis have been undertaken.

Indeed, the poisoned relationship between preterism and mainstream theological scholarship represents a case study in the erosion of theological integrity plaguing contemporary Christianity. Even Rowan Williams, the Archbishop of Canterbury (as he then was), acknowledges that when theology "resists debate and transmutation, claiming that it may prescribe exactly what the learning of its skills lead to, it is open to the suspicion that its workings are no longer answerable to what they what they claim to answer to...and thus integrity disappears."[61] This is a political problem eating away at the heart of theological hermeneutics. Unfortunately, those who have done so much to re-discover "national Jesus" and "national Paul" have failed to mount an effective political challenge to the institutional defenders of "global Jesus" and "global Paul."

Such a challenge would have to consider the possibility that the incarnation, crucifixion, and resurrection of Jesus Christ were inextricably bound up with the *national* history of Old Covenant Israel. Israel became a holy nation precisely because it served as the corporate womb giving birth in history to a divinely inspired Messiah. If Jesus really died as the representative of national Israel, it perhaps follows that some nations are more open than others to what Orthodox Christians call the process of theosis or deification.[62] According to Athanasius (296–373 A.D.), global Jesus became Man so that we might be made

---

60 See, *e.g.*, Sam Frost, "Taking on Don K. Preston's Jesus,": https://vigil.blog/2017/02/22/taking-on-don-k-prestons-jesus.

61 Rowan Williams, *On Christian Theology* (Oxford: Blackwell, 2000), 5.

62 See, *e.g.*, Veli-Matti Kärkkäinen, *One with God: Salvation as Deification and Justification* (Collegeville, MI: Liturgical Press, 2004).

God.⁶³ Or, in light of covenant eschatology, Jesus Christ became incarnate in-and-through the nation of Israel, so that at least some other nation(s) might be made in the image of God. And so, our salvation, too, could become corporate, national and *spiritual* rather than personal, individual, and *biological*—much like the resurrection of "the whole house of Israel" envisioned for the valley of the dry bones in Ezekiel 37:1–14.

Conclusion

One might imagine that having restored "national Jesus" to historical memory, scholars such as Scot McKnight could help contemporary Christians reconceive the political hermeneutics of resurrection. As it happens, however, few historical revisionists display much faith in the spiritual vitality of mainstream Christianity. McKnight, for example, denies that his own findings are of any use to the church—even if they are true.⁶⁴ The traditional ecclesiology of global Christianity rests upon the eschatological hopes and ecumenical dreams of a long-dead civilization. Awaiting their long-delayed Day of the Lord, Christian churches have no interest in a philosophy of religious history grounded in the rise and fall of nations in a world without end. This observation holds true even among Christian biblical scholars who reject futurist eschatology. Samuel Dawson, for example, rests content in the hope that when he dies his reward "will be blessedness or happiness, and rest, in the presence of Christ!" Even preterists, it seems, cannot do without the vision of a "global Jesus" as our universal, heavenly overlord.⁶⁵ Sadly, those whose only hope lies in death rather than in the

---

63 Saint Athanasius, *On the Incarnation* (Yonkers, N.Y.: St. Vladimir's Seminary Press, 2011), 167.

64 Scot McKnight, "Why the Authentic Jesus is of No Use for the Church," in Chris Keith, et. al., *Jesus, Criteria, and the Demise of Authenticity* (London: T&T Clark, 2012), 173–185.

65 Dawson, *Essays*, 455.

historical opportunity to prepare the way for our own "national Jesus" have resigned themselves to national suicide.

Perhaps it is time to take the advice of the nineteenth century English historian, J.R. Seeley, who urged the Church of England to give its parishioners a break from endless sermons on the remote and obscure history of ancient Israel. Suggesting "that every nation's true Bible is its history," Seeley urged the church to draw moral lessons and spiritual insight from England's own storied past.[66] Already, one hundred and fifty years ago, he recognized that the imperial Augustinian vision of the church universal had reached its use-by date. Nowadays, the notion that Christendom ever did or could in times yet to come unite the whole of humanity under the reign of "global Jesus" has lost all credibility. Another great reformation may be necessary if the post-Christian West is to reverse the nation-destroying forces of secular, increasingly satanic, globalism. Traditionalist Catholic E. Michael Jones justly observes that "*ethnos* needs *logos*."[67] But it is no less true that "logos needs *ethnos*."

Is it already too late to reconstitute churches throughout the Anglosphere and the wider Western world as the religious foundation for a federation of autonomous, European-descended ethno-nations? This need not mean a complete break with the "global Jesus" historically associated with the rise of European Christendom. Building upon their Christian past, the peoples of the Anglosphere should continue to venerate the Bible and national Israel's historical Messiah. Both can serve as sources of spiritual and political wisdom, providing a warrant for the distinct, ethnoreligious identity of every European people, as well as a warning of the dreadful fate awaiting nations that stray from the path of righteousness. Should the Anglican church, at home and in the old white dominions, ever heed Seeley's call "to draw largely upon

---

66 J.R. Seeley, "The Church as a Teacher of Morality," in Rev. W.L. Clay, ed. *Essays in Church Policy* (London: Macmillan, 1868), 278, 267. Available online at: https://babel.hathitrust.org/cgi/pt?id=hvd.ah4gyv&view=1up&seq=263.

67 E. Michael Jones, "Ethnos Needs Logos," (2015) 34(7) *Culture Wars* 12.

English [and Australian, Canadian, and New Zealand] history and biography for illustrations of their moral teaching," God might well be prepared to gift us our own Patriot King![68] Under such a dispensation, a restored Angelcynn church could begin to hope and pray for the resurrection of our own dead ones.

---

68 Seeley, "Church," 278. See, Henry St. John, Viscount Bolingbroke (1678–1751), "The Idea of a Patriot King," in David Armitage (ed.) *Bolingbroke: Political Writings* (Cambridge: Cambridge University Press, 1997).

PART TWO

Did Anglo-Saxon Christendom Replicate the "Project of Peoplehood" Posited by the Hebrew Bible?

5. Adam and Eve in Torah: The Lost World of Covenantal Ethnotheology

Introduction

ADAM AND EVE live in the popular imagination nurtured by childhood bible stories as the first fully human beings, created *ex nihilo* by God. Having disobeyed an express commandment from God, they were driven out of their lush and lavish Garden into a world of thorns and thistles to become our biological progenitors. Most modern biblical scholars read Genesis 2–3 quite differently, as an ancient Near Eastern myth rather than as paleo-anthropology. For them, Adam and Eve function within a literary text as bloodless archetypes.

Despite their differences, literalists and literary critics alike abstract Adam and Eve from their place in the particularistic ethno-theology of ancient, national Israel. Both camps view Adam and Eve, whether biologically or mythically, literally or figuratively, as ancestors or representatives of Everyman and Everywoman. But surely ancient Israelites writing and reading Torah conceived Adam and Eve, together, as a mythic metaphor for carnal Israel according to the flesh. Only in the retrospective view of Christian humanism can Adam and Eve function as generic human beings. Augustine pulled that hermeneutic rabbit out of the hat but only by identifying the covenantal history of Israel, figuratively and literally, with both the material origins and the salvation history of the human race. Given their traditionalist, indeed, patriarchal and tribal *Sitz im Leben*, it seems doubtful that the Hebrew authors and readers of Torah held up Adam and Eve as ideal typical proxies for men and women in all times and places. Still less would they receive Genesis 2–3 as an invitation to take sides in an eternal war between the sexes. How things have changed!

Genesis 2–3: The Biblical Foundation of Patriarchy?

The text of Genesis 2–3 has been attributed to "Yahwist" sources in ancient Israel dating from around the time of Solomon (*ca.* 1000 BC).[1] Whoever they were, the Yahwists were not historians or paleoanthropologists. Walter Vogels represents a broad scholarly consensus when he declares that the narrative in Genesis 2–3 "is not a historical report… but myth." Those two chapters "attempt to express in symbolical story form a transcendental truth reality or truth grasped intuitively."[2] In his own reading of the myth, Vogels believes that the transcendental truths revealed by the story of what happened between Adam and Eve in the Garden of Eden reveal the primal realities driving the perennial power struggle between men and women generally in all times and places.

Vogels contends that what "kills the relationship" between man and woman "is the desire to possess, to keep, to hold, to dominate, or to crush the other."[3] Just such a power struggle has erupted within the modern theological academy where feminists wage war on patriarchal

---

[1] Ann E. Gardner, "Genesis 2:4b-3: A Mythological Paradigm of Sexual Equality or of the Religious History of Pre-Exilic Israel?" (1990) 43 *Scottish Journal of Theology* 1, at 17. The "documentary hypothesis" in modern biblical criticism has rested upon distinctions between, *inter alia*, Yahwist and Priestly sources for the Old Testament text. But more recently scholars have found it "increasingly difficult to agree that an ancient Yahwist source ever existed". See, Jean-Louis Ska, *Introduction to Reading the Pentateuch* (Winona Lake, IN: Eisenbrauns, 2006), 142. I use the distinction here mainly to show that Genesis I and Genesis 2–3 can be harmonized even if they derive from different sources.

[2] Walter Vogels, "The Power Struggle between Man and Woman," (1996) 77(2) *Biblica* 197, at 198.

[3] *Ibid.*, 209.

traditions of biblical interpretation. Certainly, scholarly discourse on the subject of Adam and Eve, in particular, has been shaped by a brand of sexual politics in which feminists claim the moral high ground. Woe betides an aspiring academic who dares to place a positive prescriptive spin on the rule of husbands over wives traditionally seen as a consequence of the Fall.

Almost fifty years ago, Kate Millett put feminism into the business of biblical criticism when she declared that the myth of Eve the temptress was "designed...expressly in order to blame all this world's discomforts on the female."[4] Millett's hermeneutic of suspicion became highly influential but not all feminist theologians agreed to bin the Bible. In fact, some challenged Millett's casual acceptance of the myth that Eve tempted Adam to commit the first sin. Phyllis Trible and Jean Higgins, for example, emphasize the mutual and equal responsibility of Adam and Eve for the original sin alienating "humankind" from God.[5] Both writers, however, carefully concede the bedrock feminist presupposition that oppressive patriarchal institutions have been propped up for millennia by those presenting Eve as an archetype of (*inter alia*) feminine guile and Adam of (*inter* alia) masculine stolidity.

Male and Female Archetypes: Ontological or Covenantal?

Feminist theologians and other scholars who treat Adam and Eve as universalistic archetypes tend to draw bright-line boundaries between history and myth. Most biblical critics appear to be secular or Christian humanists who embrace the ecumenical belief that all human beings, male and female, are made in the image of God. The primary

---

4   Kate Millett, *Sexual Politics* (Garden City, N.Y.: Doubleday, 1970), 51–54.
5   Phyllis Trible, "Depatriarchalizing in Biblical Interpretation," (1973) 41(1) *Journal of the American Academy of Religion* 30; and Jean M Higgins, "The Myth of Eve: The Temptress," (1976) 44(4) *Journal of the American Academy of Religion* 639.

scriptural authority for that proposition is found in Genesis 1:27, but few now believe in the literal truth of the story that God created male and female on the sixth day of creation. Most biblical critics contend that the creation story in Genesis 1:26–27 expresses a transcendent and universal truth in mythical form. It was never intended to be an objective report on human origins on the model of natural history or physical science. According to John H. Walton, whether real persons called Adam and Eve once lived somewhere in the ancient Near East is largely irrelevant to biblical criticism; their function in the biblical text is purely archetypal.[6]

As archetypes, the couple in the Garden of Eden convey an image of God which "pertains not only to each individual but, perhaps more importantly, to the corporate species — to the human race".[7] Walton is convinced that Adam and Eve "describe and represent all of humanity throughout time, as do the roles given them (subdue, rule, etc.)." Because Adam represents "Everyman" and Eve "Everywoman" the relationship between them is neither biological nor historical; it is not even emotional. Rather, Adam and Eve represent the primordial ties between husband and wife as "the essential bond built into our nature." In a word, the biblical archetype of male and female is *ontological* in character.[8]

Note that Genesis 1:27 is commonly attributed to a "priestly" source writing centuries after the composition of the Yahwist creation and paradise stories in Genesis 2–3. An obvious problem for biblical criticism: How can two different creation stories from two different authors situated in radically different circumstances be harmonized? The conventional solution posits the latter tale as a more detailed view of

---

6   John H. Walton, *The Lost World of Adam and Eve: Genesis 2–3 and the Human Origins Debate* (Downers Grove, IL: IVP Academic, 2015), 92–95.

7   Ibid., 42.

8   John H. Walton, "A Historical Adam: Archetypal Creation View," in Matthew Barrett and Ardel B. Caneday, *Four Views on the Historical Adam* (Grand Rapids, MI: Zondervan, 2013), 90, 104.

the events on the sixth day in Genesis 1. Walton prefers to read Genesis 2–3 not as the coeval backstory to Genesis 1:26–27 but its sequel. It may be, he says, that Adam and Eve lived long after God created "man" in his own image. But that matters not. Either way, Adam was made in the image of God.[9]

Walton's states emphatically that Genesis 1 deals with neither the temporal creation of physical planet earth nor the material origins of the human race. Rather, in timelessly mythological terms that chapter describes the way in which God transforms a chaotic cosmos devoid of value, meaning, and purpose into an ordered system within which all beings have a function to perform. In effect, God works to create a cosmic temple within which he and his minions can rest in peace.[10]

As Walton reads the Genesis 2 sequel to the six days of creation, Adam is cast in the archetypally priestly role of tending to the Garden, the holy place at the heart of the cosmic temple. The Garden in Genesis, he writes, must not be imagined as a physical green space somewhere in ancient Mesopotamia. Rather, the image of the Garden denotes an archetypal sacred space; the inner sanctum of the cosmic temple, made sacred by the presence of God when "he rested from all his work" on the seventh day (Gen 2:2).[11] Having placed Adam and Eve together in the Garden temple on the sixth day of creation, Walton's account then resumes the conventional narrative of the Fall. Despite having been made in the image of God, Adam and Eve sin against him. By introducing disharmony and disorder into the holiest of holy places, Adam and Eve defy the divinely ordained purpose of creation: to produce order out of chaos.

Walton's schema is an elegantly constructed, humanist ontology of creation. He makes a sharp distinction between the functional role and the material origins of the beings created by God. But the creation

---

9 Walton, *Adam and Eve*, 63–69.
10 John H. Walton, *The Lost World of Genesis One: Ancient Cosmology and the Origins Debate* (Downers Grove, IL: IVP Academic, 2009), 23–37.
11 Walton *Adam and Eve*, 104–127.

myths in Genesis 1–3 themselves have both a functional role and material origins in the covenantal ethno-theology of ancient Israel. In that context, there is no good reason to think of the Adam and Eve story as the sequel to the six days of creation. Indeed, there is no good reason to confine either Genesis 1 or 2–3 exclusively within the genre of myth. Perhaps Genesis 1 was not just myth but also prophecy.

In other words, perhaps the priestly writers of Genesis 1 were not just looking backwards to the six days of creation as an accomplished reality but also forward to the future completion of the cosmic temple in ages to come. If so, the priestly story in Genesis 1 can best be harmonized with the Yahwist Garden narrative by situating Adam and Eve in the beginning of Genesis 1 on the first, rather than the sixth day of creation. After all, why must we accept Walton's presupposition that Adam was either the "man" made in the "image" of God in Genesis 1:27 or one of his descendants? On the other hand, if we place Adam earlier in the Genesis 1 narrative, who were the male and female created on the sixth day? Augustine provides one compelling answer: Christ and his bride the Church.[12]

Covenantal Creation

Augustine's exegesis of Genesis 1–3 fuses the Adam and Eve myth with world history and the messianic hopes of national Israel. The brief narrative in Genesis 1, he says, encapsulates the entire history of ancient Israel as recounted in both the Old and New Testaments. Believing that biblical history had yet to run its full course and that the last days were yet to come, Augustine could not get Genesis off his mind. He spent a lifetime attempting to reconcile his figurative and literal interpretations of Genesis 1–3.

From the beginning of that project, he insisted that the "whole text must first be discussed in terms of history, and then in terms

---

12   Saint Augustine, *On Genesis* eds Edmund Hill, O.P. and John E Rotelle, O.S.A. (Hyde Park, N.Y.: New City Press, 2002), 64–66.

of prophecy. In terms of history deeds and events are being related, in terms of prophecy future events are being foretold."[13] In treating Genesis 1 as a prophetic allegory, Augustine recognizes the mythic character of the narrative. However, he does not treat Adam and Eve as archetypes of man and woman *as such*. Rather, he recognizes in them the body and soul of Old Covenant Israel. Accordingly, the prophetic priestly image of God at rest in the Garden on the seventh day is a covenantal eschatology, the mythic image of the age to come in which the promise of creation will be fulfilled.

Genesis 2:1–3 performs the same role in the priestly creation story as the Book of Revelation does in the Bible as a whole. The difference is that Revelation was written in the first century AD to assure its readers that the promises of the law and the prophets were soon to be redeemed, that the cosmic temple was on the verge of completion.[14] Like the cosmic temple imagined by the priestly authors of Genesis 1, the New Jerusalem was not to be a temple made with hands (Rev 22:2; Act 17:24). But the Johannine apocalypse was embedded in history as well as myth; its prophecy of the end days was fulfilled in real time. As promised by Jesus (Luke 21:6; Matt 24:2), the inauguration of the new heaven and new earth was accomplished by the actual physical destruction in AD 70 of the temple made by hands in Old Jerusalem. The providential execution of that divine judgement ushered in the morning of the seventh day when God finally "rested from all the work of creating he had done" (Gen 2:3).

For Augustine, the six days of creation represented the six ages of world history which culminate in the advent, death, and resurrection of Jesus Christ. He did not, however, believe that the seventh and last day had arrived. Indeed, he hoped to goodness that the Day of Judgement

---

13 *Ibid.*, 72.
14 For a detailed presentation of this preterist argument see, Don K Preston, *Who is This Babylon?* (Ardmore, OK: JaDon, 2011).

"does not overtake us, provided that it hasn't already begun".[15] He feared that the fourth century world had too little faith to justify the Parousia of the Son of Man. Like most modern Christians, Augustine read Genesis 2:2 as prophecy not history. That futurist interpretation has not gone unchallenged. A minority school in biblical criticism known as covenant eschatology or preterism seeks to demonstrate that the seventh day came with the destruction of the temple in Jerusalem in AD 70.[16]

This hermeneutic framework treats Adam and Eve as covenantal rather than ontological archetypes. Covenant eschatology recognizes the importance of Walton's work on ancient cosmology but denies that Adam and Eve came into being *after* the presumptive completion of the cosmic temple in Genesis 1. In other words, Genesis 2–3 was not a sequel to Genesis 1. Instead, as in Augustine's schema, Genesis 1 is better understood as a symbolic synopsis or, in critical jargon, a proleptic summary of the Bible from Genesis to Revelation.

Augustine inserted the Adam and Eve story into the morning of the first day in Genesis 1. In Augustine's prophetic allegory, the first day corresponded to the first age of world history, from Adam until the evening came with Noah and the flood.[17] With Adam and Eve the human race began to enjoy the light of grace. It was then that God said, "'Let there be light,' and there was light" (Gen 1:3). Adam and Eve

---

15 Augustine, *On Genesis*, 66. A good online discussion of Augustine's reading of Genesis 1 as a prophetic allegory and biblical meta-narrative is, Norman Voss, "Six Days of Creation,": http://deathisdefeated.ning.com/forum/topics/the-covenant-creation-2.

16 This body of biblical criticism has been developed for the most part outside the theological academy. A useful introduction to the genre can be found in Timothy P Martin & Jeffrey L Vaughn, *Beyond Creation Science: New Covenant Creation from Genesis to Revelation* (Whitehall, MT: Apocalyptic Press, 2007).

17 Augustine, *On Genesis*, 62–67. The second age was from Noah to Abraham, the third went from Abraham to David, the fourth from David to the Babylonian exile, and the fifth from the exile until the advent of Jesus Christ which marked the morning of the sixth age.

chose to become the first light-bearers. But before they could see the light, both their eyes had to be opened. In choosing, jointly and severally, to open their eyes to the light, Adam and Eve consummated their formal *covenantal* union as husband and wife in Genesis 2:23.

Augustine compares the relationship between Adam and Eve to the relationship between Christ and his bride, the Church. Adam joined in the eating of the fruit offered by Eve without demur because he had already, in effect, "chosen to leave his father and mother and be united with his wife" in "one flesh." Christ, too, left his father and came into the world to be united with the Church. To achieve that union, it was necessary for Christ to leave his mother as well, "that is the Synagogue and her old literal observance of the law." Just as Eve was fashioned from the rib taken from his side while he slept, so too the Church came into being with the blood and water flowing from the crucified Christ, his side pierced by the spear of a Roman soldier (John 19:34).[18] In both cases, the relation between the two parties was covenantal, not ontological or biological. Adam's pledge to the woman that she was to be "flesh of my flesh and bone of my bone" was a covenantal formula concerning "fidelity to vows, constancy in purpose [and] acceptance of responsibility." In other words, to understand the nature of the relationship between Adam and Eve and the function they play in Genesis 1–3, it is necessary to "return to the covenantal categories in which Israel viewed her world and lived her life."[19]

Conclusion

Some movement in that direction has occurred among biblical scholars. Anne Gardner, for example, contends that feminist efforts to force Adam and Eve into the universalistic archetypal forms of either patriarchy or sexual equality are misguided. She suggests that "Genesis 3 can

---

18 Ibid., 96–97.
19 Walter Brueggemann, "Of the Same Flesh and Bone," (1970) 32 *Catholic Biblical Quarterly* 532, at 542.

be viewed as a mythological interpretation of Israelite religious history from the time of the settlement." In other words, the original Yahwist model for the myth of Eve the temptress did not reflect a universalistic humanist or functional ontology. Instead, the myth had its material origins and found its functional role within the particularistic concerns of Old Covenant Israel at a moment in its history when powerful women were upsetting the harmonious functioning the regime. In 1 Kings 11:4, for example, it is said "that in his old age Solomon's wives 'turned away his heart after other gods,'" thereby sowing the seeds of discord and instability.[20]

Gardner does not explore the relationship between priestly and Yahwist creation stories. Nor does she discuss the covenantal nature of the relationship between Adam and Eve. She also accepts the conventional narrative of the Fall. Sam Dragga rejects the conventional view that Genesis 2–3 is "a tragic narrative of human failure and disgrace." While his argument is couched in humanist language, it is consistent with a covenantal, ethnotheological interpretation of the bond between Adam and Eve. His effort to spin Genesis 2–3 as "a story of liberation" also fits comfortably into the prophetic allegory that Augustine teased out of Genesis 1.[21]

Briefly, he "pictures the man and the woman developing as human beings, from timid dependence to aggressive irresponsibility to courageous maturity. When her eyes were opened to the light by eating the fruit, the woman chooses fertility and the man joined the woman, "together forfeiting personal immortality, blessed and cursed with the ability of creativity, proud of their choice, and given their liberty by a sympathetic creator." God acknowledged that the couple had chosen freedom and "sent forth" (*i.e.* not "drove out" [NEB] or "banished"

---

20   Gardner, "Mythological Paradigm of Sexual Equality," 15.
21   Sam Dragga. "Genesis 2–3: A Story of Liberation," (1992) 55 *Journal for the Study of the Old Testament* 3.

[NAB]) the man to carry his small beacon of light into the dark world outside the Garden.[22]

In what is called Paradise, Adam and Eve lived like caged rats in a scientific experiment: they were provided in perpetuity with "an abundance of food and places to live and with predation and disease reduced or eliminated." Under such circumstances, rats initially show a high rate of population growth. As numbers plateau, various social pathologies appear causing them to die out.[23] Had Adam and Eve not seen the light they would have lived the life of well-fed rats in perpetuity. The good news was that, unlike rats they would never know death (even the sin death of alienation from God); the bad news was that, like caged rats, they would never procreate. Dragga's story of liberation works best if we imagine Adam and Eve in the Garden on the first day of creation. It was then that they chose to forsake the enervating comforts of life in an eternal nanny state for the burdens of freedom.

But the freedom at issue was not individual but corporate and covenantal. Woman was to bear the pain of childbirth while her husband would rule over her. He in turn would have to endure painful toil, earning his daily bread by the sweat of his brow. Augustine acknowledged that such pain and difficulties appear to be curses. But he writes, they are commandments designed to bring forth good habits, making the soul of the light-bearers "submit to the reason as to its husband."[24] In leaving "the cage of their creator,"[25] Adam and Eve did not function as archetypes representing the ordinary run of humanity. Nor are they

---

22　*Ibid.*, 11–12.

23　John B. Calhoun, "Population Density and Social Pathology." National Institute of Mental Health. https://www.ncbi.nlm.nih.gov/pmc/articles/PMC1501789/pdf/califmedoo143-0080.pdf These introductory paragraphs are part of a longer article published in *Scientific American* in February 1962. H/T Tory Scot, "Nationalism, Natalism, and the Curse of Affluence," John B. Calhoun, "Population Density and Social Pathology" http://therightstuff.biz/2016/03/15/nationalism-natalism-and-the-curse-of-affluence.

24　Augustine, *On Genesis*, 91.

25　Dragga, "Story of Liberation," 12.

our common ancestors. Rather, they were characters in the foundation myth of carnal Israel according to the flesh. The myth helped national Israel to break the mould in which other benighted peoples of the ancient Near East had been baked from time out of mind.

It seems that the priestly authors of Genesis 1 saw in the Yahwist Garden narrative the mythic cornerstone for a cosmic temple within which the seven ages of Israel's salvation history were destined to unfold. In their vision, Israel came into being, like Adam, inside the inner sanctum of a temple not made with hands. Also, like Adam, Israel would become a light unto the world. Bearing the divine light into the profane world outside the sacred space of the Garden, Adam and Eve set the unique and highly ethnocentric covenantal history of Israel into motion.

6. Exodus 34: Covenantal Ethnotheology and the (Re-) Birth of the First Holy Nation

Introduction

IN 1773, near the high-water mark of the Enlightenment in Germany, Johann Wolfgang von Goethe (1749–1832) was moved to despair by the blatant ethnocentrism on display in Exodus 34. Then a young, cosmopolitan law student, Goethe challenged the canonical understanding of Exodus 34:11–26. Conventional wisdom, then and now, presents the covenant cut between Moses and the Lord in that passage as the reaffirmation of the Ten Commandments first proclaimed by the Lord in Exodus 20:1–17. "Despite the text's own claims," Goethe convinced himself that Exodus 34:11–26 reveals not a *renewed* Decalogue but rather "the original covenant that God made with the Jews." He believed that the law proclaimed in Exodus 34 was so focused on "the *Stamm* [tribe], with its so very *particular* ritual law," that it could not be a simple restatement of the universalistic "ethical Decalogue" set out in Exodus 20. Goethe pictured an unbridgeable gulf between the punitively particularistic religious rituals of ancient Israel and the free-thinking, universalistic ethos of liberal Protestantism in enlightened Germany. He simply could not reconcile the crabbed casuistry and ritualistic cruelty endemic to the religion practiced by ancient Israelites in the Sinai wilderness with the pious Protestant narrative of covenant renewal. Goethe's ecumenical brand of Christian theology conceived the Ten Commandments (*das erste Stück unsers Katechismus!*) as the template for the apodictic rationality of the modernist *Rechtstaat*.[1]

The Meaning of Exodus 34: Original Sources or Canonical Narrative?

As an exemplar of the *Aufklärung*, Goethe took it upon himself to de-authorize the received understanding of Exodus 34. He almost succeeded. Goethe's callow essay served as the seminal expression of the far more professional, and systematically sceptical, source-critical school of modern biblical criticism, founded in the late nineteenth century by Julius Wellhausen (1844–1918). According to Wellhausen's Documentary Hypothesis, Exodus 34:11–26 was the Yahwist (J-source) counterpart to a quite different Eloist (E-source) Decalogue in Exodus 20.[2] On this account, then, Exodus tells two different Decalogue stories rather than a single continuous narrative.

Taken in isolation, Exodus 34 begins as the Lord directs Moses to chisel out two stone tablets. But the Lord specifies (34:1) that the tablets were to be like those that Moses broke, a reference to Moses' outraged reaction when he saw his people worshipping a golden calf, an idol cast, moreover, by his own brother (Exodus 32:19). On its face, therefore, this chapter appears to be about the replacement of an earlier covenant inscribed upon the original, now broken, tablets. The short story told in Exodus 34 almost begs to be set within the wider narrative context of the Sinai pericope within which its deeper theological meaning can be discerned. But even then, the source critic replies, the story does not make sense.

The Lord ordered Moses to craft the replacement tablets so that he could "write on them the words that were on the first tablets" (34:1).

---

1 Bernard M. Levinson, "Goethe's Analysis of Exodus 34 and Its Influence on Wellhausen: The *Pfropfung* of the Documentary Hypothesis," (2002) 114(2) *Zeitschrift für die altestamentliche Wissenschaft* 212, at 215–217.
2 Ibid., 214.

Just as Goethe long ago recognized, the critical problem posed by this chapter therefore "turns on the issue of the relation of the Decalogue in Exodus 20 with the laws of chapter 34". "If," as Brevard S. Childs puts it, "chapter 34 was simply a rewriting of the original laws upon fresh tablets, one would expect to find an exact repetition, which does not seem to be the case." In 34:11-26 the Lord issues a series of highly ethnocentric, ritualistic—even war-mongering—commandments. These decrees from on high have more in common with the cultic laws set out in the Book of the Covenant (Ex. 20:19-23:33) than with the ethical Decalogue of Exodus 20:1-17. The conclusion seems inescapable: the laws relating to worship in Exodus 34 are not those "those written on the first tablets which Moses broke."[3] But Exodus 34:28 compounds the confusion still further: following his encounter with the Lord, Moses is said to have written "on the tablets the words of the covenant—the Ten Commandments."

Unfortunately, the resolutely agnostic methodology of source criticism thoroughly obscures the ethnotheological significance of the Sinai narrative. It fails to recognize the complicated process of covenant formation, rescission, and renewal described in Exodus 32-34 for what it is: namely, a case-study in the ethnotheology of proto-Christian nationhood. The story deals with a practical problem: How *can* Yahweh, Moses and the apostate people of Israel work in tandem to create a holy nation? The narrative in Exodus 32-34 deals with the tense relationships between rebellion, divine presence, and covenant arising out of the providential history of ancient Israel. Goethe and Wellhausen pursued a single-minded search for the *historical* origins of the story thereby displacing its *theological* meaning.

The ethnotheological significance of the ritual Decalogue emerges only with the recognition "that a real basic unity inheres in the narrative [of Ex. 32-34] if it is approached by way of its canonical presentation." Even as a matter of source criticism, Dale Ralph Davis suggests,

---

3   Brevard S. Childs, *Exodus: A Commentary* (London: SCM Press, 1974), 605.

this "basic unity...is more likely to stem from one original hand than from a number of contributors plus the final redactor." Davis concedes that there may be a place for source analysis, but he believes that such "analysis has a tendency to begin too soon" and, as a consequence, is not prepared "really to 'hear' the text."[4]

Moses and the Practical Work of Ethnotheology in Exodus 34

Whatever its documentary sources, the entire Sinai narrative in Exodus 19–40 tells a coherent story about the divine role in the ethnogenesis of ancient Israel — a particularistic people destined by the Lord to play a decisive role in salvation history. The crisis provoked by the golden calf incident and its resolution in the encounter between Moses and the Lord on the top of Mount Sinai brings the wider narrative to its climax. Moses knew that his people needed the Lord. The question was whether the Lord needed them. Indeed, at first the Lord threatens to destroy the Israelites and in their place make Moses "into [the progenitor of] a great nation" (Exodus 32:10).

Exodus 32–34 shows clearly that the motley crew camped at the foot of the mountain needed inspired leadership if it were to fulfil its divinely appointed mission. It was through the medium of Mosaic authority that Israel too underwent an experience that Orthodox Christians might describe as "ethnotheosis," a concept that recalls "Irenaeus' famous comment about deification: God became human that we might become divine."[5] Theosis is the process through which individuals or groups come to participate in the power of the Lord.

---

4 Dale Ralph Davis, "Rebellion, Presence, and Covenant: A Study in Exodus 32–34," (1982) 44 *Westminster Theological Journal* 71, at 71. A good example of a source-critical exegesis of Exodus 34 that seems deaf to the text can be found in William Johnstone, *Exodus 20–40* (Macon, GA: Smyth & Helwys, 2014), 397–433.

5 Veli-Matti Kärkkäinen, *One with God: Salvation as Deification and Justification* (Collegeville, MN: Liturgical Press, 2004), 4.

In Exodus 32–34 we see God, via the channel of grace embodied in Mosaic authority, entering Israel according to the flesh. National Israel is thereby empowered to serve as the spiritual womb of the living God; the one to come in an as-yet far-distant future.

Unlike the public theophany in Exodus 20, in Exodus 34 "the people are nowhere in view. Yahweh appears to Moses alone." It is during this "private theophany" that Moses intercedes with the Lord on behalf of his people.[6] Passing in front of Moses on Mount Sinai, the Lord declares that he is a merciful and compassionate God. The Lord also describes himself, *inter alia*, as "slow to anger" and "abounding in love." Nevertheless, the Lord makes clear his determination not to leave the guilty unpunished, even if that means condemning "their children for the sin of the fathers to the third and fourth generation." In response, Moses falls to the ground, depending upon whatever favour he might have found in the eyes of the Lord to win forgiveness for the wickedness and sins of his "stiff-necked people" (34:5–9). Not for the first time Moses begs the Lord to "go with us" on Israel's journey up to the Promised Land.

During an earlier encounter in the Tent of Meeting, Moses had expressed fear that without the Presence of the Lord there would be nothing to "distinguish me and your people from all the other people on the face of the earth" (33:16). Then on Mount Sinai, in recognition of the trust and friendship he shares with Moses, the Lord relents. He announces his willingness to renew the covenant with Moses and his people (34:10). The narrative context of the renewed covenant looks backward to the story of the golden calf in Exodus 32 and forward, after forty days and nights on the mountaintop, to Moses' descent as the bearer of a divine light to his people (Exodus 34:29–35).

Many modern biblical critics have been as blind as Goethe to the light that shone forth from the laws and covenants proclaimed by Moses to his people in the Sinai wilderness. In fact, Old Covenant

---

6   R.W.L. Moberly, *At the Mountain of God: Story and Theology in Exodus 32–34* (Sheffield: JSOT Press, 1983), 84.

Israel according to the flesh was conceived as an embryonic expression of a proto-Christian ethnotheology. Its laws and covenant were but a shadow, type, or pattern of the new covenant in which all nations are free to seek and perhaps find their own particular and distinctive form of communion with the triune God.

Steeped as he was in the salvation history of Old Covenant Israel, the Apostle Paul understood well the providential significance of the Sinai narrative. In fact, Paul set out the foundation principle of Christian ethnotheology in Acts 17:26-27, saying that God "made every nation of men...so that men would seek him and perhaps reach out for him and find him." In Exodus 34 we see Moses not just reaching out to the Lord but also working to deflect his anger. Moses reminds the Lord that the people of Israel are his inheritance (34:9). Having himself entered the Presence of the Lord, Moses participates in the power of God by winning him over to renewed support for their common mission, the creation of a holy nation. It is through the authority embodied in Moses that the law and covenant finally come to be housed in the tabernacle of the Lord (Ex. 35-40).

The Presence of the Lord: Ethnic Chauvinism or Inner Light?

The ethnocentric character of Exodus 34 is plain to see. Few would deny that ancient Israelites possessed a distinctive "racial" and "ethnic" identity which fused biology and culture into a unique bioculture.[7] The secular mind-set easily subsumes ancient Israelite religion within the concept of culture. Modernists are less receptive to the notion that theology was a fully independent variable in the constitution of ancient Israel's national identity. Because religion tends to be perceived by modernists in functionalist terms as a dependent variable, secular

---

7   On the genetic and cultural segregation of Jews and Gentiles in the ancient world, see Kevin MacDonald, *A People That Shall Dwell Alone: Judaism as a Group Evolutionary Strategy* (Westport, CN: Praeger, 1994), 57–74.

scholars such as evolutionary psychologist Kevin MacDonald typically echo Goethe's strictures on the primitive, particularistic, and narrowly ethnocentric character of ancient Israelite religion, generally, as well as Exodus 34.

In the first volume of his ground-breaking trilogy on Judaism as a group evolutionary strategy, MacDonald took special note of Exodus 34:12–16. Like Goethe, MacDonald is struck by the nature of the Israelite God as depicted in that passage. The Lord appears to function as "a mark of separateness and is closely linked with an abhorrence of exogamy and with aggression against foreigners." MacDonald interprets the monotheism of ancient Israelite religion in functional terms. Having but one God amidst a polyglot mass of polytheistic peoples reinforced the ethnic chauvinism inherent in the highly successful group evolutionary strategy pursued by the Israelites.[8]

MacDonald believes that the Israelites had "only one purpose for God — to represent the idea of kinship, ingroup membership, and separateness from other." The "major function for Israelite theology was not to interpret the workings of nature or to bring good fortune in various endeavours but rather to represent the kinship group through historical time — clearly a unitary concept." Like Goethe, MacDonald recognizes that in Exodus 34 "Israelite theology is intimately bound up with Israelite history."[9] Unfortunately, both writers also treat the spiritual dimension of Israelite theology as a vehicle for the advancement of ethnic group interests. They are conspicuously uninterested in the heroic role played by Moses in the cultic reconstitution of the first holy nation.

It is only after repeated intercession by Moses that the Lord renews the covenant in 34:10. Moses knows that his people need the Lord. But the Lord must be persuaded that he needs them. This is the story told in Exodus 32–34. Throughout, the appeal made by Moses to the

---

8   *Ibid.*, 44.

9   *Ibid.*, 45.

Lord "focuses on the presence of God *for the people* as the crucial distinctive quality that defines the people." Without the Presence of the Lord, "there is no people."[10] Moreover, without Moses there can be no covenant. The connection between the Lord and the Israelites must be mediated by Moses. The covenantal religion of the ancient Israelites required not just a monotheistic God but his loyal servant, Moses.

> Even when standing 'face-to-face' with the Lord, 'as a man speaks to his friend,' (33:11) Moses defended his people with the same courage and vigour necessary to defeat a foreign enemy. Such a 'heroic figure instructs the faithful by his stature'. The 'heroic identification' of Moses 'with his people' made it possible for the nation as a whole to participate in the power of God.[11] As the initial term of the covenant, the Lord promises Moses that '[b]efore all your people I will do wonders never before done in any nation in all the world' (34:10). In return, the people of Israel recognize and obey Moses as the shining face of God within their midst.[12]

The Shining and Veiled Faces of Moses

Moberly remarks that the final scene in Exodus 34:29–35 "brings the narrative to the quiet close that is characteristic of a good story."[13] Dozeman, on the other hand, contends that "[t]he shining skin and veil are more than a conclusion to covenant renewal; they are also intended to influence the subsequent portrayal of Moses."[14] In other words, the pericope sets the stage for what would otherwise be the anti-climactic construction of the Tabernacle in Exodus 35–40. There the cultic constitution of ancient Israelite religion proceeds according

---

10 George W. Coats, "'The King's Loyal Opposition: Obedience and Authority in Exodus 32–34," in *idem* and Burke O. Long, *Canon and Authority: Essays in Old Testament Religion and Theology* (Philadelphia, PA: Fortress Press, 1977), 102.
11 Ibid., 106–107.
12 Thomas P. Dozeman, "Masking Moses and Mosaic Authority in Torah," (2000) 119(1) *Journal of Biblical Literature* 21, at 42.
13 Moberly, *Mountain of God*, 106.
14 Dozeman, "Masking Moses," 30.

to the covenantal blueprint received by Moses on the top of Mount Sinai. Hence, in the conclusion to Exodus 34, "Moses came down from Mount Sinai with the two tablets of the Testimony in his hands," unaware "that his face was radiant because he had spoken with the LORD" (34:29). Aaron and the leaders of the community, however, were afraid to approach him. They calm down when they recognize Moses' voice. After Moses delivers the commandments and finishes speaking, he puts a veil over his face. The veil remains in place for the rest of Moses' life whenever he is not speaking to the Lord or delivering his message to the people (34:33–35).

The significance of Moses' radiant face is contested. Indeed, some scholars dispute whether the original Hebrew text is best translated as "shining" or "horned." Seth Sanders splits the difference, pointing out that given "an ancient understanding of light as material...Moses' face could, quite literally, *radiate* horns, and the need to translate the term as *either* divine radiance *or* physical protuberance is merely a side-effect of our conceptual categories, irrelevant to ancient Israelite ideas." The important message, however, is the image of "a transformed Moses who is no longer precisely human."[15]

Other scholars demur from Sanders' suggestion that Moses shining face indicates that he had taken on divine status. Thomas Dozeman more temperately remarks that "Moses is not divinized...But he is most certainly idealized."[16] But, if one accepts George Coats' account of Moses' "participation in the power of God," something like a process of theosis must have taken place both during the encounter between Moses and the Lord on Mount Sinai and then between Moses and the people following his descent.[17]

The significance of the veil worn by Moses when he was not mediating directly between the Lord and the Israelites is also a bone of

---

15 Seth L. Sanders, "Old Light on Moses' Shining Face," (2002) 52(3) *Vetus Testamentum* 400, at 405.

16 Dozeman, "Masking Moses," 27.

17 Coats, "King's Loyal Opposition," 109.

contention among biblical critics. Some maintain that "the function of the veil is a very simple one: it is worn as a response to the Israelites' fear in 34:30 and used by Moses to conceal his face when not operating as a mediator." When the people see Moses' shining face, they know that the word of the Lord is being spoken to them. Accordingly, "Moses dons the veil only when he is not communicating Yhwh's word, that is only when he is acting as a regular, individual Israelite, unoccupied with the role of mediator."[18]

But another interpretation of the veil is possible, one related to the "ritual" character of the Decalogue in Exodus 34. William Propp observes that "the veiled, shining Moses may be regarded as a walking Tabernacle, manifesting and yet concealing Yahweh's splendour."[19] According to Dozeman, Exodus 34:29–35 is a story about two masks, not one — namely, Moses' shining skin and his veil, and...the relationship between these masks creates the paradigm of Mosaic authority in Torah." The radiant face becomes a mask which gives substance and form to the outside power which has transfigured Moses. The veil, by contrast, "cloaks the shining skin of Moses already invaded by an outside power. The veil, therefore, does not represent deity but is a covering."[20]

Many commentators have drawn an analogy between the veil worn by Moses and the veil of the tabernacle and later in the first and second temples in Jerusalem.[21] And it does seem likely that Moses wore the veil to conceal the fading nature of the glory in his own face, thereby "allowing for the construction of the Tabernacle." Dozeman argues

---

18 Joshua Matthew Philpot, "The Shining Face of Moses: The Interpretation of Exodus 34:29–35 and Its Use in the Old and New Testaments" (Doctoral Dissertation: Southern Baptist Theological Seminary, 2013), 94–95.

19 William H.C. Propp, *Exodus 19–40: The Anchor Bible* (New York: Doubleday, 2006), 621.

20 Dozeman, "Masking Moses," 23, 27–28.

21 Philpot, "Shining Face," 93–94, cites several such commentators while disapproving their opinion.

that "Moses' shining skin fades in Priestly tradition because the goal is for God to dwell in the Tabernacle cult and not in the person of Moses." In Exodus 35–40 the "transfer of divine glory from person to cult becomes a necessary stage in authenticating Moses as the founder of the cult, indicating the success of his mission."[22]

The urgency of Moses' mission was prompted by the golden calf incident. The people's request for a new god exposed "the danger of covenant without cult." No "established cultic setting" was in existence when the "ethical Decalogue" was proclaimed during the public theophany of Exodus 20:1–17.[23] Not long afterward, the prolonged absence from Israel of Moses produced a social and religious crisis. However high the "ethical Decalogue" stood in Goethe's estimation, he was wrong to believe that the original covenant laws could survive unaltered in the wake of the golden calf fiasco. On his return, Moses recognized immediately that Israel had dishonoured its covenantal obligations.

The covenant, therefore, had to be renewed in Exodus 34. But while the continuing validity of the earlier covenant was taken for granted, the new dispensation set out "*to select and emphasize those particular aspects which are relevant to the sinful tendencies which Israel has displayed.*" Yahweh renews the covenant "by demanding obedience in the area where Israel has already failed [polytheism and idolatry] and where it will be under continual temptation in the promised land to sin again [exogamy and apostasy]."[24] Moses' mission reaches its successful conclusion only with the creation of a secure cultic foundation for ancient Israelite religion.

---

22 Dozeman, "Masking Moses," 44.

23 Ibid., 33.

24 Moberly, *Mountain of God*, 95–96 (emphasis in original).

Conclusion

An ethnotheological exegesis of Exodus 34 in its canonical narrative context highlights a crucial early episode in the evolution of covenant and law in ancient Israel. Only with the advent of Jesus the Christ does the ministry of the Spirit come to fruition. Old Covenant Israel was not yet ready either to generate or to gaze upon the unveiled radiance of the triune God. Indeed, for all its glory "the ministry that brought death, which was engraved in letters on stone," dullened the minds of the ancient Israelites. Even in Paul's day, a veil still covered the hearts of the Jews when Moses was read in temple and synagogue. "It has not been removed, because only in Christ is it taken away" (2 Cor. 3:7–14).

Strangely, even Kevin MacDonald fails to grasp fully what the ripping of the veil meant either for ancient Israelite religion or for Judaism as a group evolutionary strategy. The role played by Old Covenant Israel in salvation history ended with the destruction of the Temple in Jerusalem in AD 70. The bioculture associated with the Judean Temple cult became extinct, ceasing to play any further role in the historical evolution of religion. Rabbinic or Talmudic Judaism emerged as another, altogether novel, religion. The group evolutionary strategy pursued by those who called themselves Jews after AD 70 must be distinguished from the providential role played by ancient Israelite religion.

Like Goethe, MacDonald conflates Judaism and the religion of ancient Israel. In the words of one Jewish scholar, both are "conceptualized as sterile, particularistic, and lacking in world-historical significance…The ethical, which is to say, the universal, cannot logically be Jewish." Given an evolutionary and historical perspective, this position is untenable. Neither MacDonald nor Goethe has any way to account for the historical "origins of the ethical Decalogue to which the original ritual Decalogue allegedly yielded its rightful, rite-full, place."[25] In fact, neither writer so much as raises the issue.

---

25 Levinson, "Goethe's Analysis of Exodus 34," 217–218.

MacDonald does make a powerful case for the proposition that Judaism in Christian societies has been guided by remarkably particularistic, highly ethnocentric ethos. So, too, no doubt, was the religion of the ancient Israelites; in the end, however, they suffered the wrathful judgement promised by the Song of Moses (Deut. 32:1–43). But, at the very least, ancient Israel left behind an inspired narrative of its providential history from Genesis to Revelation. The ethnotheological lessons that can be drawn from both the biblical meta-narrative and the mini-narrative of Exodus 32–34 serve as both warrant and warning to all peoples compelled to confront the most pressing problem in practical theology: How do *we* become and remain Christian nations? Is it even possible to be a nation if the Presence of the Lord no longer goes with *us*?

7. Making *Angelcynns*: How Alfred the Great Responded to the Viking Invasions of Wessex

Introduction

THE *Anglo-Saxon Chronicles* reported that in the year 793 the people of Northumbria were "wretchedly terrified" by "fierce, foreboding omens" including "excessive whirlwinds, lightning storms, and fiery dragons...flying in the sky." Such ominous signs preceded not just a famine, but the "brutal robbery and slaughter" committed by a band of pagan Vikings upon a monastery on the island of Lindisfarne. The sacking of Lindisfarne inaugurated a tumultuous and terrifying century of piracy and plunder with large areas of England subjected to occupation under Scandinavian kings. Decade after decade, with almost seasonal regularity, Viking marauders pounced at will, pillaging their choice of prime targets along a practically defenceless English coastline.[1] Eventually, however, a legendary Anglo-Saxon warrior-king repelled the heathen hordes and, in so doing, created a new people, the newly christened *Anglecynn* (meaning "kin of the Angles").

Alfred (849–899), the fifth and youngest son of pious King Æthelwulf, succeeded to the West Saxon throne in 871. His response to the ever-present Viking menace can be captured in one pithy observation: he successfully practiced the virtues of Christian kingship. In so doing, Alfred transformed the petty, squabbling and thoroughly

---

1 A. Savage ed., *The Anglo-Saxon Chronicles* (London: Guild Publishing, 1983) 75.

demoralized Anglo-Saxon kingdoms then dividing England into the most successful prototype of a holy nation to be found in medieval Christendom. A proper appreciation of that achievement — to understand why he, uniquely among English monarchs, is styled Alfred the Great — requires the suspension of the easy modern assumption that ideas such as "Christian kingship" and a "holy nation" long ago reached their use-by date.

Sacral Kingship in Anglo-Saxon England

For Alfred and his contemporaries, it was axiomatic that God "was intimately involved, even on the smallest scale, in the fate of individuals and nations on a daily basis…If this was a world into which pagan Vikings could suddenly burst forth, then it must be with God's knowledge," just as the suffering the pagans had caused throughout the various Anglo-Saxon kingdoms "must have occurred with his blessing." In other words, "the Vikings themselves were not the problem but merely the symptom of the problem."[2] Alfred, to be sure, did not minimize the military problem posed by the pagan invasions; he spent decades fighting off Viking attacks, not infrequently in hand-to-hand, personal combat. But the warrior-king never lost sight of the real problem: the spiritual void in the hearts of his people. Having turned away from God, Anglo-Saxon England became a veritable moral vacuum into which a satanic scourge rushed like rats towards decaying flesh. Late in life, having established a comparatively peaceable kingdom, he advised his subjects to "[r]emember what punishments befell us in this world when we ourselves did not cherish learning nor transmit it to other men. We were Christians in name alone, and very few of us possessed Christian virtues."[3] Having "set his mind to the true cause of the pagan

---

2   Justin Pollard, *Alfred the Great: The Man Who Made England* (London: John Murray, 2006), 233, 231.

3   S. Keynes and M. Lapidge, trans., "From the Translation of Gregory's *Pastoral Care*" in *Alfred the Great: Asser's Life of Alfred and the Contemporary Sources* (Harmondsworth: Penguin, 1983), 125.

plague," Alfred "then gave all his strength to righting those wrongs."[4] Alfred's exemplary, indeed heroic reign embodied the perfected Christian *telos* of an ancestral, Germanic cult of sacral kingship, the foundational myth of Anglo-Saxon peoplehood.

Such myths were the symbolic glue that maintained social order and cohesion in a tribal society. In pagan times, the Anglo-Saxon warrior-king was the intermediary between his people and the gods. Faith, family, and folk were fused together in the sacred body of a king. Kings belonged to a royal lineage claiming descent from a common divine ancestor. Indeed, the Anglo-Saxon word *cyning* for king originally meant "son of the *cyn* or family." Accordingly, a warrior-king combined religious and political functions in a seamless unity. Descended from the gods, a pagan king was *heilerfüllt* (literally, "filled with the sacred") and so represented "the charismatic embodiment of the 'luck' of the folk."[5] Such a fusion of religious and political authority in the Anglo-Saxon kings facilitated the conversion of their peoples to Christianity. Without royal support, conversion (or in Alfred's case, Christian regeneration) did not and could not occur. Portraying Christ as the noble Son of God made it easy for Anglo-Saxons to understand his authority in terms analogous to Anglo-Saxon kingship.[6] Even the crucifixion of Christ could be assimilated to pagan legends of ritual king-slaying, "portraying a young hero who ascends the tree of the cross to enter into combat with death and, while succumbing, prevails in the end"[7]

---

4 Benjamin Merkle, *The White Horse King: The Life of Alfred the Great* (Nashville, TN: Thomas Nelson, 2009), 207.

5 William A. Chaney, *The Cult of Kingship in Anglo-Saxon England: The Transition from Paganism to Christianity* (Berkeley: University of California Press, 1970), 14–21, 7, 34, 12.

6 Ibid., 167, 46, 19.

7 James C. Russell, *The Germanization of Early Medieval Christianity* (New York: Oxford University Press, 1994), 170. The portrayal of Christ as a Germanic warrior-king found epic expression in *Heliand*, the Old Saxon gospel written only ten to twenty years before Alfred's birth. See, G. Ronald Murphy, S.J., *The*

Like the sacrificial priest-king of ancient Germanic tribes, the Christian tribal king possessed a sacred character. God and king were fused together in Alfred's biblically suspect claim that Christ had "ordered that everyone should love his lord [*hlaford*] as He Himself did."⁸ Alfred clearly understood that the spiritual fate and political destiny of his people depended upon the influence, ability, and military strength of their king. He saw in the biblical history of Israel confirmation that only kings could "serve as effective war-leaders in maintaining and extending the position of their own people against the encroachments of surrounding tribes with their own hostile and aggressive kings."⁹ Such a king was necessarily both warrior and priest.

Well into the nineteenth century, a popular writer such as Thomas Hughes portrayed Alfred the Great as the heroic exemplar of Christianity understood as a fighting faith, someone who recognized that Christ calls his people "as clearly in the drum beating to battle, as in the bell calling to prayer."¹⁰ In Alfred's kingdom of Wessex, even priests and bishops fought the Vikings alongside the men of their parishes and diocese. Indeed, the good bishop of Sherborne, Bishop Heahmund, died at Alfred's side during a bloody clash with Viking forces. Alfred's last remaining brother, King Æthelred, was wounded in the same battle and died soon aft.erwards. Consequently, Alfred received the crown of Wessex.¹¹

Saxon Savior: The Germanic Transformation of the Gospel in the Ninth-Century Heliand (New York: Oxford University Press, 1989), and *Idem.*, *The Heliand: The Saxon Gospel. A Translation and Commentary* (New York: Oxford University Press, 1992).

8   Chaney, *Cult of Kingship*, 185, 195.
9   Judith McClure, "Bede's Old Testament Kings" in Patrick Wormald ed., *Ideal and Reality in Frankish and Anglo-Saxon Society* (Oxford: Basil Blackwell, 1983), 87.
10 Thomas Hughes, M.P., *Alfred the Great* (London: R. Clay & Sons, 1869), 70.
11 Merkle, *White Horse King*, 68–71.

Alfred became a great king because he activated the virtues of all his subjects: those who prayed, those who fought, and those who worked. By embodying, in his own person, the virtues belonging to each of those three estates, Alfred served as a charismatic channel of grace through which Providence worked to create another holy nation, "a new Chosen People," known in the vernacular propagated by Alfred, his court and his church as the *Angelcynn*.[12]

In each of his roles, as a warrior, as a priest, and as a ruler able to connect with ordinary working people, Alfred set out "to shape the English imagination." After winning the Viking wars and uniting several Anglo-Saxon kingdoms, he commissioned the *Anglo-Saxon Chronicles* to persuade the *Angelcynn* that, while they might "have had multiple early histories," they "will have one future." Sarah Foot documents how Alfred taught his subjects that "despite the differences in each [Anglo-Saxon] kingdom's past history, they all share certain common features and ultimately theirs is a collective history." In effect, Alfred "invented" an English ethno-nation by "implanting into the minds of his people a personal and cultural feeling of belonging to the *Angelcynn*, the English kind."[13] The common identity created by Alfred

---

12   Sarah Foot, "The Making of *Angelcynn*: English Identity Before the Norman Conquest," (1996) 6 *Transactions of the Royal Historical Society* 25, at 32. George Molyneaux contends the Patrick Wormald, Judith McClure, and other scholars misinterpret Alfred. It is wrong, according to Molyeaux, to put the words "new Chosen People" in Alfred's mouth. In the king's writings, he says, "the English are...treated as but one of numerous gentile nations: nothing is said to imply that their position in relation to God or Israel was different from that" of any other people converted to Christianity. Perhaps Alfred was merely modest, too humble to recognize just how path-breaking — even unique — the *Angelcynn* experience was to be perceived in the eyes of posterity (before it vanished down the memory hole in the self-understanding of contemporary Anglicanism)? See, George Molyneaux, "Did the English Really Think They Were God's Elect in the Anglo-Saxon Period?" (2014) 65(4) *Journal of Ecclesiastical History* 721, at 735. *Cf.*, Simon Keynes, "The Cult of Alfred the Great," (1999) 28 *Anglo-Saxon England* 225.

13   Foot, "Making the *Angelcynn*," 35–36.

for the *Angelcynn* was shared not just across old tribal boundaries but among the three estates of the realm. The *Angelcynn* nation created by Alfred in response to the Viking invasions embodied a trifunctional social order, "invoking a concept of Englishness particularly dependent on the Christian faith."[14] Not surprisingly, therefore, the ethnogenesis of the *Angelcynn*, understood from the inside as a lived experience, can be likened to a collective process of "deification" or "theosis."[15] The complex unity of the distinctively tripartite social order characteristic of that novel "imagined community"[16] had much in common with the theological mysteries of the triune God.

Alfred's Trinitarian Vision of Christian Nationhood

Alfred was intensely aware of the divinely ordained responsibilities of Christian rulership. But he also acknowledged explicitly that a king cannot "get full play for his natural gifts, nor conduct and administer government unless he has fit tools and the raw material to work upon." Without "a well-peopled land" comprised of virtuous, diligent, intelligent "men of prayer, men of war, and men of work," a king "cannot perform any of the tasks entrusted to him."[17] Throughout his reign, Alfred sought to ensure that the royal administration worked to provide the conditions essential to the optimal performance of the tasks entrusted to each of the three estates. A major long-term priority, of course, was the re-organization of the defence of the realm.[18] But in the short term, on Twelfth Night 878, humiliating defeat at the hands

---

14 *Ibid.*, 37.

15 *Cf.*, Veli-Matti Kärkkäinen, *One with God: Salvation as Deification and Justification* (Collegeville, MN: Liturgical Press, 2004.

16 Benedict Anderson, *Imagined Communities: Reflections on the Origin and Spread of Nationalism* (London: Verso, 1991).

17 Richard Abels, *Alfred the Great: War, Kingship and Culture in Anglo-Saxon England* (London: Longman, 1998), 259.

18 *Ibid.*, 194–218.

of the Viking king Guthrum put the very existence of Alfred's realm into question. To recover and regenerate his kingdom Alfred was compelled to find new ways to facilitate co-operation and co-ordination between those who fought, those who prayed, and those who worked.

But, first, Alfred had to recover the *heil* he had lost, having been driven into the swamps of Somerset. There he fortified a small camp on the island of Athelney, from which he waged sporadic guerrilla war for several months. Alfred demonstrated his inspirational qualities as a leader of men in the most adverse circumstances. With consummate skill, he raised an underground militia which soundly defeated Guthrum at the battle of Edington. That famous victory revealed not just Alfred's prowess as a warrior but also his ability to project an image as a man of the people.

The once-famous tale of Alfred and the cakes conveys something of the populist charisma generated by the fugitive king's sojourn in the swampy wilderness.[19] According to this popular medieval legend, Alfred was wandering incognito through the wilderness one day when he happened upon a poor swineherd's hut. He sought refuge there for the night. The next morning peasant's wife was busy outside while Alfred sat by the fire fletching arrows. Preoccupied with his own affairs, Alfred neglected to notice when the cakes the woman had left to bake began to burn. After a severe scolding by the wife, Alfred became the perfect household guest, dutifully helping with the chores for the remainder of his stay.

In the medieval English popular imagination, the story symbolized the manner in which Alfred had let his political cakes burn during the early years of his reign, utterly failing to build up the kingdom's defences against the Vikings.[20] In this wider context, it was the severe scolding that Alfred received from his people after the Twelfth Night disaster that awakened him to the dimensions of the disaster facing

---

19 David Horspool, *Why Alfred Burned the Cakes: A King and His Eleven-Hundred-Year Afterlife* (London: Profile Books, 2007).
20 Pollard, *Man Who Made England*, 177–178.

his kingdom. According to Thomas Hughes, the special function of a king is to demonstrate "sympathy for the masses." Alfred snatched victory from the jaws of defeat only by rallying swineherds, peasant, and artisans to his side while hiding in the wilderness. As Hughes puts it, he came to understand that if "all people are to bow before the king, all nations to do him service, it is *because* 'he shall deliver the poor when he crieth, the needy also, and him that has no helper.'"[21]

In the aftermath of the triumphant battle of Edington, Alfred's actions revealed that he was a king for those who prayed as well as for those who fought and those who worked. Alfred had Guthrum and his defeated followers at his mercy. In accordance with the Vikings' own practice, Alfred could have had his captives killed or sold into slavery. Instead, he allowed Guthrum and his warriors safe passage out of Wessex on condition that they be baptized. Guthrum accepted the condition and departed Wessex to rule thereafter (under his baptismal name of Æthelstan) over East Anglia and Mercia as a Christian king, faithfully keeping the peace with Alfred.[22]

Conclusion

For his own part, Alfred worked thereafter to provide innovative, often radical cures for the spiritual degeneration which had loosed God's wrath upon the Anglo-Saxon kingdoms of yesteryear. He continued to strengthen the defences of his kingdom. Towards the end of his life, he launched "a programme of educational revival and reform to encourage

---

21 Hughes, *Alfred the Great*, 11.

22 One scholar remarks "that *among Scandinavian settlers abroad* conversion was something that 'just happened' in the process of assimilation to a host culture" such as Anglo-Saxon England. This might be taken to suggest that Guthrum's baptism was a matter of slight significance, that Guthrum wasn't really likely to have been a hard-core pagan. On the other hand, his faithfulness to the baptismal oath may suggest a recognition on his part of the victorious Alfred's *heilerfüllt* character. See, Richard Fletcher, *The Barbarian Conversion: From Paganism to Christianity* (Berkeley: University of California Press, 1999), 416.

among his subjects an idea of their single past history."[23] In many other ways, he worked to improve the material and moral, cultural and spiritual conditions of the *Angelcynn*. One measure of our own sad spiritual state is that few deracinated Anglican WASPs (whether Australian or Canadian, English or American) appear ever to have heard of Alfred the Great. Fewer still venerate him as the patron saint of their once great national church (or *Volkskirche* as Germans might style it). Sadly, those modern descendants of the *Angelcynn* stranded in the spiritual swamps of our distinctly unholy nations themselves stand ever more sorely in need of a Christian king ready, willing, and able to fight for faith, family, and folk.

---

23 Foot, "Making the *Angelcynn*," 33.

8. Sanctifying the Norman Yoke: William the Conqueror, the Angelcynn Church and the Papal Revolution

Introduction

THE BRUTE MILITARY reality of the Norman Conquest received formal constitutional recognition on Christmas Day, 1066 when William, the victorious Duke of Normandy was installed as William I, King of England. At William's coronation, the bishops of the kingdom anointed him with holy oil, thereby consecrating him as an English priest king. Despite his Norman origins, William possessed a credible claim to "the loyalties inherent in English kingship." Certainly, the *ecclesia Anglicana* readily acknowledged William as the direct and legitimate successor to his royal kinsman, Edward the Confessor. He received the blessing of the kingdom's bishops as "the legitimate, and consecrated, holder of all the royal rights of the ancient English dynasty." In keeping with Old English tradition, the bishops "once more prayed that this new Norman king would foster, teach, strengthen, and establish 'the church of the whole kingdom of the Anglo-Saxons, committed to his charge, and defend it against all visible and invisible enemies.'"[1] Time would tell whether their prayers were answered.

Ironically, not long afterwards, the Pope in Rome chose "to deny that royal unction was an indelible sacrament giving the king the status

---

1   David C. Douglas, *William the Conqueror: The Norman Impact upon England* (Berkeley: University of California Press, 1964), 256–259.

of a priest." That doctrinal shift was but one corollary of the revolution in political theology foreshadowed in 1075 by Gregory VII's *Dictatus Papae*. This private memorandum, written "for an unclear purpose and never circulated," set out the foundation principles of a new-modelled papal absolutism.[2] The Pope declared in blunt and uncompromising terms that secular princes and kings were subordinate to the spiritual authority vested in the "Roman Church [which] was founded by God alone." For Gregory, it followed that "the Roman Pontiff alone is rightly to be called universal". The Pope took it as axiomatic that he alone, as the Vicar of Christ, possessed the power to "depose and reinstate bishops."[3]

Gregory's determination to assert papal control over bishops flew in the face of Old English custom. "Although bishops were technically subject to election, apparently conducted at synods before the mid-ninth century, in practice there were strong incentives for episcopal communities to favour candidates amenable to royal interests."[4] But Gregory's claims were not confined the internal constitution of the Church. He added insult to injury by boasting that "the Pope is the only one whose feet are to be kissed by all princes." Gregory's presumption of spiritual hegemony over secular rulers expressly included the power to "depose Emperors" and "absolve subjects of unjust men from their fealty."[5] This revolutionary theory of papal monarchy inevitably forced the nominally English priest-king William I upon the horns of a dilemma. Had not William I sworn to defend a particular local church? After all, it was not the universal Roman Church that had been committed to William's charge.

---

2   Gregory VII, "Dictatus Papae," in Brian Tierney, ed., *The Crisis of Church & State 1050–1300* (Englewood Cliffs, N.J.: Prentice-Hall, 1964), 49–50.

3   Gregory VII, "Dictatus Papae," 49–50.

4   David Pratt, *The Political Thought of Alfred the Great* (Cambridge: Cambridge University Press, 2007), 56.

5   Gregory VII, "Dictatus Papae," 49–50.

Was it not the church belonging to the whole kingdom of the Anglo-Saxons (i.e. the *Angelcynn* church established by Alfred the Great) that had *anointed* William, by the grace of God, King of England? If the Old English bishops who presided over royal unction at William's coronation were indeed a channel of divine grace, did the Holy Spirit come directly to them from the Father or did grace first flow through the Vicar of Christ, the Son in Rome? As a matter of Old English customary law, the holiness or *heil* attributed to Anglo-Saxon kings never had derived from or depended upon the Bishop of Rome. William I and his subjects were presented with a problem by Gregory's revolution in political theology: Was the Roman Church, henceforth, to be the inveterate enemy of the *Angelcynn* cult of sacral kingship?[6] Opinion on that issue has been divided ever since.

The Old English Church: Roman or *Angelcynn*?

In 1080, Pope Gregory VII gave practical expression to his revolutionary model of papal monarchy when he demanded "that William should do him fealty in respect of the kingdom of England." William refused to comply. The Anglo-Norman monarch had a very different "conception of his rights as a king within the Church." William believed that the Christ-centred monarchy of Old England "legitimized the control by a king over the Church throughout all his dominions."[7] To "perform his duty of securing the welfare of the Church within his dominions" a priest-king was bound to "resist any division of loyalty among his subjects." Contemplating the prospect of a disputed papal election, William announced that "no pope was to be recognized within his realm without his consent". Accordingly, ecclesiastical law was to be made by church synods convened by William while ecclesiastical

---

6   *Cf.*, Sarah Foot, "The Making of *Angelcynn*: English Identity Before the Norman Conquest," (1996) 6 *Transactions of the Royal Historical Society* 25.

7   Douglas, *William*, 340–341, 259.

penalties imposed on his barons and officials were subject to a royal veto power.[8]

One need not infer, however, that such royal resistance set William in opposition to the reforming thrust of Gregory's Papal Revolution. Indeed, while noting the inevitable friction between king and pope, staunchly Catholic biographer Hilaire Belloc does not hesitate to identify William as a life-long champion of the papacy and the Church, in turn, as "the principal support of William from the beginning." Belloc maintains that, throughout his reign, in both England and Normandy, William was the firm ally of that "universal society with its chief at Rome." In fact, he anchors William's monarchical legitimacy not in Anglo-Saxon law and tradition but in its "general acceptance throughout Christendom." Like other "triumphant Norman adventurers," William joined forces "with the reinforced Papacy, for it was the moment of the restoration of the Papacy and the great Cluniac reform, the purging and consolidation of the Church." In Belloc's eyes, William's exemplary efforts to reform and strengthen clerical organization in both Normandy and England made him "of all the monarchs of the west, the one most closely bound to the new order of the Church."[9]

Belloc's overwhelmingly positive evaluation of William's relationship with the papal monarchy seems to have won implicit acceptance within the cosmopolitan fraternity of professional historians. Belloc wrote as a Roman Catholic pan-Europeanist, de-emphasizing the importance of English national feeling. To grasp William's place in history, he urged his readers "to forget the modern ideas of nationalism." Language and race contributed less to the collective or personal identity of people in medieval Europe than the Christian monarchies governing them. England was in 1066 "a province of Christendom which has surged and tumbled, during all living memory before Edward's accession, in a sort of chaos." The whole "business from

---

8   Ibid., 342.
9   Hilaire Belloc, *William the Conqueror* (Rockford, IL: Tan Books, 1992 [original ed., 1934]), 42, 63, 31.

Hastings onwards is essentially the re-entry of Britain more fully and finally into the European unity of which of course it had always formed a part."[10] In a similar vein, David C Douglas remarks that the success of the Norman Conquest reshaped "the medieval destinies of England" as that nation was "deflected from Scandinavia towards Latin Europe by a descendant of the Viking Rolf."[11]

Of course, not everyone shares such an anodyne view of William's impact upon the *ecclesia Anglicana*. Fr. Andrew Phillips does not dispute the consensus view that William worked to advance the reform program of the papal monarchy. But as an English Orthodox priest, Phillips views the Papal Revolution as one of the principal mechanisms fastening the tyrannical Norman yoke more securely upon the whole kingdom of the Anglo-Saxons.[12] The inherited stock of spiritual capital belonging to the *Angelcynn* was captured by an increasingly centralized proto-state legitimized by the Roman Church. The newly-Norman episcopacy set over the historic *ecclesia Anglicana* joined forces with the Roman Pontiff to divide and harry the Old English nation. "Men wept as the golden age of Christianity in these islands that had lasted a millennium and more ended in blood and strife." The Faith of Old England, of the church regenerated by Alfred the Great, "the life-wisdom of noble ideal and practical sense, was perverted into the arid booklore of brain-ridden schoolmen and jurists."[13] Clearly, Fr. Phillips is no fan of the medieval papacy; he would be wrong, however, to cite the once-commonplace view that William of Normandy fought the Battle of Hastings under a papal banner.

---

10 *Ibid.*, 27, 23, 62.

11 Douglas, *William*, 159.

12 On the myth of the Norman yoke, see Christopher Hill, *Puritanism and Revolution* (New York: St. Martin's Press, 1997 [original ed., 1958]), 46–111.

13 Fr. Andrew Phillips, *Orthodox Christianity and the English Tradition* (Norfolk: English Orthodox Trust, 1995), 154–155.

William the Conqueror: Spearhead of the Papal Revolution?

As we have seen, Belloc's popular biography of William the Conqueror portrays him as a champion of the "reformed" papacy. As late as the 1960s scholarly works routinely asserted that "Duke William was to fight at Hastings under a papal banner, and with consecrated relics round his neck."[14] This story has its origins in an eleventh-century account written by "a contemporary witness of the events of 1066" and later the Conqueror's own chaplain, William of Poitiers. More recently, Catherine Morton has demonstrated that it was most unlikely that Gregory's predecessor Pope Alexander II ever gave public support to the Norman Conquest of England. "The disposition of the reforming popes to extend their power over lay rulers had not yet in the time of Alexander II plunged the church into warfare against Christians, and there was, in fact, no precedent for the church's urging one Christian ruler into battle against another." Morton pours scorn upon the discrepancies in the chronicle prepared by William of Poitiers "an unsuccessful sycophant who does not even trouble to make his various falsehoods fit together." Poitiers' lack of credibility, "as well as the total lack of confirmation of [his] story in the other eleventh-century sources…suggest that…King William's chaplain…invented it."[15]

It was, of course true that Gregory VII, or Archdeacon Hildebrand, as he was in 1066, had urged Alexander II to "sanction the aggression of a Norman war-host" set to invade England. But nowhere in the historical record "is there any hint that Alexander supported William's invasion." When Gregory VII wrote to William in 1080 soliciting the Anglo-Norman king's support on other issues, the Pope fails to cite his earlier intervention on William's behalf as a personal debt of gratitude now owing by the king to the pope. Such an omission "must of

---

14 Douglas, *William*, 188.
15 Catherine Morton, "Pope Alexander II and the Norman Conquest," (1975) 34(2) *Latomus* 362, at 365, 380, 368.

necessity mean nothing less than total failure of his efforts on William's behalf in 1066."[16] By the same token, however, it cannot be denied that from an early date William was *ad idem* with powerful figures in the Roman See, men who expected the Norman conquest of England to advance the revolutionary renewal of the papal monarchy.

William the Conqueror as Fellow Traveller in the Papal Revolution

Belloc certainly portrays William I as at the very least a fellow traveller in a military, political, and theological campaign, cosmopolitan in origins and revolutionary in its goals, to transform the Old English church, the papal monarchy and Christendom generally. A "very necessary piece of reform, part and parcel of the time, the separation of the ecclesiastical from the civil courts" was "specifically William's work."[17] Those long accustomed to the rationalist and legalistic jurisprudence of the Western legal tradition tend to minimize or miss altogether the truly revolutionary character of this program. It is easy to forget that the Old English church's Germanic Christianity was steeped in primeval, magico-religious practices and pre-modern ways of knowing resistant to analytical reasoning.[18]

Therefore, ecclesiastical jurisdiction prior to the late eleventh century "lacked precise boundaries." In fact, there "was considerable overlapping between the competence of ecclesiastical authorities and that of secular authorities." Even "within the church there was no clear division between matters that came before a priest or bishop in his capacity as father confessor and dispenser of penitential remedies, on the one hand, and matters that came before him as an ecclesiastical administrator or judge, on the other." It was the sacramental character

---

16 *Ibid.*, 374, 375.

17 Belloc, *William the Conqueror*, 63.

18 Marcel Gauchet, *The Disenchantment of the World: A Political History of Religion* Oscar Burge, trans. (Princeton, N.J.: Princeton University Press, 1997), 1–33.

attached to the *ordination* of priests and bishops that endowed them with authority, not their formal legal *jurisdiction*.[19]

Just as the king was also a priest, priests participated in the divinely inspired majesty of royal power. This situation confused and obscured the chain of command in both church and state. Reform from above was the solution to that problem. As Harold J. Berman puts it "the Papal Revolution, with its liberation of the clergy from the laity and its emphasis upon the separation of the spiritual from the secular…made it both necessary and possible to place more or less clear limits upon, and hence to systematize, ecclesiastical jurisdiction."[20]

It, therefore, "fell to William to initiate a new phase of church reform in England no less than Normandy." This was not just a matter of liberating the church from secular control; it also required the "strengthening of the ecclesiastical hierarchy. This meant reinforcing the authority of the bishop in his diocese as well as that of the pope in whole church."[21] Prior to the Papal Revolution, Christendom comprised a Commonwealth of local churches in which the Bishop of Rome made no claim to absolute and universal authority over all Christian believers. The church was "not a secular institution, but a divino-human one," as reflected in "the fact that She [had] no visible Head, but the invisible Head of the God-Man, Christ, present in the Church through the Holy Spirit."[22] The Old English church participated in the Holy Spirit in like manner. But, in accordance with the linear, rationalist logic of papal absolutism, as codified in the "reformed" system of canon law, the Holy Spirit now moved along legally prescribed channels from the Father, through the Son, to the Vicar of

---

19 Harold J. Berman, *Law and Revolution: The Formation of the Western Legal Tradition* (Cambridge, MA: Harvard University Press, 1983), 221.

20 Ibid., 222.

21 Marjorie Chibnall, *Anglo-Norman England, 1066–1166* (Oxford: Blackwell, 1986), 192–193.

22 Phillips, *Orthodox Christianity*, 225.

Christ seated in Rome and through him to bishops and parish priests administering the sacraments to the laity.

The Cultural Dispossession of the Old English Church

However useful such "reforms" were to the Norman conquerors, there is no good reason to believe that they served the spiritual needs much less the ethnic interests of the conquered *Angelcynn*. On the contrary, it has long been known that "the last phase of the Old English Church" was itself marked by "an almost continual movement of reform which presents some striking similarities to those on the Continent and yet is characterized by peculiarities which enhance its interest." R.R. Darlington credited the beginning of the indigenous recovery to Alfred the Great who "inaugurated a literary movement of which one of the chief objects was the education of the secular clergy."[23]

In the tenth century this autochthonous regeneration process continued with efforts to sub-divide dioceses in southern England. The "zeal for reform was widespread among the higher clergy" who were "to a remarkable degree...recruited from the reformed monasteries." The chief mission of these "ardent reformers" was "raising the standard of the secular clergy". Literacy programs were important to such a project. More fundamental was the need to constitute a distinctive clerical culture. The secular clergy were encouraged to conceive the priesthood as a higher calling grounded in the monastic model of common living. Unfortunately, most parochial clergy were, in fact, both married and ill-educated. As a last resort, reformers sometimes substituted monks for clerks in cathedral establishments. The higher clergy were active outside the church as well: "In the reigns of Ethelred

---

23   R.R. Darlington, "Ecclesiastical Reform in the Late Old English Period," (1936) 51 *English Historical Review* 385, at 385–386.

and Cnut the influence of the leading churchmen was great and can be traced in the legal codes of the period."[24]

It is important to note as well "the abundance of homiletic literature in the vernacular and the bulk of it was suitable for the use of educated parish priests."[25] The *Angelcynn* vernacular disappeared from the upper reaches of the Anglo-Norman church soon after the Conquest. In monastic libraries Old English as a literary language was ousted by Anglo-Norman and Latin. But the changes in those libraries went beyond "a change in language. There was a shift in interest and in monastic culture". No longer was the emphasis on "the Anglo-Saxon curriculum" devoted to moral and religious teaching. High theological culture shifted towards the patristic classics and the scholastic "moderns."[26] This intellectual shift too was the work of William. Even the holy spaces of the monasteries reflected the rationalization and legalization of Christianity under the aegis of the Roman Church working in tandem with a Norman king.

Prior to this cultural revolution, Canterbury had been "the Metropolitan Church of the English. The Irish, Scottish and Welsh had theirs." The Old English church was a characteristic product of what Fr. Phillips describes as the Age of Incarnation. Had this age continued, Western Christendom might have seen "the formation of Metropolitan Churches in different linguistic areas. European Christianity might have developed a confederal pattern of unity in diversity within the Patriarchal See of Rome, a harmony of unity of Faith and autonomy of local Metropolitans." In those days, "Europe was colonized by monasteries and ascetics" so that the *Angelcynn* and other Christian ethno-nations were "guided by theology, the knowledge of God, the inspiration of the Holy Spirit."[27]

---

24 Ibid., 386, 389, 392, 404–405, 398.

25 Ibid., 409.

26 Chibnall, *Anglo-Norman England*, 214–215.

27 Phillips, *Orthodox Christianity*, 283.

Conclusion

The Papal Revolution and the Norman Conquest inaugurated a new era. A profound world-historical shift took place in the historical trajectory of Western Christianity. William's supporting role in the Papal Revolution paved the way for the big guns of medieval scholasticism to take aim at the Old English church. Legalism and rationalist philosophy became the hallmark of the theological movement leading the frontal assault on Old English and, more broadly, Germanic Christianity, the syncretic message that the early missionaries had carried to Anglo-Saxon England.[28] The newly converted Anglo-Saxon tribes fused Christianity with a primordial belief in the ultimate unity of the visible and the invisible world. William's coronation on Christmas Day, 1066 marked the beginning in England of the Age of Disincarnation.[29]

The Old English, Christ-centred cult of sacral kingship assumed the close involvement of God in the world of his chosen people. By contrast, the Roman Catholic theology of papal supremacy deliberately distanced God from his creation, endowing the church with a monopoly over the spiritual power to mediate between the beyond and the here-below.[30] As collateral damage, the Anglo-Saxon cult of sacral kingship was hollowed-out and rendered obsolescent.

William's experience shows that the papal push to protect and preserve the freedom of the church from secular control had the paradoxical effect of freeing kings to promote their own powers and prerogatives. More broadly, in proclaiming an institutional monopoly

---

28 See, William A. Chaney, *The Cult of Kingship in Anglo-Saxon England: The Transition from Paganism to Christianity* (Berkeley: University of California Press, 1970); and James C. Russell, *The Germanization of Early Medieval Christianity: A Sociohistorical Approach to Religious Transformation* (New York: Oxford University Press, 1994).

29 Phillips, *Orthodox Christianity*, 284.

30 See, generally, Berman, *Law and Revolution*.

upon access to the other world, the Roman Church inevitably fostered a pervasive disposition among the laity to exploit to the full our earthly abode. As a result, we witness the ever-deepening disenchantment of the world.[31]

---

31 Cf., Gauchet, *Disenchantment of the World*.

9. A Choice Not an Echo: Biblical Israel as Mythic Model for Early Anglo-Saxon Christendom

Introduction

FROM ITS ORIGINS in the sixth century AD, Anglo-Saxon Christendom was grounded in a magicoreligious way of life suffused with the charismatic authority of kings. Anglo-Saxon Christendom was radically and permanently transformed in the late eleventh century by the combined impact of the Norman Conquest and the Papal Revolution following on its heels. In hindsight, the unmistakably ethnoreligious character of that Germanic Christianity stands in sharp contrast to the ever-more rationalized, universalized, and deracinated Roman Catholicism of the High Middle Ages. The revolutionary transformation of both state and church in England resulted, of course, in a formalized separation of secular from spiritual authority. At the most profound, world-historical level, 1066 and all that marked the beginning of an epochal shift. The first millennium AD of Christianity had been an enchanted Age of Incarnation. It was succeeded by our own disenchanted Age of Disincarnation, culminating, at the end of the second millennium, in the spiritual enervation of creedal Christianity and the secular irrelevance of Christendom.

In the magicoreligious world of early Anglo-Saxon England, neither Christians, nor the remaining pagan tribes, made sharp distinctions between secular and sacred. Law and religion were two sides of the same coin. Indeed, "the purpose of the first written laws of the English" had been "to integrate the new religion into the already existing social structure." Like the priest-kings of the ancient Germanic tribes, the Christian tribal king, too, possessed a sacred character.[1] The spiritual dimension of rulership went all the way down. Even fidelity to one's lord was a religious duty.

Accordingly, both the king and his warrior nobility had a stake in the sacralization of lordship, viewing "ecclesiastical offices, churches, and monastic foundations from a pre-Christian Germanic perspective, as sources of sacral charism and legitimation." Such considerations gave rise to the *Eigenkirchensytem* (proprietary church system) and the *Eigenklostersystem* (proprietary monastic system). In other words, livings in churches and monasteries were in the personal gift of the landed nobility. The essential function of the church, for both nobles and their king, was not to tutor commoners in ortho*dox* theological doctrines. Rather, their religious authority required the inculcation of behavioural ortho*praxy* through a set of cultic observances and ritual practices highlighting the *mana*-filled nature of lordship.[2]

Even after their conversion to Christianity, the common culture of Anglo-Saxon kings and peoples remained rooted in a magicoreligious way of life. Royal authority was charismatic in nature. Should a king lose his *Heil* — the magical powers of divine origin endowing him with supernatural, or at least exceptional qualities — his followers might well desert him. Descended from a god the warrior-king was seen as *heilerfüllt* (literally "filled with the sacred") and so represented "the charismatic embodiment of the 'luck' of the folk." A particularly

---

1 William A. Chaney, *The Cult of Kingship in Anglo-Saxon England: The Transition from Paganism to Christianity* (Berkeley: University of California Press, 1970), 185, 195.

2 James C. Russell, *The Germanization of Early Medieval Christianity: A Sociohistorical Approach to Religious Transformation* (Oxford: Oxford University Press, 1994), 154–155.

"unlucky" king might even be killed and hung upon a sacred tree to propitiate the gods.³

When charismatic authority became routinized, the magicoreligious-directed character of the English ruling class was replaced by a new, "tradition-directed" way of life.⁴ In post-Conquest England, the routinization of charismatic authority was associated with new forms of rationalized and traditionalized authority. By contrast, in pre-Conquest England, Anglo-Saxon law was not a distinct system of regulation nor was it a distinct system of thought. There had been no professional judges or lawyers, much less a hierarchy of courts. But, after the Conquest, "there emerged for the first time strong central authorities, both ecclesiastical and secular, whose control reached down, through delegated officials, from the centre to the localities."⁵

From the start, ruling over a restive Anglo-Saxon people, the Norman kings needed to centralize their authority. For its part, the medieval papacy already "considered itself primarily as an institution of government," holding "itself responsible for the authoritative guidance of the whole Church comprising as the notion did clergy as well as laity."⁶ Unhappily, perhaps, before the late eleventh century "the clergy of Western Christendom — bishops, priests, and monks — were, as a rule, much more under the authority of emperors, kings, and leading feudal lords than of popes." But, by then, "there was a strong movement to purge the church of feudal and local influences and of the corruption that inevitably accompanied them." Finally, in 1075, "after years of agitation and propaganda by the papal party," Pope

---

3   Ibid., 205–206; Chaney, *Cult of Kingship*, 12; Max Weber, *The Theory of Social and Economic Organization* (New York: Free Press, 1964), 358–363.

4   David Riesman, et.al., *The Lonely Crowd: A Study of the Changing American Character* abridged edition (New Haven, CN: Yale University Press, 1961), 9–13.

5   Harold J. Berman, *Law and Revolution: The Formation of the Western Legal Tradition* (Cambridge, MA: Harvard University Press, 1983), 85–86.

6   Walter Ullman, *Law and Politics in the Middle Ages: An Introduction to the Sources of Medieval Political Ideas* (London: Sources of History Ltd., 1975), 120.

Gregory VII "declared the political and legal supremacy of the papacy over the entire church and the independence of the clergy from secular control."[7]

Latin Christianity, of course, always conceived the relations between God and man as legal relations, a "framework of rights and duties...moulded into a Roman jurisprudential scheme."[8] The process of moulding that abstract presupposition into a functioning system of canon law was not fully operational until the eleventh century. Only then, could the papal party sponsor networks of scholars in the emergent universities to develop a science of law to support Gregory's revolutionary claim to papal supremacy; not just over the entire clergy, but perhaps even over "the entire secular branch of society." In response, kings and emperors marshalled ancient legal authorities in defence of their own case against papal usurpation. For centuries thereafter, recurrent jurisdictional disputes between kings, emperors, and popes over the next two or three centuries drove the development of both civil and canon law as sources of authority and instruments of control.[9]

In England, such irreconcilable constitutional conflicts eventually led to the Anglo-Protestant Reformation and its sequel the Puritan Revolution. Looking back over the almost one thousand years beginning with the Norman Conquest and the Papal Revolution, one wonders whether this chain of events baked the Anglo-Protestant deformation of Christian nationhood into the constitutional cake? More pointedly, do vested institutional interests prevent modern theologians and church professionals such as the Reverend Dr. Bruce Kaye (who capped his academic career by serving as the General Secretary of the Anglican Church of Australia for ten years) from asking, much less answering, such questions?

---

7   Berman, *Law and Revolution*, 87–89.

8   Walter Ullman, *Medieval Political Thought* (Harmondsworth: Penguin, 1975), 21.

9   Berman, *Law and Revolution*, 95.

The Missing Link

Certainly, Dr. Kaye's work itself illustrates just how far Anglo-Protestantism has departed from the Anglo-Saxon experience of Christian nationhood prior to the Norman Conquest. For starters, his most recent book, on the rise and fall of English Christendom, obscures the revolutionary character of the Anglo-Norman regime. Instead, Kaye holds "that the Norman Conquest marked more of a consolidation than a revolution and that such changes as were established in the kingdom had the effect of making the nation more coherent and organized."[10]

Kaye is reluctant to acknowledge that an English people, the *gens anglorum*, could or did come into being, as a "nation," outside and apart from the "embryonic form" of a "political entity" now known as the "nation-state." He sees nothing of spiritual significance in the history of the English people, understood as a process of ethnogenesis. There was nothing special, as far as Kaye can see, about Christianity in Anglo-Saxon England. It simply existed as one of many European "micro-christendoms," each of which could be defined as "a political entity that is christian and whose government has strong lay and clerical elements." In other words, English christians lived "in a context where royal power and church power worked hand in hand in the ordering and evangelising of the people."[11]

Note the lower-case spelling of "Christian" and "Christendom." Kaye's account is premised on Peter Brown's thesis that there was never one, unitary medieval Christianity. Rather, regionalism prevailed, giving rise to "a patchwork of adjacent, but separate micro-Christendoms," each feeling "that it possessed, if in diminished form, the

---

10 Bruce Kaye, *The Rise and Fall of the English Christendom: Theocracy, Christology, Order, and Power* (London: Routledge, 2018), 268.

11 Ibid., 48, 273–274.

essence of an entire Christian culture."[12] In Kaye's narrative, English Christendom maintains a fundamental continuity from the Venerable Bede (673–735 AD) in the early eighth century (whose *Ecclesiastical History of the English People* first imagined a future English Christian nation), through the Anglo-Saxon period and the Norman Conquest, to the late seventeenth century when it began its long, inexorable decomposition. The story ends, on Kaye's account, in the contemporary post-Christendom era, where the state maintains, at best, a neutral stance towards Christianity and other religions, all of which have been relegated to the private realm.[13]

Kaye's worldview is that of an ecclesiastical administrator in one province of global Anglicanism. His political theology is grounded in an Augustinian cosmology, paradoxically adapted to a post-christendom age. Presumably, as an ordained priest, he still holds to the ancient creeds. Certainly, he views "christians" in orthodox eschatological terms, as resident aliens in this world, awaiting the return of Christ to rule over the glorified bodies of faithful believers. He invokes the work of Stanley Hauerwas on living *After Christendom* to understand the difference between the secular stories of liberal societies and the church and its narrative. "Understanding that difference," he avers, "is the seedbed from which christians can sustain habits and training that will enable them to live faithfully as disciples of Jesus."[14]

For Kaye, the salvific life of the church has never been bound up intrinsically with the fate of this or that local "christendom." Nor, therefore, was the English Christendom ever an end in itself; rather, it "was

---

12 Bruce Kaye, *Reinventing Anglicanism: A Vision of Confidence, Community, and Engagement in Anglican Christianity* (New York: Church Publishing, 2003), 17; Peter Brown, *The Rise of Western Christendom: Triumph and Diversity, AD 200–1000* (Oxford: Blackwell, 1996), 218.

13 Kaye, *Rise and Fall*, 268, 288; Bede, *Ecclesiastical History of the English People* (Harmondsworth: Penguin, 1990).

14 Kaye, *Rise and Fall*, 286–287; Stanley Hauerwas, *After Christendom: How the Church is to Behave if Freedom, Justice, and a Christian Nation are Bad Ideas*, second edition, (1999).

a means to a mature christian community." Like the early christians in the pre-Constantinian age, the church today requires an "active sense that it lives in the kingdom of Jesus that is not of this world." He insists that "the theocracy of the God and Father of our Lord Jesus Christ is the active determining citizenship of the church" which must not "be conformed to the schema of this world." And yet, or perhaps therefore, the figure of Jesus Christ tends "to float hazily above the surface of the text rather than convincingly tying it together."[15] The pronounced, other-worldly character of Jesus Christ in the contemporary Age of Disincarnation also hovered somewhere between the lines of Kaye's earlier book on *Reinventing Anglicanism*. There, he advocated the re-configuration of global Anglicanism on the managerialist model of a "post-corporate networked organization."[16]

Accordingly, Kaye defines Anglicanism, rather vaguely, "as one of the discrete traditions within western Christianity" distinguished by its development over the past three hundred years "from national church to international Communion of churches." In that definition, there is no hint of that Anglicanism possesses a distinctive *ethnoreligious* identity. Rather, Anglicanism is conceived as a particular variant of catholic Christianity. In the realm of managerial theology, the Church, in its essential nature, is a universal theocracy under the disembodied headship of Jesus Christ. As such, ethnicity is irrelevant, either to church's institutional identity or its universal mission. He encourages Anglicans worldwide, in whichever local community they may live, to become "respectful visionaries" committed to an incarnational God whose authority is marked by open-endedness and porous borders, and tentativeness "experienced and exercised by the whole people of God."[17]

---

15 Kaye, *Rise and Fall*, 297–298; *cf.*, Bradford Littlejohn's review of Kaye's *Rise and Fall of English Christendom* in (2019) 61(1) *Journal of Church and State* 145–147.
16 Kaye, *Reinventing Anglicanism*, 259–265.
17 *Ibid.*, 3, 7, 20, 259–265.

To my mind, the theopolitical significance of Kaye's book on the rise and fall of English Christendom lies less in what he includes in his narrative than in what he leaves out. He begins the story with Bede. But he then simply ignores the entire three centuries between Bede's death and the Norman Conquest. Most egregiously, by skipping that formative era, Kaye effectively renders invisible the process of ethnogenesis through which the Old English church laid the spiritual foundations of English national identity.

It is vital to note that, in contrast, to Kaye's description of "Bede's Christendom" as "a political entity," Patrick Wormald emphasized that the most striking aspect of the English, understood as "a well-established ethnicity," was "that it had so little political basis until the first half of the tenth century." The Germanization of Christianity in Anglo-Saxon England presupposed the invisible synthesis of spiritual and royal authority in the charismatic figure of an Anglo-Saxon king. He points out that "the very name of 'English' was one of [the] fruits" of "a single English Church." But that "ecclesiastical authority would [not] would not have sufficed to instil a new ethnicity into Britain's Germanic-speaking inhabitants." Ethnicity, as we will see, necessarily exists within a culturally autonomous narrative context. The impact of ecclesiastical authority had to be reinforced "by the manufacture of a common history" which in Anglo-Saxon England first took shape in Bede's "supreme masterpiece of the world's historical literature."[18]

Naturally enough, Kaye and Bede are both interested in the ways in which the church worked with tribal kings to Christianize the various Germanic tribes settled in Britain. But Kaye seems oblivious to what a growing body of scholarship describes as the "Germanization of early medieval Christianity," a process which shaped the "common history," as described by Bede, both in England and on the continent. He makes only one oblique reference to this process when discussing a passage in Bede's *History* dealing with a letter from Augustine of Canterbury

---

18 Kaye, *Rise and Fall*, 48–49; Patrick Wormald, "*Engla Lond*: The Making of an Allegiance," (1994) 7(1) *Journal of Historical Sociology* 1, 9–13.

to Pope Gregory I. Augustine asks why customs vary in different churches and what, if anything, he should do about such diversity in ecclesiastical practices. Gregory's reply recommends recognition of whatever local customs that seem "devout, religious, and right." Kaye briefly characterizes this advice in general terms as a "significant principle of local adaptation or, in modern terms, of contextualization."[19] He remains indifferent, however, to the Germanic nature of the "context" within which the process of Christianization was taking shape.

This is a major defect in Kaye's understanding of "Bede's christendom." His abstract definition of "christendoms" as a fusion of lay and clerical power in the form of a polity or "theocracy" is utterly inappropriate to the circumstances of Anglo-Saxon Christendom.[20] After all, both Bede in the early eighth century and King Alfred in the late tenth century inhabited a Germanic ethnoculture within which religion and law were inseparable from the *Heil* of a king. As we have seen above, there was no distinction between "lay" and "clerical" authority in church prior to the late eleventh century. Even within the church, the magicoreligious authority of Anglo-Saxon kings was, if anything, more potent than that of priests and bishops.[21]

James Russell describes the Germanization process in early medieval Christianity as an encounter between folk-religious societies and a universal religious movement. His model of religious transformation identifies Germanic religions as "folk-centred" and "world-accepting" in contrast to early Christianity which "was essentially soteriological and eschatological, hence 'world-rejecting.'" Even late Christianity, as represented by modern Anglican clerics such as Bruce Kaye, insists that the church must be *contra mundum*. Russell attributes the contrast between Christian and Germanic folk-based worldviews to the fact "that the social structure of the Germanic peoples at the time of their

---

19   Kaye, *Rise and Fall*, 39; Bede, *Ecclesiastical History*, 79.
20   Kaye, *Rise and Fall*, 2–3, 267.
21   Berman, *Law and Revolution*, 88–89.

encounter with Christianity reflected a high level of groups solidarity, while the urban social environment in which early Christianity flourished was one in which alienation and normlessness or anomie flourished." In such circumstances, the ethos of "brotherly love" among Christians attracted many culturally and spiritually alienated individuals ready to reject a world steeped in sin in the hope of heavenly salvation. While early Mediterranean Christianity might fulfill "the socioreligious aspirations of a highly anomic society," it "would be dysfunctional if applied to rural, warrior, pastoral-agricultural society with a high level of group solidarity." The Germanic peoples were unlikely to accept Christianity unless it came to "be perceived as responsive to the heroic, religiopolitical and magicoreligious orientation" of their ethnoculture.[22]

Clearly, the effort to convert Anglo-Saxon pagans would never have succeeded had Christian missionaries not recognized that a Germanic warrior society asked little more from religion than prayers for victory and good crops, protection against black magic and a swift and easy death carrying them directly into the Valhalla of tribal heroes. There is an obvious contrast between the early Church's need to accommodate itself to the magicoreligious character of Germanic folk-religions and the renunciation by modern, global Anglicanism of its ancestral origins in the Anglo-Saxon *Volksgeist* in favour of a universalistic ethos of tentativeness, open-endedness, and porous borders.

From Bede to Alfred the Great, literate Anglo-Saxons viewed their own past through the prism provided by the biblical history of ancient Israel. Nothing could be further from the pacifist preoccupations of contemporary mainstream Christianity than the blood-soaked war stories of the Old Testament which fascinated early Anglo-Saxon Christians. Looking to the example of Israelite kings such as Saul, David, and Solomon, they well understood that only kings could "serve as effective warleaders in maintaining and extending the position of

---

22 Russell, *Germanization of Early Medieval Christianity*, 3–4.

their own people against the encroachments of surrounding tribes with their own hostile and aggressive kings."[23]

The Germanic warriors who invaded Britain were intensely ethnocentric, bound together by the sacred bond between the tribe and its gods. The fusion of religious and political authority embodied in Anglo-Saxon kings facilitated the conversion of their peoples to Christianity. Without royal support conversion did not and could not occur. For centuries after Augustine of Canterbury's mission to the Angles, Christianity nurtured a people incorporating several independent kingdoms. The *mana*-filled royal stirpes was the purest manifestation of the Anglo-Saxon *Volksgeist*, before and after the transition from paganism to Christianity. Every Anglo-Saxon king carried his splendour into the Church: as *fidei defensor*, he was a priest, as much as a monarch. The Norman Conquest marked the end of an era, however. Slowly but surely, the magicoreligious, heroic, and highly ethnocentric myth of sacral kingship lost its force. Having turned a blind eye to the "Germanization" of Anglo-Saxon Christianity, Kaye misses entirely "the disenchantment of the world" in the aftermath of the Norman Conquest and the Papal Revolution.[24]

In the High Middle Ages, the spiritual and temporal powers carved out separate, distinct, and autonomous spheres of jurisdiction. Just as the sacred was separated from the secular, so too religion itself became a matter of reason, not magic. Reflecting the prestige of scholastic rationalism, Catholic Christianity in England was "Romanized," becoming steadily more universalistic and less Germanic in its outlook. After all, Germanic Christendom stood as an obstacle to the imperial ambitions of the papal monarchy. Having consecrated the foreign king

---

23 Judith McClure, "Bede's Old Testament Kings," in Patrick Wormald, *et.al.*, eds., *Ideal and Reality and Frankish and Anglo-Saxon Society* (Oxford: Basil Blackwell, 1983), 87.

24 Marcel Gauchet, *The Disenchantment of the World: A Political History of the World*, Translated by Oscar Burge, (Princeton, NJ: Princeton University Press, 1997).

who seized the English throne, the papacy proceeded to drain the English church of its core ethnoreligious, *Angelcynn* identity.

Writing Scripture

Not surprisingly, Kaye views the Anglo-Norman Christendom as the consummation of Bede's vision of an English people, the *gens anglorum*, ordained by God to constitute the nation as a political entity. Bede, Kaye tells us, regarded the Bible "as an account of the providence and redemptive activity of God." In other words, Bede was pointing "to God as agent in the history of the English." Kaye describes this "this overarching framework of divine protection and [a] calling for the English" as the "key to understanding what Bede was attempting." In other words, Bede's job was to write "an account of the active providence of God in bringing to fulfilment a divine intention of creating the English people as the hegemonic Catholic Christian people in the land."[25]

Kaye attributes to Bede the presupposition that Holy Scripture represents the uniquely inspired, historical revelation of the Word of God. In passing, Kaye also opines that "of course Bede did not think he was 'writing scripture.'"[26] Kaye's certitude on that score begs any number of questions. Who decides just what "writing scripture" entails and who gets to participate in such a practice? Is "scripture" an emanation of the divine will or a human artifact? Indeed, to get down to brass tacks, is it clear who wrote the Hebrew Bible, where, when, why, and how? Is it possible to seek and find persuasive answers to such questions? If so, could it be that Bede was, in fact, doing something very much like the work of the anonymous scribe(s) who produced the Hebrew Bible (or its Greek version, known as the Septuagint, the Old Testament, or, for that matter, the New Testament)?

---

25 Kaye, *Rise and Fall*, 33.
26 Ibid., 33.

Certainly, the view that the Bible is not the supernatural Word of God, as faithfully transcribed by Moses and other inspired prophets, but a man-made, literary construct finds ample support in an ever-growing body of biblical scholarship. As it happens, one recent historical analysis of the origins of the Hebrew Bible, is particularly useful in considering whether Bede and generations of other Anglo-Saxon writers, artists, and folklorists were engaged in activities comparable to "writing scripture." In his latest book, *Why the Bible Began*, Jacob L. Wright provides a convincing alternative to the orthodox interpretation of scripture and its origins. Christians and Jews, alike, tend to assume that the Bible is a form of "religious scripture" that "exists because God wanted to reveal divine truth to us." Whether that proposition is true or not, it does not tell us why the Bible came to be written in a particular time and place. Nor does it acknowledge either that sacred texts were rarely central to ancient religions or that the much "of the Hebrew Bible has little to do with religion or theology."[27]

Wright's origins story treats the Bible as the response by "generations of anonymous scribes" to Israel's experience of defeat, devastation, and disunity. To understand the nature of that collective literary enterprise, it is important to remember "the two, very different, meanings of the name 'Israel.' One refers to the Northern kingdom, and the other to the nation (the 'Israelites') that descended from Abraham and Sarah." Wright traces the "biblical narrative, which begins with the creation of the world in Genesis" to its end "with the destruction of Jerusalem in the book of Kings," showing how it "evolved over the ages from smaller, originally independent pieces." He argues that the work blends the separate stories of "the two kingdoms, Israel and Judah, portraying their tragic ends" and "setting them in relation to an earlier 'United Monarch' from the time of David and Solomon, and beyond

---

27 Jacob L. Wright, *Why the Bible Began: An Alternative History of Scripture and its Origins* (Cambridge: Cambridge University Press, 2023), xv.

that, to a nation that evolved from a single, extended family, beginning with Abraham and Sarah."[28]

Writing as an historian, Wright rejects the idea floated by the biblical writers of a common past that antedated the two kingdoms. Instead, he demonstrates that "at the beginning, there was not one family, or one nation, as the Bible portrays it, but a wide array of unrelated clans that would later populate these two kingdoms." There might have been a special relationship between those kingdoms but the idea of a "United Monarchy" was a historical fiction. The reality was that Israel and Judah "had long been divided, and the states had repeatedly come to blows in bloody civil wars." Wright notes that "much of what became the biblical narrative originated in the Northern kingdom of Israel." After its downfall in 722 BC, at the hands of Assyrian invaders, "Northern scribes set the biblical project in motion by constructing a *prehistory of peoplehood*, one which Israel had flourished as a nation or people long before establishing a kingdom." Their "People's History" laid the groundwork for "the Family Story of Genesis and the Exodus-Conquest Account." At the same time, Judean scribes were constructing the "Palace History" as found in the books of Samuel and Kings. That narrative knows nothing of an exodus from Egypt, beginning instead "with Saul and later David liberating the nation from the Philistines (and Ammonites)." No mention is made of an exodus from Egypt. Instead, the palace narrative "presupposes that the 'Israelites' had always lived in their homeland, albeit under foreign domination."[29]

Without the special relationship between the two defeated kingdoms, the formation of the biblical narrative would not have been possible. After the defeat and destruction of their own kingdom in 586 BC, Judean scribes created a larger "National Narrative" by connecting the competing People's and Palace Histories of Israel and Judah. Driven by "a vision that the populations of these two vanquished kingdoms could

---

28   *Ibid.*, 26.
29   *Ibid.*, 149, 66.

be one people," Southern scribes endowed the early Northern tales with much of their "poignancy and power." The National Narrative was drafted as a "biblical monument to defeat," responding "to downfall and destruction by simultaneously demonstrating the culpability of the whole nation and laying out a roadmap for a viable future." Wright claims that "the Hebrew Bible represents the first attempt in world history to construct what we may properly call a 'national identity.'" In doing so, it imagines Israel as "a people not limited to its historical territory and longstanding monarchies," able to survive as a nation "without its temple and armies." The biblical narrative and literary division illustrate, "for the first time in history, a cardinal categorical distinction" between "the nation and the state" as "two separate identities, with the nation being greater than the state which governs it." Peoplehood was severed from statehood.[30]

Wright defines a state "as a polity with institutions of government and a territory that can be conquered and destroyed. Nation, by contrast, is a political community held together by shared memories and a will to act in solidarity." As such, a nation, or people "is fundamentally a work of the collective imagination — a state of mind." In other words, nations "depend on an *esprit de corps* and a collective consciousness among their members, even if that consciousness is often feeble and fails to mobilize (coherent) collective action." Wright recognizes that "nations need narratives, and in this respect, the Bible offers us a powerful case study."[31]

His account begins with the observation that many kingdoms and empires have come and gone but only "some communities have managed to survive." He contends that "one ancient community, in the aftermath of defeat and devastation, reinvented itself," claiming that, in the process of creating the Hebrew Bible, generations of anonymous scribes combined history and mythology into a National Narrative.

---

30 *Ibid.*, 27, 12, 248–249.
31 *Ibid.*, 12–13.

They thereby endowed the scattered, competing clans and communities of Judah with a unique collective identity. A literary monument to political failure and military defeat, the biblical epic "brought to light a new wisdom: the notion that a people is greater than the kings who govern it, and that a nation will survive conquest when all of its members can claim a piece of the pie and therefore have a reason to take an active part in its collective life." As with their rivals in the ancient Near East, state and society in the early kingdoms of Israel and Judah had "worked together in relative harmony and their purpose was to preserve a political order with the *palace* at its center." Competing communities were held together by "their shared duty to the throne, *not covenantal commitments or a collective consciousness.*" Following the collapse of those kingdoms, the scribes employed language and text in the biblical corpus which inspired "a project of peoplehood."[32]

Wright contends, in effect, that the Hebrew Bible invented the Jewish people. It, and they, were, therefore, the product of human choice, not an echo of Yahweh's spoken Word. Wright conceives the Bible as a multi-generational, *pedagogical* project. As such, it reflected the "shared intentionality" of many "organizational clusters" of Northern and Southern scribes. In part, that clustering may have represented an instinctive response by a Hebrew priestly caste given to ethnic nepotism who felt a strong kinship with one another. But, once an inchoate sense of peoplehood began to take shape within scribal communities, the conscious planning and development characteristic of a systematic project took on the form of what Kevin MacDonald calls an "evolutionary group strategy" in response to the Babylonian conquest of 586 BC. Prior to that catastrophe, Wright observes, a Judean was simply "one who lived in Judah. The Jew had yet to be invented."[33]

---

32 Ibid., xvi–xvii, 12, 27, 135 (emphasis added).

33 Ibid., 135–136. On "shared intentionality" see, Michael Tomasello, quoted in Richard Wrangham, *The Goodness Paradox: How Evolution Made Us Both More and Less Violent* (London: Profile Books, 2020), 166; Kevin MacDonald, *A People*

The biblical invention of the Jewish people was the work of centuries, first under Persian, then Hellenic rule, reaching completion sometime around the Maccabean revolt of the second Nehemiah 8 century BC.[34] Wright identifies the climax of the entire project as the moment when Ezra, having returned from exile, teaches the law in Jerusalem to a vast "congregation both of men and women, and all that could hear with understanding" (Nehemiah 8:1–6). Ezra the Educator, mounting the podium with the Torah scroll in his hand, thus personifies "the profile of those who crafted the biblical corpus." As that "highly symbolic account continues, the community learns to read on their own." Within a month, "the community assembles again, yet now they are reading and studying without his help." From that time on, the "text is firmly in their hands, and together they have embraced a groundbreaking paradigm for their future as a people."[35]

Wright acknowledges that the historicity of Ezra-Nehemiah cannot be taken at face value. Nevertheless, he is confident that "the book reflects a pioneering vision among a group of ancient scribes, namely, to make their beloved body of writings an object of affection for a new nation." A body of sacred writings that the priests and palace members in the now-vanquished kingdoms would previously have "guarded as their special heritage" was now to be made "available, and indeed mandatory, for the education and edification of the entire nation." Imperial powers used "arms and creeds to carve out their kingdoms, the intergenerational community of biblical authors created a community with texts and vibrant, persisting conversations that these texts prompted." Their pedagogical project "consolidated a people in the aftermath of defeat by reshaping earlier writings into a national curriculum."[36]

That Shall Dwell Alone: Judaism as a Group Evolutionary Strategy (Westport, CN: Praeger, 1994).

34 Cf., Shlomo Sand, *The Invention of the Jewish People* Translated by Yael Lotan (London: Verso, 2009).

35 Wright, *Why the Bible Began*, 206–207.

36 Ibid., 213, 226–227, 234–235.

Education became the means where Judean scribes enabled their defeated communities to compete corporately "on the international stage and demarcate themselves from surrounding peoples." Wright notes that, having lost territorial sovereignty, communities in both the North and South needed to create a socio-cultural space for themselves in a foreign empire. Written traditions became the tools used by the scribes to demarcate that space. Wright is rather coy, however, when it comes to identifying the sources of those written traditions, never adverting to the possibility that Judean scribes might have drawn on Hellenic traditions in shaping the biblical narrative.

Instead, he confines his discussion of the source question to myths, stories, and traditions arising out of the clans and communities that were eventually incorporated into one or other of the Northern and Southern kingdoms. This becomes something of a problem, as we have seen in the ahistorical story of Ezra the Educator teaching the law to his people. That story is set in the early post-exile period, somewhere around 538 BC. But Wright does accept the insights of modern biblical criticism as "summed up in the Latin expression *lex post prophetas*, meaning that the "Mosaic law" as set out in the Pentateuch (*i.e.*, the first five books of the Bible) postdates the Prophets.[37]

Scholarly scepticism as to an early date for the Pentateuch is based in part upon a large store of well-preserved documents dating from the period 495–399 BC, discovered by modern archaeologists at Elephantine, the site of a Judean military garrison guarding the borders of the Persian empire on the upper Nile not far from the Aswan Dam today. Those documents reveal that the garrison community retained close ties with priestly and lay authorities in both Judea and Samaria. But, even though the habits, laws, and religious behaviours of the Elephantine community differed "starkly from biblical teachings," they attracted no criticism from religious authorities in Jerusalem. For example, there was a temple to Yahweh (who appears to have had a

---

37 *Ibid.*, 324.

wife) in Elephantine, the members of the community worked on the Sabbath, and, despite living near an Egyptian population, they do not appear to have been aware of the exodus narrative. In fact, they demonstrate no knowledge of the biblical writings generally, much less the Deuteronomic law.[38]

Were the Writers of the Hebrew Bible Inspired by Hellenism?

Such archaeological revelations have caused many scholars to wonder whether Judean scribes drew on Hellenic literary traditions in composing their own, apparently late, version of the Pentateuch? Disappointingly, Wright does not address that question. Fortunately, other scholars have risen to the challenge. Russell E. Gmirkin, for example, in *Plato and the Creation of the Hebrew Bible*, contends "that the Pentateuch was written ca. 270 BCE, drawing on a variety of sources written in Greek and housed in the Great Library of Alexandria," possibly by "the same group of seventy aristocratic, Greek-educated Jewish scholars" traditionally credited with production of the Septuagint around the same time. Gmirkin argues that the law collections set out in the Pentateuch "are in large part based on Athenian law and on Plato's *Laws*."[39]

Gmirkin compares, in exacting detail, "constitutional features found in the biblical laws and narratives of Exodus-Joshua...with those found in the Greek world, especially at Athens." In the process, he discovered "a systematic indebtedness" between "the constitutional features of the nation founded by Moses and Joshua in the biblical account" and "Greek political and legal institutions." Athenian legal institutions seem to have provided a particularly influential model, for example: "the system of ten or twelve tribes, also found at Athens,

---

38 Ibid., 208–213.

39 Russell E. Gmirkin, *Plato and the Creation of the Hebrew Bible* (London: Routledge, 2017), 1.

command of the army under tribal generals; the dual kinship and geographical functions of the fictitious tribes" as well as "the similar extended conception of the household." In addition, he identifies "comparable judicial procedures and rules of evidence" and "broadly similar classes of officials, including priests, exegetes, prophets, civic magistrates, judges and king; and an elective kingship that lacked the usual powers and trappings of rulership in the Ancient Near East."[40]

Gmirkin notes the "absence of direct contact between Athens and Judea in either pre-Hellenistic or Hellenistic times." This suggests that "the influence of Athenian constitutional features on the biblical legal system was mediated by exposure to Greek literature on political topics during the Hellenistic Era." The commonalities between Mosaic and Athenian political systems, such as the organization of the nation into twelve tribes, seem to draw directly on Platonic legal and political ideas. Similarly, the "supreme civic powers given to the Jewish high priest" and the role of "priestly Levites entrusted with preserving and promulgating the biblical laws" seems to be "modelled on the Guardians of the Laws who have a preeminent role in the administration of government in Plato's *Laws*." In short, Gmirkin agrees with Wright's description of the Hebrew Bible as a national literature whose pedagogical aims and procedures were designed to shape "the consciousness and character of the nation." He insists, however, that the institutional design of that pedagogical project was first based upon a Platonic prototype.[41]

Russell Gmirkin is not the only historian who has discovered parallels to Greek mythology and philosophy in the Hebrew Bible. Nor are such mimetic parallels confined to Plato's *Laws*. For example, an exhaustive study by Philippe Wajdenbaum demonstrates that Greek literature contains so many narratives based upon mythical and narrative types resembling those in the Bible that one can safely "infer that the biblical authors had a direct knowledge of this literature."

---

40   Ibid., 38–39.
41   Ibid., 39, 267.

The fact "that the Bible borrows mythical, literary and philosophical themes from the major Greek authors" supports the conclusion "that it would have to have been written after the death of one of the most important of them in 350 B.C.E., Plato, and after Judea had become a Greek province" following its conquest by Alexander the Great. Wajdenbaum is convinced, therefore, that "the Bible's author(s) wanted to transpose — in the form of their own national epic — the Ideal State of Plato's *Laws*, a political and theological project initiated in the *Republic*." Moreover, to "enhance this platonic utopia with narrative, the biblical author(s) used Greek sources" including Herodotus "for myths and stories in 'historical prose.'" Inspiration for the Bible was found as well in "the great mythological cycles: the Argonauts, the Heraclean cycle, the Theban cycle and the Trojan cycle by such authors as Homer, Pindar and the Tragedian."[42]

Wajdenbaum explicitly recognizes that his analysis undermines the premise underlying Bruce Kaye's bland assurance that "of course Bede did not think he was writing scripture." In other words, the "idea of a Bible having borrowed its main themes from the Greeks goes against the belief of a divinely revealed text, or of its authentic and original character; the belief that there is something unique in the Bible, something unprecedented, precisely unprecedented by the Greeks." Of course, there *is* something original and unique in the biblical text "yet its originality and uniqueness derive from how the narratives, most of them coming from the Greek tradition, have been assembled to form a unified and coherent tradition." The implications of this insight are most unsettling for many, Christians and Jews alike. After all, Wajdenbaum observes, "if the Hebrew Bible is indeed a Hellenistic book, then Judaism and Christianity both developed in the Greco-Roman and Mediterranean worlds and both share Hellenistic and platonic roots." He attributes their failure to "recognise this

---

42 Philippe Wajdenbaum, *Argonauts of the Desert: Structural Analysis of the Hebrew Bible* (London: Routledge, 2011), 3–4.

common background" to "their shared belief in the divine inspiration of the Scriptures."[43]

That explanation does, however, beg the question as to what "divine inspiration" might work in real historical time. We already seen that Jacob Wright, for example, does not explicitly ascribe the origins of the Hebrew Bible to divine intervention. At the same time, his obvious reluctance to probe the Hellenic roots of the Hebrew Bible seems grounded in a deep need, shared by the biblical scribes themselves, to preserve and protect the identarian integrity of the text as a uniquely Jewish project. Wajdenbaum himself notes that the Hellenic origins thesis "may shatter the most deeply anchored belief in the Western mind, the belief in the Jewish origin of both the Old Testament and of Christianity." That foundational belief presupposes an essentially mythological equation between the origins of the Jewish people and the divine purposes guiding their historical development. Bede's *Ecclesiastical History* rests upon a similar mythological equation between divine purposes and the historical destiny of the *gens Anglorum*. To explain how such mythohistorical mysteries have concealed the Hellenic origins of the Hebrew Bible, Wajdenbaum turned to Claude Lévi-Strauss' approach to the study of mythology. The rules of that methodology require: (1) that the Bible is not to "be interpreted by itself, but will be analysed with regard to it variants, most of which are found in Greek literature;" (2) "the different variants of the Greek myths will be studied;" (3) examples of borrowing must be set in the Hellenistic era "to help us understand why and how the borrowing happened."[44]

To provide just one example of the way in which the meaning of a myth can only be understood in relation to other variants:

---

43 *Ibid.*, 7–8.
44 *Ibid.*, 9, 17.

> Let us take the binding of Isaac in Genesis 22. Abraham is about to sacrifice his son to Yahweh when a divine messenger stops him, Abraham sacrifices a ram, whose horns are embedded in a bush, instead of Isaac.
>
> In the Greek variant, Athamas, king of Boeotia, is about to sacrifice his son, Phrixos to Zeus because of a false oracle, when a winged ram sent by Zeus takes Phrixos on its back and takes him safely to Colchis...There, to thank Zeus for saving his life, Phrixos sacrifices the ram and hangs the Golden Fleece on an oak. We can distinguish several mythemes in this narrative: a father is about to sacrifice his son to the supreme god, a divine messenger intervenes, the son is saved, and a ram is sacrificed in his stead. But there is an inversion of one detail: in the Greek version the ram's fleece is hung in a tree after the sacrifice, whereas in the biblical version, the ram's horns are embedded in a bush before the sacrifice.[45]

According to Wajdenbaum, this "inversion is very typical of mythical transformations, and can be seen as the 'fingerprint' of the tradent" (i.e., the person responsible for preserving or handing down traditions). He suggests that "a myth or a sequence of myths cannot be understood if it were not opposable to other versions of the same myth." As one fascinating example of mythic transformation, I invite the reader to compare the Exodus narrative in the Hebrew Bible to the allegory of the cave in Plato's *Republic*. Or, as evidence that monotheism itself originated with Plato, compare the account of creation in his *Timaeus* with Genesis 1.[46]

Wajdenbaum analyses dozens, if not hundreds of other mythic transformations that appear in the Bible. All these examples, shed light on Judean reactions to the process of Hellenization in the period leading up to the Maccabean revolt in the second century BC. Like Wright, Wajdenbaum interprets the writing of the Bible as a "process of peoplehood." But, unlike Wright, he emphasizes the ways in which "Greek culture was used in order to make both a national history and a religion, as well as to resist Hellenisation and gain independence

---

45 Ibid., 18.
46 18, 158–159, 92–95.

(which eventually happened)." For Wajdenbaum, the Jewish peoplehood project was part of a reactive process of "counter-acculturation" which culminated in the Maccabean revolt. By the time that the Bible "became the official source and history of religion, Hellenism was retrospectively seen as a threat and the Hellenised character of the Bible passed into shadow."[47] The Hebrew Bible was, therefore, doubly a matter of human choice, of social intentionality, both in its composition and the subsequent effort to "forget" the Hellenic origins of its source material. If Wajdenbaum is correct, perhaps it is not at all far-fetched to suggest that Bede, too, might have thought he was "writing scripture."

Bede's Bible?

Certainly, however he understood his personal relationship with the God of Israel, Bede was engaged in an enterprise very much like the ethnoreligious "project of peoplehood" pursued by the authors of the Hebrew Bible. Stephen J. Harris, in his book on *Race and Ethnicity in Anglo-Saxon Literature*, maintains that an early medieval model of ethnicity such as that elaborated in Bede's *Ecclesiastical History* followed naturally from the widely shared "notion that behind collective identity was a divine purpose." This is another way of saying that "ethnicity is also a narrative phenomenon," putting Harris on the same page with Wright.[48]

Bede's literary tradition was subtended, supported, and enfolded by ethnoreligious boundaries. According to Harris, Anglo-Saxon ethnicity generally cannot be understood in its "irremediably unrecoverable" physical manifestations." Rather, one must "understand how an author (or group of authors) imagined a collective, and the categories by which those images came into physical being in narrative." Bede's model of ethnicity was both literary and historical. He "*chose* [emphasis added]

---

47   Ibid., 40–41.
48   Stephen J. Harris, *Race and Ethnicity in Anglo-Saxon Literature* (London: Routledge, 2003), 8,1.

to illustrate the Anglo-Saxons chiefly as a *gens*, not as a nation, or a republic or a province — although these terms were certainly available to him." While some of his contemporaries made no clear distinction between *natio* and *gens*, others held that a *gens*, unlike a *natio*, had no *regnum* (royal power). But early medieval social categories were imprecise. Tribes, for instance, "were not stable entities which could be physically isolated and catalogued." Indeed, Patrick Geary described them as "processes," constantly changing groupings "of people bound together by shared perceptions, traditions, and institutions." One such perception was that of the Anglo-Saxons as a Germanic people, yet at first, the invading tribes of Britain do not appear to have had "a common sense of "Germanity," or *Germanentum*. Even so, by the ninth century, when an explicit sense of a *gens teudisca* seems to have found its way into British texts, the tribal diversity and disunity of the fifth century was perceived in retrospect as an imagined unity.[49]

According to Harris, Bede's *History* "begins with an ethnic story of origins by differentiating the ethnically autonomous *gens Anglorum* from the other *gens* who populate the island of Britain, itself comprised of numerous kingdoms." The Angles spoke their own language and "left no portion of their *gens* waiting on the continent — while the Saxons and the *Iutae* have." Having "moved as an entire people, as *gens*, as the Israelites did during the Exodus...the Angles have a rightful and consistent claim as an originary British *gens*." As Harris reads Bede's narrative, "it is the originary and unified pagan Angles who alone among all the *gentes* of Britain are fit to receive Christianity." Accordingly, "until the arrival of Christianity, there is in Bede's account no necessary moral obligation obtaining between the Angles and any other peoples on the island." As Bede's story of the Anglian people develops, however, "the compass of his collective identity philanthropically extends to include all the *gentes Christianorum* on the island." Bede's Angles thus become "the priest among nations." He

---

49 Ibid., 9–10.

claims, in effect, "that as the family of Angles coheres under divine election, so will the family of Britain's Christians."[50]

It should be noted that Bede and other Anglo-Saxon writers, no less than their Greek, Roman, and Judean predecessors, shared "a general indifference to the distinction between history and myth." His *History* "includes reports from both verifiable sources and unverifiable oral tradition, as well as miracle stories and saint's lives." Harris reports that "vast portions of the *HE* are today treated generically as fictions (its dream visions, miracle stories, and so forth)." Myths, legends, and histories all "configure the past into narrative, and set generic conditions for the interpretation of the present." Harris suggests that Bede's historical narrative included in its "stylized evocation of spiritual truth, an important figurative sense." His readers no doubt expected him "to engage a symbolic language and to reproduce allusively the traditional discourse of Christian faith." And Bede delivered, by making "Anglo-Saxon origins into Scriptural history." Bede drew upon Scripture as the model for "the paradigmatic medieval historical narrative" while the biblical commentary tradition offered him "a way of understanding the role of history in the scheme of salvation." Harris believes that whether "there is actually a spiritual meaning to medieval historical narrative or not," they "were generally written so as to imply and read so as to infer a spiritual meaning." In the ethnic reach of Bede's voice, as well as the spiritual depth of his prototype of an English National Narrative, his work is difficult to distinguish from that of the Judean scribes who produced the Torah.[51]

In fact, Harris points to the many parallels between the Torah as taught by Ezra the Educator and Bede's *Ecclesiastical History*. In both cases, the text "becomes the undying poet, historian, and prophet to the people." According to Harris, both Jews and Anglo-Saxons found "their identity chiefly in a living book, not in a tentative collection

---

50   *Ibid.*, 15, 74, 77, 15.

51   *Ibid.*, 6, 45–46.

of stories and ideas entrusted to the fading memories of men." The Anglo-Saxon scribes "of Wearmouth and Jarrow celebrated Ezra's role as the scribe in their great pandect, the *Codex Amiatimus*, which begins with a portrait of Ezra, a painting suggested perhaps by Bede himself." Harris even toys with the thought "that Bede's *HE* may have been patterned on Ezra's story of a migration of three tribes, who re-establish a faith and reconstruct its texts." Certainly, "Bede's role as a priest to the Angles is shaped by the narrative of Hebrew election, an ethnic election, then extended to the nations of the world." But, just as Ezra saw no conflict between Torah and his Judean identity, Bede does not "forget his tribal allegiance in the face of his Christian faith."[52]

Harris argues that Bede's *History* made it clear that "Christianity does not obliterate ethnic differences but reinterprets them and reconciles them to an abstract religious order of identity." For Bede, the term *gens* is especially important in that it enables two orders of identity — ethnicity and religion — to "exist simultaneously, but not in essential contradiction." In the *History*, "Anglo-Saxons were exposed to a view of themselves as a single people [*gens*] before God — a people who, though they lived in 'Britannia' or 'Saxonia' and though they called themselves Saxons as well as Angles, were known in heaven as the 'gens Anglorum.'" Thus, "one could conceivably be a member of the *gens Saxonum* but understand oneself as part of the larger *gens Anglorum*." The "Christian imperative" here "ultimately depends for its teleological sense of cohesion not on the redesignation of *gens* as a term devoid of its tribal implications, but on a new ethnogenesis which refigured Christ and Abraham as tribal ancestors." In short, "Christianity, through its genealogy through Abraham and God the Father, becomes a mythographic vehicle for uniting divided peoples without forcing the ascetic abnegation of self and tribe upon them. In fact, it is as a unified *ethnie* that they come to spiritual election."[53]

---

52 Ibid., 55–58.
53 Ibid., 61, 64–66.

The historical sociologist, Anthony D. Smith used the French term "*ethnie*" to describe a sense of collective identity dependent on "common or shared stories, sentiments, and expressions of solidarity." Chroniclers of a communal past such as Bede employed their texts "to express what is already conceived as the natural cohesion of a group."[54] Even at an early stage in the ethnogenesis of the *gens Anglorum*, Bede perceived an essential harmony between the five books of the divine law [the Pentateuch], the five languages and four nations [English, British, Scots Irish, and Picts] in Britain. "Each of these have their own language; but all are united in their study of God's truth by the fifth (Latin) which has become a common medium through the study of the scriptures."[55] For Bede, the language of tribal identity could infuse a wider sense of community because "Christian identity was described in textual culture as familial, emphasizing the role of Abraham and Adam as ancestors of all Christians." Even "Anglo-Saxons recently introduced to the faith could have understood themselves as literally descended from both Woden and Adam." While "their physical selves" may have been "a part of the family of Angles (or Saxons)," they identified "their spiritual selves as part of the family of Christ."[56]

Germanic Christendom I: "What Has Weland to Do with Christ"?

Clearly, mythology played a crucial role in the ethnogenesis of the *gens Anglorum*. The mythology which bound Anglo-Saxon Christians together was constantly changing in tandem with their diverse tribal composition. From the time Augustine of Canterbury arrived in England, the mythos of Christian missionaries had to accommodate itself to various indigenous, pagan traditions. As we have seen that process of localization can be described as the "Germanization" of Christianity.

---

54 Ibid., 38–39.
55 Bede, *Ecclesiastical History*, I.1, 45.
56 Harris, *Race and Ethnicity*, 64–66.

Harris notes that, in the nineteenth century, William (later Bishop) Stubbs "distinguished two discrete systems of political organization in England, a Germanic one before 1066, and a Norman one after 1066," in his famous *Constitutional History of England*. There he drew a sharp contrast between the centralized, Norman feudal system based upon "involuntary bonds of fealty" and the oath-based, voluntary relationship binding Anglo-Saxon lords to their free-born subjects within the traditionally Germanic pagan *Männerbund* (Latin: *comitatus*).[57] But, *pace* Stubbs, it was not so much the Norman Conquest, as such, but the concomitant "Romanization" of the English church that undermined the mythological foundations of Anglo-Saxon Christendom.

When Bede was writing his *Ecclesiastical History* in Northumbria, however, the mythological foundations of the Germanic *Männerbund* were still solidly in place. One material manifestation of that mythology can still be seen today in the Franks Casket, a rectangular whalebone box, roughly 23 cm long, 19 cm wide, and 13cm high. This casket is most likely a product (as was Bede's *History*) of the "Northumbrian Renaissance" of the early eighth century. Medieval historian Richard Abels wonders what modern English Christians might make of the carving on "its front panel depicting, side-by-side, the Adoration of the Magi and the bloody tale of Weland the Smith." According to him, most would likely be "inspired to ask, "What has Weland to do with Christ?" Abels then offers his own "cultural explanation for why the casket's designer chose to couple a biblical tale focused upon recognition of Christ's majesty through gift giving with a Germanic story concerned with bloody revenge." The casket itself, Abels believes, could have been commissioned by monks at Jarrow-Wearmouth as a gift for a lordly benefactor. Abels argues that the noble recipient of the casket "would have recognized and appreciated the juxtaposition of a story that emphasized gifts given by faithful men to a good lord in expectation of the lord's much greater countergift (in this case salvation) with

---

57   Ibid., 39, 42, 27.

a tale that with brutal irony depicts the deadly 'gift' that a bad lord could expect from the followers whom he has abused."[58]

Abels describes the front panel of the casket as follows:

> The panel is divided into two equal compartments. In the right-hand compartment three men in profile, the first two carrying chalices and the third a branch, approach a woman and child seated within a columned building. So as to leave no doubt as to their identity, the designer placed the runic inscription *mægi* (Magi) over the first two figures...The Magi, who approach the Virgin and Christ Child sequentially from the left, are distinguished from each other by their visages, gifts, and postures...A nimbed Virgin Mary is presented frontally, seated enthroned with a cross—nimbed Christ Child in her lap...Rather than a manger, the designer places the enthroned Virgin and Child inside an elaborate arched structure reminiscent of both Herod's Temple on the back [of the casket] and the woman's inner sanctuary on the lid.
>
> On the left hand of the front panel is a scene less familiar to modern viewers and one for which there is no surviving early medieval model. Here, a bearded, bare-headed man stands bent-kneed in a forge, tongs in his left hand and a cup cradled in his right. Beneath the man's feet lies a headless body, and in the tongs, we see the head, held over an anvil. The smith is offering the cup to a robed woman, who reaches for it. Another woman stands immediately to her right, clutching a traveller's pouch. Next to her a cloaked man is strangling birds that look very much like the bird leading the Magi to the Christ Child. The audience for which the Franks Casket was intended would have quickly recognized these as episodes from the story of Weland the Smith.[59]

That story "tells how King Niðhad captured the heroic smith, lamed him by severing Weland's hamstrings, and imprisoned him in a forge

---

58 Richard Abels, "What Has Weland to Do with Christ? The Franks Casket and the Acculturation of Christianity in Early Anglo-Saxon England," (2009) 84 *Speculum* 549, 551, 550.

59 *Ibid.*, 558–559.

on an island, where he put him to work making wondrous things."⁶⁰ Not surprisingly, Weland sought revenge:

> Weland, as any proper hero would, plotted and achieved his revenge. He prepared for his escape by having his brother Egil strangle birds and collect their feathers. From these Weland fashioned wings upon which he could fly away. But before escape came vengeance. When the king's two sons visited his smithy to view his treasure, Weland killed them both. He made cups out of their skulls as gifts for their father and gems out of their eyes for their mother. When Niðhad's daughter Beadohild subsequently came to Weland with a broken ring for repair, he gave her a cup of drugged beer (in the casket the cup is made from the skull of her murdered brother) and then raped and impregnated her. Satisfied, he flew away boasting of his revenge.⁶¹

Abels explains the iconography of the Franks Casket as an expression of "the ethos of lordship and moral reciprocity...which obliged a man to do to others as they had done to him, returning *freondscipe* with *freondscipe* and *feondscipe* with *feondscipe*." Thus, "a good follower freely gave gifts to his lord as tokens of his love and loyalty. A worthy lord responded with greater gifts by which he rewarded that love and loyalty." And, of course, "enmity was to be answered with enmity." This idea would have seemed so axiomatic, even to the aristocratic culture surrounding Bede's fellow monks that he thought it necessary to explain to them "that one should forgive enemies out of Christian love and charity, not as a mechanism for calling down upon them divine vengeance." Still, Bede might have recognized "that Weland's revenge and the Magi's adoration fit together into a coherent worldview rooted in an ethos of reciprocity in which gift-giving and revenge were two sides of the same coin."⁶²

Abels emphasizes that the "scenes on the front panel are more plausibly interpreted as complementary than adversarial." On his reading,

---

60   *Ibid.*, 560.
61   *Ibid.*, 560.
62   *Ibid.*, 550–551.

the images of Weland and the Adoration of the Magi "represent two aspects of reciprocity, vendetta and gift-giving, and two models of lordship, the good lordship of the Lord Christ contrasted with the bad lordship of King Niðhad." Leaders "who emulate the former merit the love, loyalty, and gratitude of their followers, which are manifested through their gifts and offerings." On the other hand, "those who treat their men with cruelty and harshness, as King Niðhad did Weland, could expect an equally suitable response, vengeance."[63]

Consequently, the "Christianity that took root in seventh-century England not only reshaped the indigenous Germanic culture but in turn was transformed by it." Abels observes that this "was particularly true for the values and ideals of its warrior aristocracy, which derived less from pagan religion than from the sociopolitical institutions of lordship, the following, and kinship." Because "the Anglo-Saxons conceived of the Christian God as a *dryhten* (warlord)," they were generally more interested in the Old Testament than the New. Naturally enough, "the warlike ethos of the Hebrews of the Old Testament was easily assimilated with the heroic culture of the Anglo-Saxon elite."[64]

The moral lesson implicit in the front panel of the Franks Casket reflects the fact that, "throughout its history, Anglo-Saxon England had a culture that accepted the feud as right and necessary." Given "the institutional limitations on the police powers" in every kingdom on the island, "the vendetta, paradoxically, was perhaps the most effective mechanism for the prevention of violence and maintenance of order in England before the mid-tenth century." Even Alfred the Great never sought "to legislate the vendetta out of existence." Instead, he tried "regulate feuds and to bring them under royal supervision if not control." Not even the fact that "the object of Weland's vengeance was his lord" would have shocked its audience, "especially given the doubtful legitimacy of Niðhad's lordship over Weland." Of course, one

---

63 Ibid., 567.
64 Ibid., 567–568, 579.

was obliged "to serve a good lord faithfully and to express one's love and loyalty through gifts." But a bad lord such as the wicked Niðhad was another matter. In summary, Abels makes a convincing case that Anglo-Saxon Christendom "in the seventh and eighth centuries represented more than a superficial syncretism in which Christianity transformed to its uses native culture; rather, it was a fusion of different cultures in which Christianity itself was profoundly transformed."[65]

Germanic Christendom II: The Saxon Gospel

In his *History* Bede mentions the Anglo-Saxon mission sent to Germany to convert the various pagan tribes to Christianity. The most famous of those missionaries was Bede's contemporary, St. Boniface. Originally known by his Anglo-Saxon name of Wynfrid, Boniface was born in Wessex c. 675 AD and became active as a missionary in Germany after 716 AD. His approach to the pagan Germans is usually interpreted as critical of "earlier missionaries' attempts to 'accommodate' ritual and formulation to native Germanic culture." According to G. Ronald Murpy, he allegedly "insisted instead on romanization of the pagans in the preaching of the Gospel." The most notorious illustration of his supposed refusal to tolerate pagan practices was his "felling of the sacred oak of Thor at Geismar while a great crowd of pagans stood silently cursing Boniface as the enemy of their gods and concealing their shock and hatred in their hearts."[66]

James Russell disagrees with Murphy, contending that Boniface's actions at Geismar actually accommodated a fundamental premise of Germanic religion, that is, that the most powerful god should be worshipped." In addition, Boniface's decision to use the very timber of the Thor Oak in the construction of a church further supports the view

---

65 Ibid., 575–577, 581.
66 G. Ronald Murphy, *The Saxon Savior: The Germanic Transformation of the Gospel in the Ninth-Century Heliand* (New York: Oxford University Press, 1989), 13–14.

that Boniface was in fact pursuing a policy of accommodation.[67] Later in 737, Boniface undertook a mission to the old, or continental Saxons. During that mission, in 744, Boniface founded the celebrated monastery at Fulda, located on a river providing easy access to the North Sea. Despite Boniface's best efforts, however, the Saxons remained resistant to the church's efforts to convert them to Christianity. In the late eighth century, Charlemagne engaged in a sustained and brutal military campaign aimed at the forced conversion of the recalcitrant Saxons.

Sometime around the year 830, still facing passive resistance at best from the Saxons, the monastery at Fulda undertook an alternative, pacific project — commissioned by Charlemagne's son and troubled successor — aimed at persuading pagans to take a more positive view of Christianity. The result was an epic poem, amounting to almost 6000 lines of alliterative verse in the Old Saxon language.[68] It appears that, *inter alia*, the poem was often sung by itinerant monks to groups of Saxon nobles gathered in mead halls. Originally untitled, it was not

---

67 Russell, *Germanization of Early Medieval Christianity*, 94 note 38.
68 G. Ronald Murphy, S.J., *The Heliand: The Saxon Gospel* Translation and Commentary by G. Ronal Murphy, S.J. (New York: Oxford University Press, 1992). The anonymous poet who wrote this poem may have been a monk resident at Fulda and, hence, someone with some cultural connection to Anglo-Saxon England. In any case, manuscript versions of the poem were circulating in England during the tenth century: see Ciaran Arthur, "The *Heliand* in Tenth-Century England: Translation, Transmission and Turbulence," (2021) 47(4-5) *Journal of Medieval History* 509–25.
For those who can read German, there is an attractive folio edition edited by Clemens Burchhardt which provides a translation from Old Saxon into modern German. Clemens Burchhardt, ed. *Heliand: Die Verdener altsächische Evangelien-Dichtung übertragen ins 21. Jahrhundert* (Verden, 2007).
The Burchhardt edition has been described by Elisabeth Kristofferson as "unfortunately…a rather inaccurate translation strongly coloured by the editor's personal preferences as a man of the church." She nevertheless recommends it "because it puts Simrock's edition of the Hêliand and their translation side by side, making it very handy to work with if one is aware of the challenges in the German translation." 10 (full citation below in note 75) That German translation should also be compared with Murphy's translation and commentary above.

until 1830, when it was published by its first editor, Andreas Schmeller, that it became known as the *Heliand*, or "Saviour." In form, the *Heliand* was an "evangelic harmony," combining all four gospels into one coherent story. Its goal was to portray the life of Christ in a dynamic, intercultural context by transferring the original Mediterranean language and cultural references into a new, North Sea, geographical, cultural, and linguistic setting.[69]

In the mid-nineteenth century German scholar A. F. C. Vilmar eagerly embraced the *Heliand* as *das Christentum im deutschen Gewände* (or Christendom in German Clothing). On his reading, the image of Jesus had been transformed into *ein deutscher Christus* or a "German Christ." Ronald Murphy, author of the authoritative *The Saxon Savior*, acknowledges that this controversial thesis "has been largely rejected by the scholarship of the present day, and yet [he thinks] there is indeed much to be said for it." While suggesting that the author of this "*Saxon* religious epic" was unlikely to have conceived the work as an expression of anything like Vilmar's pan-Germanic ideology, Murphy does concede that the *Heliand* "can be accurately interpreted both as a *saxonization* and as a *northernization* of the Gospel."[70] Lukasz Neubauer agrees, describing the poem as "an idiosyncratic reimagining of the Gospel in which the anonymous Saxon poet chose to depict Christ as an archetypical native hero." Blending "traditional Germanic views on loyalty and courage with the purely Christian concepts of humility, forgiveness, love, and sympathy," the poet nimbly creates "a largely Saxonised portrait of the Son of God and the social milieu of His laudable deeds in the far land of Galilee (*Galilealand*)."[71]

---

69 Murphy, *Saxon Savior*, 12, 28; Douglas Hayward, "Contextualizing the Gospel Among the Saxons: An Example form the Ninth Century of the Cultural Adaptation of the Gospel as Found in the *Heliand*," (1994) 22(4) *Missiology: An International Review* 439, at 441.

70 Murphy, *Saxon Savior*, 3–4.

71 Lukasz Neubauer, "The Character of 'Iĕsu Krist' in the Old Saxon Gospel Harmony 'The Hêliand' as a Dramatic Cultural Synthesis Combining Elements

Neubaurer argues that the "unique Germanic character" of the *Heliand* can be found in the image "of a bellicose Messiah and his private entourage." As a rule, the Saxon Christ is portrayed as the *manno mahtig drohtin* (mighty lord of men), "a northern European chieftain who treads the earth with his fearless band of *sâlige gisîðos* (trustworthy retainers), performing numerous deeds of righteousness and courage." The native Saxon tone can be seen in "the hypermasculine relationship between the military lord Christ (*Krist*) and his twelve battle-hardened *thegnôs* (thegns)."[72]

Neubarer finds echoes of Bede's own description of Saxon chieftains in the poem. Bede remarks:

> For these Old Saxons have no king, but several lords who are set over the nation. Whenever war is imminent, these cast lots impartially, and the one on whom the lot falls is followed and obeyed by all for the duration of the war; but as soon as the war ends, the lords revert to equality of status.[73]

The "very idea of elective leadership" piqued Neubaurer's interest. On the one hand, this seems to run counter to "the hierarchical (perhaps somewhat Arian in its nature) relationship between the Father (king) and the Son (chieftain)" in the *Heliand*. There, God is typically referred to as "the mightiest of all kings," "King of Heaven," or "Almighty Father." Neubaurer points out that "His son Jesus may share some of His Father's epithets, but He is primarily known [as] 'God's Child' whose outstanding valour and untiring commitment to the 'All-Creator' allow him to be assigned by the Lord as His Sacrificial Lamb." On the other hand, the poem has Christ being "subsequent elected (not the other way round) by the two brothers, James and John who 'chose for

---

of Deep Christian Piety and the Germanic Code of Heroic Honour," in *Marvels of Reading: Essays in Honour of Professor Andrzej Wicher*, 71–84. Downloaded from The Central and Eastern European Online Library at: https://www.ceeol.com/search/chapter-detail?id=1076694, at 74.

72 Ibid., 74.

73 Bede, *Ecclesiastical History*, V 10, 281.

themselves, Christ the Saviour.'" Matthew, too, "chose Christ as Lord" to be both their mighty chieftain and 'Lord of mankind.'"[74]

It is not uncommon for such emphasis on the Germanic character of the *Heliand* to provoke shocked, even horrified reactions. One classic example of academic pearl-clutching can be found in a master's thesis in Nordic Studies completed in 2013 at Oslo University by Elisabeth Kristoffersen. In her preface, Kristoffersen salutes the *Heliand* as "one of our earliest, most contemporary, best preserved and therefore most important sources of early medieval thought and religious mentality in what is now northern Germany." She is concerned, however, that the study of this subject "for some reason is still overshadowed and quite resiliently so even among scholars by the prejudices, romanticisms and misconceptions of the 19th century and those of the Nazis." Worried that the "subject itself seems to be tainted in the public mind," she set out to redeem the reputation of the *Heliand* as an important intellectual resource. She hoped to accomplish that task both "by renewing interest in the subject and removing the brown stain." Such language seems to imply that any interpretation of the *Heliand* as part of the historical process now known as the "Germanization of Christianity" is tantamount to academic crypto-Nazism. In combatting that moral menace, Kristoffersen argues that the goal of the *Heliand*'s author was the pacification or, in effect, the Christianization of the Saxons. To attain that end, she explains, the storytelling of the *Heliand* presents a vision of conversion to Christianity as something other than racial conquest; namely, "the more 'peaceful' way of submissiveness and assimilation."[75]

A major problem with Kristoffersen's thesis is that the "Germanization of Christianity" was not confined to Germany; nor

---

74 Neubauer, *Old Saxon Gospel Harmony*, 75–76. On the Arian question, *cf.*, Stephen Pelle, "The *Heliand* and Christological Orthodoxy," (2010) 27 *Florilegium* 63–89.

75 Elisabeth Kristoffersen, "Pacifying the Saxons: An Interpretative Reading of the Hêliand," Master of Arts Thesis, University of Oslo (15 November 2013), viii, 11, 26. Downloaded from: https://www.duo.uio.no/handle/10852/38506.

can it be equated with war, conquest, and racial supremacy. As we have seen, the Germanization of Christianity also featured in the history of Anglo-Saxon England. Moreover, in that context, the history of Germanization had to do not merely with a people's intergenerational experience of their own ethnogenesis but also with the way in which at least some Anglo-Saxons once conceived the history of war and peace in the world-at-large. There we see that, *pace* Bruce Kaye, it was the confluence of *ethnicity* and Christianity, not "the coalescence of power and authority of the lay and clerical elements of a christian polity," which gave rise to Anglo-Saxon Christendom.[76]

Germanic Christendom III: The Old English History of the World

Mythology and narrative are constitutive elements of ethnic identity. According to Stephen Harris, evidence for that proposition can be found in the ninth-century reconfiguration of an Anglo-Saxon ethnic identity which had its beginnings in the authoritative Latin text of Bede's *Ecclesiastical History of the English People*." In that text, the Anglo-Saxons "came from three very powerful Germanic tribes, the Saxons, Angles, and Jutes (*Iutis*)."[77] This "textual kernel of tradition" was refashioned one hundred and seventy years later in the Old English translation of Bede's *History* commissioned by King Alfred. There the translator declared that the Anglo-Saxons came from the three incoming tribes identified as "that of the *Seaxum*, and of the *Angle*, and of the *Geatum*," meaning the Saxons, the Angles, and the Goths. Citing Jane Acomb Leake, Harris tells us that the "Geats appear to have been a mythological result of "misinterpretations of Latin works of literature, geography, and theology dating from the classical and early Christian periods."[78]

---

76 Harris, *Race and Ethnicity*, 84; Kaye, *Rise and Fall*, 2–3.
77 Bede, *Ecclesiastical History*, I 15, 63.
78 Harris, *Race and Ethnicity*, 84–85.

A long mythological tradition which included *Beowulf* had been incorporated into the common Germanic heritage of "a *gens teudisca*, a community of German-speaking *people*." The ethnographic myths of origins of several peoples, including the Longobards, the Danes, and the Angles, all begin with the figure of Geat, whose progeny was said to have included Theodoric the Great, Emperor of Rome. Ethnographic tradition thus even validated "a link between Germanic ethnicity and Roman *imperium*." But group identity required both a religious and an ethnic component. Harris contends that King Alfred's court found the basis for the reconfiguration of Anglo-Saxon ethnoreligious identity in the Old English translation of a fifth-century Latin work (itself commissioned by Augustine of Hippo), Paul Orosius' *Seven Books of History Against the Pagans*. The translation of this book (hereafter *World History*) was completed sometime between 889 and 899 AD. Its reconfiguration of Anglo-Saxon group identity turned on the concept of Christendom, an order of ethnoreligious "identity established by Charlemagne and which, like the Geatish genealogies, combined Germanic *imperium* with Roman Christianity."[79]

Harris argues that adherence to Christendom "offered an Anglo-Saxon not only Christian identity, born of Latin textual culture, but also a Germanic identity, which was nonetheless intimately tied to an ancient Christian past." He adds that "the Old English word for this ethno-religious order of identity is *Cristendom*" which "first appears in texts of the ninth century and is used in the *World History* thirty-seven times." Over the next three centuries, the word had varying uses but in the ninth century it did not "properly refer to a political community comprised of Christians." As "a domain or community of believers," Christendom was often conceived "in theoretical opposition to heathendom." When established "among a people, as its ethnic or national religion," Christendom could also be "imagined as the Church." In

---

79 Ibid., 86; See also, Malcolm R. Godden, Editor and Translator *The Old English History of the World: An Anglo-Saxon Rewriting of Orosius* (Cambridge, MA: Harvard University Press, 2016.

the original Latin edition of Orosius' book, however, Christ and the Church were rarely mentioned. The Alfredian *World History* configured "identity and morality within Christendom" and, especially when dealing with the fifth-century sacking of Rome, offered "an ethnic (especially Anglo-Saxon) response to Christian history; that is, a sense of Germanic community shapes the Latin into a story of the origins of Christendom." In short, the *World History* shifted the focus of the original "from a Roman Christ to a Germanic Christendom."[80]

In the original, Orosius portrayed the political condition of Rome in his time, the early fifth century, as "a consequence of divine and secular history coming to a single point, the birth of Christ within the Empire. Furthermore, the later decline of the Christian faith… was the cause of the Germanic invasion." But the Alfredian translation totally excises "the passages extolling the centrality of Rome to God's historical plan." The birth of a Roman Christ, the "one essential piece of historical evidence which grounds Orosius' larger argument is nowhere to be seen." Orosius claimed "that Christ was historically a Roman citizen, and thus tied implicitly and exclusively to the fate of Rome." But, if so, the Alfredian translator was bound to ask himself: What "role could the historical Christ play in the course of Western history after the fall of Rome?"[81]

The translator of the *World History*, unlike Orosius writing in the year 415 AD, knew that the Roman Empire had collapsed. Rome was no longer "considered — although it may once have been — the conduit for God's historical presence." Orosius might try to convince himself that the Empire had not fallen because of the sacking of Rome by the Gothic king Alaric in 410 AD. But Alfred's ninth-century translator "would have been identified ethnically with the Goths rather than with the Romans, and religiously with Christendom." For him, the Anglo-Saxons were descended from the Goths. Given that identification with

---

80 Harris, *Race and Ethnicity*, 88–91.
81 Ibid., 95, 100.

Alaric, it comes as no surprise that "the sacking of Rome is characterized as an entirely peaceful affair" in the *World History* or that "Alaric is called the most Christian king, *se cristena cyning*."⁸²

Not only did Alaric not burn Rome but no one was slain. To cap it all, "the Goths left of their own accord, not explicitly by God's hand." The *World History* unites "Christian and Germanic identity in the person of Alaric, the most Christian of kings." In this account, then, the Roman past no longer spoke to the Germanic present. The ninth-century Anglo-Saxon identification with historical, Carolingian Christendom created "an order of identity that [had] left the senate and people of Rome far behind." Hence, the *World History* had no good reason to treat Rome or Greece as the centre around which history revolves. Instead, the religious and ethnic logic of Christendom, a "combined sense of Christian kingship and Germanic Christendom seems to have shaped the historical record of Alfred's leadership."⁸³ Alfred the Great *chose* to pursue a Christian "project of peoplehood" based on the mythic model of biblical Israel. Tragically, that vision was doomed. Within little more than a century and a half, it was, like Alfred himself, dead and buried.

Conclusion: To Be or Not to Be?

Ten years ago, a young Englishman with an Anglo-Norman name and an Oxonian academic pedigree to match, ran counter to an established scholarly consensus by denying that the English of the Anglo-Saxon period really thought that they, like the Old Testament Israelites, were God's elect. At the time, I brushed his argument aside. Now, I must admit that George Molyneaux was not altogether wrong. He does make a strong case in opposition to Patrick Wormald and others "who contended that long before the Norman Conquest, the notion that the English had a 'special relationship with the Almighty' was already

---

82 *Ibid.*, 100, 96–97.

83 *Ibid.*, 99, 105.

firmly established." In fact, there really does not seem to be a great deal of evidence that most Englishmen living between the early eighth and the late tenth century ever believed that England was a "chosen nation," distinguished from other Christian nations in that they enjoyed God's special favour. There may be some scattered sources, such as Bede or in works produced by the court of King Alfred, containing such language. But Anglo-Saxon England clearly failed to produce a body of sacred literature remotely comparable to the Hebrew Bible testifying to its elect status.[84]

On the other hand, if we can believe Jacob Wright, prior to the production of the Hebrew Bible during the Hellenic era (*i.e.*, perhaps as late as the second century BC), Judeans never claimed to be descendants of an elect nation, led out of slavery in Egypt by the prophet Moses to enter a covenant with Yahweh. Nor did they claim that, a millennium earlier, Joshua had led them into the land long before promised to Abraham's seed. Wright makes a convincing case that the myth of the chosen people was a man-made literary creation deliberately designed to create an Israelite national identity. In other words, the Hebrew Bible was written to advance a group evolutionary strategy of survival, or a "project of peoplehood," as Wright puts it. Wright also demonstrates that Israel was chosen, not by God, but by an intergenerational, anonymous body of religious scribes, pursuing a clear ethnoreligious agenda in geopolitical competition with other groups for land, resources, power, and prestige.

During the Anglo-Saxon period in England, Bede, King Alfred, and those he employed as translators and writers, were similarly engaged in their own peoplehood project. To that end, they produced a body of ethnoreligious literature, hoping to inspire the fusion of a Germanic ethnicity with the Christian religion. Their goal was to produce a *gens Anglorum*, or what Alfred the Great hoped might become an *Angelcynn* Christendom. The anonymous poet who wrote the *Heliand* was also

---

84 George Molyneaux, "Did the English Really Think They Were God's Elect in the Anglo-Saxon Period?" (2014) 65(4) *Journal of Ecclesiastical History* 721–737.

engaged in an ethnogenetic enterprise. All of them *chose* to act in ways they hoped might inspire their respective peoples to become an elect nation, or, at least, a nation as elect as possible. As a matter of historical fact, it was not God who *chose* either to bestow "chosen" status upon biblical Israel or to deny it to the embryonic English nation.

Instead, whether it was Bede, Alfred, or the *Heliand* poet, all *chose* to bestow their special favour (whatever it was worth) upon their respective Germanic Christendoms. Unfortunately, despite having the Bible as a mythic model of ethnoreligious nation-building outside and apart from a national state apparatus, the Anglo-Saxon project of peoplehood failed. Anglo-Saxon scribes simply lacked anything like the institutional, cultural, and motivational resources available to their Judean counterparts during the Hellenic era. And, of course, the Norman Conquest certainly didn't help matters. But, well before William the Conqueror was crowned as King of England, the Anglo-Saxon peoplehood project was already foundering. Indeed, by the end of the tenth century, the linkage between Anglo-Saxon, or even Germanic, ethnic identity and the Christian religion had already been strained, and finally severed, by a problem sadly all-too-familiar to all the once-British peoples of the Anglosphere today.

By the late tenth century it was no longer possible to deny, much less ignore, "that the English were a racially diverse community, the home of what one scholar describes as "multi-national inhabitants," Danes, Angles, Saxons, and, even pagan Viking pirates, some of whom also chose to settle in the Danelaw. Notionally common Germanic origins and fictive royal and biblical genealogies were not capable of papering over ethnic rivalries. In 1014, Archbishop Wulfstan of York delivered a famous sermon, the Sermon of the Wolf to the English. In the *Sermo*, he emphasized that the "binding force of this ethnically diverse community is a common subjection to the law of God and man." As Harris observes, "this logic takes no account of ethnic differentiation among Englishmen: it makes a single body out of three ethnicities." Unlike Bede, Wulfstan did not define his community "as an *ethnie*, nor as an essentially Germanic community like Alfred's *Angelcynn*, but as a multi-ethnic Christian group whose individuals were jointly and actively responsible for the community's fate."[85]

As revealed in his *Sermo*, Wulfstan's notion of English identity subordinated collective *ethnic* identity to a *legal* and *moral* identity. This view "which diminishes ethnicity in the face of a moral and legal community, seems to have played a fundamental role in the transfer of dominion from the Anglo-Danes and the Anglo-Saxons to the Normans." At that point, Harris observes, "issues of ethnicity and ethnogenesis arose anew." Although the process of Germanizing Christianity came to an end, receiving its formal obituary in its replacement by a novel Anglo-Norman myth of origins. Seventy years or so after the Battle of Hastings, a fictive romance, now attributed to Geoffrey of Monmouth, and then written in Latin, recounted what purported to be the history of the kings of Britain, from Brutus of Troy to King Arthur, holding his plenary court at Caerleon-on-Usk in a mythical pre-Saxon era. This historical fantasy managed to put "the centre of English identity in the antique Mediterranean, thus giving new English origins a sense of authority as ancient as Rome's own origins."[86] In this new world order, the Normanized proto-state was paired with a supercharged and Romanized Church. Together, they set out the separate spiritual and secular pathways which led, over the next millennium, to the managerial, globalist, disenchanted, and thoroughly deracinated theology reflected in Bruce Kaye's account of *The Rise and Fall of the English Christendom.*

So much for the magicoreligious world we have lost. Or dare we hope to recover, repair, or, indeed, resurrect the racially distinctive spirit of our long-forgotten *Angelcynn* ancestors? Do we, as the British-descended peoples of the Anglosphere, still have such a choice? Does God truly help those peoples who help themselves? Where do we go

---

85   Harris, *Race and Ethnicity*, 121, 122, 124.

86   Ibid., 129, 132. See also, Geoffrey of Monmouth, *The History of the Kings of Britain* (Harmondsworth: Penguin, 1966).

from here, and how do we get there? Perhaps it is time that Anglican theologians took the advice of the nineteenth century historian, Sir John Seeley, and set about their own mytho-historical project of peoplehood by creating a long overdue British Bible.[87]

---

[87] See, J.R. Seeley, "The Church as a Teacher of Morality," in Rev. W.L. Clay, ed., *Essays in Church Policy* (London: Macmillan, 1868), 267.

PART THREE

Beyond Creedal Christianity: Neo-Angelcynn Political Theology versus Globalist Churches and the Transnational Corporate State

10. Who are We? Restoring the Ethnoreligious Dimensions of WASP Identity in the Spiritual Wastelands of the Anglosphere

Introduction

THE MOVE BY the Canadian government to criminalize "condoning, denying, or downplaying" the Holocaust is not just an infringement of civil liberties supposedly guaranteed by the Charter of Rights and Freedoms. More importantly, it endows a distinctively Jewish political theology with legal protections now denied to traditional Christian beliefs. The fact that this development has not been opposed either by mainline Protestant or Catholic churches is highly significant. Still, once upon a time, the Catholic Church did possess a distinctive political theology of its own, one identifying the Jewish people as an actual or, at best, a potential foe. The Second Vatican Council put an end to that "antisemitic" article of faith. But in principle, at least, Catholics could return to their historic political theology on the Jewish Question. Things are quite different among the Anglo-Protestant people of Canada and of the Anglosphere, generally.

Anglo-Protestantism has long since been captured by cosmopolitan humanism, a liberal theology refusing to accept the intractable, existential character of the distinction between friend and foe. Accordingly, Anglo-Protestants shy away from the traditional Christian belief that the Old Covenant with Israel according to the flesh was superseded by a New Covenant between God and the Church. Having rejected such "supersessionism," Anglo-Protestants generally recognize the Jews as elder brothers in the faith whose Covenant with God remains in force. The Holocaust Mythos, therefore, has been received as the story of a monstrous crime committed against a people of God representative of humanity-at-large. Mainline Anglo-Protestant churches inhabit a moral universe in which a loving God confronts the "perpetrators" of genocides against innocent "victims" who may or may not receive aid, comfort, or justice from "bystanders."

The Jewish people, on the other hand, perceive their lifeworld as one characterized by a sharp division between "philosemitic" friends and "antisemitic" enemies. Since the mid-twentieth century, Jews have persuaded Anglo-Protestants that "antisemitic" prejudice has no rational basis. Accordingly, the anti-Jewish policies of the Third Reich led our governments to portray German "Nazis" and Prussian "militarists," to this day, as "enemies," not just of the British peoples, but of humanity itself.

Now that the Palestinian President (while sharing a platform with the German Chancellor) has charged Israel with inflicting "50 Holocausts" upon his people, one might well wonder whether the Germans copped a bum rap over the Holocaust 1.0.[1] To reach any firm conclusion on that issue, we should reflect upon the historical development of Anglo-Protestantism and the theological presuppositions that have prevented the church from developing an ethnoreligious theology capable of reliably distinguishing "friend" from "foe".

The Church of England created the original model of Anglo-Protestantism during the sixteenth century. Its clergy and parishioners came to be known as "Anglicans," a Latinism derived from the old Anglo-Saxon term "Angelcynn," meaning literally "kin of the Angles." In retrospect, this nomenclature begs the question as to whether Anglo-Protestant political theology retains the capacity to draw any

---

1   Chris Jewers, "German Cops Launch Probe into Palestinian President Mahmud Abbas over Holocaust comments," *Daily Mail* (August 19, 2022).

distinction between "friend" and "enemy" now that the Anglican "brand" has been drained of its ancestral, biblically based, ethnoreligious meaning.

Nations are rooted in historical myths, symbols, and ethnoreligious traditions which, in the case of England, developed over many centuries. Leading authorities in support of that thesis are Anthony D. Smith on *The Ethnic Origins of Nations* and Martin Lichtmesz on *Ethnopluralismus*.[2] The concept of ethnopluralism must be distinguished sharply from modern secular policies of multiculturalism as defended, for example by James Tully.[3]

Official multiculturalism in the Anglosphere refuses to recognize the political dimensions of Anglo-Protestant ethnoreligious identity. But the Israeli historian, Azar Gat has documented the long history and deep roots of both political ethnicity and nationalism.[4] He provides all Anglo-Protestants with good reasons to recover a political theology anchored in their shared ethnoreligious identity. As things stand, every Protestant denomination, Anglican and dissenting churches alike, have united with the state to deny the legitimacy, indeed even the reality, of any such need.

Carl Schmitt is generally credited with the invention of the term "political theology".[5] But what exactly did Schmitt mean by political theology? German scholar Heinrich Meier suggests that Schmitt was looking for the legitimate foundations of political action. In European civilization, he found a conflict between political philosophy, ostensibly

---

2   Anthony D. Smith, *The Ethnic Origin of Nations* (Wiley-Blackwell, 1988); Martin Lichtmesz, *Ethnopluralismus: Kritik und Verteidigung* (Schnellroda: Antaios Verlag, 2020).

3   James Tully, *Strange Multiplicity: Constitutionalism in an Age of Diversity* (Cambridge University Press, 1995).

4   Asar Gat, *Nations: The Long History and Deep Roots of Political Ethnicity and Nationalism* (Cambridge University Press, 2012).

5   Carl Schmitt, *Political Theology: Four Chapters on the Concept of Sovereignty* (tr. George Schwab). (Cambridge, MA: MIT Press, 1985).

based in the universal principles of rational discourse, and revelation anchored in particularistic ethnoreligions.[6] To speak of revelation, of course, takes us into the realm of biblical theology. What is the relationship between biblical revelation and political theology? Did the historical Jesus preach a political theology? Did Jesus the Christ and his followers, before and after the Cross, have friends and enemies? While the historical Jesus seems to have focused on the destiny of his own people, the global Jesus, as worshipped by contemporary Anglo-Protestants, came to save the whole of humanity.[7] But what if "humanity" must manifest its corporeal and spiritual identity through the medium of families, tribes, and nations, such as those found in medieval and modern England, Scotland, Wales, and Ireland? Not infrequently, those peoples regarded each other as deadly foes spawned by the forces of evil.

Political Theology in British History

For that reason, ancestral Anglo-Protestant churches, kings, and queens practiced political theology as an intractable fact of life, if only subliminally, *avant la lettre*. Indeed, the theology of the Old English nation is best understood as the theopolitical prerequisite for their historical ethnogenesis. The story of the emergence of the English nation, no less than the biblical narrative of ancient Israel, was and remains a *process* moved by "the lure of God."[8] Ethnoreligious divisions long defined friends and enemies, thereby shaping the demographic

---

6   Heinrich Meier, *Die Lehre Carl Schmitts: Vier Kapitel zur Unterscheidung Politischer Theologie und Politischer Philosophie* (Stuttgart: Verlag J.B. Metzler, 2012).

7   *Cf.*, Scot McKnight, *A New Vision for Israel: The Teachings of Jesus in National Context* (Grand Rapids, MI: William B. Eerdmanns, 1999) and Andrew Fraser, "Global Jesus versus National Jesus: The Political Hermeneutics of Resurrection," (2021) 21(1) *The Occidental Quarterly* (Spring 2021), 55–76.

8   Lewis S. Ford, *The Lure of God: A Biblical Background for Process Theism* (Philadelphia: Fortress Press, 1978). Available online at: https://www.religion-online.org/book/the-lure-of-god-a-biblical-background-for-process-theism.

development of the English nation. Neither the English nor, later, the British state created the English nation. Instead, an embryonic English *ethnos*, working in and through both the early *Angelcynn* church and the king, became the prototype of an English "state," well before the Norman Conquest.

Over the centuries, the identity of those deemed to be enemies of the English changed. During the reign of Alfred, the Great, the Vikings were perceived as the greatest threat.[9] When William the Conqueror invaded England, the Norman enemy was victorious. The Norman Conquest in combination with the Papal Revolution transformed the ethnoreligious culture of England.[10]

Following the upheavals of the Reformation and Civil War, the division between Protestants and Catholics largely defined the distinction between friend and enemy both domestically and internationally for Britons.[11] With the expansion of England, a Greater Britain emerged in the settler colonies around the world. From the eighteenth century onwards, the British Empire competed for power and resources with continental rivals such as France and Germany. Religious differences were no longer central to such conflicts. Indeed, since then, the process of secularization advanced to the point where historians have pronounced the death of Christian Britain.[12]

In the Empire at large, one might even ask whether Australia, for example, was ever a Christian community on its road to nationhood.[13]

---

9   Andrew Fraser, "Making Angelcynns: How Alfred the Great Responded to the Viking Invasions," (2016) 2(1) *Anglican Tradition* 1.

10 Andrew Fraser, "Sanctifying the Norman Yoke: William the Conqueror, the Angelcynn Church, and the Papal Revolution," (2016) 2(2) *Anglican Tradition* 7. n.

11 Linda Colley, *Britons: Forging the Nation, 1707–1837*, 2nd ed. (Yale University Press, 2009).

12 Callum G. Brown, *The Death of Christian Britain: Understanding Secularisation, 1800–2000*, 2nd ed. (Routledge, 2009).

13 Andrew Fraser, "Was Early NSW a Christian Community?," (2015) 1(7) *Anglican Tradition* 1.

Ever since World War II, the declining Anglican confession throughout the Anglosphere has celebrated its escape from "Anglo-Saxon captivity,"[14] to the point where it has been absorbed into a form of global Christianity hostile to any suggestion that the Anglican church should be of, by, and for the white British peoples of the Anglosphere. "White racism" is now the proclaimed enemy of mainstream Anglican political theology.

Indeed, contemporary Anglican political theology, in the person of the Archbishop of Canterbury, Justin Welby, manifests itself as the kinder, gentler face of post-Christian globalist bioleninism.[15] In other words, it is difficult to distinguish between the public face of Anglican political theology and the Woke political ideology governing "Our Democracies."

In the realm of academic theology, however, Oliver O'Donovan's *The Desire of the Nations* offers a much more sophisticated model of Anglican political theology, but one no less opposed to an ethnoreligious understanding of the Anglican tradition.[16] O'Donovan contends that the point and purpose of every nation's existence has been determined once and for all by the "Christ event." "Membership in Christ," he declares, "replaced all other political identities by which communities knew themselves."[17] Because the church is "catholic" it "leaps over all existing communal boundaries and forbids any part of the human race…to think of the Kingdom of God as confined within its own limits and to lose interest in what lies beyond them." Strictly speaking, according to O'Donovan the church is an "eschatological"

---

14 Kevin Ward, *A History of Global Anglicanism* (Cambridge University Press, 2010), Chapter 15: "The Anglican Communion: Escaping the Anglo-Saxon Captivity of the Church?" 296–318.

15 Nicholas R. Jeelvy, "On Bioleninism," *Counter-Currents* (July 31, 2020). https://counter-currents.com/2020/07/on-bioleninism.

16 Oliver O'Donovan, *The Desire of the Nations: Rediscovering the Roots of Political Theology* (Cambridge University Press, 1996).

17 Ibid., 148.

rather than a political society: it can be "entered only *by leaving* other, existing societies."[18]

For O'Donovan, in the modern world, not even those other "political" societies constituted by governments are based on shared blood, language, and religion. Instead, the only form of "nationalism" open to modern "nation-states" such as Australia, Canada, or the United Kingdom is a "civic nationalism" defined by a common political will. Nationalism, therefore, is sometimes said to be in trouble. But, O'Donovan maintains, this is nothing new. "The truth is," he remarks, "it has been in trouble ever since Christ rose from the dead."[19] In the eschatological society of the church, "no people's identity as a people can be assumed; community identity is no longer self-evident. It is called into question by the existence of a new people, drawn from every nation, which by its catholic identity casts doubt on every other."[20] In stark contrast, to that "catholic" vision of Christian identity, I contend that the *Volksgeist* of the English nation (and other British-descended peoples) was once, and could be again, an important medium through which God works in this world. Accordingly, my thesis rests on a set of presuppositions that differ in certain fundamental respects from those underlying O'Donovan's approach to political theology.

A realist political theology presupposes a Christian ethnotheology capable of distinguishing between the "friends" and "enemies" of a particular family, tribe, or nation. Such an appeal to ethnotheology is beyond the ken of most white nationalists, especially those in the USA. Repulsed by the facile universalism promoted by mainstream Christianity, it has been all too easy for white nationalists to mimic the fatal obsession with one — biological — dimension of racial identity. Racialists all too often forget that in days of yore the foundations of national and racial identity were laid by the Church. Until recently

---

18 *Ibid.*, 178 (emphasis in original).

19 *Ibid.*, 241.

20 *Ibid.*, 235.

perhaps, the identity of most white Americans has been that of a "people of plenty," defined not by common descent and kinship but by their unprecedented material wealth.[21] Nevertheless, dissident whites still long for the restoration of a racially homogeneous Constitutional Republic made of, by, and for white people.

But American white nationalism has yet to enjoy even the first hint of success in its struggle to restore the Old White Republic. Indeed, both white racial advocacy and the original, Anglo-American model of civic republicanism have been thoroughly marginalized in America by a cosmopolitan corporate culture of perpetual innovation altogether unfettered by parochial loyalty to either race or nation.

Thirty-some years ago, American open-door imperialism finally wore down the closed, command economy of Soviet-style Communism.[22] The collapse of the Soviet Union removed the last significant barrier to the free movement of capital, technology, and labour around the world, thereby handing a handsome prize to transnational corporate capital. By then, the neo-communist left, too, had already won a decisive victory. From the mid-Sixties onward, the mass migration of even the most unproductive Third World peoples into every white country was no longer open to effective political challenge. Consequently, white nationalism has been vacuum-sealed inside an intellectual bubble from whence it gazes upon a world gone mad.

Unfortunately, racial nationalists throughout the Anglosphere have deprived themselves of the spiritual oxygen needed to start political brushfires. They have become mired in the secular biopolitics of race. Of course, race *is* a biological reality, and white racial realists *are* routinely demonized and viciously defamed in politics, the courts,

---

21 David Potter, *People of Plenty: Economic Abundance and the American Character* (Chicago: University of Chicago Press, 1958).

22 The best introduction to American foreign policy as the theory and practice of open-door imperialism remains William Appleman Williams, *The Tragedy of American Diplomacy* [50th Anniversary Edition] (New York: WW Norton, 2009).

the media, or in academia. But white nationalists must not deny or downplay the importance of two other, equally important, dimensions of racial identity: namely, race-as-ethnicity and race-as-theology.[23]

Race is a three-dimensional, trinitarian phenomenon. Assuredly, race is a fact of life encoded in the DNA of every human being. But, like it or not, race is *also* a "social construct." After all, every major continental "race" — whites, blacks, and Orientals — includes many sub-races or ethnic groups. Tribes, *ethnie*, and nations emerged as the contingent products of historical, cultural, and linguistic evolution. Such ethno-cultural groupings create marked differences between peoples who may be closely related in genetic terms. Such observations are, of course, grist for anti-racist propaganda mills. But the deeply entrenched secular perspective shared by white racialists *and* their anti-racist opponents blinds both to the *third* dimension, race-as-theology.

The New Race of Christians

The history of European civilization preserves the documentary and archaeological record of the moment when God breathed life into the white race. Only in Europe did the reciprocal interaction of biology, ethnicity, and religion create a unique family of Christian nations. The early Church was the corporate seedbed of a new race (Greek: *laos, ethnos, genos*; Latin: *genus, natio*).[24] Within little more than a century, Christians from every corner of the known world (*oikumene*) were re-born as a new people possessed of a history stretching back millennia and a destiny grounded in the Great Commission delivered by Christ to his apostles. The divinely ordained mission of the Church was to "go and make disciples of all nations, baptizing them in the name of the Father and of the Son and the Holy Spirit and teaching them to obey everything I have commanded you" (Matthew 28:19–20).

---

23 Colin Kidd, *The Forging of Races: Race and Scripture in the Protestant Atlantic World, 1600–2000* (New York: Cambridge University Press, 2006), 19.

24 Denise Kimber Buell, *Why This New Race: Ethnic Reasoning in Early Christianity* (New York: Columbia University Press, 2005).

Over the course of the next few centuries, the new Christian *genos* was incubated within the Church wherein it spread throughout the Roman Empire. By the close of the Golden Age of Christendom — the first millennium AD — virtually every European ethny traced its spiritual if not its biological ancestry to the once-persecuted and politically powerless race of Christians.

It is, therefore, a mistake to detach "the white race" from its history as a family of European nations baptized by the Church. In turn, the white race provided the indispensable biocultural medium for the rise of Christendom. It is important to remember, however, that the white race never possessed a cohesive or conscious collective identity. As a collective noun, the white race is a modern social construct; as a biological sub-species, it existed in nature and pre-history as a collection of closely related ethnic groups. Of necessity, the first members of the new race of Christians were compelled to break with the ancestral religious practices at the heart of their pre-existing ethnic identities, whether Jewish, Greek, or Roman. In their adoptive spiritual kingdom, Gentiles became descendants of the righteous patriarchs and prophets of Old Covenant Israel. Jews, on the other hand, had no claim to special status in the kingdom of God simply because they were the physical seed of Abraham. Most of those who called themselves Jews responded to the perceived insult by rejecting the lordship of Jesus Christ. They turned away from God to worship carnal Israel. Those who worshipped the Israel of God's heavenly kingdom, Jews and Gentiles alike, had to "overcome the world" (1 John 5:4–5). Few would have predicted that Christians, a small minority scattered throughout the Roman Empire, would create a spiritual kingdom that transcended ethnic boundaries in the Near East and spread into the northern reaches of Europe as well.

The gospel message of the apostles revealed to early Christians that all members of this new race were kin to the righteous remnant of Old Israel. From the apostle Paul in the first century to the church historian Eusebius, writing in the fourth century, Christians constructed a myth of shared descent from Abraham. Eusebius contended that, even if Christians were an admittedly new people, "their life and method of conduct, in accordance with the precepts of religion, has not been recently invented by us." On the contrary, the righteousness of the new Christian race reflected their devotion to the law and the prophets in the sacred history of Israel. "At the present moment it is only among the Christians throughout the whole world that the manner of religion that was Abraham's can actually be found in practice."[25] Christians, in other words, affirmed their spiritual kinship with all those who love the God of Israel.

The advent of Christ entailed a profound transformation in what it meant to be a Jew. Old Israel's covenant with God was sealed by circumcision of the flesh. Christ offered a new covenant sealed by a circumcision of the heart. Hard-hearted Jews rejected Jesus because he refused the messianic kingship of carnal, nationalistic Israel. But those who shut Jesus out of their hearts ceased to be Jews in the eyes of God. Eusebius took it as axiomatic that God was finished with physical Israel when she was re-born (superseded) as the Church, the spiritual Body of Christ. Led by the risen Christ, the righteous remnant of Old Israel began a New Exodus from the old heaven and the old earth into a new creation. The New Israel reached its promised land in AD 70. The siege of Jerusalem in that year was a colossal disaster for Jews of Old Israel. The apocalypse came as no surprise to first century Christians, however. In the Book of Revelation — written before the catastrophe[26] — the apostle John described his vision of Christ's return in clouds of glory: he saw the New Jerusalem coming "down out of heaven from God, prepared as a bride beautifully dressed for her husband".(Revelation 21:2) Forty years earlier, standing outside the Temple with his disciples, Christ had foreseen that "not one stone here will be left on another" when he came again at the "end of the age". The

---

25 *Ibid.*, 77.
26 John AT Robinson, *Redating the New Testament* (Eugene, OR: Wipf & Stock, 2000), 221–253.

Day of the Lord's return was not to occur in some far distant future, perhaps thousands of years later. Christ assured the crowds who heard him that "this generation will certainly not pass away until these things have happened" (Matthew 24:2-3, 34).

Even the contemporary Jewish historian Josephus registered the providential significance of what happened in Jerusalem. He reported several signs and portents of the coming disaster. One day, for example, "before sun-setting, chariots and troops of soldiers in their armour were seen running about among the clouds and surrounding of cities." Christians had already fled the city. They knew that Israel had played the harlot in its covenantal relationship with God. Yet again, she had ignored the prophets who warned her not to "sow the wind" lest she "reap the whirlwind" in the coming Day of the Lord. When Judgement Day arrived, the Temple was burned, and Old Covenant Judaism ended abruptly. Josephus estimated that the dead during the siege numbered more than a million, most of whom were, by his lights, "pure and holy" Jews. The survivors were scattered to the four winds.[27] "Israel is swallowed up; now she is among the nations like a worthless thing" (Hosea 8:7-8). No longer is God hidden behind a veil in a temple made by hands. A new temple was built for a New Israel *in the hearts* of the new race of faithful Christians — the spiritual Body of Christ.

Corporate bodies of Christian believers still affirm their spiritual kinship, their holy communion, with Christ by eating and drinking his flesh and blood, reconstituted symbolically from the mundane materials of bread and wine. In the first century, the blood of Christ played a central role in the social construction of a Christian people. Like any other *ethnie*, the Christians created "a sense of the collective self" by viewing themselves through the prism of "myths, memories, values and symbols." Some cultures "derive communal solidarity from alleged ties of kinship and genealogical descent." Others ground their collective identity in "an ideological affinity to allegedly similar cultures in

---

27 Flavius Josephus, *The New Complete Works of Josephus* translated byWilliam Whiston (Grand Rapids, MI: Kregel, 1999), 898-899, 906-907.

archaic eras of communal history." The Christian gospel blurred "the distinction between biological and cultural modes of tracing descent and customs" by drawing on the Old Testament to construct a "myth-symbol complex." It was just such a "corpus of beliefs and sentiments" which the Church preserved, diffused, and transmitted to future generations. Together with the blood of Christ, Spirit and water became the master symbols in what ethnologists call the *mythomoteur* of a socially cohesive Christian *ethny*.[28]

Christian Nationhood and the Theopolitical Process of Ethnogenesis

According to the apostle John, the Lord is "the one who came by water and blood — Jesus Christ. He did not come by water only, but by water and blood." The Holy Spirit testified to the truth: only through communion with Jesus Christ, the Son of God, could the world be overcome. Indeed, "there are three that testify" to the new Kingdom coming on clouds of glory: "the Spirit, the water, and the blood: and the three are in agreement" (1 John 5:6–8). The apostle Paul taught first-century Christians that "to live outside Christ is to die, in Christ is to live."[29] Believers were prepared therefore to endure, even to welcome persecution.[30] Before long, the blood of the martyrs was spilled in sufficient quantities to become the water that fertilized the seed of the Church. When Constantine granted official status to the Church in the fourth century AD, the new race of Christians had established itself in large numbers in settled communities across Europe and Asia Minor. Before long, spiritual kinship among Christians was

---

28 Anthony D Smith, *The Ethnic Origins of Nations* (Oxford: Blackwell, 1988), 14–15, 58.

29 Thomas J Heffernan and James E Shelton, "*Paradisus in carcere*: The Vocabulary of Imprisonment and the Theology of Martyrdom in *Passio Sanctarum Perpetuae et Felicitatus*" (2006) 14(2) *Journal of Early Christian Studies* 217.

30 But, see Candida Moss, *The Myth of Persecution: How Early Christians Invented a Story of Martyrdom* (New York: Harper One, 2014).

transmitted across generations, creating embryonic Christian nations in which belonging was based on blood and consecrated by the holy water of infant baptism.

By such means, the new race of Christians *did* overcome the world. In effect, Christian theology created a new *ethnos*. People drawn from different biological races and from many diverse ethnic groups took on an altogether novel ethnoreligious identity. The boundaries of the new Christian *genos* were both fixed and fluid. Christians learned to use various forms of "ethnic reasoning" to distinguish themselves from other groups.[31] But, like almost every other people in the ancient world, Christian ethnicity/race was deemed to be produced and sustained by its own distinctive religious practices. But neither the Old Testament God of Israel nor the Lordship of Jesus Christ could be assimilated into pagan pantheons. In pagan societies, "certain divine beings, the gods of the family and of the state" were connected intimately to the human members of one's social circle of kinfolk and fellow citizens. When "a god was spoken of as a father and his worshippers as his offspring… the meaning was that the worshippers were literally of his stock, that he and they made up one natural family with reciprocal family duties to one another." But the spiritual bond between the God of Israel and his people was not "natural" but "artificial," not fixed but fluid. The gods of the Greeks could never be anything else but Greek gods, but Yahweh exists eternally "as a God independently of Israel."[32]

Even so, it was common ground among pagans and Jews that blood was the basis for membership in an ethnoreligious community. Membership in the early Christian communities, however, was, in the first instance, the work of Spirit and water. Consequently, Christian identity was markedly more mutable than in other contemporary peoples. Conversion and baptism functioned as "rebirth." In the first few centuries, a distinctive juxtaposition of fixity and fluidity allowed

---

31 Buell, *Why This New Race, passim*.
32 Tom Holland, *Contours of Pauline Theology: A Radical New Survey of the Influences on Paul's Biblical Writings* (Fearn, UK: Mentor, 2004), 104.

Christians to make universalizing claims, arguing that anyone can, and everyone should become a member of the Christian "people." Christian identity became both distinct from yet comparable to the racial/ethnic identity of other peoples. The dynamic and malleable character of Christian identity gave the new race a distinct advantage in the unique circumstances of the Mediterranean world of late antiquity.

Already the spread of the Roman Empire had laid the foundation for a universal religion, most obviously in the pagan cult of the emperor. The late Roman Empire had created an urban civilization as well based on slavery in which grinding poverty for the many produced great wealth for the few. Corruption, political instability, and recurrent social upheavals were endemic. The result was chronic anomie and widespread status inconsistencies (e.g., educated slaves in upstart wealthy households), both of which favoured the spread of an egalitarian salvation religion.[33] The new race itself undermined existing racial/ethnic identities because holy men replaced warriors in its social hierarchy while slaves and women were admitted to communion alongside free citizens and wealthy men.

But there were limits to the plasticity of Christian racial/ethnic identity. The early, world-rejecting brand of Christianity had little appeal to the Teutonic peoples of north-western Europe. It was the conversion of those pagan peoples, however, which unleashed the dynamic rise of medieval Christendom. Compared to the clapped-out, anomic racial/ethnic cultures of late antiquity, the Germanic tribes who overran the Roman Empire exhibited remarkable social cohesion. Their world-accepting culture was hierarchical and rural, giving pride of place to warriors. In their pagan pre-history, tribal identity was rooted in biological ties of kinship, descent, and blood. Accordingly, when the Germanic peoples were brought into the fold of

---

33 James C Russell, *The Germanization of Early Medieval Christianity: A Sociohistorical Approach to Religious Transformation* (New York: Oxford University Press, 1994), 83–84, 87–88.

the Church, Christian identity became less fluid and more fixed.[34] By the end of the first millennium of the Christian era, Spirit, water, *and* blood were the constituent elements of every Christian nation. Those three-dimensions of Christian racial/ethnic identity reflect the unity in diversity of the three persons of the triune God.

The Three Dimensions of Racial Identity

Race-as-biology promises to shed light on the relationship between blood and behaviour as manifested in measurable group differences such as average intelligence, temperament, and reproductive strategies.[35] By contrast, race-as-ethnicity deals with the cultural myths and symbols which move men to collective action. As Hannah Arendt observed, to act, in the "most general sense, means to take an initiative, to begin…to set something in motion."[36] The actor is someone who starts something new. Applied to the birth of an ethno-nation, her insights suggest that action promotes the process of ethnogenesis in two stages: (1) the beginning, made by a charismatic leader; and (2) the subsequent construction of a novel collective identity by his followers. No wonder, then, that the imagined community of Christians in late antiquity appeared "in the guise of a miracle."[37] Not even the most devout Jews longing for the messianic restoration of national Israel expected what actually came to pass. Against all the odds, this new race of men was moved by the Spirit to accomplish their divinely appointed mission. Race-as-theology helps us to understand how Spirit and blood mingled with the life-giving power of water to sustain the first, embryonic Christian communities. Since then, Christian nationhood has been nourished by the continuing interplay of Spirit, water,

---

34 Ibid., passim.

35 J Phillipe Rushton, *Race, Evolution, and Behavior: A Life History Perspective* Third Edition (Port Huron, MI: Charles Darwin Research Institute, 2000).

36 Hannah Arendt, *The Human Condition* (Chicago: University of Chicago Press, 1958), 177.

37 Ibid., 189, 178.

and blood. But disorder or dysfunction in one or more of these three elements has led many nations to defeat and destruction. Even the mostly atheistic practitioners of race-as-biology concede that a shared religious faith is likely to enhance the inclusive fitness of any race or nation.[38]

Conversely, the essential trinitarian character of Christian nationhood is subverted when the unitarian logic of biology suppresses the theological dimension of racial/ethnic identity. A single-minded Darwinian focus on the survival of the fittest in a pitiless process of group selection can justify all manner of crimes committed in the name of racial solidarity. But the inescapable fluidity of racial classifications undercuts any misplaced faith in the unimpeachable objectivity of race-as-biology. German National Socialists sometimes conflated race-as-biology (*Rasse*) with race-as-ethnicity (*Volk*) while sidelining race-as-theology. They insisted, for example, that neither Jews *nor* Slavs were Aryans even though both were recognized as White, in law and custom, under *apartheid* in South Africa and Jim Crow in the American South. Nor could Christianity bridge the racial gulf between Jews and Germans; under National Socialism not even baptism could wash away the indelible stain of Semitic origins. Both the American and the German experience teach us that race-as-Christian-theology must temper both the irrational impulses of unrestrained ethnic chauvinism and the imperial claims of biological science.

But a one-dimensional obsession with race-as-theology is no less productive of disastrous consequences. In particular, the currently dominant unitarian theology asserts that there is only one race: the human race. The denial by "anti-racists" of the fixed, intractable, biological, character of the observable differences between various population groups provides ideological cover for the deliberate displacement of white populations in favour of non-white immigrants. But in acknowledging that racial identities can be fluid at the margins,

---

38 David Sloan Wilson, *Darwin's Cathedral: Evolution, Religion, and the Nature of Society* (Chicago: University of Chicago Press, 2002).

one need not deny the enduringly distinctive biological and ethnic characteristics of various human population groups. Admittedly, when dealing with hybrid individuals, it can be difficult to identify bright-line biological boundaries, even between whites and the other major continental races. The fuzziness of racial categories, however, provides no theological warrant for the abolition of the white race. White racial identity is not merely, as anti-racists would have it, a social construct invented by European colonialists to justify the exploitation of the Other. Racial diversity should be seen as a gift from God not just a randomly evolved datum of modern biological science. Differences between Negroes, white Europeans, and Orientals are part of the divinely created order of things. Race is a theological not just a biological or cultural phenomenon. Those who refuse to recognize the theological significance of race do so at their peril.

In times past, our ancestors understood that God may turn his back on *any* nation which turns its back on him. Such was the exemplary fate of Old Covenant Israel. The expulsion of Adam and Eve from the Garden of Eden foreshadows the final destruction of the Jerusalem temple in AD 70, the very apocalypse promised by the Book of Revelation. Perhaps this, too, should be taken as a warning that even nominally Christian nations such as Germany and the United States can incur the wrath of God. Indeed, both the presently accelerating decay of the American Constitutional Republic and the earlier, crushing defeat of Nazi Germany attest to the continuing role of divine Providence in human history.

The idea of providential history is, after all, an inescapable corollary of the belief that in Jesus Christ the divine became human. God entered history by becoming a man of flesh and blood. Jesus was the perfect incarnation of Spirit, water, and blood. After the Spirit left Christ as he hung on the cross, a Roman soldier pierced his side with a spear, whereupon water and blood poured out of his body (John 19:34). His suffering and death revealed that all men can become alienated from God, falling into the state of spiritual death called sin.

Spiritual *life* depends upon the mutual indwelling of the divine and the human. It was no accident, therefore, that, after carnal Israel rejected Jesus Christ, his Spirit found another earthly abode in the hearts of the European peoples. Providence had prepared the ideal medium for the incubation of Christian nations in the pre-historic, triadic character of Indo-European religions and societies. The future heartland of Christendom was to be established not just in England, France, and Germany but in a host of city-states, principalities, kingdoms, and empires stretching from Spain to Holy Russia.

The Tripartite Structure of Indo-European Societies

From time out of mind, the many, widely dispersed, Indo-European peoples have shared a distinctive, tripartite cosmology. Georges Dumézil revealed the remarkable congruence between the gods of ancient Rome and Scandinavia that extends to the Vedic religions of India 3,000 years ago. In each case, gods were divided into three ranks, each playing its own distinctive role in the cosmos. The gods representing the sovereign function of maintaining unity and harmony were in the first rank. The second type of god commonly found in Indo-European mythology was associated with war. Gods of the third rank performed the functions which provided the practical foundations for the other two roles. In this grouping were found the gods of fecundity and abundance. The trifunctional character of the pantheon presupposed the interdependence and unity of the three ranks of gods and goddesses. The boundaries separating the three functions were not set in concrete precisely because interaction and interpenetration of the three divine archetypes was essential to produce a harmonious equilibrium.[39]

---

39 Georges Dumézil, *Mythes et Dieux des Indo-Européens*, edited by Hervé Coutau-Bégarie (Paris: Flammarion, 1992), 155–65, 137, 176–177, 192. See also, John Milbank, "Sacred Triads: Augustine and the Indo-European Soul," (1997) 13(4) *Modern Theology* 451.

The tripartite structure of Indo-European ethnoreligions embodied a social ideal that was translated at one time or another, with greater or lesser fidelity, into the organization of social life. The pagan priest-kings of the Teutonic tribes represented both aspects of the premier function, magic and sovereignty; a king might also represent a mélange of elements drawn from all three functions, particularly the second since he was invariably drawn from the warrior class. Even after the conversion of the Anglo-Saxons to Christianity the divine triad of the pagans retained its imaginative power to shape the organizational life of Old England by echoing the trinity of Spirit, water, and blood.

Alfred the Great gave explicit recognition to the prehistoric ideal of a trifunctional social structure. Just as a man cannot practice a craft without materials and the tools of his trade, Alfred knew that the king cannot govern without "a well-populated land; he must have men of prayer, men of war, men of labor." Those "three pillars of the community are the ruler's tools; as for materials, he must have enough land to provide an adequate supply of arms, food, and clothing." Otherwise, the king "cannot keep these tools, and without these tools he cannot do any of the things he is responsible for doing." In Alfred's schema the king is presented as above and apart from the trifunctional structure supporting the throne just as three legs support a stool.[40]

The triadic ideal of social order persisted in early modern England in the form of the Anglican ideal of a united Church and Commonwealth both of which necessarily rested upon and included the people as the indispensable element which supported the whole structure. Just as the Church represented "those who pray" and the Commonwealth "those who fight," all "those who labour" were simultaneously members of the Church of England and of the Commonwealth creating "a figure *triangular*" in which "the base does not differ from the sides thereof" but in which every line is "both a base and also a side." Richard Hooker's "triangular" figure replicated the equilibrium between three functions

---

40 Georges Duby, *The Three Orders: Feudal Society Imagined* (Chicago: University of Chicago Press, 1980), 100–102, 276.

that regulate the order of the cosmos.[41] The trinitarian ideal of social order was embodied as well in the three estates comprising the *ancient regime* in France. Unfortunately, beginning with the seventeenth century Puritan Revolution, modernist egalitarianism "progressively" flattened the antique tripartite structure of both religion and society.

For whites, generally, as well as for Anglo-Saxons and Christians, the results have been catastrophic. One-dimensional man has become the template for normality in the post-Christian, transnational Empire. Spiritual barbarism is not a phenomenon peculiar to whites; nor can it be blamed on a failure of political leadership among WASP elites. Nor is the one-dimensional character of postmodern life simply an ideological disorder or theological heresy which can be cured through a return to doctrinal orthodoxy. For all those embedded in the high-intensity commodity culture of corporate capitalism, the once-powerful idea of providential history now appears mainly in the guise of a postmodern cargo cult.[42] The globalized economy is now regarded with religious reverence. Consequently, an abyss has opened up between the white race and God. The hidden God cannot be reached "by insight, by knowledge, by intelligence, by courage, by politics, [or] by tradition." One-dimensional man has been thrown back on faith in the mysterious powers animating the transnational Empire: "Awesome, inscrutable, self-impelling, the system invite[s] adoration." A pantheistic "wish for plenty" becomes "the wish not to have to wish wishes of one's own at all." Spirit, water, and blood have disappeared into a spiritual void in which the Lordship of Jesus Christ is little more than a quaint medieval superstition.[43] Such a built-in

---

41 Richard Hooker, *Of the Laws of Ecclesiastical Polity*, edited by Arthur Stephen McGrade (Cambridge: Cambridge University Press, 1989), 130.

42 William Leiss, *The Limits to Satisfaction: An Essay on the Problem of Needs and Commodities* (Toronto: University of Toronto Press, 1976).

43 Donald Meyer, *The Positive Thinkers: A Study of the American Quest for Health, Wealth, and Power from Mary Baker Eddy to Norman Vincent Peale* (New York: Anchor, 1966), 194–195, 207.

disharmony between God and man positively invites a providential response. Somehow the equilibrium between heaven and earth in the new creation must be restored.

Towards the Restoration of Anglo-Saxon Christendom

Any theological schema of civic action aimed at the restoration of Anglo-Saxon Christendom must draw upon one or more *orienting concepts* if it is to achieve its objectives.[44] Historically potent examples of such orienting concepts, can be found in the lives and works of men such as Martin Luther, John Calvin, and John Wesley. Calvin's theology was oriented around the concept of the "majesty or sovereignty of God." Luther oriented his theological theory and practice around "justification by faith," while Wesley's work revolved around the notion of "responsible grace." Each of these concepts oriented new approaches to practical theology, each sparking its own theological revolution. Unfortunately, those revolutions oriented as they were, each in its own way, to personal salvation has run its course. Evangelical Protestantism is dying on the vine.

An *Angelcynn* Reformation seeking the collective redemption of British-descended peoples requires a more comprehensive strategy; it must be oriented around not just one but four concepts. This multi-pronged approach can be grounded in several existing yet separate streams of White Anglo-Saxon Protestant theology. The four key theological concepts are: (1) process theism; (2) preterism; (3) kinism; and (4) royalism. When these already intellectually compelling challenges to theological orthodoxy merge into a single popular current of ethnoreligious experience, the next Great Awakening in British religious history will be in the offing.

---

44 Randy L. Maddox, "Responsible Grace: The Systematic Perspective of Wesleyan Theology," (1984) 19(2) *Wesleyan Theological Journal* 7–22.

In what follows, I give a brief account of each of those four orienting concepts:

Process Theism

Process theism builds on the historical theology of the nineteenth-century Anglican broad-church movement in rejecting traditional Christian theism. The early creeds of the Church established an image of God, outside time and space, the omnipotent, omniscient, and omnipresent source of being itself, who created the world out of nothing.

The doctrine of *creatio ex nihilo* cannot be found in either the Old or the New Testament. It appeared suddenly in the latter half of the second century B.C. Its appearance "can best be explained as a defense of the most controversial part of the Christian kerygma, the resurrection of the dead."[45] Only a God who created the world out of nothing could accomplish the bodily resurrection of the dead. Oliver O'Donovan's vision of the universal church as an eschatological society preserves that creedal linkage between God's created order and the bodily resurrection of believers in the new creation.

By contrast, process theism denies that the doctrine of *creatio ex nihilo* can be grounded in Genesis One. Instead, creation is conceived as an ongoing process within which God remains actively involved with all forms of conscious life.

Biologist Bruce G. Charlton suggests that process theism can provide his discipline with the metaphysical framework it desperately needs to solve fundamental problems such as group selection. Natural selection is comparatively easy to explain at the level of individual organisms. But "true group selection … entails a purposive mechanism that can predict, can 'look ahead' several generations, and infer what is likely to be good for the survival and reproduction of the species."

---

45 James Noel Hubler, "Creatio ex nihilo: Matter, creation, and the body in classical and Christian philosophy through Aquinas" (1995) at: https://repository.upenn.edu/dissertations/AAI9532205, 143, 107.

The theory of natural selection "*lacks teleology — a goal, direction or purpose.*"[46]

If the idea of purpose demands an organizing entity or deity, then "evolution across history is best explained as a directional process of development" at both the individual (ontogeny) and group (phylogeny) level.[47] The comparative evolutionary success of ethnic groups is probably affected, therefore, by the nature and intensity of their religious connection to the theistic organizing entity.

God is not omnipotent, however. Hence the evils of the world cannot be charged exclusively to his account; moreover, he is affected by his interactions with us and the wrongs we do unto others and ourselves. Robert Gnuse demonstrates that the Old Testament provides a revealing account of the processes of communication between the Israelites and the divine.[48] Perhaps white Anglo-Saxon Protestants, too, could and should create a national bible recording our own communication — or lack thereof — with the divine.

Indeed, process theism provides grounds for doubting that the "Christ-event" (i.e., the Incarnation, Passion, and Resurrection of Jesus) must be conceived as a singular happening, occurring, once and for all, in the history of but one nation located in the ancient Near East on planet Earth. Nevertheless, Protestants and Catholics still share the Augustinian metanarrative grounded in the proposition that "Jesus is Lord" is "a universally true statement."[49] In his discourse on *Dominus Jesus*, Cardinal Joseph Ratzinger (as he then was) declared that:

---

46 Bruce G. Carlton, "Reconceptualizing the Metaphysical Basis of Biology: A New Definition Based on Deistic Teleology and a Hierarchy of Organizing Entities, *The Winnower* (February 25, 2016). https://www.thewinnower.com/papers/3497-reconceptualizing-the-metaphysical-basis-of-biology-a-new-definition-based-on-deistic-teleology-and-an-hierarchy-of-organizing-entities.

47 *Ibid.*

48 Robert Gnuse, *The Old Testament and Process Theology* (Eugene, OR: Wipf & Stock, 2000).

49 Stephen Wolfe, *The Case for Christian Nationalism* (Moscow, ID: Canon Press, 2022), 120.

There is only one salvific economy of the One and Triune God, realized in the mystery of the incarnation, death, and resurrection of the Son of God, actualized with the cooperation of the Holy Spirit, and extended in its salvific value to all humanity *and to the entire universe*.⁵⁰

In a book dealing with the problems posed to Catholic faith by the possibility that extraterrestrial life has, or may appear, on other worlds, Paul Thigpen comments that

This statement does have an explicit cosmic scope and could indeed be read as support for a "cosmic Christ"...God's salvation in Christ on Earth makes a contribution to His greater redemptive plan for the cosmos...[But] it cannot be ruling out multiple incarnations; the Church has never definitively settled or even addressed the issue.⁵¹

Indeed, who knows whether other singular incarnations for other unique nations or even other worlds have been forever excluded from the realm of possibility by divine decree? There is only one historical Jesus, but, if "creation" is an ongoing process, there may be future Christ-events in some other "holy nation" on this or some other planet. Thigpen warns that

...if the day should come when the world has a public, undeniable encounter with [extraterrestrial intelligence] or an official disclosure of its existence, Catholic and other Christians must be prepared to assimilate that new empirical information through careful reflection and prayer. Just as their spiritual ancestors had to grapple with the theological implications of the Copernican revolution or the new encounter with peoples in the Western

---

50 Quoted in Robert Sungenis, "The Problem of an Incarnate God," (2022) 41(11) *Culture Wars* 34, at 37 (emphasis added).
51 Paul Thigpen, *Extraterrestrial Intelligence and the Catholic Faith: Are We Alone in the Universe with God and the Angels* (Gastonia, NC: TAN Books, 2022), 333. Sungenis, "Problem of an Incarnate God," defends Catholic orthodoxy and denies the possibility of multiple incarnations in his lengthy review of Thigpen's book.

Hemisphere, they will have much to ponder that will require a response of "faith seeking understanding."[52]

Preterism, or Covenant Eschatology

Preterism (from the Latin, *præter* or "past") is a biblical hermeneutic or interpretive method consistent with process theism and even the possibility of multiple incarnations. A preterist biblical theology denies that the Bible sets out the story of humanity from the creation of planet earth when God breathed life into the first human until the end of the world at the Second Coming (the *Parousia*) of Jesus Christ. Rather, the biblical narrative has to do with the rise and fall of Old Covenant Israel. On a preterist reading, the bible story will not support a futurist eschatology which still awaits the return of Christ at the end of the world. Preterists hold that the clear text of Scripture shows that all the biblical prophesies of a new heaven and a new earth, not just those in Revelation, were fulfilled in AD 70.

In that year, Christ returned to oversee the destruction of the Temple in Jerusalem, the physical centre of the old heaven and old earth occupied by God's first people. In the Book of Revelation, we see the Old Covenant world of Israel sinking into lakes of fire, while the New Covenant world enters history. The Jerusalem Temple makes its exit in a spectacular cataclysm; a new creation becomes incarnate in the church, the ecclesiastical Body of Christ. There the bible story ends.

The preterist hermeneutic is also known as "covenant eschatology." That is to say, the biblical narrative is consummated by the fulfillment of the covenant promises to carnal Israel. This was the end of the old age; it was then, that "the first heaven and first earth" long symbolized by the Jerusalem Temple, "passed away." It was with the end of the Old Covenant that the promised resurrection of the saints was fulfilled. This was a process of spiritual renewal, begun by the resurrection of

---

52 Thigpen, *Extraterrestrial Intelligence*, 379.

Jesus the Christ as "the first fruits of those who have fallen asleep" (1 Cor. 15:20). As the "Holy City, the new Jerusalem" came down from God, "a new heaven and a new earth" came into being (Rev. 21:1–2) thus inaugurating the church age.

This preterist vision of the resurrection at "the end of the age" is quite different from O'Donovan's mainstream futurist eschatology. On his reading, it is given to nobody but the risen Christ to raise the dead, the church's authority does not rest in exercising that power by delegation, but in pointing to its future exercise in an act of testimony.[53] O'Donovan, like another well-known Anglican theologian, N.T. Wright, looks forward to the *parousia* of a "global Jesus" at some point in our own future.[54] Wright portrays Paul as the one who prophesies the still-future transfiguration of the entire cosmos, the moment when all those who belong to the Messiah "are themselves raised bodily from the dead." Wright very explicitly ties the victory over death promised by Paul and Jesus to a physical resurrection of the dead. If death is to be defeated, he declares, then "anything other than some kind of bodily resurrection, therefore, is simply unthinkable."[55] In stark contrast, preterists contend that the covenantal eschatology of national Israel offers a much more persuasive hermeneutical framework within which to interpret Paul's understanding of the resurrection body.

Samuel G. Dawson, for example, points out that Paul publicly declared that he was saying that nothing except that which the prophets and Moses did say would come about (Acts 26:22). As a result, Dawson contends that "Paul's concept of the resurrection wasn't that fleshly (or even transfigured) bodies would come out of holes in ground at all, because that's not what Moses and the prophets taught. Instead, Paul

---

53 O'Donovan, *The Desire of the Nations*, 217.

54 N. T. Wright, *Paul and the Faithfulness of God* (Minneapolis: Fortress Press, 2013), 408..

55 N.T. Wright, *The Resurrection of the Son of God: Christian Origins and the Question of God*, Vol. 3 (Minneapolis: Fortress Press, 2003), 336, 313–314.

taught that "the resurrection of Old Covenant Israel from the death of its fellowship from God."[56]

Dawson breaks even more dramatically from Wright when he observes that Paul never speaks of resurrected "bodies." Instead, Paul refers only to "the resurrection of one body, the Old Covenant faithful who were being transformed into the body of Christ." The hermeneutic problem here, Dawson concludes, "comes down to whether the resurrection Paul spoke of was *one body* in his *present time* or *billions of bodies* more than *two thousand years* in the future."[57]

If Dawson is right, then the early church effectively replaced Israel as the people of God. The God of history ordained that old national Israel fulfill its *telos* through one final, fiery sacrifice on the Temple Mount. A new age dawned in which the historical process of interaction between God and national Israel, as recounted in the biblical narrative, expanded to incorporate both the Greek and Latin civilizations of the Mediterranean basin. In effect, Old Covenant Israel was superseded by the development of European Christendom.

O'Donovan explicitly rejects any such supersessionist interpretation. National Israel, he asserts, can never be replaced. The Old Covenant remains in force for the Jews. Because Jesus the Christ represents God the "Kingdom's representative must suffer the resistance of Israel on God's behalf; but representing Israel's cause, too, he must suffer God's resistance on Israel's behalf." In the end, however, O'Donovan returns to the utterly ahistorical claim that the representation of Israel "opens out to the representation *of the human race*."[58] In this new creation, however, O'Donovan insists that "the continuing Israel…is not to be dismissed as an irrelevant survival from the past." The Gentiles have been grafted onto Israel's root; we only await the

---

56 Samuel G. Dawson, *Essays on Eschatology: An Introductory Overview on the Study of Last Things*, 3rd ed. (Amarillo, TX: SGD Press, 2017), 105, 109.

57 Ibid., 144–146.

58 O'Donovan, *The Desire of the Nations*, 130.

moment when carnal Israel comes to see "the possession of the law fulfilled in Christ."[59]

O'Donovan maintains that "until the last reconciliation the two communities must coexist." Gentile Christians "cannot ignore the community into which they have by faith been grafted."[60] In effect, therefore, when carnal Israel speaks, Christians must listen. One might expect, therefore, that even if O'Donovan's political theology does not require the criminalization of acts which "deny" or "downplay" the Holocaust, he would never condone such blasphemy.

Indeed, O'Donovan explicitly joins with Christian Zionists to accord carnal Israel a theological-political status unknown to other nations comprising the eschatological society of humanity. Whether other families, tribes, and nations have an eternal destiny may be open to debate; but there is no doubt in his mind that "Israel has one—is that not enough?"[61] A positive response to that rhetorical question, turns on the truth or falsity of the futurist eschatology upon which O'Donovan's political theology rests. My own view is that Old Covenant Israel is not the only nation through which God has worked in this world. The English, too, once saw themselves as a "holy nation." With the grace of God, other British-descended peoples can and should strive to emulate that godly objective.

Kinism

Process theism, when combined with the historical theology inherent in preterism, leads inexorably to Kinism, or, as some would have it, "the Christian doctrine of nations."[62] The Old Covenant bound the holy nation of Israel to God; the New Covenant offered the grace of

---

59 Ibid.,131.

60 Ibid., 132.

61 Ibid., 132, 219.

62 H. A. Scott Trask, "The Christian Doctrine of Nations," *American Renaissance* (July, 2001). https://www.amren.com/news/2018/04/christian-doctrine-racism-identity-bible.

God to every nation (*ethnos*) of the known world (*oikumene*). The leaves of the tree of life in the New Jerusalem were to serve for "the healing of nations." Old Israel was no more. On Judgement Day, Christ sentenced the stiff-necked synagogue of Satan to spiritual death. Only a righteous remnant was left to carry the holy seed of Israel unto the nations. For almost two thousand years, every Christian nation adjured Jews within the realm to recognize their Redeemer, thus ending their age-old rebellion against God. In sharp contrast to the Jews, Anglo-Saxons eagerly entered the new covenant world.

Attuned to racial and ethnic differences, kinists understand the powerful biocultural affinity between the early Christian church and the pagan tribes of Anglo-Saxon England as well as the prominent place occupied by covenants in tribal social structures. Conversely, once their churches downplayed the importance of *blood* covenants to the spiritual life of both family and nation, the ancestral attachment of Anglo-Saxon Protestants to the Body of Christ was bound to fade away. The creedal religion of the modern Anglican church denies that either faith or political allegiance is passed on through the blood of the large, partly inbred extended family that constitutes the Anglo-Saxon ethny. No modernist "proposition nation" grounded in the universalist ideology of secular humanism, least of all the one abjuring its ethnoreligious roots in the sacred blood and faith of the Old English people, can ever again be a holy nation in the eyes of God.

For kinists, the Christian nation rests upon a covenant, under God, between the dead, the living, and the unborn. The living members of the nation, according to R.J. Rushdoony, "see themselves as the trustees of the family blood, rights, property, name, and position for their lifetime. They have an inheritance from the past to be developed and preserved for the future."[63]

---

[63] Rousas John Rushdooony, "The Family as Trustee," *Journal of Christian Reconstruction* (1977–78) 3(2) 16–23, 20.

Royalism

Royalty plays a central role in the bible story. Jesus the Christ traced his descent to King David. As the very model of an English David, Alfred the Great established a Christian kingdom in England. The hereditary monarch of the British dominions once served as trustee-in-chief for his realm. The ecclesiastical significance of the monarchy was given formal recognition when Henry VIII, his heirs, and successors were declared to be Supreme Governors of the Church of England. The Royal Supremacy played a significant role in the rise of the broad-church movement in Victorian England. It has since become little more than a mere manifestation of the shapeshifting Crown manipulated for its own ends by the government of the United Kingdom.[64]

Anglican royalists should create an *Angelcynn* Network of ethnoreligious activists to liberate the captive Crown in right of the Royal Supremacy. The Crown has become little more than a rubber stamp for corrupt politicians with no discernible interest in the spiritual welfare of Anglo-Saxons "at home" or in the diaspora. Once the Royal Supremacy over the Church of England has been insulated from state control, it should be extended to every reformed *Angelcynn* Church, not just in the United Kingdom, but throughout the British dominions as well. In time, it may become possible for the Crown to charter *Angelcynn* churches even among the Anglo-American remnant population in the failing American republic.

In the eighteenth century, Henry St. John, Viscount Bolingbroke hoped that a Patriot King would re-awaken the English nation from its spiritual slumbers.[65] The appearance of such a patriot prince would have been a miracle indeed. In our own time, it is doubly hard to imagine

---

64 Chris Shore & David A. Williams (eds.), *The Shapeshifting Crown: Locating the State in Postcolonial New Zealand, Australia, Canada and the UK* (Cambridge University Press, 2019).

65 Viscount Bolingbroke, "The Idea of a Patriot King," [originally published 1749] in David Armitage, ed., *Political Writings* (Cambridge University Press, 1997), 217–294.

a British prince daring to stand against a government determined to maintain its control over the royal prerogative in ecclesiastical affairs. But, as Bolingbroke wrote, those who pray for such a deliverance must not neglect such means as are in their power "to keep the cause of reason, of virtue, and of liberty alive." The blessing of a patriot prince might indeed "be withheld from us" but to "deserve at least that it be granted to us, let us prepare to receive it, to improve it, and to co-operate with it."[66]

Bolingbroke knew that were a patriot prince to campaign in defence of the monarchy, he would be subject to a raging torrent of criticism and abuse. Yet when a good prince is seen "to suffer with the people, and in some measure for them...many advantages would accrue to him." For one thing, the cause of the British peoples generally "and his own cause would be made the same by their common enemies."[67]

What is the nature of that cause? In short, a patriot prince will call forth a spirit of resistance to both managerial statism and the abstract universalism of globalist plutocracy. He will do everything in his power to civilize those wild and immoral forces. But the appearance of a Patriot King is not inevitable. Indeed, only a people whose lost liberties are restored to memory will recognize his coming as an opportunity to reshape their allegedly preordained future.

Angelcynn political theology could and should resurrect the messianic mythos of a nation reborn through the advent of a Patriot King. A diasporic network of *Angelcynns* would work to establish the British monarch as Supreme Governor of their ancestral church throughout the Anglosphere. Of course, as a matter of legal formality, the King already plays this role in England. Constitutional reality is quite otherwise; his role as head of the church has been usurped in practice by the Prime Minister.[68] The Crown has been reduced to a rubber stamp.

---

66 *Ibid.*, 222.

67 *Ibid.*, 239.

68 I must confess that it was a pleasure to change the draft reference to "the Queen" in this sentence to "the King" only a few days after the death of Queen Elizabeth

Pending the constitutional reformation of the ecclesiastical body politic, the *Anglecynn* Network must develop a political theology which conceives the existentially political friend-enemy distinction as constitutive of the relationships between *Angelcynn* peoples and other peoples or states (including "our own" states which now employ their power over us, in part, by admitting alien peoples, in huge numbers, to citizenship on equal terms with British-descended host populations).

In other words, an authentic, autochthonous, *Angelcynn* political theology would understand the church as an ethnoreligious institution safeguarding the ethnic interests, spiritual welfare and godly character of the British-descended peoples. The theological justification for such a church polity is essentially biblical. The Bible tells the story of a historical process of interaction between the divine, God, or Yahweh, (whichever name you prefer) and a particular people or nation; namely, the Israelites. That nation developed into a medium through which God manifested his real presence in the world.

Significantly, the *Angelcynn* people in the time of Alfred the Great modelled themselves on ancient Israel. During the Golden Age of the early *Angelcynn* church—the Age of Incarnation—the Church was seen as the spiritual avatar of the emergent English nation, working in partnership with the King. That ethnoreligious symbiosis of nation, church, and kingship was disrupted radically during the eleventh-century by the Norman Conquest and, shortly thereafter, by the Papal Revolution which created a church-state claiming jurisdiction over the whole of Christendom.[69]

II. For years I have waited impatiently for the moment when the appearance of a Patriot *King* might become more than a pipe dream. While King Charles III seems unlikely to earn such a title, there is some hope, at least, that his son, William, or grandson, George may do so. One thing is certain: for the last seventy years, the idea of a Patriot *Queen* has been little more than a contradiction in terms. Now, however, the idea of a Patriot King seems much less of a political fantasy.

69 Harold J. Berman, *Law and Revolution: The Formation of the Western Legal Tradition* (Cambridge, MA: Harvard University Press, 1983).

The old symbiosis was not, however, restored by the substitution of a state church for the Papal church-state during the Reformation. By that time, the Age of Disincarnation driven by the scholastic rationalism and legalistic absolutism of the papal church-state had all but eliminated the explicitly ethnoreligious character of the English church. Anglican Protestantism became just another creedal religion, inevitably spawning countless doctrinal schisms down to the present day.

A genuinely *neo-Angelcynn* political theology would aim to restore the spirit, if not the letter, of the original symbiosis between British-descended peoples, the church, and a British monarchy. Such a church might even be capable of regenerating a *Volksgeist*, the essential seedbed for the advent of the Patriot King envisioned by Viscount Bolingbroke in the eighteenth-century.

Conclusion

Under present circumstances, every once-proud Anglo-Saxon country throughout the Anglosphere is now subject to states which have reduced the White Anglo-Saxon Protestant founding stock to a *de facto* stateless people. Both the globalist state and cosmopolitan Anglican churches embrace the multiculturalist program, according no special status or formal recognition to the British-descended peoples. The informal alliance between British states and Anglican churches has, in effect, transformed WASPs into an invisible race.[70] That process was well underway by the early twentieth century.

In retrospect, had an ethnoreligious *Angelcynn* political theology existed as an autonomous force (*i.e.*, one not bound hand and foot to the imperial state) during the first half of the twentieth century, church leaders might have recognized that the British and Dominion

---

70 Andrew Fraser, *The WASP Question: An Essay on the Biocultural Evolution, Present Predicament, and Future Prospects of the Invisible Race* (London: Arktos, 2011).

governments were acting in opposition to the best interests of the British peoples by declaring war on Germany.

Prior to 1914 or 1939, Germany did not conceive itself as an enemy of the British people. Both the Kaiser and Hitler declared themselves ready, willing, and able to recognize, defend, and co-operate with the governments and peoples of the British Empire. Indeed, in the late nineteenth century, many leading figures in both Britain and the United States (e.g., Cecil Rhodes, W.T. Stead, H.G. Wells, and Andrew Carnegie) not only promoted greater unity between the Anglo-Saxon nations but also believed that they should ally with their racial cousins in Germany.[71] Accordingly, Rhodes included students from Germany as well as those from America and the Commonwealth in his famous scholarship program. Unfortunately, other, more powerful interests within the British state were determined (think Churchill, in both wars) to treat Germany as an enemy that must be destroyed (ideally by re-creating the fragmented statelets that existed prior to 1870).

Clearly, the idea of a Greater Britain withered away because of the world wars of the twentieth century. For a time, during the century-and-a-half following the American revolution, the Anglo-Saxon world developed a unique geopolitical personality. The Anglo-Saxon peoples anchored their collective identity in constitutional exoskeletons, creating a commonwealth of states sharing a common "British" civic identity. In all those nations, civic identity has been progressively drained of ethnoreligious meaning.

In the nineteenth century, the Church of England, and its colonial, dissenting, and American offshoots endorsed a secularized "political theology of cosmopolitan nationalism." Anglo-Catholics, evangelical Protestants, and Christian Zionists jointly hailed the ecumenical lordship of global Jesus while awaiting his return in power and glory at the end of history. What they did not expect was the First World War.

---

71 Duncan Bell, *Dreamworlds of Race: Empire and the Utopian Destiny of Anglo-America* (Princeton, NJ: Princeton University Press, 2020).

With the foundation of the *Kaiserreich*, however, the German Question reared its ugly head; it was not at all clear how the mercantile, thalassocratic ideal of cosmopolitan nationalism could be reconciled with telluric power of a militarized German Empire. Unfortunately, the Anglican political theology of cosmopolitan nationalism did not preclude the defeat and destruction of that Empire. Indeed, it eventually spawned the global hegemony of a godless, increasingly demonic, transnational corporate plutocracy.

11. Was Early New South Wales (1788–1850) a "Christian Community"?

Introduction

IN THE EARLY 70S a CBC radio personality asked his listeners to complete the phrase "As Canadian as…" The hands-down winner: "As Canadian as possible under the circumstances,"[1] Amusing though the simile seemed, it also revealed the inescapable ambiguity at the heart of Canadian national identity. Similarly, when asked "To what extent can the early colony of New South Wales be considered a 'Christian community'" one is tempted to answer, "As Christian as possible under the circumstances." And, here too, when examining the circumstances affecting the religious life of early New South Wales, one must tackle the ambiguity which attaches to the notion of a "Christian community."

The term "Canadian" has become a legal appellation to which millions of people answer while remaining devoid of any ethno-religious content. Likewise, the concept of a "Christian community" in early colonial New South Wales is a statistical artefact embracing a mixed multitude of particularistic, sometimes competing, and often mutually antagonistic groups defined both by theological affiliations and their membership in the constituent nations at home in Great Britain.

---

1 See: http://www.cbc.ca/newsblogs/yourcommunity/2013/06/as-canadian-as.html.

Among the most significant of the many deep historical, cultural and racial differences represented within the population of the young penal colony, was the profound religious divide between the English Christianity of the majority—free men and convicts alike—and the Roman Catholicism of the Irish convicts and emancipists who amounted to a quarter of the population. That Catholic identity survived for decades before the arrival of officially sanctioned priests in the 1820s.[2]

Anglo-Irish Protestants constituted yet another distinct sub-culture among clergymen. They were nominally affiliated with the Church of England but typically hailed from Trinity College Dublin. There Anglo-Irish Protestants were also well-represented in the military garrison and among civil officials—most importantly by Governor Richard Bourke (1831–1837).[3] Such pan-British ethno-religious diversity among convicts, colonists, and clergymen did not discourage efforts by the first few Anglican chaplains to establish the early *de facto* ascendancy of the Church of England as a permanent situation. It was not long, however, before denominational diversity combined with representative government destroyed all hopes that an established national (indeed imperial) church might rival the rising religion of secular humanism. Some historians view another circumstance—the infamous if not indelible convict stain stamped on most of the early settlers—as the seedbed for secular scepticism, the greatest obstacle to the creation of *any* recognizably Christian community in colonial Australia.

---

2 Ian Breward, *A History of the Churches in Australasia* (Oxford: Oxford University Press, 2008), 19.

3 Michael Gladwin, *Anglican Clergy in Australia 1788–1850* (Woodbridge, UK: Boydell Press, 2015), 47–51; Brian Fletcher, "The Anglican Ascendancy, 1788–1835," in Bruce Kaye, ed., *Anglicanism in Australia: A History* (Melbourne: Melbourne University Press, 20020, 17.

Convicts and Christianity

Allan M Grocott paints a pathetic portrait of the plight plaguing colonial clergymen ministering to the convict population. "In general," he wrote, "the attitude of convicts and ex-convicts towards the churches and the clergy in New South Wales between 1788 and 1851 ranged from apathy, through cynicism and distrust, to violent hostility." Few convicts "were converted in any deeply religious or spiritual sense" despite the fact that "religious instruction was put on a more official and systematic basis" as time went on. In fact, according to Grocott, "[c]hurch services were sufficiently regular and repelling to be regarded as part of the punishment." Catholic convicts were especially hostile towards "the regular and compulsory Church of England services." But the colonial churches were no more successful in their efforts to win the hearts and minds of English felons. "Prisoners and old hands were plainly not interested in God the Father, or God the Son, or God the Holy Ghost." The problem was simply that the "evangelical and moralistic message of the Protestant Churches especially, was unappealing and unacceptable to the convict world."[4]

Grocott's thesis may overstate the case for convict anticlericalism by measuring outcomes in accordance with an "excessively nice" evangelical standard of religiosity.[5] He notes himself that irreligion among the lower orders was not confined to the colonies. Back in England too, "the mass of the working class were not outwardly religious and never attended church."[6] But Grocott forgets that in a "confessional state" such as eighteenth-century England the point of the ecclesiastical polity was not to generate religious enthusiasm.[7] The Church was

---

4   Allan M Grocott, *Convicts, Clergymen and Churches* (Sydney: Sydney University Press, 1980), 280–284.

5   Hilary M Carey, *Believing in Australia: A Cultural History of Religions* (St Leonards: Allen and Unwin, 1996), 14.

6   Grocott, *Convicts*, 280.

7   *Cf.*, Richard Hooker, *Of the Laws of Ecclesiastical Polity* Arthur Stephen McGrade ed. (Cambridge: Cambridge University Press, 1989).

expected to promote public decorum by shoring up a politically stable and hierarchical social order powered by the invisible hand driving the divine economy.[8] In its theology and liturgy, Anglicanism still sanctified the ancient Anglo-Saxon vision of a tripartite social order comprised of those who pray, those who fight, and those who work. Colonial convicts no less than the working poor in England were expected to absorb the Christian religion through a process of osmosis simply by rubbing shoulders with the higher orders in compulsory church services.

Still, given the special difficulties associated with a sullen and hostile convict population, it was probably fortunate that the penal colony in New South Wales attracted clergymen mainly associated with the evangelical wing of the Church of England. Gladwin demonstrates that "Evangelicalism was probably the dominant force in the Australian Church even during 1836–1850, when all bishops but one…were of a High Church or moderate Tractarian stamp."[9] Evangelicals were possessed by the indomitable will to win converts to the faith among the heathen, foreign and domestic. Of course, even fervent evangelicals such as Richard Johnson and Samuel Marsden were depressed and dispirited by personal contact with their convict charges. But the disciplinary compulsion of a temporarily transplanted confessional state combined with the missionary fervour of colonial chaplains had some positive outcomes. At the very least, the Anglican chaplaincy became "part of the process of transplanting the institutions and culture of the mother country."[10] The dogged efforts of Anglican chaplains before 1820 must have had some subliminal influence on convict culture while having a more explicit impact on the religiosity of upwardly

---

8   John Gascoigne, *The Enlightenment and the Origins of European Australia* (Cambridge: Cambridge University Press, 2002), 23–26.

9   Gladwin, *Anglican Clergy*, 41.

10 JD Bollen, "English Christianity and the Australian Colonies, 1788–1860," (1977) 28 *Journal of Ecclesiastical History* 361, at 362.

mobile emancipists and respectable free settlers, the wave of the future in New South Wales.

Evangelical Mission Accomplished?

Alan Atkinson observes that at home and in the colonies, clergymen preaching the Word of God had to span the cultural divide between "two worlds, two types of sensibility, one nourished by writing and the other by living conversation." Men such as Johnson and Marsden laboured to imprint their written culture on the oral culture of even the most degraded convicts. They were willing "to learn their language, to listen to their common conversation and, under the guidance of a higher civilisation, to work to do them good."[11] Inspired by a sense of mission, the work of evangelical clergymen became "the religious success story of the Australian colonies."[12]

Naturally, both evangelical Anglican clergymen with "their characteristic emphasis on…the missionary work of preaching the gospel" and colonial governors who identified "good order" with religious observance were appalled by oral cultures impervious to the written word, such as the debauched community living "above all restrictions" on the remote reaches of the Hawkesbury River.[13] But in time official pragmatism in religious matters would be content if such communities merely carried sufficient cultural baggage from their British origins to "found a type of order among themselves."[14]

The Whig triumph in British party politics in the years from 1828 to 1832 meant that the original commitment of the imperial authorities to the creation of a "Christian community" (implicit in the appointment of Anglican chaplains) in New South Wales was now most definitely

---

11 Alan Atkinson, *The Europeans in Australia: A History* Vol. 1 (Melbourne: Oxford University Press, 1997), 174–175.

12 Carey, *Believing*, 10.

13 *Ibid.*, 5; Atkinson, *Europeans*, 171–173.

14 Atkinson, *Europeans*, 173.

negotiable. Catholic emancipation and the removal of civil and political disabilities from Protestant Dissenters hollowed out the Christian ecclesiastical polity in Great Britain and encouraged the formal legal establishment of a pan-British secular humanism in the colonies. The Church, Commonwealth, and Commons of England ceased to be the visible embodiment of an organic "Christian community" of spirit, water, and blood (1 John 5:7–8).

Following the American Revolution, the evangelical language of religious liberty justified demands throughout the British Empire for the formal legal separation of church and state in the name of tolerance.[15] In New South Wales, the confessional state was replaced first by a multiple establishment of several Christian denominations and later by the uncontrolled proliferation of private, voluntary, religious associations which may or may not be Christian churches. Not surprisingly, it was the Anglo-Irish Whig Governor Richard Bourke who set out to deconstruct the Anglican establishment model of "Christian community" in New South Wales.

The Rise of Voluntarism

The evangelical success story turned out to be something of a mirage celebrated in the bloodless and bureaucratic language of census statistics. Taking such numbers at face value, in the last quarter of the nineteenth century Australia was a "Christian society." Reportedly, "more than 95% of the population of the Australian colonies identified with one or other of the denominations of Christianity."[16] This certainly did not in most cases translate into active church membership. Indeed, the significance of the superficially impressive number lies mainly in the reason why a question relating to religious affiliation was asked by official statisticians in the first place.

---

15 *Cf.*, JCD Clark, *The Language of Liberty 1660–1832: Political Discourse and Social Dynamics in the Anglo-American World* (Cambridge: Cambridge University Press, 1994).

16 Ken Inglis, "The Colonial Religion," (1977) 21(12) *Quadrant* 65.

By the late 1820s Catholic priests, Methodist and other Dissenting preachers, along with other evangelical ideologues such as the Presbyterian radical, John Dunmore Lang had made their presence felt in New South Wales. In 1833 Governor Bourke concluded that "in a New Country to which Persons of all religious persuasions are invited to resort, it will be impossible to establish a dominant and endowed Church without much hostility and great improbability of its becoming permanent."[17] He set out to end the informal Anglican ascendancy of the early years. The Church Act proposed by Bourke "created a sort of multiple religious establishment, a polygamous union between churches and the state."[18] Bourke's scheme gave public financial "support…as required to every one of the three grand divisions of Christianity [Anglican, Presbyterian, and Catholic] indifferently" while leaving "the management of the temporalities of their Churches…to themselves." The Governor acknowledged the theoretical objection that "in granting assistance to more than one Church, a claim is given for assistance upon the same principle to every Congregation of Dissenters and Jews,"[19] In practice, however, no such immediate extension of the scheme was deemed necessary to the peace, order and good government of the colony. In any case, Bourke probably "looked forward to a purely voluntary system in the future development of the colony,"[20]

The bureaucratic logic of such a hydra-headed religious establishment required a census "to determine which churches qualified for public money, and for how much. The grants were withdrawn later in the century, but the census counting went on," if only because the

---

17 Governor Richard Bourke, "More Equitable Funding of Churches," Document 155 in J Woolmington, ed., *Religion in Early Australia: The Problem of Church and State* (Stanmore: Cassell Australia, 1976) 93, at 94–95.

18 Inglis, "Colonial Religion," 65.

19 Bourke, "Equitable Funding," 95–96.

20 RB Walker, "The Abolition of State Aid to Religion in New South Wales," (1962) 10 (38) *Historical Studies: Australia and New Zealand* 165, at 166.

various churches acquired a vested interest in knowing where they stood in the league table of inter-denominational religious competition.[21] Given that state aid to churches had ceased by the final quarter of the nineteenth century, the census might be said to reveal the collective strength of Christian churches then dependent solely upon the voluntary support of their members.

On the other hand, there is good reason doubt that the overwhelmingly Christian character of the New South Wales population — before or after 1850 — can be inferred from responses to an official census. Almost by definition, evangelical Christianity, however important it may be to the personal identity of individual believers, provides a very shallow foundation for a communal way of life. In any case, evangelical Christian churches in the early nineteenth century were living on borrowed capital. No "Christian community" could have survived in early New South Wales without assistance from English Christian mission societies halfway around the world.

Bollen demonstrates that "English aid, human and material, was an essential part of the build-up of religious capital in the new settlements. It smoothed the adjustment of the Church of England to a voluntaryist environment and helped to bring religious supply and observance in nineteenth century Austalia to something like their levels in Victorian England," Not only did the English Churches perpetuate "themselves abroad; they reinforced the cultural ties of mother country and colonies."[22] Unfortunately, those cultural ties were not always conducive to the creation of a Christian community at home or in New South Wales.

---

21 Inglis, "Colonial Religion," 65–66.
22 Bollen, "English Christianity," 385.

Conclusion

The religious revolution of 1828–1832 in Great Britain set in motion a chain of events which within two decades erased the traditional Christian character of the English polity. Jews quickly moved to enlist the support of Protestant Dissenters and English liberals in a campaign lasting over two decades to remove their own civil and political disabilities; they sought to capture "the crowning symbol of political equality...in a bill to admit Jews to parliament."[23] That movement was matched in New South Wales by Jews who pushed on the door left open by Governor Bourke in soliciting state aid for their synagogue. Despite the hopes of Anglican loyalists, not only was the Church of England not "the Established Religion of the Empire," but the concept of the "Christian State" was obsolescent once "claims for support for the Jews were advanced on the ground of their rights as equal citizens. In 1846 a building grant was made for the synagogue and in 1855 a salary for a Jewish minister was included in the Estimates."[24] From that point, the formal constitutional establishment of secular humanism was merely a matter of time.

Not long after the controversy over Jewish emancipation released members of Parliament from the traditional obligation to swear allegiance to the Crown "on the true faith of a Christian," some members of the Broad-Church movement in England could see the writing on the wall. In an essay on the church in the colonies, John Westlake contended that no "Christian community" worthy of the name can exist apart from a national church which concentrates "all the intellectual activity which has grown up on the soil and under the influence of Christianity." If, as in the colonies, there is no scope for such a national church, "that would be as much as to say that the moving spiritual forces of the nation have diverged too widely for common action in

---

23 Ursula R.Q. Henriques, "The Jewish Emancipation Controversy in Nineteenth-Century Britain," (1968) 40 *Past and Present* 126, at 127.
24 Walker, "Abolition of State Aid," 177.

any yet recognised direction; that, in short, any further development must be outside of Christianity."[25] Westlake's observation sums up the trend line in the subsequent history of Australia. It will require much more than evangelical fervour to reverse that trend.

---

25 John Westlake, "The Church in the Colonies," in W.L. Clay, ed., *Essays on Church Policy* (London: Clay and Taylor, 1868), 237–238.

12. The White Australia Policy in Retrospect: Racism or Realism?

Introduction

OVER THE PAST THIRTY YEARS, Australia, along with just about every other Western society, has been transformed by a revolution engineered from the top down by the leading echelons of the corporate welfare state.[1] New Class cadres of managers, professionals, politicians, and academics have dismantled the foundations of Australian nationhood laid down at the time of Federation.[2] The arbitration system, the protective tariff, and the White Australia Policy: all have gone in order to facilitate the free flow of capital, technology, and labour in a globalist economy.

---

1   On the first stage of the managerial revolution, see James Burnham, *The Managerial Revolution: What Is Happening in the World* (New York: John Day & Company, 1941). But the use of mass immigration and multiculturalism as weapons in that revolutionary movement assumed primary importance from the 1960s onward *After Liberalism: Mass Democracy in the Managerial State* (Princeton, NJ: Princeton University Press, 1999) and idem, *Multiculturalism and the Politics of Guilt: Towards a Secular Theocracy* (Columbia: University of Missouri Press, 2002); see also Samuel Francis, "Power Trip," *The Occidental Quarterly* 3(2) (Summer 2003): 69; and Andrew Fraser, "A Marx for the Managerial Revolution: Habermas on Law and Democracy," *Journal of Law and Society* 28 (2001): 361.

2   On the New Class, see Alvin W. Gouldner, *The Future of Intellectuals and the Rise of the New Class* (New York: Continuum, 1979).

The most revolutionary, by far, of these radical changes has been the decision to open Australia to mass Third World immigration. In taking this step, the managerial regime has, in effect, followed the wry advice tendered by Bertolt Brecht to the East German government on the occasion of the workers' revolt in 1956: rather than relying on crude repressive measures, Brecht suggested, the Communist regime should simply dissolve the people and elect a new one.[3] Indeed, since the end of the Second World War a strange alliance of Communists, Christian churches, ethnic lobbies, and other pressure groups working through the corporate sector and within the centralized apparatus of state power set out deliberately to flood the Anglo-Australian homeland with a polyglot mass of Third World immigrants.

Chief among the ideological weapons deployed in that campaign have been the interwoven myths of equality and universal human rights.[4] The official ideology of the globalist regime has been enshrined in the *International Convention on the Elimination of All Forms of Racial Discrimination*.[5] According to that document, "any doctrine of superiority based on racial differentiation is scientifically false, morally condemnable, socially unjust and dangerous." There can therefore be "no justification for racial discrimination, in theory or in practice, anywhere." Those who subscribed to the doctrine of racial egalitarianism were bound to oppose a color bar on immigration to Australia as being both immoral and pointless: it was axiomatic that "racial differences are not significant differences that need divide mankind."[6]

---

3   Bertolt Brecht, *The Solution*, quoted in Peter Brimelow, *Alien Nation: Common Sense about America's Immigration Disaster* (New York: Harper Perennial, 1996), 58.

4   See, generally, Samuel Francis, "Equality As a Political Weapon" in *Beautiful Losers: Essays on the Failure of American Conservatism* (Columbia: University of Missouri Press, 1993).

5   Included as the Schedule to the Racial Discrimination Act, 1975 (Cth).

6   Immigration Reform Group, *Immigration Control or Colour Bar?* Kenneth Rivett, ed. (Melbourne University Press, 1962), 92–3.

Racial egalitarianism rather obviously flies in the face of the more realistic premises of the White Australia Policy. The founding fathers of the Australian nation regarded racial differences as a fact of life and racial conflict as the inevitable consequence of a multiracial society. In their view, ethnic homogeneity was one of the great strengths of the Australian nation, one that ought to be preserved and not squandered or thrown away in pursuit of utopian visions of universal harmony in which lions could be re-educated to lie down with lambs.[7]

Forty years after Australian governments began to distance themselves from the White Australia Policy, advances in genetics, paleoanthropology, psychology, and medical science are placing the universalist doctrines of racial egalitarianism under serious pressure. A vast range of studies in a number of disciplines have revealed real and important differences between the races in cognitive and athletic ability, behaviour and temperament.[8] Faced with such intellectual challenges, defenders of the ruling orthodoxy are resorting to social ostracism, legal repression, and even the sort of physical coercion employed against members of the One Nation Party some years back.[9] The time is clearly ripe for a courageous and well-informed

---

[7] Douglas Cole, "The Crimson Thread of Kinship: Ethnic Ideas in Australia, 1870–1914," *Historical Studies* 14 (1971): 511.

[8] For an introduction to this literature, see, e.g., Vincent Sarich and Frank Miele, *The Reality of Human Differences* (Boulder: Westview, 2004); Michael Levin, *Why Race Matters: Race Differences and What They Mean* (Westport: Praeger, 1997); J. Philippe *Race, Evolution and Behavior: A Life History Perspective* (New Brunswick, NJ: Transaction, 1997). The entire June 2005 issue of *Psychology, Public Policy and Law* is devoted to the issue of racial differences in cognitive ability. See, in particular, the lead article by J. Philippe Rushton and Arthur Jensen, "Thirty Years of Research on Race Differences in Cognitive Ability," *Psychology, Public Policy and Law* 11 (2005): 235. See also Charles Murray, "The Inequality Taboo," *Commentary* (September 1, 2005); a fully annotated version is available online at http://www.aei.org/publications/ pubID.23075,filter.social/ pub_detail.asp.

[9] See, e.g., Tim Dick, "Uni Suspends Outspoken Academic," *Sydney Morning Herald* July 30–31, 2005, 9; Bernard Lane, "African Groups Take Aim at Uni

reappraisal of the White Australia Policy and the decision to dismantle it. Unfortunately, racial realists, concerned to bring common sense to contemporary Australian debates over race and immigration, will be disappointed with two recent books on the White Australia Policy. Both promise much but deliver little because of their authors' determined refusal to take race seriously.

Was the White Australia Policy "Racist"?

The first of these books to appear was written by Keith Windschuttle, former Marxist academic turned independent neoconservative writer. Hot on the heels of his controversial revision of the "black armband" view of Aboriginal history, Windschuttle has upset yet another academic applecart.[10] In *The White Australia Policy,* he sets out to refute the orthodox leftist charge that the immigration legislation enacted shortly after Federation was "racist."[11] On the formal level that is easily done, since the Immigration Restriction Act, 1901 (Cth) did not explicitly prohibit nonwhite immigration. Instead, prospective immigrants were required to pass a dictation test by writing out fifty words in any European language selected by immigration officials.

But because both the intent and the practical effect of the dictation test were to sharply limit coloured immigration, Australia was open to attack from progressives around the world and, especially during the Cold War, from newly assertive postcolonial regimes in Asia and Africa. Over the last forty years, a homegrown generation of New Left historians routinely portrayed Australia as a racist pariah nation on a par with South Africa. Ever since the Sixties generation began its long march through the institutions, Australians have been taught to

Lecturer," *The Weekend Australian,* August 6–7, 2005, 3; Andrew Fraser, "The Trials and Tribulations of Populism in Australia," *Telos* 127 (Spring 2004): 119–148.

10 Keith Windschuttle, *The Fabrication of Aboriginal History* (Sydney: Macleay Press, 2002).

11 Keith Windschuttle, *The White Australia Policy* (Sydney: Macleay Press, 2005).

approach their past in a self-hating mood of enthusiastic shame. To his credit, Windschuttle has been one of the few historians to resist this form of intellectual self-flagellation.

Unfortunately, Windschuttle's rehabilitation of the White Australia Policy is premised on a familiar, if pernicious, tenet of neoconservatism: like those who claim that the United States is a "creedal nation," Windschuttle maintains that the operating premise of Australian society is the proposition that all people are equal in principle and in potential.[12] Supposedly, Australia's national identity is "based on a civic patriotism," thereby fostering "loyalty to Australia's liberal democratic political institutions rather than to race or ethnicity." He contends that the White Australia Policy, far from being the reactionary spawn of an irredeemably racist nation, grew out of a long-established, progressive program aiming "to extend both the freedom and the dignity of labour."[13]

Earlier movements to end slavery throughout the British Empire and the transportation of convicts to Australia culminated in a concerted campaign to prevent the importation of cheap coolie labour from Asia and the Pacific islands. Windschuttle claims, therefore, that opposition to Asian immigration was not grounded in fears of "racial contamination." Rather, politicians were concerned both to protect the standard of living of Australian workers and to prevent the emergence of "a racially-based political underclass" that would undermine Australia's egalitarian democracy.[14]

---

12 See, e.g., Ben J. Wattenberg, *The First Universal Nation* (New York: Touchstone, 2001).

13 Windschuttle, *White Australia*, 5–6. The suggestion that the White Australia Policy was based upon a civic rather than ethnic nationalism was made earlier in Robert Birrell, *A Nation of Our Own: Citizenship and Nation-Building in Federation Australia* (Melbourne: Longman, 1995).

14 Windschuttle, *White Australia*, 6, 8.

This argument rests upon a false dichotomy. Australia's egalitarian democracy was conceived as a new and better Britannia.[15] Who could have doubted that antipodean Britons, too, were white Europeans? By the turn of the twentieth century, references to the "crimson thread of kinship" binding Australians to the mother country had become a staple of political rhetoric.[16] Most Australians hardly needed to be reminded that blood is thicker than water; nevertheless, Windschuttle portrays their leaders as proto-Boasian anthropologists, rejecting any suggestion that racial differences marked a permanent or intractable barrier between different branches of the human brotherhood.[17] Windschuttle maintains that most early twentieth century Australians were confident that Chinese and Indian labourers would become indistinguishable from white Australians of British stock once they were detached from the environments fostering their historic cultures of servility.[18]

---

15 Humphrey McQueen, *A New Britannia: An Argument Concerning Australian Radicalism* (Melbourne: Penguin, 1970).

16 Cole, "The Crimson Thread of Kinship."

17 Franz Boas was a Jewish anthropologist who played a key role in the anti-Darwinian remaking of American social science. According to Carl Degler, "Boas' influence upon American social scientists in matters of race can hardly be exaggerated." He engaged in "a life-long assault on the idea that race was a primary source of the differences to be found in the mental or social capabilities of human groups." It was "through his ceaseless, almost relentless articulation of the concept of culture" that he effectively expunged race from American social science. See Carl Degler, *In Search of Human Nature: The Decline and Revival of Darwinism in American Social Thought* (New York: Oxford University Press, 1991), 61, 71. Boas did not approach his work in the neutral spirit of objective scientific inquiry. On the contrary, his pronounced "out-group sensibility" led him to transform anthropology into a formidable ideological weapon, thereby promoting Jewish ethnic interests in what he conceived as a struggle against anti-Semitism. See Sarich and Miele, 86–91l and Kevin MacDonald, *The Culture of Critique: An Evolutionary Analysis of Jewish Involvement in Twentieth-Century Intellectual and Political Movements* (Westport: Praeger, 1998).

18 Windschuttle, *White Australia*, 174–181.

Windschuttle concedes that the immigration restriction movement did attract support from "unequivocally racist" elements. Indeed, he savours the irony in the fact that in early twentieth-century Australia, the most sympathetic audience for racial nationalism was found among the bohemian writers, artists, and intellectuals of the leftist intelligentsia. That elite minority, then famously associated with the *Bulletin* magazine, bears an "uncanny resemblance" to the "chattering classes" now: "they agree on almost everything, with the conspicuous exception of immigration policy, where their positions are reversed."[19]

Revolution from Above?

By contrast, Windschuttle insists, mainstream Australians have never subscribed to biological theories of race. Influenced instead by the universalistic principles of both evangelical Christianity and the Scottish Enlightenment, they have refused to treat white Europeans as superior and other races as innately and permanently inferior. This, then, is the crux of Windschuttle's argument: because the White Australia Policy was never based on racial nationalism, it could be — and was — readily jettisoned once the original political, economic, and cultural justifications for its adoption lost their potency. "The proof that Australia wore the policy lightly was the ease with which it discarded it."[20]

In other words, if the White Australia Policy really had been steeped in "racist paranoia," it would be difficult to explain the fact that dismantling it in the twenty years from the mid-1950s onward "required no major cultural upheaval and was accomplished with a minimum of fuss by liberal politicians with values similar to those held by the original sceptics and critics when immigration restrictions were introduced in 1901."[21]

---

19 Ibid., 5, 82.
20 Ibid., 67–74, 326.
21 Ibid., 9.

Windschuttle is mainly concerned with the rise of the immigration restriction movement. His argument with the academic establishment is pitched as a simple matter of historical fact: was the White Australia Policy "racist" or not? *The Long, Slow Death of White Australia*, by Gwenda Tavan, deals with its demise. In her first chapter, Tavan differs from Windschuttle on the reasons for the ascendancy of White Australia, insisting that racism and xenophobia were driving forces in the campaign to restrict non-white immigration. But, like Windschuttle, she is struck by the ease with which opponents of the White Australia Policy were able to overturn it. Her brief is to rebut the most obvious explanation for the lack of massive popular resistance to such a fundamental change: namely, that the White Australia Policy was dismantled by an elite conspiracy operating in stealth, leaving the Australian people in the dark concerning the nature and magnitude of the mass Third World immigration soon to be inflicted upon them.[22]

Tavan is not especially convincing in her effort to demonstrate that the Australian public readily accepted higher non-European immigration as early as the 1970s. Her main evidence is the fact that the Whitlam government was re-elected in 1974, even after its Minister for Immigration, Al Grassby, publicly proclaimed his determination to bury the White Australia Policy. Of course, Whitlam's Labor government was soundly rejected by the electorate in 1975. The incoming Fraser government certainly had no mandate to promote a massive influx of non-white immigrants. Nevertheless, it joined with the Australian Labor Party to forge a bipartisan consensus in favour of Third World immigration.

For decades, there was no effective political opposition to the revolution from above in immigration law and policy. Among the managerial and professional classes, a complacently "cosmopolitan" consensus reigned supreme; the political equilibrium was not upset until the meteoric rise of the One Nation party in the late 1990s. Then,

---

22 Gwenda Tavan, *The Long Slow Death of White Australia* (Melbourne: Scribe, 2005), 227–229.

for a brief, shining moment, the patriotic instincts of the more "parochial," outer suburban, white Australians found a political voice.[23] Much to the relief of the political class, however, that too often tongue-tied voice of populist protest was largely ineffectual and, in any case, was soon silenced.

Concerned to counter suggestions that the new regime lacked popular support from the beginning, Tavan cites opinion polls from the mid-1970s favouring the then-current rate of Asian migration. When weighing such evidence, one wonders how citizens then would have responded to pollsters had they been presented with an accurate picture of how Sydney and Melbourne would look after thirty years of colonization by Third World immigrants. Tavan acknowledges that "debate still continues" over how many non-whites should be allowed to enter while insisting that "a majority of Australians since the 1960s have unequivocally rejected any policy that would completely bar non-Europeans from settling." White Australia, she maintains, is no longer a "dominant worldview"; at most, it persists as a "residual cultural form." Even so, she concedes that "the battle against White Australia is not completely won." From Pauline Hanson to the *Tampa* incident, recent events have revealed that "the [white, Anglo-Celtic] racial-cultural ideals" of Australian nationhood have never been completely extinguished.[24] Tavan fears that, like the slow, silent combustion of an

---

23 On the conflict between "cosmopolitans" and "parochials" in contemporary Australia, see Katharine Betts, *The Great Divide* (Sydney: Duffy and Snellgrove, 1999).

24 In August 2001, a Norwegian freighter, the *MV Tampa*, picked up 460 predominantly Afghani "asylum-seekers" from a boat that sank in Indonesian waters before it could reach Australia. Rather than return the passengers to Indonesia, the ship's captain ought to land them in Australian territory. Prime Minister John Howard refused permission, and the resulting standoff was only resolved when New Zealand and the tiny Pacific island nation of Nauru agreed to take the would-be illegal migrants. His firm stand contributed to the government's victory in the November 2001 election. Since then, however, many, if not most of the *Tampa* passengers have wheedled and cajoled their way into Australia.

underground coal seam, the fiery force of white racial consciousness may burst, without warning, through the surface somnolence secured, so far, by the multiracialist mullahs of the media, the human rights industry, and the educational establishment.[25]

Tavan clearly shares Windschuttle's conventionally progressive views on the nature and significance of race. As committed racial egalitarians, both writers desperately want to drive a stake through the heart of racial realism, once and for all. Tavan and Windschuttle still worry that, despite having been in a state of suspended animation for several decades, residual forms of racial identity might someday reawaken in the hearts of white Australians, perhaps even with renewed vigour and enhanced vitality. For that reason, Windschuttle happily joins the left in its attack upon race as "an unscientific category," as a thoroughly modern, bad idea "engendered by the new social sciences and brought to maturity by the evolutionary biology of the nineteenth century."[26] In the battle between racial realism and racial egalitarianism, former Professor Windschuttle joins his old revolutionary comrades on the barricades, resolutely denying that differences between "races" have a biological or genetic foundation.

In his thoroughly orthodox opinion, nineteenth century anthropology and biology took a wrong turn when they denied "Enlightenment and Evangelical ideas about the unity of humanity." For him, the evident differences between the various races of mankind are the malleable product of their cultures and the state each may have reached in the long ascent from savagery to civilization. No race is permanently incapable of change and development. Somewhat imprudently, Windschuttle suggests that to take any other view on this question "is to betray one's ignorance of the subject."[27] In fact, to anyone familiar with the rapidly expanding literature on the genetic character of racial

---

25 Tavan, *Long Slow Death of White Australia,* 210, 225.

26 Windschuttle, *White Australia,* 28–35.

27 Ibid., 34, 27.

differences, Windschuttle's dogmatism is a clear case of what American commentator Steve Sailer calls racial flat-earthism.²⁸

Biology and Culture

There is still room for debate on the precise genetic contribution to any given racial difference in, for example, intelligence, temperament, criminality, and athletic ability. But that such racial differences do exist and that they have a biological basis is not any longer open to serious scientific question. As Vincent Sarich and Frank Miele put it, "the case for race hinges on recognition that genetic variation in traits that affect performance and ultimately survival is the fuel on which the evolutionary process runs." Without that "functional genetic variation, there can be no adaptive evolution." Variation "is the norm...and not...the exception in the case of humans." In fact, Sarich and Miele suggest that the range of genetic variation between different races of *Homo sapiens* much greater than for any other species, including domesticated dogs. They observe that commonly used genetic tests can determine with great precision not just an individual's race but also "the percentage of racial background in people of mixed ancestry." But until very recently it was impossible to detect the genetic markers distinguishing a cocker spaniel from a wolf.²⁹

Race exists and it matters across a wide range of public policy issues. It is of relevance to any analysis of immigration law and policy. Windschuttle, however, is determined to remain uncontaminated by the new sciences of racial difference. He does recognize the seemingly insuperable *cultural* barriers alienating mainstream Australians from other racial groups, particularly the Chinese. Nevertheless, he asserts that it is a fundamental error "to slide from the concept of culture to

---

28 Steve Sailer, "Race Flat-Earthers Dangerous to Everyone's Health," http://www.vdare.com/sailer/medicine_and_race.htm.

29 Sarich and Miele, *Race*, 8, 21, 184–7.

that of race."[30] Since cultural differences are not inbred and immutable, there is no insuperable barrier to the assimilation of large numbers of non-white migrants into Australian society. But what if Windschuttle is wrong? What if racial differences are, in large part, biologically or genetically grounded? What if even culture is not simply a social construct but, rather, a phenomenon with a substantial biological component? Windschuttle does document the dominance of Enlightenment and Christian influences in middle Australia, demonstrating that explicitly racialist ideologies have had little appeal to opinion leaders in Australia. But that may mean only that Australians, like other ethnic groups tracing their ancestry to Northwestern Europe, are predisposed to individualism, exogamy, and small nuclear families and, consequently, display a relative lack of ethnocentrism.

Thus, what Windschuttle describes as a creedal commitment to racial egalitarianism may be a defining characteristic of a distinctive European racial identity not shared by other peoples. Kevin MacDonald explains Western "cultural" traits as an evolutionary adaptation to the

---

30 Windschuttle, *White Australia,* 285. Windschuttle's dogmatic insistence that there is an impassable gulf between the concepts of "race" and "culture" is repeated endlessly not just by orthodox leftists and timid academics but also by nominally "conservative" figures such as former National Party Senator John Stone. Mr. Stone deplores the growth of large Muslim colonies in Australia. He calls for strict limits on further Muslim immigration and other measures requiring immigrants to assimilate into Australian society. On the other hand, he has no objection to large-scale nonwhite immigration so long as it seems good for the economy. Mr. Stone is a former Treasury Secretary known for his "economic rationalist" outlook. Probably for that reason, he makes it clear that his concerns are "not about race, but about *culture.*" To reinforce that point he warns that "some real racists may also seek to inject themselves into the debate, but their advocacy...should be set aside if we are to reach sensible outcomes." John Stone, "Solutions to the Muslim Problem in Australia," *National Observer* 66 (Spring 2005): 20. Mr. Stone was as good as his word when I asked him, in his capacity as Honorary Secretary of the Samuel Griffith Society, to include the present paper in the proceedings of the society's conference in 2006. He flatly refused, saying it was out of place–even though earlier conferences had included several papers dealing with immigration law and policy.

rigors of life in cold, ecologically adverse climates. Natural selection worked there to favour the reproductive success of those individuals capable of sustaining "non-kinship-based forms of reciprocity."[31]

Over time, individualistic social structures encouraged the emergence in England of the common law of property and contract and, later still, the emergence of impersonal corporate forms of business enterprise, all requiring cooperation between strangers. The distinctive culture that emerged from the interaction between the genotype of the English people and their environment can be understood as what Richard Dawkins calls an extended phenotype.[32] Like the spider's web or the beaver's dam, the extended phenotypes of Western civilization are part of a biocultural feedback loop linking our genes with our environment over countless generations.[33]

The extended phenotype produced by the English people finds its greatest political expression in the phenomenon of nationhood. Appearing first of all in England, the idea of the nation could be understood as what Richard Dawkins might call a "meme"[34] that has been only imperfectly or not at all replicated in the bioculture of other, particularly non-European, races. Some scholars, however, deny that English nationhood is the product of a primordial English ethnicity. It is often remarked that there are very few nations that seem to be ethnically homogeneous, and that England is not one of them. On

---

31 Kevin MacDonald, "What Makes Western Culture Unique?," *The Occidental Quarterly* 2(2) (2002) http://theoccidentalquarterly.com/vol2no2/km-unique.html.

32 Richard Dawkins, *The Extended Phenotype* (New York: Oxford University Press, 1989).

33 Louis R Browning, "*Bioculture:* A New Paradigm for the Evolution of Western Populations," *The Occidental Quarterly* 4(1) (2004):31. http://theoccidentalquarterly.com/vol4no1/lrb-bioculture.html.

34 Dawkins defines a meme as follows: "A unit of cultural inheritance, hypothesized as analogous to the particulate gene, and as naturally selected by virtue of its 'phenotypic' consequences on its own survival and replication in the cultural environment," Dawkins, *Extended Phenotype,* 290.

this view, the English nation "emerged out of populations deposited by successive waves of alien conquest." It was "through the merging or assimilation of peoples who were originally distinct" that a single English nation arose. According to Margaret Canovan, English nationhood "was in no sense a reflection of primordial ties of blood." On the contrary, the English nation was remarkably *in*clusive, taking in not only the scions of Danish, Norman, Saxon, and some Welsh stock, "but also (and, at the time, more significantly) nobles and commoners." Canovan's case would appear to be clinched by the "subsequent expansion of English into *British* identity," carrying "the nation even farther away from anything resembling primordial ethnicity."[35]

Constitutional Patriotism

It seems, then, that civic rather than ethnic nationalism has been the defining feature of not just Australian but British identity as well. Roger Scruton lends support to that suggestion when he remarks that modern citizenship presupposes a society of strangers: "The good citizen recognizes obligations towards people who are not, and cannot be, known to him." Such a society of strangers cannot survive without "the kind of courage, discipline and self-sacrifice that stem from civic patriotism."[36] But neither Canovan nor Scruton embraces the bloodless vision of constitutional patriotism promoted by Keith Windschuttle and the American neo-conservatives. For her part, Canovan acknowledges that nations "are political communities that are experienced as if they were communities of kin." She adds, however, that "the 'as if is vital."[37] In doing so, she seeks to mark out a middle position between ethnic and civic nationalism.

---

35 Margaret Canovan, *Nationhood and Political Theory* (Cheltenham: Edward Elgar, 1996), 58, 75–77.

36 Roger Scruton, *The West and the Rest: Globalization and the Terrorist Threat* (Wilmington: ntercollegiate Studies Institute, 2002), 52, 56.

37 Canovan, *Nationhood and Political Theory*, 59.

Neither Canovan nor Scruton believes that a nation can be grounded in an abstract loyalty to a particular political regime or constitutional order. Under the label of constitutional patriotism, Windschuttle is marketing a thoroughly artificial nationhood. Inhabiting an ancestral homeland, a real nation binds its citizens together in an inherited community of memory, language, culture, and, indeed, of blood. Citizens are members of a pre-political community that includes the living, their ancestors, and their unborn offspring. Absent generations are among the strangers to whom the good citizen is bound in "a common web of rights and duties."[38] Canovan, too, affirms both that within any nation, "many fellow-nationals really will be blood relations" and that "nations depend upon the symbolism of kinship for much of their emotional appeal." But she rejects the claims of ethnic nationalism, pointing out that "much of that kinship is imagined kinship, and a good deal of it is always fictitious."[39]

The problem with Canovan's argument is that she does not give sufficient weight to the "peculiarities of the English."[40] As a consequence, like Windschuttle, in relation to the White Australia Policy, she sets up a false dichotomy between ethnic and civic nationalism. In the case of England and the old white dominions settled by people of British stock, including the United States, there is simply no contradiction between the two. That is part of the reason why, for two hundred years after the emergence of the English nation, it was the *only* nation.[41] Even those citizens of a modern nation who are blood relations are expected to treat each other publicly "as if" they were strangers bound together by a willingness to recognize the fundamental constitutional norms associated with the rule of law, representative government,

---

38 Scruton, *The West and the Rest*, 51.
39 Canovan, *Nationhood and Political Theory*, 59.
40 On which, see Alan Macfarlane, *The Origins of English Individualism: The Family, Property and Social Transition* (Oxford: Basil Blackwell, 1978). The phrase itself was coined by E. P. Thompson.
41 Canovan, *Nationhood and Political Theory*, 63.

and individual rights.⁴² Only a people such as the English, characterized by the "non-kinship based forms of reciprocity" associated with Protestant Christianity, monogamy and companionate marriage, nuclear families, a marked de-emphasis on extended kinship relations, and a strong tendency towards individualism, could possibly succeed in creating such a "society of strangers."⁴³

It is true, of course, that the English nation was the hybrid product of many preexisting ethnic groups. But the fact is that the ingredients in the ethnic stew that ultimately produced the English people and, later still, British nation, were not all that genetically remote from one another. Indeed, the Danes, the Saxons, and the Normans were closely related Germanic peoples and the genetic distance between the English, the Scots, and the Irish was not much more significant. Precisely because all the Germanic peoples were relatively individualistic and comparatively less ethnocentric than Eurasian and African races, they were able to overcome their group differences when they encountered each other in England, merging into a new ethny possessed of its own distinctive language, religion, and way of life.

The relative inclusiveness of English national identity was replicated in the settler dominions. In fact, the English, Irish, Scottish, Welsh, and even continental European settlers in colonial America, English Canada, Australia, and New Zealand fused together to become more British than the British in their new homelands. The creation of those colonial British cultures was an important first step on the road to creating new national identities as Americans, Australians, Canadians, and New Zealanders.⁴⁴ Civic nationalism was, therefore, a meme replicated best and most easily through the vehicle provided by the Anglo-Saxon genotype. This exposes a fundamental paradox built

---

42 Scruton, *The West and the Rest*, 51.
43 MacDonald, "Western Culture."
44 Donald Harman Akenson, "The Historiography of English-speaking Canada and the Concept of Diaspora: A Skeptical Appreciation, " *Canadian Historical Review* 76 (1995): 377.

into the free and open societies of the West: the only racial groups able to fit seamlessly into the society of strangers constituting a civic nation are those whose members can easily shed the deeply ingrained ethnocentrism and xenophobia characterizing most non-European peoples. Receptivity to civic nationalism, in other words, is found only in a relatively few, mainly northwestern European, ethnic or racial groups.

Unfortunately, over the past two centuries the nationhood meme has undergone a monstrous mutation. Originally, the English nation created the state as a medium for political self-expression. Since then, the transnational corporate welfare state has taken on a life of its own, asserting its power and right to recreate the nation and its people in whatever form it chooses. The result in Australia was the covert decision by political, corporate, and cultural elites to abandon the White Australia Policy.

The Downside of Diversity

The conventional wisdom holds that "race" is merely an imaginary social construct; all significant group differences are the malleable products of "culture." Therefore, it is said, social engineering by enlightened policymakers can overcome racial divisions in polyethnic societies. Now, it is true that biology is not destiny; morality and character also work to shape individual and group behaviour. But they, too, are intertwined intimately with the predispositions built into "racial" genotypes. Consequently, ethnic conflict is an inescapable fact of life. Unfortunately, those who abandoned the White Australia Policy were riven by a dogged determination to deny the reality of racial differences in favour of a sweeping cultural revolution. According to the *Shorter Oxford English Dictionary*, "culture" denotes "the refinement of mind, tastes and manners." Clearly there can be no "mind, tastes or manners" without a brain and the body that houses it. And, if the biology of the brain and the body differs between "races" (or sexes, for that matter), as it does,[45] it will be reflected in their respective cultures. This would be a thoroughly uncontroversial proposition but for the ideologically driven efforts of Boasian anthropology to treat "culture" as a "super-organic" phenomenon altogether detached from human biology. As Roger Sandall remarks, "the anthropological concept of culture is far too general for its own good, a fact which makes its 'explanatory importance' hard to evaluate — because it explains everything, it also tends to explain nothing."[46]

One need not resort to a crude genetic determinism to recognize the deeply entrenched character of cultural differences between racial groups. The culture of any given racial group is never static; it changes and develops, for better or for worse. Black Africans, for example, have been present in large numbers in America for almost four hundred years. During that time, their culture has been transformed in countless ways. But never have they been successfully integrated into the common culture of white Americans. It remains an open question whether other races can be absorbed into either the American or the Australian nation more easily than the now militantly hyphenated African-Americans.

Experience with the overseas Chinese diaspora throughout the Pacific Rim also gives cause for concern.[47] As the numerous Chinese colonies in Australia's largest cities grow, in size, wealth, and power, even their Australian-born members may be reluctant to dissolve their ancient collective identity into an individualistic society of strangers owing allegiance to nothing beyond a modern paper constitution, now divorced from its own ancestral roots. Thousands of years ago, the

---

45 See, generally, Rushton.

46 Roger Sandall, *The Culture Cult: Designer Tribalism and Other Essays* (Boulder: Westview, 2001), 156.

47 See, generally, Sterling Seagrave, *Lords of the Rim* London: Corgi, 1996); Joel Kotkin, *Tribes: How Race, Religion and Identity Determine Success in the New Global Economy* (New York: Random House, 1992); Thomas Sowell, *Migrations and Cultures: A World View* (New York: Basic, 1996)

Chinese took an evolutionary path favouring the growth of centralized, authoritarian regimes; not surprisingly, the Chinese today place a premium on clannish behaviour and downplay the worth of individual creativity. The result has been a people marked by higher average intelligence — but more conformity, hierarchy, and racial solidarity — than that found in northwestern European societies.

Even when faced with competition from highly cohesive ethnic groups such as the Chinese, a great many individualistic Australians remain utterly oblivious to their own genetic interest in a racially homogeneous society. The demographic threat to that interest grows as immigrants are drawn from racial groups whose genotypes are ever more distant from Australia's largely European gene pool. Like any other ethno-nation, white Australians constitute a large, partly inbred, extended family[48] Since an ethny is "analogous to a population of cousins," even distant kin "carry genetic interests for each other." But, because — at any given level of technology — the Australian landmass has a finite carrying capacity, mass immigration must replace future Australian children

The damage caused by Third World immigration to the genetic interests of European peoples can now be quantified with considerable precision. Frank Salter has calculated that if England, for example, received 12.5 million closely related Danish immigrants, the genetic loss to the remaining English would be relatively low, amounting to the equivalent of 209,000 children (still a large family to lose). But the

---

48 See, e.g., Steve Sailer, "It's All Relative: Putting Race in Its Proper Perspective" at http://www.vdare.com/sailer/presentation.htm Note that Sailer's definition of "race" as an inbred extended family means that some such descent groups are closely related, such as Catholics and Protestants in Northern Ireland, while others, such as the classic continental races (Africans, Europeans, and East Asians) that evolved separately for 40,000 years or so were relatively remote from each other both genetically and geographically. Race is a fuzzy category precisely because any genetically distinct descent group could be classified as a race. Remember, however, that the concept of a species is no less fuzzy: Are dogs, wolves, and coyotes separate or members of the same species?

same number of immigrants from India would cause a corresponding loss of 2.6 million children. Since black, sub-Saharan Africans are even more genetically distant from the English, an influx of 12.5 million Bantus would displace the equivalent of 13 million English children. The genetic losses to the English would be greater still if Indians or Bantus had fertility rates higher than the host population.[49]

Apart from the objective genetic interests at stake, a multiracial society forces white Australians to bear other, more subjectively painful, social, economic and political costs. At the high end of Australia's immigrant intake, a growing cognitive elite of East Asians threatens to become similar to "market-dominant minorities" such as the overseas Chinese in Southeast Asia, Jews in Russia, or Indians in East Africa.[50] Faced with competition from a growing East Asian population, white Australians now find themselves outgunned: Western-style "old boy" preference networks are only weakly ethnic in character and, thus, permeable, making them no match for the institutionally directed, in-group solidarity or "ethnic nepotism" practices deployed by other groups. Endowed with an edge in IQ and a temperament conducive to rigorous regimes of coaching, rote learning and stricter parental discipline, young East Asians already dominate the competition for places in universities and professional schools. Within two or three decades, it is not unreasonable to expect that Australia will have a heavily Asian

---

49 Frank Salter, *On Genetic Interests: Family, Ethny and Humanity in an Age of Mass Migration* (Frankfurt am Main: Peter Lang, 2003), 47, 42, 59–75.

50 On "market-dominant minorities," see Amy Chua, *World on Fire: How Exporting Free-Market Democracy Breeds Ethnic Hatred and Global Instability (*London: William Heinemann, 2003). Matt Nuenke's excellent review of Chua's book is available online at: http://home.comcast.net/~neoeugenics/wof.htm On Jews as the classic "market-dominant minority": see Kevin MacDonald, *A People That Shall Dwell Alone: Judaism As a Group Evolutionary Strategy* (Westport: Praeger, 1994); and Yuri Slezkine, *The Jewish Century* (Princeton, NJ: Princeton University Press, 2004).

managerial-professional ruling class that will not hesitate to promote the interests of coethnics at the expense of white Australians.[51]

There is no shortage of Chinese authority for such predictions. A recent book by the Philippine-born Chinese American Amy Chua provides a striking discussion of the intractable conflicts between the overseas Chinese and the host populations of just about every country in Southeast Asia. In the Philippines, for example, the Chinese minority, representing only 1 percent of the population, controls over 60 percent of the economy. Such a lopsided situation generates widespread resentment among Filipinos. This simmering tension boiled over onto Chua's own family when an elderly aunt was murdered by her Filipino chauffeur, a crime all but ignored by Filipino police.[52] Similar conflicts are an inescapable fact of life almost everywhere in Southeast Asia, most famously in Malaysia, where locals became so incensed over the dominance of the overseas Chinese that governments were forced to protect the ethnic interests of native Malays by adopting official preferential policies.[53]

Winners And Losers

In his online review of Chua's book, Matt Nuenke suggests that the best explanation for the ability of the Chinese to establish and maintain their position as a "market-dominant minority" throughout the region is the significant IQ gap (in favour of the Chinese) between them and the native populations.[54] The IQ differential between Chinese and white Australians is not as large, but it does exist, and already it has had a striking effect on the competition for places in higher education

---

51 Frank Salter, ed., *Welfare, Ethnicity and Altruism: New Findings and Evolutionary Theory* (London: Frank Cass, 2004).

52 Chua, *World on Fire*, 1–5.

53 Thomas Sowell, *Preferential Policies: An International Perspective* (New York: William Morrow, 1990), 45–51.

54 Nuenke, http://home.comcast.net/~neoeugenics/wof.htm.

and access to professional careers — with white Australians being the big losers.

Prominent Chinese leaders, such as the former prime minister of Singapore, Lee Kuan Yew, now boast openly that East Asians share with Jews "a place at the top of the racial pyramid." In Australia, too, one Chinese writer has escribed the xenophobic, even downright "racist" attitudes long harboured by his people.[55] That ingrained racial realism reinforces age-old tendencies towards ethnic nepotism among Asian peoples. If a British-style representative democracy had been grafted onto Singapore's multiracial society, Lee Kuan Yew is sure that Malays would always vote for Muslims, Indians for Indians, and the Chinese for Chinese, even at the expense of other economic or social interests.[56]

Such ethnocentric attitudes have been powerfully reinforced in recent times in China by a Communist government that, having lost its Marxist ideological mooring, is fearful of losing control over its vast empire. Immigrants from mainland China have been taught to hate "the foreign devils" and cherish the Motherland, "which never has done, and never could do, any wrong." Steeped from childhood in an ever more aggressive Chinese nationalism, such immigrants are unlikely to resist powerfully ingrained habits of ethnic nepotism. Indeed, even the British-American writer John Derbyshire, who has a Chinese wife, warns that mass Chinese immigration brings with it the very real danger of an imported Sino-Fascism.[57]

That danger must become ever more pronounced as China itself advances in military and economic might. But even if we leave that geopolitical dimension of the problem aside, there is no denying that

---

55 Michael D. Barr, "Lee Kuan Yew: Race, Culture and Genes," *Journal of Contemporary Asia* 29(2) (1999): 145–147; Sang Ye, *The Year the Dragon Came* (St. Lucia: University of Queensland Press, 1996), vii–viii.

56 Lee Kuan Yew in *Der Spiegel* 32/2005 (August 8, 2005).

57 John Derbyshire, "Importing Sino-Fascism?," http://www.vdare.com/derbyshire/sino-fascism.htm.

individualistic white Australians, taught from infancy that white racial pride is a grave moral failing and that ethnic nepotism is an unlawful form of racial discrimination, will be extraordinarily vulnerable to competition from a much more cohesive cognitive elite of overseas Chinese. Janet Landa points out that in overseas Chinese society, Confucian ethics prescribe "differences in patterns of mutual aid obligations between people with *varying degrees of social distance within a well-defined social structure* — near kinsmen (e.g., family members), distant kinsmen in extended family and lineage, clansmen, fellow villagers, and people speaking the same dialect."[58]

The strongest ties are within the family, where social distance is at a minimum. Trustworthiness in trade relations is generally measured in terms of concentric circles extending outward from family and near kin. On Landa's analysis, "Chinese social structure, unlike Western social structure, which is individualistic in nature, consists of a careful ranking of people who are classified according to distinct categories of social relationships."[59] Outside the framework of established relationships, the overseas Chinese are brutal competitors.[60]

Steep hierarchies and inequality are accepted as a normal part of life so that strangers cannot expect to be treated on a par with friends and family. Accordingly, Indonesian Chinese bankers experience no ethical difficulty in forwarding "[a stranger's] loan application as strategically important information to members of their business networks doing business in the same area and industry as the loan applicant." Armed with that information, the banker's associates might

---

58 Janet T. L Landa, "Cognitive and Classificatory Foundations of Trust and Informal Institutions: A New and Expanded Theory of Ethnic Trading Networks," in Frank Salter, ed. *Risky Transactions: Trust, Kinship and Ethnicity* (New York: Berghahn, 2002), 134–5.
59 Ibid., 135.
60 George T. Haley, Chin Tiong Tan, and Usha C.V. Haley, *New Asian Emperors: The Overseas Chinese, Their Strategies and Competitive Advantage* (Oxford: Butterworth Heinemann, 1998), 68.

not only move into the business but set out as well to implement the business plan submitted along with the stranger's loan application.[61]

The strongest ethical obligation among the overseas Chinese is to preserve social harmony. But strangers falling outside the circle of ethically significant others are fair game; their disappointment and anger cannot disrupt social harmony. Clearly, the greater in-group solidarity of Chinese operating within such a social structure will give them a powerful edge in competition with unorganized, individualistic white Australians. Even the nuclear family has lost much of its former power to bind white Australians together into cohesive units capable of meeting stiff competition from East Asian cognitive elites.

Middle-class Australians face little competitive pressure from the low end of the market for Third World immigrants, but the downside for the nation is even more obvious. Tensions are already appearing between white Australians and the growing numbers of black, sub-Saharan Africans settled here by the transnational refugee industry.[62] One can safely predict that, no matter how large this Third World colony becomes, black Africans will never become a "market-dominant minority" in Australia. On the contrary, experience "practically everywhere in the world tells us that an expanding black population is a sure-fire recipe for increases in crime, violence and a wide range of other social problems."[63] Unfortunately, experience also demonstrates that any such suggestion will produce nothing short of a hysterical reaction among Australian journalists and academics.[64]

For Australian intellectual and cultural elites, it does not seem to matter that support for such observations can be found in countless

---

61 Ibid., 135.
62 Greg Roberts, "Refugees from Africa Focus of Hate Campaign," *The Weekend Australian*, July 23-24, 2005, 6.
63 Andrew Fraser, "Refugees and Anglo-Australians," *Parramatta Sun*, July 6, 2005, 6.
64 Greg Roberts, "Top Academic Accused of Neo-Nazi Links." *The Australian*, July 20, 2005, 6.

academic and official sources. After all, it is hardly news that violent criminals of any race are likely to be people with low IQs who display poor impulse control.[65] Nor is it difficult to establish that, on average, black sub-Saharan Africans score around 70–75 on IQ tests while white Europeans have a mean score of 100 and East Asians about 105.[66] It is equally well known that young black men have higher levels of serum testosterone — often associated with impulsive behaviour and poor judgement — than whites or East Asians. Now, this does not mean that black Africans carry a "crime gene." Nor can one say that "blacks are genetically more crime-prone than whites." But, as Michael Levin points out, "it does make sense to say that blacks are more prone to behaviour that is in fact criminalized in virtually all societies.[67]

Australians will ignore these racial realities at their peril. In *The White Australia Policy,* Keith Windschuttle sees no cause for concern in the ethnic replacement of white, Christian Europeans by Chinese or Muslim newcomers. He has "accepted mass Third World immigration

---

65 Levin, *Why Race Matters,* 291–332.
66 Rushton and Jensen, "Thirty Years of Research on Race Differences in Cognitive Ability"
67 Levin, Why Race Matters, 148, 105–6; Rushton, Race, Evolution and Behavior, 169–170, 267–8. Authorities in many Western countries, including Australia, do not collect or publish comprehensive and reliable statistics showing the relationship between ethnicity and crime. Where statistics on black crime rates, in particular, are available clear patterns emerge. See, e.g., the data sets available online at http://www.ojp.usdog.govbjs/abstract/cvus/rape_sexual_ data sets available online at http://www.ojp.usdoj.gov/bjs/abstract/cvus/rape_sexual_assault700.htm One analysis of U.S. government crime statistics concluded that blacks were responsible for 90 percent of the incidents of violent interracial crime involving blacks and whites. Blacks in the United States "are as much more violent than whites (four to eight times) as men are more violent than women." See New Century Foundation, The Color of Crime: Race, Crime and Violence in America (Herndon, VA: New Century Foundation, 1997) available at: http://www. amren.com/color.pdf.
British experience with black crime can be examined at: http://www.homeoffice.gov.uk/rds/pdfs05/s95race04.pdf.

with equanimity," perhaps even "with a sense of self-congratulation."[68] Utterly confident that non-white migrants can be assimilated into the individualistic norms of Western culture, Windschuttle looks upon both "racial prejudice" and "religious intolerance" not as essential ingredients in collective identity but as embarrassing social diseases.[69]

Managerial Multiculturalism

Like the managerial class generally, Windschuttle does not experience his membership in the Australian nation "as if" he belongs to a community of kin. Unlike the bourgeois pioneers of Anglo-American capitalism, managerial-professional elites are no longer rooted in particular communities; they are "at best indifferent and actually hostile to...specific identities...derived from class, ethnicity and race, religion, region and gender."[70] This requires the repudiation not just of ethnic nationalism but also of any civic nationalism grounded in "pre-political loyalties of a territorial kind—loyalties rooted in a sense of the common home and of the transgenerational society that resides there."[71] The flip side of the universalism and egalitarianism sponsored by the managerial regime is, therefore, the multicultural politics of identity. Doctrines of racial egalitarianism and official multiculturalism may appear to contradict one another but the social and political function of both is to undermine the white, Christian, masculine, and bourgeois values and institutions "that remain the principal constraints on managerial reach and power."[72]

Under the aegis of the globalist regime, the shared civic culture that is the greatest achievement of Anglo-American constitutionalism is being displaced by a neofeudal system of group representation.

---

68 Keith Windschuttle, *White Australia*, 25.
69 Immigration Reform Group, 123.
70 Francis, "Power Trip," 76.
71 Scruton, *The West and the Rest*, 60.
72 Francis, "Power Trip," 76–7.

Promoting this program, James Tully attacks modern Western constitutionalism because it threatens "the extinction or assimilation of different cultures." Not only did modern constitutionalism authorize "imperial rule of former colonies over Indigenous peoples," it still underwrites "cultural imperialism over the diverse citizens of contemporary societies."[73] Tully's ideal of "intercultural negotiation" aims to replace the individualistic society of strangers with the politics of cultural recognition. Significantly, the only culture that cannot be accommodated within what Tully calls the convention of mutual recognition is the common civic culture of Anglo-American constitutionalism. Modernist universalism will be supplanted by postmodernist particularism.

Faced with the reality of cultural diversity, the Anglo-American civic culture has been *expansive* in nature. In other words, it has been "geared toward the assimilation of difference." Tully's multicultural constitutionalism, by contrast, is *separatist* or *exclusive* in that it is "geared toward the magnification and encouragement of difference." These two very different constitutional cultures cannot coexist; a choice between them must be made. Anglo-American civic cultures developed "a strong momentum towards political connectedness" to "overcome the separatist pull of diversity and disagreement." Building on long experience with non-kinship-based forms of reciprocity, the civic cultures of British-derived societies stimulated the "development of imaginative empathy" among citizens. Everyone was required to imagine himself "in the position of a person whose starting point is radically different" from his own.

Multicultural constitutionalism, by contrast, is already causing our shared civic culture to fragment; the momentum towards separatism is growing.[74] Managerial elites have an obvious interest in dividing

---

73 James Tully, *Strange Multiplicity: Constitutionalism in an Age of Diversity* (Cambridge: Cambridge University Press, 1995), 70, 96.

74 Cynthia V. Ward, "The Limits of 'Liberal Republicanism': Why Group-Based Remedies and Republican Citizenship Don't Mix, *Columbia Law Review* 91

subject populations, the better to dominate them. In line with that strategy, multicultural constitutionalism "encourages the citizenry to divide itself into groups in order to win politically controlled benefits." Not surprisingly, once interest groups succeed in "winning special benefits, the separatist pull grows stronger." Group representation spawns new elites with a vested interest in thickening the boundaries between citizens. One corollary of the perennial process of intercultural negotiation is that there can be no possibility of general agreement on public goods. Multicultural constitutionalism assumes "that diversity can be acknowledged and empowered only through constant political battle pitting the races and genders against each other in a never-ending contest for recognition and public benefits."[75]

Tully maintains the pious hope that every group will be able to stand on an equal footing in the contest over recognition and the political rewards that flow from it. But it has long been an axiom of corporatist interest intermediation that not all groups possess equal procedural status. Groups lacking functional relevance to the globalist system (or which are dysfunctional) will be shunted aside unless they possess some other resource that enables them to generate destabilizing conflict.[76] The basic premise that interest groups are not all created equal is particularly true of racial and ethnic groups. Tully is careful to cite William McNeill to make the point that polyethnicity has been the rule rather than the exception in the life of all advanced civilizations. He does not dwell on McNeill's companion observation that ethnic intermingling has produced a "complex ethnic hierarchy" whenever it has occurred.[77]

(2991): 585–6.

75 Ibid., 593, 606.

76 Julian Triado, "Corporatism, Democracy and Modernity," *Thesis Eleven* 9 (1994): 33.

77 William H. McNeill, *Polyethnicity and National Identity in World History* (Toronto: University of Toronto Press, 1986), 76.

Any constitutional order that sets out deliberately to grant special privileges to certain ethnic groups inevitably will produce a still more complex ethnic hierarchy. The relative standing of any given group probably will depend to a significant degree on its performance within the global system of needs. There can be no automatic right to consent or cultural continuity or even recognition of group rights within the context of that dynamic system. A group that is functionally relevant or possesses a significant conflict potential today may find itself in the dustbin of history tomorrow. While it may be difficult to predict permanent winners in the incessant competition for increasingly scarce resources in a multiracial Australia, we can be sure that the civic culture created and nurtured by generations of white Anglo-Australians will be the sure loser.

As continued Third World immigration provides further impetus to the multiracialist politics of identity, the individualistic society of strangers will be extraordinarily vulnerable to competition from other, tightly knit, racial groups. In retreat from "the rising tide of colour,"[78] white Australians may be forced to reinvent themselves as a people *comme les autres*, shedding their customary civic universalism in favour of a less natural but more powerfully particularistic racial consciousness. Windschuttle would be among the first to deplore any such development, even as his deracinated model of civic patriotism becomes an ever more maladaptive threat to the survival of the historic Australian nation.

Racial realists who read Windschuttle's book will discover ample evidence that, if his tender-minded attitudes prevail, white Australians are destined to be displaced by immigrant groups much less sensitive to charges of racism and xenophobia. One example: Windschuttle informs us that the most violent race riots in Australian history were led, not by murderous white racists, but by Japanese pearl divers determined to eliminate competition from Timorese rivals. There were

---

78 See the prescient work by Lothrop Stoddard, *The Rising Tide of Color* (New York: Charles Scribners' Sons, 1920).

three such riots in Broome, Western Australia, in 19907, 1914, and 1920. The last continued for a week and involved more than half the town's population of five thousand. Seven people were killed and more than sixty were seriously injured, dwarfing the casualty figures for the worst if the anti-Chinese goldfield riots of the mid-nineteenth century.[79]

Almost every immigrant group encountered in Windschuttle's narrative, not to mention the Aboriginal population, displays a strong sense of racial solidarity and an aggressive determination to advance its ethnic genetic interests. Much the same can be said for the postwar governments in Japan and the Third World leading the diplomatic offensive against the White Australia Policy. Throughout her book on the deconstruction of the White Australia Policy, Gwenda Tavan is, of course, sympathetic to the relentless attacks by non-white nations on Australia's immigration policies; she remains strangely uninterested in their simultaneous determination to retain tight control over their own borders.[80] Unfortunately this is par for the academic course; "educated" white Australians, leftist "idealists," and right-wing "ratbags" alike remain, at best, resolutely indifferent and, at worst, actively hostile to the survival of their own ethnonation. Indeed, immigration enthusiasts bend every effort to hasten "the long, slow death of white Australia." The brazen "treason of the intellectuals" marching under the banner of managerial multiculturalism has transformed a successful society of sociable strangers into an alphabet soup of self-assertive and mutually indifferent aliens.[81]

Conclusion

Given the relentless and revolutionary assault on their historic national identity, white Australians now face a life-or-death struggle to preserve their homeland. Whether effective resistance to their displacement and

---

79 Windschuttle, *White Australia*, 201.
80 Tavan, *Long Slow Death of White Australia*.
81 Julian Benda, *La Trahison des Clercs* (Paris: J.J. Pauvert, 1965, originally published 1927.

dispossession can be mounted is another question. Unlike other racial, ethnic, or religious groups well-equipped to practice the politics of identity, white Australians lack a strong, cohesive sense of ethnic solidarity. Consequently, ordinary Australians favouring a moratorium on non-white immigration cannot count on effective leadership or support from their coethnics among political, intellectual, and corporate elites. On the contrary, our still predominantly Anglo-Australian rulers are indifferent; some profit from, and others take pride in, their active collaboration with the Third World colonization of Australia. None of the major parties, indeed not one member of the Commonwealth Parliament, offers citizens the option of voting to defend and nurture Australia's Anglo-European identity.

The problem, in short, is clear: the Australian nation is bereft of a responsible ruling class. The solution is, in principle, no less obvious: namely, the restoration of a ruling class rooted in the reinvigorated folkways of an authentically Anglo-Australian civic patriotism, a ruling class reattached to the history and destiny of its own people. Only time will tell whether and how any such constitutional reformation could take place.[82]

But the problem of an irresponsible ruling class wedded to open borders is not confined to Australia; it threatens the survival of European civilization. The growing Islamic presence throughout the West is perhaps the most visible sign of our spiritual decline.[83] As the secular crisis of European modernity deepens, the soul of our society cries out, unheeded, for salvation. Like the Soviet empire before it, the managerial regime in the West rests upon a shaky foundation of deception and fraud. Charles Murray puts the point bluntly. Western elites, he charges, "are living a lie, basing the future of their societies

---

82 For one possible strategy, see Andrew Fraser, *Reinventing Aristocracy: The Constitutional Reformation of Corporate Governance* (Aldershot: Dartmouth/Ashgate, 1998).

83 Scruton, *The West and the Rest*; Serge Trifkovic, The Sword of the Prophet: History, Theology, Impact on the World Boston: Regina Orthodox Press, 2002).

on the assumption that all groups of people are equal in all respects.[84] A great many politicians and scholars know or suspect, privately, that there are real differences between racial groups; still they support immigration policies demanding public prevarication about the putative evils of racial discrimination even though immigration policy — short of completely open or completely closed borders — inevitably favours some groups over others). Such mendacious elites pose a greater threat to Western civilization than the Islamic militants they choose to harbor in the heart of the citadel.

Unfortunately, so long as the postmodernist boundary between fact and fiction remains in the eye of the beholder, the truth about that threat becomes a mere matter of opinion. The directorate of the globalist regime draws its deepest inspiration from Hollywood dream factories, where manufactured mages become the new reality. Organized social and political life in the Western world is largely driven by the psychic power of carefully crafted illusions. One fears, therefore, that it may take a serious systemic breakdown to free us from the self-destructive taboo against discussion of innate group differences.

The orthodox doctrine that race is only skin deep is only one of the official fictions underpinning the transnational system; more fundamental to the regime's legitimacy is the cornucopian myth of endless economic growth. Seen through the eyes of the managerial class, Australia is an *economy,* not a *country.* Nevertheless, a folk memory still survives of a time when Australia was "the lucky country," the homeland of a particular people of British stock with their own way of life. Should the globalist economy first falter and finally fail, regime change may yet become possible for this and other Western countries. It may well be that only a miracle can save us now; even more reason, then, to recall that God helps only those who help themselves. The capacity to act remains the key to our political salvation.[85]

---

84 Murray, "The Inequality Taboo."
85 Andrew Fraser, "Monarchs and Miracles: Australia's Need for a Patriot King,"chapter 15..

13. Puritans in Babylon: The Impact of Global Christianity on Sydney Anglicans

Introduction

THE CONCEPT of "global Christianity" came to public prominence in 2002 when historian Philip Jenkins celebrated the advent of a new era in the history of Christendom. Happily, to his mind at least, the time when most Christians were to be found in white European nations is now past. Religious decline in the affluent, increasing secular, global North has been more than matched by the rapid expansion of Christianity among "people of colour" in the Third World. In the last half of the twentieth century "the centre of gravity in the Christian world has shifted inexorably southward, to Africa, Asia, and Latin America." The largest Christian communities today are to be found in the global South, especially in Africa and Latin America. Jenkins predicts that a list of the world's leading Christian countries in 2050 will no longer include Britain, France, Spain, and Italy, the historical heartland of what Jenkins calls Old Christendom.[1]

Sydney Anglicans and Global Christianity

The Sydney Diocese of the Anglican Church of Australia fits somewhat oddly into the postmodern narrative of a global Christianity no longer

---

1   Philip Jenkins, *The Next Christendom: The Coming of Global Christianity* (New York: Oxford University Press, 2002), 1–3, 217.

circumscribed, geographically or theologically, by its Eurocentric past. Geographically, Sydney Anglicans are in the global South. Most, however, trace their biological and cultural ancestry to the British and European peoples of the global North. In the most literal sense, Sydney Anglicans pioneered the global expansion of Christianity from global North to global South when a one-man offshoot of the Church of England was transplanted with the First Fleet to New South Wales in January 1788. Richard Johnson, the first chaplain to serve the Church of England in Sydney, and Samuel Marsden, the second, obviously shared a strongly evangelical disposition towards foreign missions. Marsden, in particular—besides discharging his heavy civil and ecclesiastical workload among convicts, soldiers, and Aborigines in Sydney—was personally engaged over several decades in a mission to the Maori of New Zealand.[2]

The low church Anglican evangelicalism seeded in Sydney souls by Johnson and Marsden continues to thrive in local parishes throughout the sprawling Sydney Diocese. The relatively healthy state of Sydney Anglicanism stands in stark contrast to the liberal Anglo-Catholicism found in most other Australian Anglican dioceses. Even so, up until the 1960s, the "old evangelical pattern of what was termed 'low church' worship had been prayer book based and thoroughly liturgical". In those days, evangelical Anglican clergy "dressed soberly but correctly in black cassocks, white surplices and black scarves."[3]

Today, the absence of most of the "formalities of traditional Anglican liturgy" often surprises visitors to Sydney Anglican churches. With some exaggeration, Muriel Porter, a Melbourne High Church Anglican deeply involved in progressive church politics, sniffs that "[i]nstead of distinctive robes, clergy usually wear street dress. There are no prayer books or organ music and relatively few hymn books."

---

2 John Rawson Elder, ed., *The Letters and Journals of Samuel Marsden 1765–1838* (Dunedin, N.Z.: Couls, Somerville Wilkie, 1932).

3 Muriel Porter, *A New Exile? The Future of Anglicanism* (Northcote, Vic: Morning Star, 2015), 4–5.

Porter's critical observations are not always accurate. But apparently, she struck close enough to the mark. Her critique triggered Michael Jensen's book-length defence of the paradoxical proposition that Sydney Anglicans really are Anglicans.[4] Many outsiders, however, still suspect that the ecclesiology of Sydney Anglicans owes more to Geneva than to Canterbury.[5] In 2004, the then Archbishop (and father of Michael) Peter Jensen further fuelled such suspicions with the reply he gave to a journalist asking why he was an Anglican. "I am not sure," he said. "I could just as easily be a Presbyterian."[6]

Throughout the colonial period and well into the twentieth century, there was no question whether Church of England clergymen in Sydney belonged to the spiritual estate of the historic English nation. When the first Australian bishop of the Church of England took his seat in Sydney in 1836 the New Britannia in the Southern Ocean received recognition as an ecclesiastical province of the Second British Empire.[7] Clearly, therefore, from the late eighteenth century onward the Church of England had a global reach. But the long and bitter struggle between the English Church and Rome had left it with a highly particularistic vision of its mission in this world. Certainly, it had no desire nor was it in any position to become the religion of humanity-at-large.

Over the past fifty years much has changed. In the present "era of remarkable innovation and experimentation in the name of mission," Sydney Anglicans have embraced "global Christianity." By strengthening ties with African and Asian and South American Anglicans, the diocesan leadership expects "to profit considerably from the Christlike example and witness of faithful Christians in other parts of the world."

---

4   Michael P. Jensen, *Sydney Anglicanism: An Apology* (Eugene, OR: Wipf & Stock, 2012), 90–118.

5   Porter, *New Exile*, 32.

6   Muriel Porter, *The New Puritans: The Rise of Fundamentalism in the Anglican Church* (Carlton: Melbourne University Press, 2006), 146–147.

7   Tom Frame, *Anglicans in Australia* (Sydney: UNSW Press, 2007), 52.

The "promise of the future," according to Michael Jensen, is that support for "gospel work in some of the most difficult parts of the world for Christian witness" has "provided the opportunity for a renewal of the notion of a global *confessing* Anglicanism."[8]

Global Christianity as the Religion of Humanity

What exactly is "global Christianity"? Philip Jenkins conceives of global Christianity, first, as an accomplished demographic *fact*. More importantly, however, Jenkins also views the emergence of "the next Christendom" as an ongoing world-historical *project* of apocalyptic significance. He suggests that a new heaven and a new earth are emerging before our eyes in the global South. There "the book of Revelation looks like true prophecy on an epic scale…In the South, Revelation simply makes sense, in its description of a world ruled by monstrous demonic powers" whether they "be literal servants of Satan, or symbols for evil social forces." For Jenkins, it seems "as if we are seeing Christianity again for the first time." The image of God is re-appearing to us in the lives of African and Latin American Christians.[9]

In contrast to the advice the apostle Paul gave to the Athenians in Acts 17:26–28, Jenkins believes that we must seek and perhaps find God not in the bosom of our own white European-descended, once-Christian, nations but in the global multitude, the teeming masses of poor and persecuted people trapped in the sprawling slums and desolate landscapes of the Third World. In Jenkins' eyes, these desperate souls "are people for whom the New Testament Beatitudes have a direct relevance inconceivable for most Christians in Northern societies."[10]

Understood as an open-source project in political and practical theology, global Christianity is centred in the global North, the

---

8 Jensen, *Sydney Anglicans*, 105–106 (emphasis in original).
9 Jenkins, *Next Christendom*, 214–219.
10 Ibid., 216.

cultural homeland of antipodean Sydney Anglicans. For Christian Northerners, global Christianity exists both as a *report* of demographic facts on the ground and as a *response*. In evangelical protestant parishes throughout the Sydney Diocese, global Christianity manifests itself as a low-intensity religious *movement* in which opinion leaders have been influenced by the branch of cultural Marxism known as liberation theology.[11] From the detached perspective of a sociology of contemporary religions, one might classify believers in global Christianity according to the intensity of their faith, ranging from moderate, relatively uninvolved, local parishioners to sectarians, deeply committed to a cult of the Other. In the more socially engaged realm of contextual and public theology, global Christianity has become synonymous with the progressive political theology of Christian humanism.[12]

The Christian humanist cult of the Other is both enshrined in law and public policy and promulgated by the mainstream media. Most Sydney Anglicans perceive global Christianity as an opportunity to the sort of good works expected of those who accept Jesus Christ as their Lord and Saviour. Such well-meaning projects are not always well-conceived. One thinks of the ladies of St. Matthews at West Pennant Hills who organized "an evening to pack birthing kits for pregnant women in Africa."[13] As far as one can tell, these women were entirely unaware that the massive population explosion in sub-Saharan Africa

---

11 The ideological convergence between the theology of global Christianity and the ideology of contemporary cultural Marxism becomes evident when one compares Jenkins' apocalyptic rhetoric with Michael Hardt and Antonio Negri, *Empire* (Cambridge, MA: Harvard University Press, 2000) and its companion volumes, *Multitude: War and Democracy in the Age of Empire* (New York: Penguin, 2004) and *Commonwealth* (Cambridge, MA: Harvard University Press, 2009).

12 See, for example, Glenn Morrison, "Living at the Margins of Life: Encountering the Other and Doing Theology," (2006) 6 *Australian eJournal of Theology* 1–4 and Chris Budden, *Following Jesus in Invaded Space: Doing Theology on Aboriginal Land* (Eugene, OR: Pickwick, 2009).

13 "Birth Kits for Africa," *Southern Cross* March 2016, 10.

already represents a recruiting ground for the current mass invasion of Europe by "refugees" seeking a "better life" in post-Christian Europe. Such well-meaning out-group altruism comes at a cost.

White Anglo-Saxon Protestants — the WASPs who are still the core demographic backbone of Sydney Anglicanism — are now under a presumptive moral obligation to accord special priority to the (perhaps covertly self-interested) voice of the global South. The routine expectation that one will prefer the moral claims of the stranger and the alien to those of one's co-ethnics smacks of the pathological altruism popularly associated with cat ladies.[14] Incorporated within the moral universe of WASPs in local parishes throughout the Sydney Diocese, the humanist cult of the Other fosters a collective spiritual disorder best described as ethnomasochism, or perhaps Anglo-Saxon Anglophobia. The most obvious symptom of this ethno-pathology is the automatic invocation by church-going WASPs of the Good Samaritan parable whenever news breaks of another Third World disaster. Invariably, the allegedly other-directed altruism of the Good Samaritan becomes the master model of Christian witness in our relationships with the global coalition of the marginalized.[15]

Membership in this cult of the Other offers materially rich but spiritually barren white folks living in the post-Christian West the opportunity to find new life in service to the poor and powerless people of colour in the global South. Today, Jenkins avers, it is only in Southern churches familiar with the biblical themes of "martyrdom, oppression, and exile...that the Bible can be read with any authenticity and immediacy." For that reason, "the Old Christendom" of the global North

---

14 See, e.g., Jane N. Nathanson and Gary J. Patronek, "Animal Hoarding: How the Semblance of a Benevolent Mission Becomes Actualized as Egoism and Cruelty," in Barbara Oakley, *et.al.*, *Pathological Altruism* (New York: Oxford University Press, 2012), 107–115.

15 For a useful corrective to the conventional wisdom on the Good Samaritan parable, see, Bruce W. Longenecker, "The Story of the Samaritan and the Innkeeper (Luke 10:30–35): A Study in Character Rehabilitation," (2009) 17 *Biblical Interpretation* 422.

"must give priority to Southern voices."[16] Western churches, Catholic and Protestant alike have heeded that call for ecumenical solidarity with "the wretched of the earth."[17]

Even the reputedly "radical conservative" and "fundamentalist" Sydney Diocese gladly glorifies the false gods of Christian humanism: Equality, Diversity, Tolerance, Inclusivity, and Progress. Here, even the nominally Anglican neo-Calvinist evangelicals in most local parishes enthusiastically embrace a religion of humanity practically indistinguishable from the human rights ideology promoted by the transnational corporate welfare state.

Consider, for example, the Christmas 2014 message from the then Anglican Archbishop of Sydney, Dr. Glenn Davies. Jesus does not appear in this short essay as the Christ, the anointed Messiah called to save the lost sheep of carnal, national Israel in the first century AD. Dr. Davies is not much interested in the historical Jesus whose vision for the nation of Israel owed more to ancient Jewish nationalism than to the modern religion of humanity. He teaches instead that "God the Father sent God the Son...so that he might save us from our sins and restore the broken relationship between God and humanity, and every dysfunctional relationship that thwarts the human condition."[18] This abstract and timeless Christology is even more striking considering that it comes from the leader of an ostensibly "bible-believing" denomination.

Sydney Anglicans pointedly give priority to the preaching of the Word over the traditional sacramental and liturgical life of the church. Unfortunately, the Word is often ripped from its historical context as if the Bible is addressed either to humanity in the abstract, in all times and places or, more specifically, to people in pews throughout the Sydney Diocese on Sunday mornings. But, as biblical scholar Scot

---

16 Jenkins, *Next Christendom*, 214–217.
17 *Cf*., Frantz Fanon, *The Wretched of the Earth* (New York: Grove Press, 1963).
18 Dr. Glenn Davies, "Mission Impossible," *Southern Cross* (December 2014), 17.

McKnight reminds us, the historical Jesus was not "thinking down the road thousands of years, to our own time, when Christianity would have gone through a multitude of mutations and denominations and when the Church would be interacting with cultures and ideologies" utterly remote from the biblical land of Israel in the first century AD.[19] Instead, Jesus sent out the Twelve (Matt. 9:35–11:1) not as "evangelistic preachers sent out to save individual souls for some unearthly paradise." As fellow-Israelites, his disciples "were couriers proclaiming a national emergency and conducting a referendum on a question of national survival."[20]

Globalism as the New Localism in Sydney

In a world where global has become the new local for white Western Christians generally and Sydney Anglicans, in particular, a narrow focus on the parochial issue of national survival is deemed to be anachronistic and old-fashioned.[21] This development is paradoxical in the extreme, given the obvious ethno-national character of the biblical narrative from Genesis to Revelation. Nevertheless, the ethno-nation is no longer valued as a divinely ordained order of creation by WASP Anglicans, in Sydney or elsewhere in the global North. Here one should be recall that in times past it was the lived experience of Christian nationhood that brought heaven down to earth for the English and other European peoples.

Nowadays, "the rhetoric of nationalism and race" regularly receives ritual condemnation from official Anglicanism in the global North. Global Christianity is determined, it seems, to "nurture a loathing of the sin of racism."[22] For most good-thinking Christians ethnon-

---

19 Scot McKnight, *A New Vision for Israel: The Teachings of Jesus in National Context* (Grand Rapids, MI: William B. Eerdmans, 1999), 5.
20 G.B. Caird, quoted in *ibid.*, 11.
21 *Cf.*, David Neff, "Global is the New Local," (2009) 53(6) *Christianity Today* 38.
22 House of Bishops, Church of England. "Affirming Our Common Humanity," A Theological Statement (6 January, 2011. s. 15, available online at: https://www.

ationalism is little more than a synonym for racism. As a matter of historical fact, however, evangelical clergymen in colonial and early national Sydney, unlike most Anglican WASPs today, did not pursue the egalitarian and inclusive vision of social justice embedded in the Other-directed religion of humanity. Their understanding of Christian witness to the heathen peoples of the world had more in common with Kipling's notion of the White Man's Burden.

Certainly, Samuel Marsden was no racial egalitarian. He recognized clear racial differences not only between the British colonists in Sydney and the Australian Aborigines but between the latter and the Maori people of New Zealand. He was particularly contemptuous of what psychologists call the "high time preference" (*i.e.* an unwillingness or inability to defer gratification) which characterized Aborigines. He was particularly frustrated by the prevalence of this trait among the young Aborigines enrolled as students in his Parramatta seminary. He wrote that when the natives of this colony "attain the age of thirteen or fourteen years," they "always take to the woods." Nothing could persuade them "to live in any regular way." His despair over the degenerate state of Australian Aborigines must be set against the high regard for the Maori students he brought to Parramatta. Unsurprisingly, because those Maoris shared Marsden's low opinion of the Australian natives, he reported that, even if it were possible to confine the young Aboriginals to the seminary, the Maori students "would never be induced to live with them."[23]

Such racial realism encouraged an unapologetic ethno-religious ethic of in-group solidarity (more specifically, of British race patriotism) among Sydney Anglicans. These attitudes prevailed until well into the twentieth century.[24] Sixty or so years ago, rather abruptly,

---

churchofengland.org/media/1165806/gs%20misc%20972.doc.

23 Samuel Marsden, "Letter to the Secretary, Church Missionary Society," February 24, 1819, in Elder, *Marsden Letters*, 231.

24 See, *e.g.*, Robert S. Withycombe, "Australian Anglicans and Imperial Identity, 1900–1914," (2001) 25(3) *Journal of Religious History* 286 and Brian H. Fletcher,

things changed. WASPs in the Sydney Diocese, as elsewhere, found in "global Christianity" an escape route from "the Anglo-Saxon captivity" of the Anglican church.[25] Ironically, no matter how hard today's Sydney Anglicans try to shed their implicitly WASP image, their critics continue to insist that the "Anglican ethos is that of the English middle class."[26] Should the Archbishop of Sydney offer an anodyne tribute to the Queen's achievement in becoming the longest -serving British monarch, parishioners steeped in the cult of the Other can be counted on to provide conspicuous displays of Anglo-Saxon Anglophobia in letters to the diocesan monthly magazine, *Southern Cross*. Most recently, a WASP parishioner from Kingsgrove warned that "[i]n multifaith and multicultural Australia, the Anglican Church needs to avoid any suggestion that it is an Anglophile enclave."[27] Clearly, if only for public relations purposes, "global is the new local" in Sydney.

Why, then, have Sydney Anglicans become internationally notorious for their stubborn local resistance to key elements in social justice campaigns associated with global Christianity? As it happens, persistent tensions between globalism and localism in the Sydney Diocese over the past sixty years reflect the grand but often bumpy convergence between global Christianity, the social justice warriors (SJWs) of the political left, and the transnational corporate welfare state.

The Grand Convergence

Leading Sydney Anglicans have not always looked with favour upon the social justice agenda. Indeed, Broughton Knox, principal of Moore College between 1959 and 1985 disdained the progressive obsession

---

"Anglicanism and Nationalism in Australia, 1901–1962," (1999) 23(2) *Journal of Religious History* 215.

25 *Cf.*, Kevin Ward, *A History of Global Anglicanism* (Cambridge: Cambridge University Press, 2006), 296–318.

26 Caroline Miley, *The Suicidal Church: Can the Anglican Church Be Saved?* (Annandale, NSW: Pluto Press, 2002), 58.

27 James Moore, "Letter to the Editor," *Southern Cross* November 2015, 16.

with "social justice." He insisted that "the teaching and actions of Jesus nowhere show a concern for 'social justice.'" Indeed, he charged that a religious passion for social justice, grounded as it is in envy rather than compassion, has no basis in Christian theology.[28] Knox was right. The concept of social justice had its explicit origin in the philosophical radicalism of John Stuart Mill rather than in the recorded teachings of Jesus Christ. Social justice, therefore, has more in common with secular progressivism than with the ethical foundations of Christian nationhood.

Mill made it plain that social justice is a humanist programme with universal application. It follows that merely traditional human relationships stubbornly resistant to the values of equality, diversity, tolerance, and inclusivity must be transformed. He set out a mini manifesto for modern SJWs as follows:

> Society should treat all equally well who have deserved equally well of it, that is, who have deserved equally well absolutely. This is the highest abstract standard of social and distributive justice; towards which all institutions, and the efforts of all virtuous citizens, should be made in the utmost possible degree to converge.[29]

To put it mildly, rock-ribbed Sydney Anglicans such as Broughton Knox were not keen to converge with the progressive social justice agenda, especially in its contemporary incarnations. Indeed, Michael Jensen somewhat shame-facedly reveals that Knox taught his students that apartheid in South Africa "was not an evil system."[30] One of those students (later a persistent and prominent public critic of the Sydney Diocese) vividly remembers "him saying often in classes that he could see no problem with white people ruling over coloured people, as long

---

28 Jensen, *Sydney Anglicans*, 119.
29 John Stuart Mill, *On Liberty and Other Essays*, (Oxford: Oxford University Press, 2008), 198.
30 Jensen, *Sydney Anglicans*, 120.

as they were not cruel or harsh."³¹ One suspects as well that Knox, if asked, might have defended the White Australia Policy.³² Certainly, he would not have been the only Sydney Anglican to support a racially exclusive immigration policy. As late as 1971, the *Australian Church Record* ran a leading article which "reaffirmed the right of governments to decide where migrants were to come from even if this was discriminatory."³³ Knox placed the principle of in-group solidarity higher than the pursuit of social justice in his hierarchy of Christian virtues. But not even such a prominent figure as the principal of Moore College could prevent the convergence of the great majority of Sydney Anglicans with the social justice warriors and corporate interests demanding the abolition of the White Australia Policy.

Sydney Anglicans offered little or no apparent resistance to the abolition of the White Australia Policy in the mid-70s. Most took the path of least resistance, reflecting a chronic institutional preference for "happy collaboration with the state" over the preservation of a racially homogeneous Australian ethno-nation.³⁴ They were easily persuaded that Mills' "highest abstract standard of social and distributive justice" endows the whole of humanity with a "human right" to migrate freely to Australia (and other white countries). By 1973, the General Synod of the Anglican Church "together with provincial and diocesan synods, leading churchmen, and church newspapers, welcomed federal

---

31 Dr. Kevin Giles, "An Outsider's Response to an Insider's Defence of the Anglican Diocese of Sydney," 7. Available online at: sjks.org.au/wp-content/uploads/2015/.../Giles-Looking-at-Sydney-from-the-inside.pdf.

32 Broughton Knox's now politically incorrect views on race and immigration also surface occasionally in Marcia Cameron, *An Enigmatic Life: David Broughton Knox. Father of Sydney Anglicanism* (Brunswick East, Vic: Acorn Press, 2006), 54, 147, 214, 222.

33 Brian H. Fletcher, "Anglicanism and National Identity in Australia Since 1962," (2001) 25(3) *Journal of Religious History* 324, at 334.

34 Jensen, *Sydney Anglicans*, 119.

government moves to abolish the White Australia policy, the last remnants of which disappeared in 1975."³⁵

Since then, the drumbeat of support among Sydney Anglicans for the demographic transformation of their city and country into an egalitarian, diverse, inclusive, and tolerant multiracial society has been loud and continuous. Although, his critics describe former Archbishop Peter Jensen as a "fundamentalist" and a "radical conservative," he publicly proclaimed that Sydney Anglicans have "embraced multiculturalism, and I myself am delighted by the new and different Australia that is emerging as a result of our immigration policies."³⁶ He worked hard to erase the public perception of the Anglican Church as an Anglo-Saxon ghetto. When Jensen retired, he called for the creation of "120 ethnic congregations in the next decade."³⁷ By "ethnic congregations," Archbishop Jensen did not mean exclusively WASP parishes or churches. On the contrary, Jensen urged Sydney Anglicans "to be universal in our outlook and not restricted to people of our own kind, race or class." In his view, "we are too restricted to the professional and middle class; we are too limited to European and English- speaking tribes."³⁸

Sydney Anglicans now present their evangelical faith as a religion for humanity at large. Working to perform the Great Commission of Matthew 28:1 is longer restricted to foreign missions. Global Christianity enthusiasts endlessly thank God for the abolition of the White Australia Policy. In his wisdom, they say, God is "bringing the

---

35 Fletcher, "Anglicanism and National Identity Since 1962," 334.
36 Peter Jensen, "Lecture 1: Jesus the Prophet at the End of the World," *Boyer Lectures* (ABC Radio National, 13 November 2005), transcript available online at: http://www.abc.net.au/radionational/programs/boyerlectures/lecture-1-jesus-the-prophet-at-the-end-of-the-world/3316056#transcript.
37 Peter Jensen, "Archbishop's Presidential Address 2012: Last Words," 15, transcript available on-line at: http://sydneyanglicans.net/images/uploads/pres_address_2012.pdf.
38 Peter Jensen, "Presidential Address to Synod 2001," available on-line at: http://sydneyanglicans.net/seniorclergy/articles/77a.

nations to us" thereby offering the Australian church the "unique opportunity to fulfil the Commission in its own backyard."[39] Refugees, especially, give Sydney Anglicans a chance to serve as a Good Samaritan to the Other right here at home. In response to the foreshadowed influx of Syrian refugees into western Sydney, Archbishop Davies, together with the Principal of Moore College, pledged allegiance to the social justice program of equality, diversity, inclusion, and tolerance by highlighting "the importance of a non-discriminatory approach in deciding who should or should not come to Australia." Not even Muslim refugees should be excluded from the hospitality and practical care offered by the church-state partnership in Sydney. "Our response needs to be immediate, generous and unquestioning with regard to race, ethnicity, or religion."[40]

How could it be otherwise, one might ask, in a society where "every church, every elementary school, every Boy Scout troop, every university, every science journal, every corporation, every movie, every television advertisement, every video game site, are preaching the exact same message of diversity, equality, and tolerance."[41] John Stuart Mills' insistence on the absolute imperative of convergence now carries ominous undertones of totalitarian thought control. Worse still, the single-minded pursuit of social justice in every domain of life turns out to be "utterly incompatible with personal freedom, societal wealth, and advanced technological civilization." Once every church, university, school, and corporation "converges towards the highest abstract standard of social and distributive justice, the less it is able to perform its primary function."[42]

---

39 Bruce Hall, "Ministry for Muslims," *Southern Cross* June 2016, 13.
40 "Archbishop Calls for "Warm and Generous Welcome," *Southern Cross* October 2015, 3.
41 Vox Day, *SJWs Always Lie* (Kouvola, Finland: Castalia House, 2015) Kindle Edition, 233 of 2848.
42 *Ibid.*, 2135 of 2848.

Even Archbishop Glenn Davies wondered why a "naïve enthusiasm" for same-sex marriages leads a significant number of corporations to publish endorsements calling for such a fundamental change to the institutions of marriage and family. Without providing an answer, he asks, "how does such a position have anything to do with the core business of these companies"?[43] Sadly, the Archbishop did not understand the forces driving the convergence of global Christianity, transnational corporatism, and the social justice agenda of the political left. Nor did he appreciate the dangers of even a partial and limited convergence between the human rights ideology of the SJWs and the theological presuppositions of Sydney Anglicanism.

The deep antagonism between Sydney Anglicans and the homosexual and feminist lobbies over the past forty years reflects what Vox Day calls "the Impossibility of Social Justice Convergence." Just as "no man can serve two masters…no institution can serve two different functions."[44] Sydney Anglicans, however, maintain that the "plain meaning" of the Bible disapproves both the open practice of homosexuality and the ordination of women ministers.[45] For them, the Bible trumps social justice. Accordingly, the Sydney Synod has stuck to its position despite massive social pressure to converge with the feminist and homosexual SJWs based within the national church. Synod insists that to cave in to same-sex marriage and the ordination of female ministers would be to distort and betray the saving Word of our Lord and Saviour Jesus Christ.

The intractable problem Sydney Anglicans face, however, is that already they have accepted the SJW demand that the Anglican Church anathematize the evil of racism (because Equality, Diversity, Inclusivity, Tolerance etc.). By refusing to apply those same values

---

43 Archbishop Glenn Davies, "We Commit Ourselves Afresh…," Presidential Address, *Southern Cross* November 2015, 24.

44 Day, *SJWs Always Lie*, 2135 of 2848.

45 Muriel Porter, *Sydney Anglicans and the Threat to World Anglicanism: The Sydney Experiment* (Farnham: Ashgate, 2011), 64–67, 113–134.

to the institutions of marriage and the ministry they remain open to charges of sexism, homophobia and hypocrisy.[46]

Sydney Anglicans are fighting a rear-guard action. Not so long ago, they unsuccessfully resisted calls, all framed in the name of social justice, for the de-criminalization of homosexuality, abortion-on-demand, and no-fault divorce.[47] Predictably, once Sydney Anglicans gave SJWs an inch on the issue of non-white immigration, homosexual activists and feminists immediately demanded a mile on issues falling directly within the province of the church. Thus far, only the constitutionally entrenched autonomy of the Sydney Diocese within the Anglican Church of Australia has insulated Sydney Anglicans against total convergence with the SJW agenda. Unhappily, merely formal legal barriers to convergence are unlikely to stave off the final victory of the SJWs within the Sydney Diocese.

The Future of Social Justice Convergence in the Sydney Diocese

The fact that sworn enemy of the Jensen ascendancy in Sydney and doyenne of ecclesiastical SJWs, Muriel Porter, greeted the 2013 election of Archbishop Dr. Glenn Davies with cautious optimism should be cause for concern among evangelical traditionalists in the Sydney Diocese.[48] For years, Porter has portrayed Sydney's hard-line opposition to same-sex marriage and the ordination of women as a threat to the harmony of global Anglicanism. Her hope appears to have been that the danger of an open break with world Anglicanism would recede under the leadership of Archbishop Davies.

---

46 Miley, *Suicidal Church*, 85–100.

47 See, David Marr, *The High Price of Heaven* (St. Leonards, NSW: Allen & Unwin, 1999), 151–178 and David Hilliard, "Sydney Anglicans and Homosexuality," (1997) 33(2) *Journal of Homosexuality* 101.

48 Muriel Porter, "The End of the Jensen Ascendancy? What the Election of Sydney's New Archbishop Means," *ABC Religion and Ethics Report* 7 August 2013: http://www.abc.net.au/religion/articles/2013/08/07/3820211.htm.

Porter's optimism may have been well-founded. In a church which denies the sacramental status of a priestly order and dresses its clergy in street clothes as visible recognition of the priesthood of all believers, it is hard to see how claims to tolerance, inclusivity, and equality of status by women and homosexuals can be defeated by invoking "the authority and timelessness of Scripture." For their part, Anglican SJWs flatly deny that the Bible has a "plain meaning" valid and binding upon all believers in all times and places.[49]

Even orthodox evangelicals such as Michael Jensen are noticeably wobbly on the issue of female ordination. He denies that evangelicals "hold to a primarily hierarchical view of humanity, or of the church, or of the ministry." On the contrary, Jensen claims, they insist upon "the profound equality of all human beings in God's eyes." He points out that, in the nineteenth century, evangelical egalitarians were "in the vanguard of the movement for female enfranchisement." Evangelicals, he adds, also uphold the SJW ideal of inclusivity which when applied to the woman question means that "*a godly church politics ought to seek the inclusion of women as well as men, and the young as well as the old.*"[50] Having denied the special priestly status of Anglican ministers, affirmed the equality of women, and accepted their inclusion in church politics, how can one consistently block their access to the ministry. It seems mere sophistry to resist the ordination of women while blandly accepting "women's involvement in the entire public arena." Why, Porter asks, should the male claim to leadership be limited to the church and the home?[51] Indeed, why should male leadership not be restored in the Commonwealth and State Parliaments, the courts, and the universities?

Jensen's political theology all but completely converged with the social justice agenda. So much so that he declined even to address the

---

49 Porter, *New Puritans*, 26–27.

50 Jensen, *Sydney Anglicans*, 127, 170 (italics in original).

51 Porter, *New Puritans*, 103.

issue of homosexual rights. This is an important omission because it was "the toxic combination of gay rights and libertarian economics [that] effectively destroyed the Left [in the 70s], just in time for the resurgence of capitalism under Reagan and Thatcher." Under the influence of prestigious homosexual intellectuals such as Michel Foucault "gay liberation became a Satanic parody of the revolutionary movements of the '60s, including the American Civil Rights Movement." In effect, the left in America and in Australia abandoned "classical Marxism's economic critique of capitalism in exchange for the ability to engage in unlimited perverse sex." Dr. Davies founds the willingness of transnational corporate elites to promote the gay liberation movement "inexplicable." Ever-pragmatic globalist elites, however, were happy to make a deal in which the New Left "got unlimited sex in exchange for the loss of political power."[52]

E. Michael Jones warns that the globalist program of the transnational corporate welfare state can be summed up in the slogan "Sodomy and Low Wages."[53] Low wages have been secured, first, by the feminist campaign to have women abandon motherhood; instead entering the labour market in competition with their own fathers, husbands, and sons. Mass Third World immigration too helps to lower or cause wages to stagnate by massively increasing the supply of labour. As an added bonus to capital, increasing demographic diversity also undermines the in-group solidarity of once racially homogeneous working classes. Sydney Anglicans have acquiesced in — when they have not actively supported — the campaign to lower wages by promoting feminism and mass immigration. Even so, the Sydney Diocese still infuriates SJWs by dragging its feet on the normalization of ever-more perverse forms of sexuality.

---

52 E. Michael Jones, "Like Father, Like Son: The Cultural Revolution Comes to South Bend," (2015) 34(9) *Culture Wars* 10, at 23–25. See also, James Miller, *The Passion of Michel Foucault* (London: Flamingo, 1994).

53 E. Michael Jones, "Sodomy in Berlin and South Bend," YouTube Interview, August 19, 2016, available online at: https://www.youtube.com/watch?v=htUbL166axQ.

Conclusion

Given their experience thus far with the brand of global Christianity favoured by Muriel Porter, Sydney Anglicans were perhaps wise not just to resist "social justice convergence" but also to form strategic alliances with ostensibly traditionalist churches in the global South. Much to the chagrin of liberal Anglo-Catholics such as Porter, Sydney Anglicanism is not only experiencing significant growth locally but is expanding its influence nationally, in part through the export of Moore College graduates. Meanwhile, Porter's brand of "catholic Anglicanism" has been in sharp decline — as measured by numbers of clergy and church attendance — both in Australia and elsewhere in the global North. Porter notes that "almost all the Anglo-Catholic youth groups, student ministries, religious orders and organisations have either gone or become absorbed into other, more generic, bodies."[54]

Why is Anglo-Catholicism declining? "For a complex set of reasons that are closely interrelated," Porter answers, rather lamely. She conspicuously declines to consider whether the decline has to do with the Impossibility of Social Justice Convergence. In other words, churches which converge completely with SJWs will soon find it impossible to perform their core functions. It is no accident that the decline is happening in precisely those churches most open to convergence with social justice campaigns for homosexual rights and female ordination.

In his study of Sydney Anglicans and homosexuality, David Hilliard found that the "observable association of homosexually inclined men with churches at the high end of the Anglican spectrum was one of the reasons for evangelical dislike of Anglo-Catholicism." Throughout the 70s and 80s in Sydney, "the homosexual debate gradually became intertwined with the debate on the ordination of women...those who were most strongly opposed to homosexuality were usually against the ordination of women."[55] The Sydney experience suggests that

---

54 Porter, *New Exile*, 26–28.
55 Hilliard, "Sydney Anglicans and Homosexuality," 105, 115.

liberal dioceses promoting homosexual rights and female ordination are bound to become increasingly alien to the sensibilities of straight, white Anglo-Australian men. Not surprisingly, many such Anglicans vote with their feet to leave churches which seem less traditional than trendy, if not decadent.

Despite Porter's predictions of global schism, Sydney Anglicans, far from precipitating a fatal fissure in world Anglicanism have become much more receptive to theological voices from the global South than liberal Anglo-Catholics. Many African and Asian churches within the Anglican Communion share their unease of the Sydney Diocese with the Babylonian culture of pornography and sexual perversion associated with homosexuality. But it is far from clear whether membership in either the Global Anglican Futures Conference (GAFCON) or the Fellowship of Confessing Anglicans (FAC) will save Sydney Anglicans from eventual complete Social Justice Convergence.

If same-sex marriage is legalized in Australia, it seems likely that most of the other-directed WASPs in the Sydney Diocese will acquiesce in the change rather than "make waves." If so, can female ordination be far behind? By embracing the anti-racist cause decades ago, Sydney Anglicans enrolled as part-time SJWs. In fleeing its supposed "Anglo-Saxon captivity," the Sydney Diocese has already abandoned its traditional core function: to disciple *Angelcynn* nations. Sydney Anglicans appear to have forgotten, if they ever knew, that the name of their church is derived from an old Anglo-Saxon word meaning "kin of the Angles," a term first applied to the church in England by Alfred the Great.[56] Clearly the great royal patron of the *Angelcynn* church was no stranger to the "rhetoric of nationalism and race." To rescue themselves from the Babylonian cult of global Christianity, Sydney Anglicans would do well to emulate his heroic defence of Christian nationhood.

---

56   Sarah Foot, "The Making of *Angelcynn*: English Identity Before the Norman Conquest," (1996) 6 *Transactions of the Royal Historical Society* 25.

# 14. Anglo-Republicanism and the Rebirth of British History: Why Virtuous WASPs Must Challenge the Corrupt Globalist Plutocracy Misgoverning the Anglosphere

Introduction

IN THE AFTERMATH of the 2020 American Presidential election, conservative websites and Trump loyalists loudly lamented the "mostly peaceful" collapse of their Constitutional Republic. One such commentator, Angelo Codevilla, worries that "laws, customs, and habits of the heart that had defined the American republic since the 18th century are [now] things of the past." No longer do Americans live "in a republic, in which life's rules flow from the people through their representatives." Instead, a new ruling class of oligarchs and experts has seized power over the putatively sovereign people, shamelessly, nay, proudly proclaiming "themselves the arbiters of truth." As such, they are "entitled and obliged to censor whoever disagrees with them as systematically racist adepts of conspiracy theories," such as the "baseless" belief that the election had been stolen from former President Trump. Once Trump was driven out of office, the oligarchy was free finally to consolidate a coalescence of public and private power prioritizing corporate and bureaucratic interests over those of the people-at-large.[1]

---

1   Angelo Codevilla, "Clarity in Trump's Wake," January 19, 2021, https://amgreatness.com/2021/01/19/clarity-in-trumps-wake.

On this view, the republic has fallen victim to a domestic colour revolution. By means of a slow-motion *coup d'état*, the powers that be have transformed the American form of government. No longer a Constitutional Republic, America is now governed by a corrupt corporatist plutocracy. Henceforth, elections will become ceremonial fig leaves disguising the reality of oligarchical control. The *modus operandi* employed by those on high is now plainly evident. The oligarchy, Codevilla observes, simply "acted to take the presidential election's outcome out of the hands of those who would *cast* the votes and to place it as much as possible in the hands of its members who would *count* the votes."[2] Should the hostile takeover of the republic succeed, he expects the notion of popular sovereignty to fade away into a historical figment of our collective imagination.

Codevilla assumes that the American "republican" form of government must be grounded in the principle of popular sovereignty. But it is not at all obvious that the ostensibly *democratic* principle of popular sovereignty is essential to a distinctively *republican* form of government. Republics, after all, have long been associated with "mixed and balanced" forms of government, incorporating not just the *many* embodied in the people-at-large but also the aristocratic *few*, as well as the monarchical *one*. In any case, whether founded as a republic or a democracy, America has become a transnational corporate welfare state. The current regime barely pretends to be either republican or democratic. Instead, the public realm has merged with the putatively private corporate sector to produce a high-tech system of anarcho-tyranny in a multiracial mass society altogether detached from its now-superseded American history. What has become of "American" history in the Age of Woke Capital?

---

2   *Ibid.*

Have WASPs Become a "Stateless" People?

America's new ruling class has no use for a patriotic past. Hence, all traces of the historic "white man's republic" are demonized by the cosmopolitan, plutocratic oligarchy set over a rootless population bereft of a collective memory. Under the new dispensation, white Anglo-Saxon Protestants, the founding stock of the American republic, dare not speak their name, much less defend the deeds of their once-honoured and revered forbears. Recently, two GOP members of Congress floated the idea of an America First Caucus, citing the importance of the nation's "Anglo-Saxon political heritage." They were accused immediately of racism, nativism, and bigotry by academics, the media, and their own party leadership.[3]

To avoid the multiple stigmata attached to such a thought-crime, even dissident websites cautiously employ anodyne cryptonyms (*e.g.*, the "historic American nation") when referring to their pale-skinned forbears. Having been officially memory-holed, this crypto-nation is now dangerously exposed to demographic and political isolation. Its members have been left lost and leaderless, amidst an ever-swelling, multi-hued multitude of alien newcomers. In the Age of Woke Capital, Anglo-Americans are regularly subjected to conspicuous displays of callous indifference (and, increasingly, naked enmity) orchestrated by the professional-managerial class in collusion with racial and deviant minorities.

White Anglo-Saxon Protestants in America are not alone in their fall from grace. Their British-descended co-ethnics throughout the Anglosphere are also experiencing the rude shock of dispossession. Once honoured as the founding race of several successful nations, white Anglo-Saxon Protestants are everywhere targeted for collective

---

3   James Kirkpatrick, "Mind Must Be the Stronger" — "Anglo-Saxon" Caucus Fiasco Shows GOP Bent on Losing," April 18, 2021. https://vdare.com/articles/mind-must-be-the-stronger-anglo-saxon-caucus-fiasco-shows-gop-bent-on-losing-but-also-the-way-forward.

shaming, public disgrace, and personal dishonour. The rising tide of colour now threatens to submerge the historic nations of Australia, Canada, and New Zealand — even of the United Kingdom itself. "People of colour" are far from friendless; they have found allies among other groups competing for resources, prestige, and power against WASPs. Having thrown open the gates to mass migration in the post-war period, every formerly Anglo-Saxon country now hosts racial, ethnic, and religious groups from every corner of the world, some harbouring hostility towards its old stock inhabitants.

In the high-stakes, globalist game of identity politics, even some European-descended ethnic groups rarely side with the few Anglo-Saxon Protestants daring openly to resist their racial replacement. In fact, many "fellow whites," notably Jews and Irish Catholics, have long nursed ancestral grudges against WASPs. Nor do relative latecomers to the American melting pot — the generically "white" descendants of late nineteenth century Ellis Islanders from southern, central, and eastern Europe — generally respect the honorific constitutional status once attached to the seed of Albion. Much the same observation applies to non-Nordic European migration into all of the historic dominions of the British Crown throughout the "old white Commonwealth."

For many hyphenated-Americans, America is self-evidently a "nation of immigrants." Angelo Codevilla's article exemplifies that frame of mind. Born in Italy, Codevilla emigrated to the USA with his parents in 1955, taking out American citizenship in 1962 at age nineteen.[4] Unsurprisingly, therefore, Codevilla is a civic nationalist. He identifies his "fellow Americans" by their legal citizenship not by ancestry, religion, or language. He is ill-equipped to understand that the collapse of the Constitutional Republic has plunged Anglo-Americans into a deepening *ethnoreligious* identity crisis. He should be excused, however. After all, far too many American WASPs themselves fail to understand just how much of their collective biocultural capital has

---

4   https://en.wikipedia.org/wiki/Angelo_Codevilla.

been sunk into a literally faithless Constitutional Republic. Indeed, the institutional architecture of the American republic emerged as an "extended phenotype" of the white Anglo-Saxon Protestant, in somewhat the same manner as the dam is an extended phenotype of the beaver, or mounds of a termite colony.[5] Perhaps a republic way of life should be seen as a distinctively WASP thing; something other ethnic groups just wouldn't understand.

From its colonial foundation, America possessed a predominantly white Anglo-Saxon Protestant population. But, having just renounced their ancestral allegiance to throne and altar, they faced a unique problem: they were to be the "first new nation."[6] Bioculturally speaking, Anglo-Americans remained a British people; but, having achieved independence, they became a politically sovereign "nation with the soul of a church." It has been said that, "just as the ideal of America has been that 'of moulding many peoples into the visible image of the citizen,' so it was implied that the religious ideal was that of melding the many diverse sectarianisms into one cosmopolitan religion."[7] The secular humanist religion of the republic presents the United States as an asylum; it has become "a home for the homeless" of all the world. A new nation was to be created "literally out of [the people of] any old nation that comes along".[8]

The founding fathers were not atheists; they still regarded nations as spiritual entities. But the religion of the new republic must "include every religion that these diverse peoples brought along."[9] Of course, the expectation at first was that these diverse peoples would

---

5   Richard Dawkins, *The Extended Phenotype: The Long Reach of the Gene* (Oxford: Oxford University Press, 1999).
6   *Cf.*, Seymour Martin Lipset, *The First New Nation: The United States in Historical and Comparative* (Garden City, N.Y.: Anchor Books, 1967).
7   Sidney E. Mead, "The 'Nation with the Soul of a Church,'" (1967) 36(3) *Church History* 262, at 263.
8   G.K. Chesterton, quoted in *ibid.*, 262.
9   *Ibid.*, 262–263.

be white European Christians. But the tragic flaw in the character of the Constitutional Republic was its "cosmopolitan, inclusive, universal theology." Neither the state nor the church could be recognized explicitly as an expression of a white Anglo-Saxon Protestant people and no other. This spiritual aporia could be resolved only by creating a republic bereft of any ethnoreligious identity; its "spiritual core...is thought to transcend and include all the national and religious particularities brought to it by the people who come from all the world to be 'Americanized.'"[10]

For quite a long while, this spiritual Ponzi scheme worked. Unfortunately for contemporary Anglo-Americans, the empty shell of a fake, transnational, Constitutional Republic not only does nothing to nurture their historic, ethnoreligious identity; it now actively works to destroy the bioculture underpinning their entire way of life. An existential crisis confronts every historic Anglo-Saxon nation; the spiritual foundations of their entire civilization have been corrupted. That problem cannot be understood, much less resolved, so long as the WASP Question is ignored by one and all.

Remarkably, when assessing a public policy, corporate institution, or religious practice, WASPs never imitate certain other, much more socially cohesive, and, hence, more powerful, ethnic groups by asking: Is it good for the WASPs? Until they free themselves from that self-denying ordinance, Anglo-Saxon civilization is doomed. But, in identifying what might be good for WASPs in the future, one must first ask: What is bad for them in the here and now? The short answer to the latter question is that every state throughout the Anglosphere, republic or monarchy, eschews its Anglo-Saxon origins, leaving WASPs bereft of effective political representation. Everywhere denied legitimate constitutional recognition as an ethnonation, WASPs are incapable of defending their ethnic interests and identity. Even the predominantly WASP churches of the Anglican communion, whether in the American

---

10   *Ibid.*, 270, 273.

republic or in the old white Commonwealth, have severed themselves, theologically, liturgically, and practically, from their spiritual roots in the blood and soil of Old England.

In doing so, these nominally Anglican churches do no more than follow the lead of the established Church of England. Safeguarding tax exemptions and lucrative partnerships with the charitable and educational arms of the corporate welfare state, no church will dare to identify itself as the spiritual guardian of the white Anglo-Saxon Protestants peoples. WASPs must pursue their collective welfare on their own, outside and apart from the state, on the terrain of civil society, if they are to recover their ethnoreligious identity. But it will remain difficult, perhaps impossible to determine just what is good for WASPs so long as they remain isolated from each other, in separate, supposedly sovereign nation-states.

From the USA to Northern Ireland to remote New Zealand, whether they realize it or not, WASPs have become an invisible race; *de facto*, if not yet *de jure*, a "stateless" people. Only if WASPs can somehow reconstitute their spiritual unity as a global network of Anglo-Saxon tribes will they recover the world-historical character of their British ancestors. Strange to say, however, the spirit that Hegel identified as "the cunning of reason" may at work within the globalist regimes currently governing Australia, Canada, New Zealand, and the United Kingdom. Adapting to the post-Brexit geopolitical realities and economic imperatives, the old white Commonwealth countries may be on the verge of creating a transnational civil society. Under the guise of a CANZUK treaty citizens, goods, and services may soon flow freely within and between the four countries. Even such a patently materialistic arrangement may sow the seeds of spiritual unity among WASPs around the world. We must pray that some of those seeds will blow over the borders into the USA, touching the hearts of hapless American WASPs trapped in an increasingly fake republic.

American WASPs, even those who identify as racially conscious "white nationalists," now seem oblivious to the congenital disease eating away at the soul of their own particular people. WASPs in America, as elsewhere, are forbidden to taste, much less savour, the fruits of in-group solidarity. The fact is, however, that Anglo-Americans can lay claim to a unique ancestral interest in, and communal responsibility for the constitutional and spiritual crisis besetting the entire Anglosphere; no other racial or ethnic group can claim a direct line of descent from the overwhelmingly British-descended founding generation of every Anglo-Saxon country.

One of the hereditary privileges that old-stock Americans possess is the membership they share with Anglo-Canadians, Anglo-Australian, and Anglo-New Zealanders in a global diaspora stemming from the British Isles. It is time for Americans of British descent to emerge from the darkness of geopolitical defeat and spiritual despondency. They could, if only they would, step once again onto the stage of history. Do they not have a divinely ordained duty to reassert their world-historical standing as the founding people of, *inter alia*, the American republic? In other words, can the ethnoreligious soul of the American republic be resurrected? The answer to such a question assumes, of course, that some such phenomenon is actually known to history.

The Constitutional Republic: What's in a Name?

Many members of the putatively sovereign people consecrated by the new American republic believed that they lived in a democracy. Others claimed it was a republic. At first, the Constitution of 1787 was presented as a modernized model of the mixed and balanced governments pioneered in ancient Greece and Rome. The founders appealed as well to the spirit of the ancient constitution of England. But they dispensed with the "natural" hierarchy of king, lords, and commons associated with the British Parliament. That superseded constitutional design was replaced by a functional separation between executive, legislative, and judicial powers, supplemented in both federal and state governments by a system of checks and balances. The result was a far cry from direct democracy. Prior to the Civil War, even the highly demagogic Jacksonian democracy spawned under the First (Federal) Republic was a sprawling, highly decentralized "state of courts and parties".[11] Even then, the American people-at-large stood outside and apart from the institutions of government. All governmental powers, legislative, executive, and judicial alike, were to be exercised in the name of the sovereign people by those occupying the seats of power.

In other words, the people were to be sovereign in name only. The founders ensured that the people could rule only indirectly, if at all, through their representatives in government. James Madison justified this double-dealing in the language of classical republicanism, declaring that only a state ruled directly by the people can be a democracy. America was to be a republic, one defined, however, in the most minimalist, modernist manner, as a state ruled by (elective and non-elective) representatives of the people.[12] This, too, was a far cry from the classical Aristotelian idea of the republic (or *polis*) as an association of persons formed with a view to some good purpose.

Aristotle taught that "the highest conceivable form of human life was that of the citizen who ruled as head of his *oikos* or household and ruled and was ruled as one of a community of equal heads making decisions which were binding on all". Through his political activity, the citizen contributed to the creation of public goods available to others while himself enjoying the values generated within the society. Civic "activity was concerned with the universal good". Participation in public life was itself, therefore, "a good of a higher order than the

---

11 Stephen Skowronek, *Building a New American State: The Expansion of National Administrative Capacities, 1877–1920* (New York: Cambridge University Press, 1982), 23–25.

12 James Madison, "The Federalist, No. 10," in Alexander Hamilton, et. al., *The Federalist: A Commentary on the Constitution of the United States* Introduction by Edward Mead Earle. (New York: The Modern Library, [orig. pub. 1788]). 58–59.

particular goods that the citizen as a social animal might enjoy". Simply by exercising his own citizenship, every member of the *polis* "enjoyed a universal good". According to J.G.A. Pocock, because citizenship was a "universal activity," the republic was a "universal community," existing "to realize for its citizens all the values which men were capable of realizing in this life."[13]

By the same token, the republic, like the individual citizen, retained a particular identity. Both were "finite and located in space and time." Universal and particular were fused together in both individual citizens and the republic as a whole. As universal beings, citizens were certainly alike; but they were not identical. As particular beings, citizens inevitably remained dissimilar in terms of the individual priorities they might elect to pursue. Their activity in pursuit of the common good could not be divorced from the particular goods each might prefer.[14]

For that reason, citizens both ruled and were ruled. But, because there were inescapable qualitative and quantitative distinctions between citizens, there was a broad division between the one, the few, and the many. Every group within each of those categories was allotted its own distinctive role in decision-making. Both the few and the many included several groups, each of which had power to pursue its own "particular good in such a way as to involve it in the pursuit of other goods by other groups." The goal was to ensure that "each group like each citizen must be subject to power as well as the exerciser of it." No one group was to be "able to exercise an unshared, and hence despotic, power over the whole." Each group was "to contribute as its character best fitted it to the attainment of particular and general goods."[15]

---

13   J.G.A. Pocock, *The Machiavellian Moment: Florentine Political Thought and the Atlantic Republican Tradition* (Princeton, N.J.: Princeton University Press, 1975), 68.

14   *Ibid.*, 3, 68.

15   *Ibid.*, 71, 70.

There was always, of course, the possibility of conflict between the goods pursued by the individual and "his concern for and awareness of the common universal good" that he sought in common with his fellow citizens. The very fact that the contradiction between the two inevitably defied a final solution meant that the *polis* or *res publica* must be a moral community. In the classical republican tradition, "the polity was a relationship between values, and…the good of citizenship — of ruling and being ruled — consisted in a relationship between one's own virtue and that of another. It was in this sense of the mutual and relational character of virtue that only the political animal could be truly a good man." Pocock makes it clear that this "theory was bought at a high price; it imposed high demands and high risks. The polity must be a perfect partnership of all citizens and all values." If failed to attain such perfection, "a part would be ruling in the name of the whole." Any such situation would push the polity towards despotism, corruption and injustice.[16]

Ideally, the republic could provide its citizens with a stable and universal harmonization of values. But as against that hope, there was always an expectation that the polity, "being a work of men's hands, must come to an end in time." Stability depended upon the willingness of citizens to abstain from "preferring his particular values to the common good." Everything turned on the cultivation of civic virtue. But "it was the predicament of civic virtue that it could only be practiced with one's fellow citizens, and consequently might be lost as surely in consequence of another's dereliction as of one's own." The fact was "that the citizen could not be forever sure of the self-maintained virtue of his fellow, let alone of his own". Corruption was "an ever-present possibility." The emergence and survival of a virtuous citizenry in a stable republic always depended on a myriad of particulars.[17]

---

16 Ibid., 74–75.
17 Ibid., 73–76.

A peculiarity of the ancient Greek city-state was that mutual trust among citizens was facilitated by two conditions which no longer obtain in modern civil societies: citizens were relatively few and shared a common ethnicity. In fact, it makes little sense to speak of an ancient Greek "state," a term that presupposes the existence of a civil society over which it rules as "an abstract entity constituted by power." In classical Greece, "there was no such thing as civil society." Constituted as a civic community whose claims were, "in principle, total," the *polis* was certainly "not a conspiracy of self-seeking individuals joined for mutual profit and protection in a temporary legal partnership that would be dissolved when it ceased to suit their interests." In ancient Athens, only the household stood outside the political realm, providing "one refuge of privacy for the procreation, rearing, and nourishment of its future citizens." Because the *polis* consisted of comparatively few, ethnically homogeneous, citizens, even Aristotle was an outsider in Athens; as a Macedonian, he remained a *metic* or resident alien.[18]

Athens possessed another peculiar institution: its political culture was founded upon slavery. The "visible *polis* constituted by the male citizens rested on an invisible and politically inarticulate body of slaves condemned to labour in private so that their masters might be free to devote time and effort to speech and action in public."[19] Only because the institution of slavery implied the absolute loss of individual liberty did the paradoxical existence of a realm of public freedom become possible. As Perry Anderson put it, "it was precisely the formation of a limpidly demarcated slave sub-population that conversely lifted the citizenry of the Greek cities to hitherto unknown heights of conscious juridical freedom."[20] Euripes recognized as much when he remarked,

---

18 Paul A. Rahe, "The Primacy of Politics in Classical Greece," (1984) 19 *American Historical Review* 265, at 268–269; *cf.*, Hannah Arendt, *The Human Condition* (Chicago: University of Chicago Press, 1958), 28–38, 68–73.

19 Rahe, "Primacy of Politics," 271.

20 Perry Anderson, *Passages from Antiquity to Feudalism* (London: New Left Books, 23.)

"As free men we live off slaves."²¹ Outside the *polis*, the law of slavery ruled supreme — the very antithesis of the free zone of interaction standing outside and apart from the modern state.

The inescapable fact that the realm of Greek freedom rested upon the historically contingent development of their peculiar slave mode of production led the ancients to regard the flux of secular happenings as inscrutable and, to all appearances, perhaps even unjustifiable. In fifteenth-century Italy, embryonic civil societies were emerging within a complex network of city-states, duchies, kingdoms, and empires. But even early modern political thinkers such as Niccolò Machiavelli (1469–1527) still identified the mysterious forces directing the endless variations of particulars as Fortune. Willy-nilly, men resigned themselves to the uncomfortable reality that the civic virtues upon which the perfection of the polity depended were always hostage to the unpredictable contingencies of fortune.²² Christians could comfort themselves with the thought that the apparently unintelligible contingency of earthly life was somehow directed by Providence towards the goal of their heavenly salvation. For secular political thinkers, however, the classical image of *Fortuna* "was the atheist's version of providence". Her feminine image "was regularly invoked to 'explain' — or to denote the inexplicability of — political change."²³

In the end, "the problem of *fortuna* [was] a problem in virtue." As J. G. A. Pocock puts it, "*virtus* was that by which the good man imposed form on his *fortuna*." In effect, those who identified "the good man with the citizen politicized virtue and rendered it dependent on the virtue of others." Only within the frame of the *vivere civile* could the good man practice his virtue. Should the civic frame of political action collapse, "whether through violent innovation or through the creeping dependence of some upon others...the virtue of the powerful as well

---

21 Quoted in Rahe, "Primacy of Politics," 271.
22 Pocock, *Machiavellian Moment*, 76.
23 J.G.A. Pocock, *Politics, Language, and Time: Essays on Political Thought and History* (Chicago: University of Chicago Press, 1989),85.

as the powerless" was bound to be corrupted. It was precisely because the tyrant had no fellow citizens that he could never be a good man. Should the *res publica* fall victim to a corrupt tyrant, only a new prince, possessed of exceptional and extraordinary qualities, of *virtù* in a word, would be capable of imposing form on the matter of *fortuna*.[24]

The Ideological Origins of the American Republic

The Renaissance revival of the classical republican tradition exercised a powerful influence on what came to be called the Commonwealth tradition in seventeenth century England associated with political thinkers such as James Harrington (1611–1677). This classically republican movement remained influential throughout the eighteenth century in England, lending support to the civic-minded Country party in its political battles with whiggish Court interests. Throughout this entire period, dissident political discourse drew heavily upon the language of civic virtue. Across the Atlantic, in the British North American colonies, the generation of men who fought the revolutionary War of Independence and framed the founding documents of the American republic were no less familiar with the Roman and Renaissance connotations of such terms as virtue, *virtus*, and *virtù*. But a significant intellectual shift took place within the Anglo-American republican tradition. Given the dynamic expansion of a commercial civil society, the antithesis of civic virtue was no longer seen as "circumstantial *fortuna* so much as historical corruption."[25] The sources of civic corruption had become much more intelligible within the systemic logic of political economy.

Even in Machiavelli's time, it had required the *virtù* of a new prince to impose form on the bad fortune which led to the corruption of the old order. But, in a world of illegitimate power relationships, the

---

24   Pocock, *Machiavellian Moment*, 157, 161.
25   Ibid., 405.

prince must establish virtue as the principle of active life for all citizens if he was to maintain the forms of his newly minted *res publica*. All too often, it was through arms alone, whether his own or those of his supporters, that Machiavelli's prince enjoyed the independence, leisure, and virtue necessary to acquire his position as an innovator.[26] Civic virtue everywhere requires a material foundation; Machiavelli found it in arms. Two thousand years earlier, slave labour laid the foundation for the Athenian *polis*. In seventeenth-century England, Harrington located the material foundations of civic freedom in the ownership of land. The freeholding English Commonwealthman became the paradigmatic image of the civic individual. The rise of the English gentry class rested on an independence made possible by possession of heritable real or landed property protected by common law and their "membership in the related structures of the militia and the parliamentary electorate, thus guaranteeing civic virtue.[27]

By the 1760s, the political culture throughout Anglophone civilization "possessed all the characteristics of neo-Harringtonian civic humanism." In the eighteenth-century American colonies, no less than "at home," a civic and patriot ideal reigned "in which the personality was founded in property, perfected in citizenship but perpetually threatened by corruption." Paradoxically, government came to be seen "as the principal source of corruption…operating through such means as patronage, faction, standing armies (opposed to the ideal of the militia), established churches…and the promotion of a monied interest."[28] Throughout most of the colonial period, Americans had little reason to fear the British government whatever corrupt ministers might do "at home," so long as colonists were free to manage their own affairs.

---

26 *Ibid.*, 185, 162.

27 *Ibid.*, 450.

28 *Ibid.*, 507.

The British conquest of Quebec in 1759 freed the American colonies from the French threat. Thereafter, they were inclined to resent any reassertion of imperial authority. When Parliament became more intrusive, mercantile interests and radical patriots alike charged that ministers at Westminster were encroaching upon colonial liberties. Convinced that "corruption was being attempted from the other side of the Atlantic," they drew upon the language of civic virtue to explain their plight. Malign agencies were conspiring to subvert the ancient liberties belonging to every free-born Englishman. Prominent colonists concluded that the imperial government and the society supporting such a conspiracy "must themselves be hopelessly corrupt." If colonial patriots were to preserve the fundamental principles of the ancient British constitution, they were bound "to reconstitute that form of polity in which virtue would be both free and secure." As a consequence, Americans "repudiated parliamentary monarchy in favor of an English-derived version of *vivere civile*," (*i.e.*, republican way of life).[29]

Eighteenth-century parliamentary monarchy, after all, was already notorious for the pragmatic acceptance of patronage, to the point that it earned the sobriquet of "Old Corruption." As Pocock points out, in Britain "Court and Country themselves were in symbiosis, and the country gentlemen never as radically independent as they liked to pretend."[30] In the American colonies, by contrast, politically minded gentlemen constituted "a Country without a Court". They were accustomed to a certain practical independence within the imperial polity. The metropolitan regime created its colonial offshoots at a distance. Thus, colonists were not face to face with modern government as a force they must and could find means of living with, but, while created by it at a distance, [they] were not in a relation of immediate symbiosis. The greater their apparent independence, the greater their sense that

---

29 *Ibid.*, 507–508.
30 *Ibid.*, 508.

their virtue was their own; but the more active a government in which they did not directly participate, the greater their sense that their independence and virtue were threatened by a force they could only call corruption; and, as Machiavelli and Cato had taught them, once they mistrusted government there was nothing they should not fear. Tyranny was indeed to be dreaded "in every tainted breeze."[31]

Pocock's description of the ideological climate in the colonies in the years before the Revolution seems somehow appropriate to the current constitutional crisis of the American republic. Fear of unknown forces unleashing malignant conspiracies once again stalks the land. Then as now, "modern and effective government had transplanted to America the dread of modernity itself." Then, however, the colonial expression of that dread much more clearly identified corruption as a threat to virtue. The difference now is that the descendants of the founding generation of white Anglo-Saxon Protestants no longer understand the classical republican language of civic virtue. Instead, they speak the liberal language of natural jurisprudence, concerned as it is with the vindication of rights and reconciliation of interests rather than the cultivation of the civic virtues. They have more in common with worldly-wise, eighteenth-century Whig politicians than with crusty colonial patriots. For contemporary WASPs, even those on the dissident right, political corruption is just a fact of life, as American as apple pie.

Virtue and Commerce in the American Republic of Letters

In that context, J. G. A. Pocock's (1924–2023) personal and professional experience of the USA is instructive. Pocock was a quintessential WASP of the old school, born in London in 1924. Three years later, his family emigrated to New Zealand where his father was appointed professor of Classics at Canterbury College in Christchurch. Reared in a peaceable kingdom of solidly middle-class WASP respectability and

---

31 Ibid., 509.

classical learning, Pocock earned his bachelor's and master's degrees in New Zealand. After the war, Pocock pursued highly successful doctoral studies at Cambridge University under Sir Herbert Butterfield. He then taught history and political science at universities back home, before moving to the USA in 1965.[32] Ten years later, he published *The Machiavellian Moment*, his highly influential history of "the Atlantic republican tradition." He was now a star in the Anglo-American academic firmament.

Pocock soon learned, however, that his revisionist interpretation of political culture in the early republic irritated many of his American professional peers. For example, one well-worn theme in American historiography had to do with Jeffersonian opposition to Alexander Hamilton's Federalist program. In Pocock's mind, it was hardly controversial to claim that, when Hamilton supported "a national debt, a standing army, and a system of patronage that would [ensure] a permanent presidential party in Congress," he was simply following in the footsteps of the Court party in England.[33] Similarly, Jefferson's oppositional rhetoric clearly echoed the English Country party language of civic virtue.

In American universities, "liberal and Marxist historians — in this respect curiously different to tell apart," were committed to a whiggish interpretation of their history "in which nothing counts except the rise of liberal individualism and the triumph of the bourgeoisie." They found Pocock's talk of virtue versus corruption suspiciously alien, too evocative of the so-called "paranoid style" of populist politics found in fly-over country. Viewing American politics as an expression of the dominant culture of "possessive individualism," they were easily triggered when Pocock expatiated on the "neo-Machiavellian critique" of the Federalist scheme to install a "corrupt" English system

---

32 https://en.wikipedia.org/wiki/J._G._A._Pocock.

33 J.G.A. Pocock, "From *The Ancient Constitution* to *Barbarism and Religion*; *The Machiavellian Moment*, the History of Political Thought and the History of Historiography," (2016) 43(2) *History of European Ideas* 129, at 143.

of government" in the new republic.³⁴ Pocock compounded the offence when adding the seemingly mild observation that the Anglo-American republican language of civic virtue "persisted" in American political discourse. Any such suggestion was received as akin to "a proposal to perpetuate" the influence of classical republican thought. Indeed, Pocock "was attacked, with a vehemence at times amounting to anger, by those who wished to claim that American political values could never have been other than Lockean."³⁵

Pocock readily conceded the influence of Lockean liberalism in American political culture. But, even as an outsider in 1960s America, Pocock soon decided that American intellectuals were kidding themselves. Their pose of hard-boiled realism was no more than skin-deep; "the American psyche...suggested less a nation of pragmatic Lockeans than one of tormented saints," compulsively reliving the built-in contradictions of a revolutionary republic grounded in the suppositious sovereignty of the people.³⁶ Pocock contended that the inescapable tension between the civic virtues presupposed by the *vivere civile* and the no less essential pursuit of private interests in a modern political economy generated a congenital anxiety among Americans. Because the republic "was founded on principles rather than precedents," Americans were prone to fret over "the fragility of the republic and the precariousness of its future."³⁷ To explain how the new nation had managed to cope with the corrosive influence of personal and political corruption in a rapidly expanding commercial republic, Pocock

---

34 J.G.A. Pocock, *Virtue, Commerce, and History: Essays on Political Thought and History* (Cambridge: Cambridge University Press, 1985), 218. *Cf*., C.B. Macpherson, *The Political Theory of Possessive Individualism: Hobbes to Locke* (Oxford: Clarendon Press, 1962).

35 Pocock, "*Ancient Constitution* to *Barbarism and Religion*," 143.

36 Mira L. Siegelberg, "Things Fall Apart: J.G.A. Pocock, Hannah Arendt, and the Politics of Time," (2013) 10(1) *Modern Intellectual History* 109, at 111.

37 *Ibid.*, 122, 125.

invoked his own variant of Frederick Jackson Turner's still-controversial "frontier thesis."[38]

For many generations, Pocock argued, the fact that a Hamiltonian "Constitution entailed an abandonment of virtue [was] more than compensated for by the *virtù* of the frontier." For more than a century and a half, Americans believed that westward expansion of the frontier would guarantee the material foundation of civic virtue. Given an abundance of new land for settlement by a citizen yeomanry, "the partnership between agrarian virtue and commercial industry could be maintained." At the very least, a dynamic, expanding fee-simple empire "could perpetuate the illusion that the American 'new man' had re-entered Eden."[39] But territorial expansion did come to an end; by 1920 America was a predominantly urban nation. How could a republic designed for expansion overcome finite limits to growth?

There were, of course, many prominent proponents of westward expansion who feared a future in which "sooner or later the reservoir of land must be exhausted, and the expansion of virtue will no longer keep ahead of the progress of commerce". Jefferson expected that when that point was reached, "the process of corruption must be resumed; men will become dependent upon each other in a market economy and dependent on government in great cities." Other more optimistic souls prophesied that "the fee-simple union of virtue and commerce" would create a global role for America, assuring "the perpetuation of that union even after the Pacific shores had been reached."[40] By the late seventies, many Americans believed that the gloomiest predictions had come to pass. A national crisis of confidence emerged, reflected, most famously, by President Jimmy Carter's "Malaise Speech". Given

---

38 Frederick Jackson Turner, "The Significance of the Frontier in American History," American Historical Association, *Annual Report for the Year 1893*, (Washington, 1894), 199–227.

39 Pocock, *Machiavellian Moment*, 539–540.

40 Ibid., 541, 542.

the national mood, Pocock probably did himself no favours by pouring salt on a wounded psyche pandemic among his fellow historians.

In such a depressive atmosphere, Pocock prudently avoided further tense debates with American colleagues over the fundamentals of their government. Whether they realized it or not, he thought, Americans were debating "who they essentially are". Since Pocock had no intention of becoming an American himself, it seemed "fitting to leave the debate to them."[41] He turned his attention instead to his other pet project, the production of a new British history.

Inventing a Political Science of "British History"

Given his youthful immersion in New Zealand academia and his subsequent identification with the Cambridge School in history and political thought, Pocock was understandably sensitive to the insular perspective of English historians. They simply took as given that "English history" could be written without explicit reference to "British history". Pocock recognized that such unconscious arrogance left a huge gap in our historical understanding, one that could be filled only by making "British history" a new subject. The premise of that sub-discipline should be that "there have been Celtic, archipelagic, American, and oceanic regions of social and historic experience with which what we call 'England' has interacted." Pocock recommended that the term "British history" be used "to isolate this series of interactions."[42] Exactly what he meant by the adjectival use of "British" was not immediately obvious.

As for his personal identity, Pocock described himself as being of "English-South African and Anglo-Norman-Channel Island descent and of New Zealand cultural formation". Accordingly, while he knew

---

41 Pocock, "*Ancient Constitution* to *Barbarism and Religion*," 143.
42 J.G.A. Pocock, "The Limits and Divisions of British History: In Search of the Unknown Subject," (1982) 87(2) *American Historical Review* 311, at 312, 317.

himself "to be British," he was "neither English, Irish, American, nor European".[43] Within such a cosmopolitan matrix, his British identity does seem biocultural in nature, though he never uses such terminology. Professionally speaking, however, Pocock presents British identity as a contingent historical phenomenon rather more civic than ethnic in nature.

As a young historian of English political thought, Pocock acquired a life-long resistance to whiggish notions of national character. He was disinclined to believe that either the "antiquarian fundamentalism" invoked by seventeenth-century common lawyers in defence of the ancient constitution or the modernist liberal faith in the inevitability of progress had stamped the English with an enduring national identity.[44] His principled "avoidance of whiggism" inoculated him against "the twin temptations of nationalism and teleology." Historians, he warned, commit a cardinal sin when they treat "history [a]s the servant of an ethical vocation embodied in a determinate national teleology."[45] He pointed to the "disastrous" example of the German idealists who foolishly assumed "that the state (even the state at war) was the highest expression of the personality."[46] Eschewing such folly, Pocock wrote history in the emotionally detached, impersonally professional language of a political scientist. He was most definitely *not* an ethnohistorian.

And, yet Pocock well knew that one of the whiggish paradoxes of modern "society is its appetite for expansion coupled with a deep nostalgia for the past." Having been deprived of a secure anchorage in religion and a traditional way of life, some of us still look to the

---

43   Ibid., 319.

44   Cf., Pocock, *Virtue and Commerce*, 215.

45   Richard Bourke, "Pocock and the Presuppositions of the New British History," (2010) 53(3) *The Historical Journal* 747, at 754.

46   J.G.A. Pocock, "Law, Sovereignty and History in a Divided Culture: The Case of New Zealand and the *Treaty of Waitangi*," (1998) 43 *McGill Law Journal* 481, at 505.

future, to the idea of posterity to ensure "that deeds will live on and memories are kept alive". But such a teleological aspiration only makes sense "within a chain of like deeds and memories, which stretches back into the mists of obscure generations of ancestors and forward into the equally unknowable generations of descendants."[47] By contrast, Pocock's work was set in conscious opposition to an "exemplary" ethnohistory relating the dramatic story of recurrent conflicts between the Anglo-Saxon peoples and their rulers.[48]

Indeed, given his coolly detached, cosmopolitan WASP predispositions, Pocock slipped easily into the role of the court historian. He grounded his writing on "the historiographical principles that should inform how the formation of British citizenship" might be better understood by those with a need to know by those participating in the exercise of sovereign authority. Historians conforming to that job description are *ipso facto* members of the political class. Pocock's new British history set out to analyse the changing intellectual contexts governing the development over time of a particular national and imperial tradition.[49] Its subject was the expansion (and contraction) of a multi-polar *polity*; most emphatically not the origins, development, and destiny of a particular *people*.

Unlike the ethnohistorian, Pocock's goal was never to trace chains of connections between the various Anglo-Saxon-Celtic peoples who, over the course of centuries, have expanded, in tandem, around the world. Rather, his concern was with the relationship between historical events and political consciousness of those who rule and are ruled at any given moment in time. Summing up his first book on *The Ancient*

---

47 Anthony D. Smith, *The Ethnic Origin of Nations* (Oxford: Blackwell, 1988), 174, 176.

48 *Cf.*, G.H. Nadel, "Philosophy of History before Historicism," in *Studies in the Philosophy of History* ed. G.H. Nadel, (New York: Gannon, 1965).

49 Bourke, "Presuppositions of New British History," 753; *cf.*, J.G.A. Pocock, "The Historian as Political Actor in Polity, Society, and Academy," (1996) 20 *Journal of Pacific Studies* 89.

Constitution and the Feudal Law, he described his intellectual project as an exercise in abstract academic humanism: "the book seems to be an essay in a certain species of historical inquiry…into how human beings live within the possibilities of their language systems, and the systems of historical time which their language articulates for them."[50] Apart from persistent warnings about the dangers of whiggism, Pocock had nothing to say about how the "language system" associated with the ancient British constitution could or should shape the destiny of his fellow WASPs throughout the contemporary Anglosphere.

Only those who possess a sense of "anamnestic solidarity" with their ancestors, only those who feel duty bound to honour their memory, are likely to be at all concerned with the good opinion of their posterity. Ethnohistories are based upon the premise that there is an essential thread of continuity binding the present to both the past and the future.[51] A British ethnohistorian aims to be both a moral teacher and a spiritual dramatist; his role is to present the audience with "a temporal and terrestrial drama of salvation". He is not a disinterested social scientist pursuing a professional inquiry into the past "as it really was"; rather, both the ethnohistorian and his readers are possessed by "a yearning desire to re-enter into a living past". A British ethnohistory strives to make the past respond to the needs of the living by recreating the peculiar atmosphere and distinctive setting associated with the Anglo-Saxon-Celtic peoples and no others.[52]

Pocock's new British history presented itself as a sub-discipline in a political science. The historian as political scientist denies that there exists any "predetermined relationship between contingent historical process and specific forms of political consciousness." In

---

50 J.G.A. Pocock, *The Ancient Constitution and the Feudal Law: A Study of English Historical Thought in the Seventeenth Century* A Reissue with a Retrospect (Cambridge: Cambridge University Press, 1987), 387.

51 Christian Lenhardt, "Anamnestic Solidarity: The Proletariat and its *Manes*," *Telos* 25 (Fall 1975), 133–154.

52 Smith, *Ethnic Origins*, 179–182.

other words, there was nothing intrinsically "British" or even "English" about the political language spoken by seventeenth-century English Commonwealthmen or eighteenth-century revolutionaries in British North America. Accordingly, when writing either British or American history, Pocock's "focus was on the formation of kinds of political allegiance" in particular polities at particular times.[53]

For Pocock, it followed that, once Americans of British descent renounced their ancestral allegiance to the parliamentary monarchy, they effectively re-constituted themselves as a new people. Thereafter, their collective identity was anchored in the institutional exoskeleton of the new state. Conversely, colonial Tories in exile from the new republic and re-settled in Upper Canada, Lower Canada, New Brunswick, or Nova Scotia remained firmly embedded within British history. In neither case were the historically contingent forms of citizenship created by successor polities confined to those possessed of a particular ethnic identity or religious consciousness.[54] As shown by the "emancipation" of Jews and Catholics in Britain and of Negro slaves in the USA, political allegiance is not a fusion of blood and belonging. Contingent historical events led to the extension of both American citizenship and British subject status to persons possessed of radically alien ethnic identities and religious faiths.

The Globalist Convergence of Parliamentary Monarchy and Constitutional Republic

If one accepts Pocock's equation of national identity with political allegiance, the unity of the British and American peoples seems to have been severed at the root not long after the foundation of the republic. Pocock conceded that "the American Revolution and the act of American political union belonged to the wider context of British history," but he maintained that the subsequent "American continental

---

53 Bourke, "Presuppositions of New British History," 753, 748.
54 Ibid., 752–753.

expansion represented a definite departure from [that] historical arena". Pocock knew, of course, that, for most of its history, the United States, has had a predominantly white Anglo-Saxon population. He also readily acknowledged that the newly created American polity drew upon British political and legal traditions. Nevertheless, for him, the fact remained that "it was only in leaving the sphere of British history that the United States became an effective and durable empire."[55] Remember, however, there is more than one way to interpret history. If peoples not polities are the focus of attention, the relationship between "British" and "American" history will be understood very differently.

As we are constantly reminded by anti-racist activists, the history of both the USA and Greater Britain is stamped with the mark of Cain; it was *white* Anglo-Saxon Protestants who inflicted slavery and colonial oppression on the coloured peoples of the world. To this day, their descendants throughout the Anglosphere bear the burden of that original sin. Whether British or American in their formal political allegiance, all WASPs allegedly share in that ancestral guilt.

From a less judgemental biocultural and ethnographic perspective, it is not at all obvious that British and American histories took separate paths after the American Revolution. British immigration to the USA continued apace (if rather anonymously) and the historical mingling of the Canadian and American peoples was a well-known phenomenon.[56] Henry James left behind a literary record of the interactions between English and American elites during the Gilded Age. And, for decades now, the entire Anglosphere has been subsumed within the history of a globalist American empire. A central theme in that history turns out to be the demographic displacement and political marginalization of the founding race in every formerly Anglo-Saxon country. Remarkably enough, Pocock's historical sensibility seemed untouched by the rapid decline in the status of his co-ethnics around the globe.

---

55 Siegelberg, "Things Fall Apart," 122.
56 Marcus Lee Hansen, *The Mingling of the Canadian and American Peoples Vol I Historical* (New Haven: Yale University Press, 1940).

That blind spot reflected his determinedly professional focus on civic rather than ethnic identities in modern British history.

Wilful blindness cannot hide the grim fact that throughout the Anglosphere, the civic identity of every British-descended people has been hollowed out. Citizenship, whether for WASPs or the multitude of dusky newcomers, is now merely a formal legal status. Our civic status has been detached, "progressively," from ties of blood and belonging, from religion, language and history. Moreover, the core responsibilities of citizenship have been diluted to the vanishing point. In "the land of the free and home of the brave" citizens may soon not be expected even to encounter one another in public; private voting by smartphone (or no-excuse mail-in ballots for less sophisticated or "undocumented" voters) has been held out by the putative President of the United States as a legitimate expression of American democracy.

Trapped together in mass multi-racial societies, both core and replacement populations of the Anglosphere are governed by and for a transnational corporatist plutocracy. Jefferson's premonition was all too prescient, if insufficiently pessimistic: the American republic has succumbed at long last to the very sort of corruption it was created to escape. In presiding over the decline and fall of Anglo-America, those who misgovern the USA today resemble the Court Whigs who shrugged their shoulders at the loss of the American colonies in the eighteenth century. American oligarchs have joined forces with the conspicuously multi-racial, globalist government of the United Kingdom and Northern Ireland. Their self-propelling globalist system is programmed to destroy what remains of the continuity of "British history" with the ancient constitution and people of Old England.

The *vivere civile*, the republican way of life, the framework within which virtuous citizens in both the American republic and the British parliamentary monarchy once resisted old forms of corruption, has been deprived of its material and spiritual foundations. A vanishing white Anglo-Protestant identity no longer provides the indispensable biocultural bedrock of a republican constitution. Political allegiances, it now appears, do turn, crucially, on race and ethnicity. Pocock knew, of course, the Atlantic republican tradition originated in ancient Greek and Roman civilizations, themselves the creation of the even-more ancient Indo-European peoples. But he refused to recognize either American republicanism or the English Commonwealth movement as the spiritually unique product of what was not-so-long ago recognized, even idealized, as the white Anglo-Saxon Protestant race. On the contrary, those political traditions are merely "language systems," available, in principle, to human beings anywhere given the appropriate historical circumstances.

But what if the modern civic republican tradition was the unique outgrowth of a WASP bioculture? All those threatened by the totalitarian tendencies manifest in the transnational corporate welfare state should ponder that uncomfortable possibility. In the present Age of Woke Capital, WASPs may be the only ethnic group capable of or interested in resisting the corruption and degeneracy permeating political and civil life everywhere in the Anglosphere. True, far-too-many WASPs are embedded within the upper reaches of the globalist plutocracy together with the middle-ranking managerial-professional classes doing their bidding. But no other ethnic group holding sway within the ruling circles of the Anglosphere (certainly not Jews, Chinese, or Indians) can claim to have created stable and enduring democratic or crowned republics in which the *vivere civile* became a way of life.

Pocock's approach seemed to take the higher ideals of a historically distinctive WASP bioculture for granted, almost as if they represent a set of possibilities encoded in every human embryo. Yet, the reality is that only white Anglo-Saxon Protestants invented the state as a surrogate for their collective identity. It might be argued that, as an upper-crust WASP, Pocock was ill-equipped to conceive the historical development of the British empire otherwise than as "the expansion of a *polity*". He viewed British history "as a recounting of past politics in which 'politics' is taken to mean a shared enterprise in ruling and being ruled".[57] Yes, the British people were distributed in polities around the globe; but those *polities* were embedded in a rapidly developing system of political economy. The result was an intractable clash between civic ideals and market realities.

The *vivere civile* of the British polities found its material foundation in the independence, leisure, and virtue of their citizens, almost always male heads of households possessed of landed property. The civic virtues presupposed by the polity were typically associated with a masculine code of honour binding upon all those who ruled and were ruled. By contrast, the modern political economy, if not dishonourable by nature, remained somewhat suspect in the eyes of gentlemen of property and standing. Conceived as an autonomous system of production, distribution, and exchange, the free market was governed, not by virtue, but by the pragmatic pursuit of selfish personal interests. A sense of honour was never deemed necessary to — and might have impeded full participation in — the market-based system of needs celebrated by eighteenth-century political economists.

Indeed, everyone resident in a modern commercial republic, whatever his or her personal character (or, nowadays, pronouns), is deemed entitled to equal dignity and equal rights before the law. It is hardly surprising, then, that the *vivere civile* prized by both the classical republican tradition and early modern parliamentary monarchy soon dissolved into the sordid factional conflicts, petty party divisions, and intractable racial discord characteristic of contemporary liberal democracy. Formal legal codes asserting the equal dignity of every human individual have replaced an unevenly distributed, aristocratic sense of personal honour. "The basic concept in republican thinking is *virtus*; the basic concept of all jurisprudence is necessarily *ius*." Lawyers in the American republic had to recognize that "there is no known way of representing virtue as a right," either in oneself or in

---

57 Bourke, "Presuppositions of New British History," 749.

one's fellow citizens.[58] In both the American republic and the British parliamentary monarchy, that iron rule remains binding to this day. Or, more accurately, the communal cultivation of the civic virtues is a cultural practice unknown, perhaps even inconceivable to denizens of the borderless society of the spectacle.

Ulsterization: The Recurrent Problem of Asymmetrical Allegiance in British History

In the twenty-first century, few Anglo-American intellectuals take seriously suggestions that classical republican ideas have any role to play in the resolution of the current constitutional crisis. Even Pocock treated civic republicanism as a largely spent force. Fears of corrupt conspiracies in high places may still prompt periodic anxiety attacks among old-stock Americans, but, typically, their responses are confined to cynical resignation, sullen resentment, or apathetic indifference. Even heated debates over Second Amendment gun rights typically have less to do with the antiquarian ideal of an armed citizenry than with rising paranoia over personal security in a crime-ridden multiracial society. Those packing concealed weapons rarely regard fellow citizens as paragons of civic virtue.

Although Pocock became increasingly pessimistic over the future of the American republic, he dared to hope that the civic identity of the British peoples could be secured by the survival of those sovereign political communities sharing an imperial past. Informed by ancient and modern models of the *res publica*, he had long been convinced that a durable form of sovereignty could still be "founded on civic involvement in its exercise". But, once the government of the United Kingdom resolved to join the Common Market, he lost his political confidence.

---

58 J.G.A. Pocock, "Cambridge Paradigms and Scotch Philosophers: A Study of the Relations between the Civic Humanist and Civil Jurisprudential Interpretation of Eighteenth-Century Social Thought, " in Istvan Hont and Michael Ignatieff, eds. *Wealth and Virtue: The Shaping of Political Economy in the Scottish Enlightenment* (Cambridge: Cambridge University Press, 1983), 248.

The European Union assumed "the form in Pocock's mind of an assault on British autonomy," the loss of which impacted his native New Zealand as much, if not more than the United Kingdom itself.[59]

Before Britain joined in the European project, Pocock retained an antipodean faith in the "commonwealth experience of global Britishness." After all, he was born a British subject; there was no such thing as New Zealand, Australian, or Canadian citizenship before the late 1940s. Until then, the Commonwealth approximated a multi-polar form of democratic sovereignty that was "an expression of the ideal of equality."[60] All British subjects were presumptively endowed with a shared capacity to make a common history. By contrast, the European Union, and neo-liberalism globalism, generally, offer nothing more than an ahistorical universalist consumer culture. Eventually, Pocock came to recognize that "British history" is dissolving into a vast, transnational corporatist system. No less than Americans, the British peoples, too, have been stripped of political agency in the present as well as sovereignty over the past.

Presumably Pocock greeted the Brexit vote with some satisfaction. Unfortunately, the protracted process of extricating Britain from the EU has exposed the intertwined illusions of both national sovereignty and democratic equality. British sovereignty has been compromised, shamefully, by the Northern Ireland Protocol to the Brexit deal. By accepting the EU demand for a custom's boundary in the middle of the Irish Sea, the British government effectively betrayed Protestant Loyalists in Ulster. Apparently, this peculiar decision was designed to avoid a hard land border between Northern Ireland and the Irish Republic. Not only does the arrangement complicate Ulster's trade with the rest of the UK, it represents a symbolic victory of Irish republicans over a Loyalist population no longer entitled to equal treatment with their fellow British citizens in England, Scotland, and Wales.

---

59 Bourke, "Presuppositions of New British History," 752.
60 *Ibid.*, 754.

Richard Bourke, a UK based Irish academic, suggests that Pocock's commitment to the civic ideal of equality causes him to overestimate its ability to inspire "commitment and allegiance." One must recognize, he reminds us, that "it has also occasioned divisiveness and hostility." The Northern Ireland Protocol is but the latest illustration of "a recurrent pattern of asymmetrical allegiance" in British history. In fact, Bourke contends, "this process is encapsulated by the concept of Ulsterization." But Ulster's experience is merely emblematic; the phenomenon can be observed far beyond Ulster. Metropolitan betrayal of the periphery has become "a paradigmatic process in British history." As such:

Ulsterization concerns the fate of allegiance under conditions of imperial retrenchment. It points to a situation of unreciprocated commitment. The situation has arisen among settler societies from North America in the eighteenth century to Northern Ireland and New Zealand in the twentieth...it cannot be conceptualized in terms of the standard preoccupations of contractual theories of government. The common concern of contractual theories is with the conditions of allegiance. However, Ulsterization is based on an asymmetrical relationship in which allegiance is staked in the absence of a final assurance of protection. This kind of loyalism amounts to a unilateral pact of submission.[61]

Indeed, the treachery synonymous with Ulsterization affects the Anglo-Saxon-Celtic inhabitants of Great Britain itself. Not even their loyalty to the governing classes of the UK has been reciprocated. Instead, the "white British" are being replaced through mass Third World immigration. Over the past seventy years, the rising tide of colour reflected the constitutional reality that almost anyone from anywhere can become British; some particularly vexatious BAMEs (Black, Asian, and Minority Ethnics) even have the hide to describe themselves as English. As a result, the indigenous English, Scottish,

---

61   Ibid., 754–755.

and Welsh peoples have lost sovereignty not just over their homelands but their past as well.

State and corporate media organizations now regularly portray English heroes and heroines as black Africans. Public policies promoting the corrosion of British identity now proceeding at a breakneck pace have been in place for a very long while. Catholic emancipation and the admission of Jews to membership in Parliament in the nineteenth century were but the thin edge of the wedge in a long campaign by cosmopolitan elites to declare their independence from the native English, Scottish, and Welsh peoples. Neither throne nor altar have protected the white Anglo-Saxon Protestant people of England from alien invasion. Such a brazen betrayal is symptomatic of a situation of ever-more-asymmetrical allegiance which has transformed the claim that the British peoples are involved in the exercise of sovereignty into a hollow fraud.

I do wonder, however, whether Pocock was ready to concede that increasing demographic diversity in the United Kingdom amounts to the replacement of the first, authentically British, peoples in their ancestral homeland. On his purely political understanding of civic identity, Québécois in Canada, Maoris in New Zealand, as well as the Muslim masses in the cities of England, must count, for the time being at least, as British peoples. After all, they do participate on equal (or better) terms in the exercise in a sovereign authority formally emanating from the British Crown. This raises the possibility that the sovereign authority exercised by the Crown in any or all of its dominions may itself cease to be "British" in any meaningful ethnoreligious sense of the term. In fact, an increasingly hollow Crown meekly takes the rap for the ritual humiliation and physical dispossession of every British-descended people.

The "Shapeshifting Crown" and the End of "British History" in New Zealand

New Zealand provides a textbook example of royal assent to Ulsterization. The "shapeshifting Crown" is regularly invoked to deconstruct New Zealand's historically and demographically British identity.[62] Adding insult to injury, J.G.A. Pocock, ONZM, the native doyen of British history bestowed his academic imprimatur upon this tawdry process. In his inimitably professorial manner, Pocock described New Zealand as a land in which law, history, and sovereignty now reflect a "divided culture". He was careful not to take sides, remaining, as ever, the detached observer. This British historian had no visible personal or tribal interest at stake in the fate of his own British-descended people.

The intractable cultural cleavage in New Zealand is anchored in the *Treaty of Waitangi*, signed in 1840, between the British Crown and various indigenous tribes coming to be known, collectively, as Maori. The Crown had been invited to assume sovereign authority over New Zealand by several tribal chieftains seeking protection from the violence and depredations they were suffering from certain other tribes making war on them. There was more than one version of the *Treaty*; the official English document and several others were translated into missionary Maori. Before long, Maoris loudly complained that they were being unfairly dealt with in land transactions allegedly contrary to the terms of the *Treaty*. Such disputes produced decades of intermittent warfare between British government and settlers versus various Maori tribes, gangs, and cults.[63]

Despite such recurrent, often violent, clashes, the Crown honoured its treaty obligations to protect the proprietary rights of the Maori peoples, granting them all the rights and privileges of British subjects,

---

62 Cris Shore and David V. Williams, eds., *The Shapeshifting Crown: Locating the State in Postcolonial New Zealand, Australia, Canada, and the UK* (Cambridge: Cambridge University Press, 2019).

63 See, generally, Kerry Bolton, *The Parihaka Cult* (London: Black House, 2012).

including representation in Parliament. Until recently, however, it was held that, as a matter of strict law, there was no native title to the lands and waters of New Zealand in the absence of a formal Crown grant. The Crown alone could solemnize the land rights of the Maori tribes through the exercise of its sovereign authority. New Zealand courts took the view that the *Treaty of Waitangi* had no independent or binding legal force. The Maori chieftains who signed the *Treaty*, each on behalf of his own tribe, did not represent an independent sovereign authority that could be recognized in international law. Native title would be secured instead through participation by the Maori, as equals, in the exercise of sovereign authority.[64]

But in recent decades the British identity of New Zealand law, history, and sovereignty has come under challenge. The unquestioned allegiance of New Zealand to the British Crown was repaid with betrayal when Britain joined the Common Market, ending imperial preferences for New Zealand trade goods. Simultaneously, WASP intellectuals in New Zealand were swept up in a permanent pandemic of post-colonial ethnomasochism. The myth of the Noble Savage was resurrected just as the traditional Maori practice of cannibalism was deemed dead and buried. In polite society, one turned a blind eye to the massive damage that the Maori had inflicted upon the flora and fauna of New Zealand in the few short centuries before the arrival of the British. And, above all, it was no longer morally or politically acceptable to deny the right of the Maori to formal legal recognition as the customary custodians of their ancestral lands.[65]

---

64 Pocock, "New Zealand and the *Treaty of Waitangi*," 488–493; see also, Grant Morris, "James Prendergast and the Treaty of Waitangi: Judicial Attitudes to the Treaty During the Latter Half of the Nineteenth Century," (2004) 35 *Victoria University of Wellington Law Review* 117.

65 Kerry Bolton, "New Zealand Histories, II, January 30, 2021 https://theeuropeannewzealander.net/2021/01/30/new-zealand-histories-ii/ ; Paul Moon, *This Horrid Practice: The Myth and the Reality of Traditional Maori Cannibalism* (Kindle Edition) Penguin Books Australia (2008); Andrew Mitchell, *A Fragile Paradise: Nature & Man in the Pacific*, Collins, London, 1989; B. McFadgen,

The modern Maori interpretation of the *Treaty* seeks to impose "a retrospective and retroactive" understanding of native title.[66] The pre-emptive title of the Crown to the lands and waters of New Zealand is now disputed by Maori activists and their ethnomasochistic WASP supporters. The latter typically signal their submission to Maori demands by adopting *pakeha* as their preferred ethnonym. Pocock provided a sympathetic statement of Maori claims. He certainly deferred to Maori norms by adopting the (significantly uncapitalized) Maori nomenclature for the founding stock when referring to his own white British-descended people.

He accepted at face value the Maori complaint that "what looked like a guarantee of possession to the *iwi* [tribes] has in practice meant to them the imposition of a greater capacity for alienation than they desired." The Maori, he said, "did not think they were conceding to the Crown any ultimate authority over or title to the lands of the two major islands." They assert that the *Treaty* recognizes their "right to possession, not of lands, forests, and fisheries alone, but of the norms and values, the social structure and culture, inherent in the occupancy of the land." The pre-emptive title of the Crown amounted to unjust dispossession." Allegedly, they have been dispossessed of their very identity as a people.[67] They claim, therefore, that the *Treaty* entitles them to repossession of both land and cultural identity (which are inseparable) where repossession is possible, and to compensation and resources to use in building a new identity where it is not. A new problem instantly arises. Claims under a treaty or under a Common Law, are in principle negotiable; claims to a unique and all-inclusive cultural or spiritual identity easily become non-negotiable.[68]

Impact on the Landscape, in *From the Beginning: The Archaeology of the Maori*, J. Wilson (ed.) Penguin Books, 1987; B. Gill, P. Martinson, *New Zealand's Extinct Birds*, Random Century, 1991.

66 Pocock, "New Zealand and the *Treaty of Waitangi*, 492.

67 Ibid., 492–493.

68 Ibid., 493.

New Zealand now confronts an existential problem; namely, "whether the Maori and the *pakeha* occupy a single history of interaction, or two histories incompatible with each other." The WASP community in New Zealand must ponder what may become of its "capacity either to make or to write its own history if its political sovereignty should be surrendered to forces from without or radically challenged by forces from within."[69] A quasi-judicial body known as the Waitangi Tribunal has been "empowered to hear claims by Maori arising out of performance or non-performance of the *Treaty*'s provisions." The Tribunal "investigates whether the Crown has or has not been discharging conditional obligations subject to which sovereignty was transferred to it in the first place." Strangely enough, the Crown itself has endowed the Tribunal with "a real if limited capacity to query the legitimacy of the sovereign's jurisdiction." In other words, the British Crown, having treated the *Treaty of Waitangi* for most of New Zealand's history as "a simple nullity," now enshrines the very same document as "New Zealand's ancient constitution, its *Magna Carta*, its fundamental law, its original contract."[70]

Pocock's apparent approval gave a doubly ironic twist to this curious turn of events. He accepted the current interpretation of the *Treaty* as a bicultural contract whose meaning is highly unstable and open to continual revision. Such a present-minded hermeneutic stood in sharp contrast to the "Cambridge method" governing Pocock's work as an historian of political thought. In that context, his concern was always, not with our own questions and answers with respect to the classic texts in political thought, but with the intentions of their authors. The task of the historian then is to reconstruct the culture and historical situation in which any given political text was originally written. This

---

69 Ibid., 493, 496.
70 *Wi Parata v. The Bishop of Wellington* (1877) 3 NZ Jur (NS) 72, at 78; *cf.*, Pocock, "New Zealand and the *Treaty of Waitangi*," 496–497; and David V. Williams, *A Simple Nullity: The* Wi Parata *Case in New Zealand Law and History* (Auckland: Auckland University Press, 2011).

detached outsider's perspective runs contrary to the ethnohistorian's preference for an insider's viewpoint sensitive to the shifting interests of his people over time. Even the most significant political writers of the past may well have vanished from the modern reader's view; professional historians labour to describe once-influential authorial projects now utterly boring and irrelevant to the public-at-large. Conversely, a text dismissed by the professional historian as unimportant at the time of its composition may suggest fascinating political possibilities never imagined by the author to those of us in the present.[71]

Not all historical texts are created equal, however. A constitution or a treaty is not a treatise in political theory. Carefully drafted legal documents in general are designed to convey stable meanings, jointly crafted by multiple framers, through time and across generations. The *Treaty of Waitangi* is one such document. If so, it is ironic that legal scholars are turning to the "Cambridge method" as an aid to the textual interpretation of constitutions understood as historical documents just as lawyers and historians in New Zealand are discarding the original understanding of the *Treaty* as drafted and signed in 1840. Were Pocock to analyse the text and legal-historical context of the *Treaty* in accordance with the hermeneutic norms of the Cambridge school, it "would be understood on its own terms, without regard to today's controversies. This necessitates a rigorous understanding of historical context. Only with such an approach can an accurate understanding of what a constitution [or *Treaty*] was intended to mean be possible."[72]

But few Anglo-New Zealanders are prepared to defend the original understanding of the *Treaty*, least of all the Crown as it bows to escalating demands from Maori activists and, *inter alia*, their ethnomasochistic

---

71   *Cf.*, Andrew Fraser, *The WASP Question: An Essay on the Biocultural Evolution, Present Predicament, and Future Prospects of the Invisible Race* (London: Arktos Media, 2011), 351–355.

72   Benjamin B. Saunders and Simon P. Kennedy, "History and Constitutional Interpretation: Applying the 'Cambridge School' Approach to Interpreting Constitutions," (2020) 40(3) *Oxford Journal of Legal Studies* 591, at 593.

WASP enablers in the media, the legal professions, and academia. Such a surrender comes at the cost of white Anglo-Saxon Protestants whose British ancestors were promised that the Crown would act as a trustee for the collective ethnic interests of their posterity. While prepared to join his professional peers in subordinating the expressed will of the *Treaty* signatories to present-day political expediency, Pocock did, to his credit, convey a sense of unease.

As an historian, Pocock knew that the past provides reminders aplenty "of how easily a challenge to sovereignty in the name of [fundamental law] can become a dissolution of government, an appeal to heaven, and a lapse into civil war and the state of nature." Maori claims have now become so sweeping that they threaten to remove the founding stock of New Zealand from the ambit of British history. They assert that "a tribe's occupancy of the land furnishes it with a spiritual substance or continuity (*mana*), which in turn is extended as power over that land (*whenua*) and becomes a mode of appropriating it and constituting personality on its foundation." The corporate personality belonging to each tribe "is that of a group whose communion with the ancestors and the land is constantly being renewed." Consequently, the Maori concept of *tangata whenua* (people of the land) allegedly "entails a relationship with the cosmos so close and exclusive as to contain both space and time within itself." The extension in time of such a relationship constitutes not a history but something more like the dreamtime of the Australian aborigines. The *pakeha* may be compelled to respect this Maori dreamtime, but they cannot possibly submit to it without abolishing their own historical identity.[73]

The Historian as Political Actor

Unfortunately, British-descended New Zealanders have been dispossessed of the power to command the past. History, Pocock taught us, "is the memory of the state." The state in New Zealand, as elsewhere,

---

73 Pocock, "New Zealand and the *Treaty of Waitangi*," 497–499.

is accustomed to intervening "in the authorisation of narratives that supported its authority." Historians are found mainly in academia where "their activity becomes professionalised...so that there exists a guild, estate or republic of historians." Cloistered within public universities, the historical profession has powerful incentives to serve as "a functionary, a dependent, a beneficiary of the state." Maori, too, have established their own relationships with the state as mediated through the metonymic image of the Crown. Over the past forty years, the image of the Crown in New Zealand has been utterly transformed, from that of a "colonial aggressor," pre-emptively seizing title to the lands and waters belonging to the *tangata whenua*, to that of a "postcolonial apologist," forever seeking forgiveness for its past misdeeds, duplicity, and failures in its relationship with the Maori people.[74]

As the editors of *The Shapeshifting Crown* remark, it is noteworthy that in countless deed of settlement ceremonies in which wrongdoing is acknowledged and forgiveness sought, "the wrongdoing is always attributed to the Crown, never to the government or its officials or any named individual." The shapeshifting character of the Crown is a metonym for the state; as such, it has turned out to be a "useful fiction" for the political class. Hiding behind the majestic image *du jour* of the Crown enables governments "to distance themselves from direct responsibility for obligations under the Treaty." The political class stands in the shadows, the self-interested source of a new metanarrative which "invalidates history as the colonisers have perceived it."[75] Attributing the collective construction of the past to the many faces of the Crown helps to disguise what Pocock called "the politics of history."[76]

Pocock encouraged his professional peers in New Zealand to recognize their role as political actors living through a cultural revolution. Fortunately for political elites, *pakeha* historians have been all-too

---

74 Pocock, "Historian as Political Actor," 91, 97, 107.
75 Shore and Williams, *The Shapeshifting Crown*, Introduction.
76 Pocock, "Historian as Political Actor," 92.

willing to embrace a culture of guilt. They readily condemn the crimes allegedly committed in the name of the Crown by their own ancestors in pursuit of selfish interests. Historians have carried out their function of rewriting the formerly British history of New Zealand "so far as to delegitimise it altogether." Pocock noted as well that they have declined — quite rightly of course — "to delegitimate the culture of the colonised," sometimes going so far as "to represent it as guiltless, and even without the capacity for guilt and self-condemnation."[77](107-8)

In the academic republic of professional historians, there is always another way of telling a story.[78] It comes as no surprise therefore that (under the joint auspices of historians and government, and in the name of the Crown) postcolonial history has migrated from the universities into the schools. The previously hegemonic British history of New Zealand is being replaced by a Maori history of "Aotearoa". New Zealand's leading dissident intellectual, Kerry Bolton, readily acknowledges that one must recognize that two different peoples will naturally construct two different histories:

However, the way these 'histories' will be taught will be at the expense of the Euro-New Zealander and particularly the Anglo-Saxon-Celtic heritage. Hence there is a denial to this element of what is being avidly promoted among all non-European elements: a sense of place and identity. This double-standard is rationalised on the premise of 'white privilege', and the notion that White identity in New Zealand cannot exist as anything other than one of colonial invasion and exploitation. What this assumes is that Whites can be lumped into an indistinguishable mass who have all profited from the legacy of colonialism. To right this alleged historical wrong it is necessary to deny Whites any form of consciousness other than that of collective shame and guilt.

---

77   *Ibid.*, 107–108.
78   *Ibid.*, 110.

When several generations of White youth have been inculcated with the feeling that their heritage is of no account in the future of Aotearoa (the days of 'New Zealand' are surely numbered) then they will at last be *passé* as an ethnic component and exist as nothing other than to serve the economic system.[79]

It is noteworthy that neither Bolton nor Pocock reference their co-ethnics as "British". But, at least, Bolton identifies with them and their plight. For his part, Pocock, too, long recognized and deplored the tragic circumstance that neo-liberal globalism has dispossessed both Maori and *pakeha* of "political communities where we were — supposedly — members as individuals of the sovereign which determined its role in history."[80] Bolton, of course, would jib at the notion that Maori ever regarded themselves as individual members of the sovereign. He knows that Maori have long been organized as tribal entities; Pocock appeared not to recognize that his fellow WASPs and the Maori are enemies in a rapidly escalating culture war.

Maori and their allies treat WASPs as defendants in a post-revolutionary Truth and Reconciliation Tribunal. Pocock found it ironic that, even as Maori and *pakeha* are in the process of "renegotiating sovereignty…it is being sold out from under them." He did not notice that the principle of equality does not apply when one party to "negotiations" cannot appear under its own name. "Both peoples" are not, as Pocock claimed, fated "to live in economic communities where our role as self-enacting individual has yet to be defined as other than the consumer."[81] He was probably right that a "nation" of consumers is unlikely to determine its own destiny. But he should have acknowledged that Maori may survive as a *tribal* nation of consumers. Receiving support neither from the Crown nor the republic of historians, New Zealand WASPs might well degenerate into deracinated *pakeha* who

---

79 Kerry Bolton, "Aotearoa New Zealand Histories," January 3, 2021. https://theeuropeannewzealander.net/2021/01/03/aotearoa-new-zealand-histories.

80 Pocock, "New Zealand and the *Treaty of Waitangi*," 505.

81 Ibid., 505–506.

dare not speak their real name, much less that of the memory-holed Dominion of New Zealand.

Still, it seems a pity that, despite their differences, both the preeminent British historian of the Atlantic republican tradition and New Zealand's most prominent dissident rightist should have presented themselves as cultural pessimists. The one refused to believe that the spirit of republicanism still inheres in the ethnonation which gave birth to both the America republic and the British parliamentary monarchies. The other seems resigned to the solitary confinement of British-descended *pakehas* on remote South Pacific islands, far from their Anglo-Saxon-Celtic cousins elsewhere in the Anglosphere. But who can blame them? No "British polity" is likely to endow New Zealand WASPs once again with the capacity to control their own past or future. Salvation if it is to come at all, will depend upon their ability to make common cause with other Anglo-Saxon tribes. It may yet be possible for WASPs everywhere to reconstitute a *vivere civile* within ethnic networks with global reach, operating outside and apart from the state, within the corporate institutions of a transnational civil society.

Republicanism as a Conditionally Operative Schema of Civic Action

Earlier we saw Pocock mourning the demise of British national sovereignty entailed by membership in the European Union. He believed that Europeanization would entail "the end of self-determination; and with this the end of the capacity to make history."[82] Pocock presumed, in effect, that only a British *polity* can make a "British history." He never considered whether an ethnically "British" *people* can create or sustain a civic identity apart from an identifiably British state. Like far too many of his fellow WASPs, Pocock tied civic identity to formal allegiance to some sovereign political authority.

---

82 Bourke, "Presuppositions of New British History," 752.

Over Pocock's lifetime, those descended from the founding stock of both the American republic and the British parliamentary monarchies possessed formal legal citizenship in ostensibly sovereign states. Meanwhile, they paid little attention and certainly offered little resistance to the transformation of their historic nations into multiracial mass societies. Fortunately for WASPs, however, civic identities are not in the exclusive gift of putatively sovereign political authorities. In any case, the formal legal membership in any sovereign political authority has lost much of its value to British-descended peoples. None of their shape-shifting sovereign states have repaid their loyal allegiance; no sovereign state, whether constitutional republic or constitutional monarchy, has honoured its promise of protection from alien invasion and ethnoreligious dispossession. Forms of government seem to have little bearing on the quality of civic life.

Certainly, there is no clear consensus on whether the American form of government is best described as a republic or as a democracy or even on whether that is a distinction without a difference. Whatever label was attached to the new American nation in its first few decades, all agreed that politics and government there bore little resemblance to the absolutist regimes found in eighteenth-century Europe. Indeed, most foreign observers described a peculiar illusion of statelessness in America.[83] American republicanism did not manifest itself as a distinctive form of the sovereign state. Instead, "republicanism" manifested itself as much in the realm of civil society as in the constitutional forms of sovereign authority.

Especially in the early republic, politics in America, presented the spectacle of a vast welter of competing individual and factional interests engaged in mutual backscratching, legislative log-rolling and pork-barrelling. Individuals preoccupied with the struggle for material advantage allowed their relation to the common good to become mediated through a class of professional politicians. The inevitable

---

83 Andrew Fraser, *The Spirit of the Laws: Republicanism and the Unfinished Project of Modernity* (Toronto: University of Toronto Press, 1990), 143–150.

result, in many minds, must be the corruption of the body politic. Even then, outside the circles of courthouse cronies and party insiders, most members of the supposedly sovereign people had no way to *be* republicans or to *act* as citizens.[84]

Instead, the stability and well-being of the polity soon depended upon the speculative pursuits of trade, credit, and commerce. Avowed republicans were beset by anxiety over this situation "but it was far from clear how the practice of virtuous and independent citizenship could be married to the institutional forms of a modern commercial society."[85] Even in seventeenth-century England, republicans feared that an unbridled commerce would release a speculative lust for private gain that would inevitably erode the material foundations of civic virtue in landed property. In post-revolutionary America, the appearance of those forms of mobile property associated with a developed market economy seemed even more likely to reduce all individuals, even those who owned landed property, to a condition of utter dependence on the vagaries of the marketplace.

Historians of Anglo-American republicanism typically doubt its capacity to resolve modern tensions between absolutism and liberty, virtue and commerce. They are convinced that the ineradicable "dread of modernity" allegedly characteristic of the republican mind left it unable to overcome the antinomic opposition between virtue and commerce. Thus, Pocock portrayed "the American Revolution less as the first act of revolutionary enlightenment than as the last great act of the Renaissance." In his view, the Country ideology was hamstrung by "a Renaissance pessimism concerning the direction and reversibility of social and historical change." Republicans generally assumed that the longevity of a balanced constitution turned on "the independence of its parts; should a change or disturbance bring one of these into dependence upon another, a degenerative trend would commence which

---

84 Hannah Arendt, *On Revolution* (Harmondsworth: Penguin, 1973), 253.
85 Fraser, *Spirit of the Laws*, 109.

would soon become almost impossible to remedy."[86] In other words, the Atlantic republican tradition was unambiguously aligned with the forces of reactionary anti-modernism.

According to this "republican synthesis" in American historiography, the interpretive schema associated with republican ideas was cast in essentially pre-modern terms.[87] Republicans could not easily come to grips with the decay of their civic ethos attendant upon the growth of a complex modern industrial society. And they were soon faced with the rapid growth of massive industries and concentrated, multi-ethnic, urban populations. No place had been provided for a vast, propertyless working class in the dominant republican vision of a fee-simple empire. Under such circumstances, the republican mind could only retreat further into its archaic "obsession with corruption and disorder, its hostile and conspiratorial outlook, and its millennial vision of a regenerated society."[88] Historians such as Pocock concluded that the backward-looking ideology of American republicanism was simply ill adapted to cope with, much less reverse, the tide of political and economic modernity.

But conspiratorial thinking was not confined to avowed republicans, then or now. Belief in plots reflected the belief, common to almost all enlightened thinkers of the period, in a pervasive duplicity assumed to exist in all human affairs. The political world "was expanding and changing faster than its natural modes of explanation could handle."[89]

---

86 J.G.A. Pocock, "Virtue and Commerce in the Eighteenth Century," (1972) 3(1) *Journal of Interdisciplinary History* 119, at 120–121.

87 Robert Shalhope, "Towards a Republican Synthesis: The Emergence of an Understanding of Republicanism in American Historiography," (1972) 29 *William and Mary Quarterly* (3d ser.) 49.

88 Gordon S. Wood, "Rhetoric and Reality in the American Revolution," (1966) 23 *William and Mary Quarterly* (3d ser.) 3, at 23; Pocock, *Machiavellian Moment*, 509.

89 Gordon S. Wood, "Conspiracy and the Paranoid Style: Causality and Deceit in the Eighteenth Century," (1982) 39 *William and Mary Quarterly* (3d ser.) 401, at 425–429.

In any case, any conceivable republican schema of civic action faced formidable obstacles. After all, the civic role of the people-at-large had been restricted to the exercise of an electoral franchise, itself largely confined, at first, to adult white male property-owners. Accordingly, if republicanism is to be identified either with a distinctive form of government or with some fixed or canonical form of political ideology, America always has been a republic in name only.

Accordingly, it is a mistake to blame the fall of the Constitutional Republic solely on the 2020 presidential election. The supposedly singular American republic has experienced more than one constitutional revolution, each of which produced "progressively" more radical forms of the republic. The original First (Federal) Republic, established in the name of constitutional *liberty*, was overthrown in 1865 with the defeat of the Southern Confederacy. It was replaced by a Second (Bourgeois) Republic, formally inaugurated in the name of *equality* by the ratification of the Fourteenth Amendment in 1868. Then, a Third (Managerial/Therapeutic) Republic was inaugurated by the New Deal during the critical years during the Great Depression. Because of that revolutionary upheaval, constitutional guarantees of legal equality were transcended by the infinitely manipulable ideal of *fraternity*.[90]

During the 1930s, the New Deal laid the foundation of the fraternal ideal by, *inter alia*, encouraging labour solidarity through trade unions and, later, by waging war against fascism in alliance with the Soviet Union. Subsequently, the rapidly expanding corporate welfare state in America sought to consolidate popular support and boost its geopolitical legitimacy through the perpetual civil rights revolutions of the post-war era. Before long, however, the anodyne ideals of inter-racial harmony gave way to public policies promoting racial solidarity among minority groups. Curiously, the ideal of fraternity was deployed by the managerial revolutions in both corporate America and the communist

---

90 Fraser, *The WASP Question*, 280–326.

Soviet Union. In both countries, appeals to fraternity turned out to be radically unstable and contradictory. In neither case, could the administrative state contain the resultant social tensions and political pressures. Eventually both managerialist systems succumbed to constitutional crisis.

In recognition of its globalist provenance and cosmopolitan character, the current oligarchical regime in the United States (foreshadowed by Obama's Presidency and rudely interrupted by the Trump Interregnum) can be described as a Fourth (Transnational) Republic. Thus far, its guiding principle seems to be a neo-Manichean *antiwhiteness*. Patriotic white Americans have become a collective Public Enemy Number One. The gathering momentum of this anti-white mood among political and corporate elites has led Gregory Hood to conclude that "We European-Americans are *a stateless people*. We have citizenship, but no country." Hood renounces all loyalty he may once have felt towards the American Regime which he refuses to dignify by calling it a republic. The people (whom he has described, variously, as the "historic American nation," as "whites," "European-Americans," or even "Amerikaners") would, he believes, "be better off without it."[91] Dissident right intellectuals and activists have come to similar conclusions in the various once-British parliamentary monarchies. WASPs, everywhere it seems, have become a stateless people. What is to be done?

Above all, we must not follow in Pocock's footsteps by conceiving republicanism either as an archaic and superseded *form of government* or else as a failed pre-modern *ideology*. The republican ideal of the *vivere civile* is not irrelevant to the historical destiny of the British-descended peoples. Self-described republics and republican ideologies are many and various, whether in ancient Athens, early modern Italy, the English Commonwealth tradition, or the American republic. The historical meaning of republicanism cannot be identified solely with

---

91 Gregory Hood, "An Open Letter to Trump Supporters," January 20, 2021:https://www.amren.com/features/2021/01/an-open-letter-to-trump-supporters.

the constitutional forms it inspired, or even with the various ideological expressions of its civic ideals. Rather, its importance for us lies in the activist impulse it releases into a body politic.

Even though it never became an accomplished, distinctive, and stable form of government in post-revolutionary America, the republic has been a feature of the actually existing realities of American political life for over two centuries now. It exists, in other words, as a special language of political action. As such, it communicates a knowledge of the existing world and of the conditional realm of action which might make possible its transcendence. Republican discourse recasts "the real relations between fundamental principle and factual appearance" into "hypothetical conditions of action" open to free citizens possessed of the majestic attributes of political power.[92]

David Hume (1711–1776) recognized long ago that there is no simple equation between constitutional forms and the realized substance of the civic ideal of personal and political liberty. He insisted that the modern absolutist monarchies of continental Europe were more receptive to those civic ideals than the ancient republics. The realization of those civic ideals need not rest, therefore, upon their genesis in a sovereign *res publica* set over and above society at large. Hume was clearly numbered among those who believed that the telic, developmental demands of modern politics required the corruption of the classical ideal of a mixed and balanced government. A modern *re-publica Anglorum*, he believed, required a sovereign authority capable of acting as an enlightened despotism with its attendant vacillation between the poles of absolutism and constitutional liberty. In effect, he sought to transplant republican principles of liberty into other forms of government.[93]

---

[92] Fraser, *Spirit of the Laws*, 111; cf., Leonard Krieger, *An Essay on the Theory of Enlightened Despotism* (Chicago: University of Chicago Press, 1975), 83–85.

[93] Fraser, *Spirit of the Laws*, 112–116; David Hume, *Political Essays* Charles W. Hendel, ed. (New York, 1953), 68–71, 49.

Hume knew that the idea of a perfect commonwealth he was sketching might not be realized as an accomplished fact nor as a utopian ideal transcending the existing political realities. WASPs, too, can adumbrate an idea of a perfect commonwealth for our time by transplanting republican ideals of civic freedom from the formal constitutional structures of the state into the institutional life of a transnational civil society. While a WASP idea of the perfect commonwealth might not be an immediate possibility, it could still be said to represent "the rational structure of actual political reality". That being so, any modern idea of the perfect commonwealth must be presented as a model or idea towards which intellectuals and activists might seek to bring the institutional life of modern civil society as near as possible. Like Hume's enlightened despotism, a modern WASP reading of the classical republican tradition would identify conditional possibilities occupying "the intermediate status of a unifying reality inseparable from the facts of political life but yet existent on a different plane, operative at once behind and through them."[94]

WASPs must employ that conditional mode in thinking about republicanism. They should describe "political reality in words that [have] been devised to transmit knowledge of the existing world but that [are] now applied to convey the possibilities in this world for action to change it."[95] WASPs today need a novel form of republicanism. They must conceive conditionally operative schemas of civic action adapted to the needs of British-descended peoples in the age of identity politics. They might begin by turning their attention away from the secular history of sovereign state.

Imagining an *Angelcynn* Reformation

Having become stateless, Gregory Hood's cryptonomous and orphaned people are not utterly bereft of institutional surrogates for

---

94 Krieger, *Enlightened Despotism*, 84.
95 Ibid., 89.

their collective identity. In principle, at least, they could rediscover and nurture the ethnoreligious soul of their nation within the ancestral church of the Anglo-Saxons. This will be no easy task, however. The Church of England could, but usually does not, trace its roots back to the *Angelcynn* (Old English for "kin of the Angles") church of Alfred the Great (844–899).[96] Most histories of the Church of England ascribe its origins to the sixteenth-century English Reformation. Today, both throne and altar are politically controlled by the multiracialist government of the United Kingdom. Prudence and demographics alike demand that the Church not display, much less celebrate its Old English roots. Indeed, Archbishop Justin Welby regularly confesses to the shameful history and "deeply institutionally racist" character of the Church he heads.[97]

Things are not much better in the Anglican churches of Australia, Canada, and New Zealand. The Synod of the Sydney Diocese of the Anglican Church of Australia, for example, has just elected as Archbishop, the Dean of Sydney, the Very Reverend Kanishka Raffel. A Sri Lankan, born in London, the Archbishop-elect is a convert from Buddhism.[98] He personally reflects and applauds the fact that "[g]lobally, Anglican Christianity is ethnically diverse and our multiculturalism in Sydney mirrors that". Naturally enough, he is pleased as well that "Our team of Bishops is almost equal part Asian-background and Anglo. That is contemporary Australia."[99] Clearly, Reverend Raffel has only the most tenuous personal or ethnoreligious connection to the *Angelcynn* origins of the Anglican confession. In fact, even white Anglo-Saxon Anglicans in Australia deliberately severed their constitutional ties to the Church of England more than sixty years ago.

---

96 See chapter 7.
97 Giles Udy, "How Critical Race Theory Captured the Church," April 21, 2021: https://unherd.com/2021/04/how-critical-race-theory-captured-the-church/.
98 This is not a surprise. See chapter 13.
99 Russell Powell, "Like every Christian, I gladly trust in Jesus,": http://sydneyanglicans.org/news/like-every-christian-i-gladly-trust-in-jesus/51245.

Queen Elizabeth, Supreme Governor of the Church of England, played no role in Reverend Raffel's ascension to archepiscopal rank.

In my own experience as a parishioner in several churches within the Sydney Diocese, I learned that a monumental struggle will be required to persuade even other WASPs that they should reconnect with their ancestral roots in the *Angelcynn* church, established in England well before the Norman Conquest. The large cathedral church in which I was baptized, for example, has four congregations, divided into language groups. Services are held in English, Cantonese, Mandarin, and Persian (Farsi). The latter three congregations are ethnically homogeneous, while the English-language congregation is an anomic and atomized ethnic hodgepodge. The institutionally entrenched and competing material, spiritual, and ethnic interests at stake in any conflict over the ethnoreligious identity of Anglican churches at the parish and national level present enormous obstacles to change.

Even so, "objective conditions" (as Marxists used to say) are ripe for the creation of a federal ecclesiastical republic uniting British-descended peoples around the world in spiritual communion. Such a network of civil bodies ecclesiastic and politic requires the incorporation of associations of persons to promote novel forms of civic action that will be (spiritually, morally, politically, and perhaps even economically) good for WASPs. If successful, such a program will amount to a postmodern *Angelcynn* reformation. Fierce resistance can be expected from the various Anglican establishments in the old white Commonwealth. In the United States, *Angelcynn* reformers will be greeted with complacently arrogant disbelief by an Episcopalian establishment that has long since renounced even its remotely Anglican identity.

For as long as anyone can remember, leaders of the "global Anglican communion" have been desperate to escape their "Anglo-Saxon captivity."[100] The result in Anglican churches everywhere has

---

100 Kevin Ward, *A History of Global Anglicanism* (Cambridge: Cambridge University Press, 2006), 296–318.

been theological timidity and ever-deepening spiritual anomie. The Anglican church must be reformed, root and branch; how else can a widely scattered and demoralized people who know not their own name reconstitute their historic ethnonation? Patriotic WASPs now face implacable opposition, not just from disloyal leaders of their own race (in both church and state), but from a host of other rival groups outfitted by a hostile globalist regime with legitimate (racial/ethnic/gender *etc.*) identities and organizational resources. As a consequence, even Anglo-Americans, too, have been Ulsterized. We are all Anglo-New Zealanders now! WASPs of the world, unite! You have nothing to lose but your ethnomasochism!

Towards a Church with the Soul of an Ethnonation

Anglo-Americans have been reduced to existence as an ethnonation "in itself," bereft of the life-giving spirit belonging to an ethnonation "for itself." For far too long they projected their collective identity onto the Constitutional Republic. With the transformation of the American republic into a globalist plutocracy, American WASPs lost their institutional surrogate and with it their standing as the "historic American nation." Their co-ethnics in the rest of the Anglosphere have been dispossessed in much the same way. If each of the various Anglo-Saxon peoples is to become an ethnonation "for itself," each will have to create novel institutional forms capable of nurturing and preserving their distinctive biocultures.

Over the past few centuries, the several WASP ethnonations have accumulated massive stocks of biocultural capital. Much of that social capital lies dormant simply because WASPs everywhere now lack the collective imagination, capacity, and will, effectively to unlock and deploy the ethnoreligious resources built into their biocultures. Heightened awareness among WASPs of their shared ethnic interests would produce a massive spike in the value of that social capital.

Happily, geopolitical developments in the American republic and the British parliamentary monarchies are creating the conditions for just such a boost to ethnic consciousness among WASPs around the world.

One particularly interesting emanation of implicit WASP identity (as yet visible only in elite circles) comes via the post-Brexit discussions in Canada, Australia, New Zealand, and the United Kingdom aimed at an alliance, enabling, *inter alia*, the free movement of citizens between the four British dominions.[101] As one might expect, the present proponents of this arrangement — known by the unlovely name of CANZUK — are promoting a neo-liberal free-trade agenda. Significantly, however, many of those involved feel compelled to deny that the project is motivated by covert imperial nostalgia. But, despite such denials, the scheme instinctively appeals to most WASPs. Should CANZUK become a reality, bred-in-the-bone Anglos in those four countries will be best-placed personally to pursue enhanced opportunities in a new-modelled, transnational civil society. Should CANZUK succeed, citizens of the four dominions will enjoy, jointly and severally, significantly greater geopolitical clout; a circumstance that will lead, no doubt, to accusations of WASP privilege.

Another geopolitical factor should be borne in mind. Should the accelerating collapse of the Constitutional Republic in America lead to the complete or partial disintegration of the American Union, a successful CANZUK alliance will provide an attractive bolt-hole to those American states or regions with significant WASP or WASP-adjacent populations.

Given the ever-increasing salience of identity politics, a WASPish alliance of the CANZUK countries, with or without Anglo-American participation, would represent a new departure in British history. Modern Anglo-Saxon tribes remain in embryo, but, whether they realize it or not, their shared British ancestry endows them with a biocultural aptitude in the planning and execution of conditionally

---

101 https://www.canzukinternational.com.

operative schemas of civic action. In the medium- to long-term, the transnational civil society of the Anglosphere can become the medium through which a rejuvenated, culturally British, *vivere civile* comes to life.

A confident, self-respecting, and healthy British bioculture is a form of social capital that actively generates moral and spiritual goods. That spiritual wealth can be good, not just for WASPs, but for their ethnic rivals as well. A WASP bioculture provides the best possible material foundation for the exercise of the civic virtues in a transnational mass society. Consider the historically given alternatives: slavery in Athens, arms in Florence, and heritable landed property in England and America. In the competitive game of identity politics, WASPs working together in teams and tribes will acquire a trustworthy reputation for honourable behaviour and a virtuous commitment to the common good. (Here, too, consider the alternatives: has the Jewish Century benefited the WASPs — or any other racial/ethnic group?)[102] Given time and the appropriate ethnoreligious matrix, a reformed Angelcynn church together with allied institutions, including schools, colleges, and hospitals, will produce white Anglo-Saxon Protestant elites ready, willing, and able to displace the corrupt globalist plutocracy currently misgoverning the Anglosphere. Any such peaceful revolution requires the regeneration of a responsible WASP ruling-class-in-waiting eager to assume civic responsibility for the good governance of the Anglosphere.[103]

A reformed Angelcynn Church must play a vital role in preparing WASPs to work together in the planning and execution of that

---

102 Yuri Slezkine, *The Jewish Century* (Princeton: Princeton University Press, 2004); *cf.*, Kevin Macdonald, *The Culture of Critique: An Evolutionary Analysis of Jewish Involvement in Twentieth-Century Intellectual and Political Movements* (Westport, CN: Praeger, 1998); and *idem.*, *Individualism and the Western Liberal Tradition: Evolutionary Origins, History, and Prospects for the Future* (Kindle Direct Publishing, 2019), esp. chapter 8.

103 Fraser, *The WASP Question*, 373–402.

revolutionary project. No such spiritual and ecclesiastical reformation can occur overnight, as if by magic. It will emerge, if at all, only because associations of virtuous WASPs create conditionally operative schemas of civic action designed to achieve that end. As it happens, nineteenth-century British history provides a useful model of just such a republican project of spiritual renewal within the established Churches of England and Scotland.

The Broad-Church movement in the United Kingdom offers both inspiration and cautionary lessons to a similar project in our time. The most prominent leaders of that movement regarded the Church of England as a church of, by, and for the English nation. They believed "that neither the high church nor the evangelical parties gave sufficient attention to the national aspects of religion". As mostly liberal Anglicans, they "sought to define a new Christian ideal with emphasis on the established church as the moral educator of the nation." By the 1850s, circumstances favoured the growth of this movement: increased prosperity and social stability caused many to turn away from earlier "pessimistic, atonement-based theologies of human depravity and eternal punishment." Large numbers of laymen were ready to embrace "instead the more inclusive, world-affirming, broad church teachings, with their emphasis on the moral example of Christ, the benevolence of God, and the potential for moral improvement in this world." The fundamental idea driving "the broad-church movement was a commitment to a comprehensive national Church, which would be as inclusive of different varieties of belief as possible."[104]

Combined with unwavering support for the establishment of the Church of England among broad-churchmen, their "optimistic, tolerant, humane, and world-affirming broad church theological positions" appealed to the "educated laity, many leading Liberal politicians, and

---

104 Stewart J. Brown, "The Broad Church Movement, National Culture, and the Established Churches of Great Britain, C.1850-C.1900," in Hilary M.Carey and John Gascoigne, eds., *Church and State in Old and New Worlds* (Brill's Series in Church History, Vol. 51), 99, at 102–103.

the queen." All those fed up with "clerical narrowness and excessive dogmatism...appreciated the efforts of broad-church clergy to bridge the gap between Christianity and educated middle-class opinion, and also to reach out to the labouring classes through social activism." It helped greatly, of course, that "broad-church Christianity was powerful in the political and social establishment, not least at Court."[105] Queen Victoria lent highly visible public and personal support to the movement.

Broad church thinkers took the view "that the purpose of the national Church was the spiritual and moral cultivation of the nation, the preservation and interpretation of its history, and the defining of its highest aspirations...For them, Christianity was a social and historical religion, as well as a personal faith; it was about the redemption of nations as well as individuals."[106] The Cambridge historian, Sir John Robert Seeley (1834-1895), was a leading broad-churchman. He saw religion as "much less personal and much more national and political than was commonly supposed." Religions were essentially, he believed, "nationalities in an idealised form."[107]

Biblical theology should be based, therefore, on the premise that "the Hebrew Bible...owes its peculiar force to the fact that it embodies a treatment of national history more intense and more ideal than that which can be found in any other literature."[108] Another Cambridge professor, Frederick Denison Maurice (1805-1872) agreed, adding that church and nation were one in England, just "as had been the case with ancient Israel and Judea." Moreover, he insisted, "we have as much right to call England a holy nation as the prophets had to call Judaea a holy nation. I believe it is holy in virtue of God's calling."[109]

---

105 *Ibid.*, 109.

106 *Ibid.*, 112.

107 H.A.L. Fisher, quoted in *ibid.*, 112.

108 *Ibid.*, 113.

109 *Ibid.*, 115; see also, Jeremy Morris, *F.D. Maurice and the Crisis of Christian Authority* (Oxford: Oxford University Press, 2005).

Today, anyone who still believes in the civilizing mission of the Anglo-Saxon peoples or, more modestly, the spiritual regeneration of the vanishing race of WASPs, will find those homiletic themes more than congenial. Unfortunately, they also reveal a touching but untenable faith in the unity of state, church, and nation. In our time, British state and church join forces against the nation, invoking the name of the shapeshifting Crown to betray the very British peoples whose monarchs have sworn to protect and preserve. In such circumstances, one may applaud the broad-church movement's efforts to fuse the church with the nation. On the one hand, that program suggests solutions to many of our contemporary problems; the naïve belief that the sovereign state is a trustworthy surrogate for the nation, on the other hand, has turned out to be the biggest problem (or curse) confronting contemporary WASPs.

Whatever the limitations of the broad-church movement in its own time, we need a comparable ecclesiastical insurrection today. This time around, of course, any such movement will be opposed by both the political and ecclesiastical establishments, drawing support instead from a motley crew of ecclesiastical outsiders. It is important to remember, therefore, that the nineteenth-century movement encountered stiff resistance from all levels of the ecclesiastical hierarchy.[110] Broad-churchmen were supported by powerful figures among the laity but, as far as the Church itself was concerned, they stood on the outside looking in. Sticking to their guns, however, the movement did, in time, achieve a significant measure of ecclesiastical and social reform. Patriotic WASPs today owe it to their ancestors, their posterity, and themselves to match and better the broad-church record in the reform of their ancestral church. It is the task of the present and rising generations to infuse an ancient Christian church with the resurrection soul of the *Angelcynn* nation.

---

110 Brown, "Broad Church Movement," 100, 107.

Conclusion

A contemporary counterpart to the broad-church movement might be called the *Angelcynn* Network. It will differ significantly from its English and Scottish predecessors, first, in its design as a globe-girdling movement, requiring participation from would-be Angelcynns in all four CANZUK countries as well as from American WASPs. It will also draw upon a very different understanding of British history.

As we have seen, members of the broad-church movement took the spiritual unity of state, church and nation as a given. It seems strange, therefore, that Pocock believed that his conception of British history as the history of the British state had been pioneered by Seeley.[111] It is true, of course, that Seeley rejected the notion that history should "investigate all the causes of human well-being alike." Instead, Seeley considered "that history has to do with the State, that it investigates the growth and changes of a certain corporate society, which acts through certain functionaries and certain assemblies." History was interested in Englishmen as individuals only "in their capacity of members of a State...By England I mean solely the state or political community that has its seat in England."[112] But Seeley, unlike Pocock, situated the State within an implicitly ethnohistorical context uniting past, present, and future.

Today, no "true Englishman," one might say, could accept Pocock's narrowly political view of British history. No one now can simply assume, as Seeley did, that members of the English state are, and will continue to be overwhelmingly of English ancestry. He would almost certainly have recoiled in horror from a future in which state and church employ the sovereign authority of the Crown to Ulsterize the peoples of the countries he proudly called Greater Britain. Seeley viewed the British historian as a patriot not, as did Pocock, a professionalized

---

111 Bourke, "Presuppositions of New British History," 748, 751.

112 Sir John Robert Seeley, *The Expansion of England: Two Courses of Lectures* (New York: Cosmo Classics, 2005 [orig. pub. 1891]), 5, 7.

"political actor," tempted always to become a mere functionary of the state.[113]

Members of the *Angelcynn* Network will resent and resist efforts by shapeshifting sovereign states to assert their accustomed control over the past, even as they don the mask of the British Crown to betray their own historic nations. They will counter Pocock's spiritually disembodied political science of British history with an ethnohistory of what has been and could be once again, a holy nation. Having severed the history (as made *and* written) of the British state from any organic connection to church and nation, Pocock's "new British history" is withering away in a globalist cul-de-sac. By contrast, the *Angelcynn* Network will call upon a revitalized *Angelcynn* Church, not the state, to oversee the reconstruction of Anglo-Saxon ethnohistory.

A reborn British ethnohistory sponsored by the *Angelcynn* church will connect history and destiny to the here and now. In doing so, the church will fuse Christian moral teaching with a patriotic sense of civic responsibility to the British-descended peoples. Clergymen will heed Seeley's advice "to draw largely upon English history and biography for illustrations of their moral teaching. Carlyle has said that every nation's true Bible is its history." Just as the Hebrew history recounted in the Bible provides a cosmopolitan vision of Israel serving as a light unto the nations, every subsequent Christian nation deserves its own Bible as well. Seeley could imagine "no more proper and nobler task for a clergy than the perpetual shaping and elaborating of such a national monument."[114] For Seeley, history is not just a branch of the academic discipline of theology; it is the very root of religious experience and Anglo-Saxon identity.

A British historical theology, then, must be cognisant of specific problems faced by the British peoples in the church of our day, as well as in the past and the future. Those committed to the resurrection of

---

113 Pocock, "Historian as Political Actor," 97.

114 J.R. Seeley, "The Church as a Teacher of Morality," in Rev. W.L. Clay, ed., *Essays in Church Policy* (London: Macmillan, 1868), 278.

the Angelcynn Church will be confronted with "the vital task of rendering theological judgements on the life and practice of the church." They will need a practical rather than systematic theology to win over their WASP co-ethnics.

15. Monarchs and Miracles: Australia's Need for a Patriot King

Introduction

IN THE 1999 REFERENDUM on the republic, defenders of the monarchy failed to drive a stake through the heart of the Australian republican movement. The votes had hardly been counted before republicans were invoking their presumptively perennial right to demand a rematch at a time and on terms of their own choosing. If monarchists are ever to achieve a decisive victory, they must not rely upon republicans to shoot themselves in the foot, once again, with another deeply flawed model of the "politician's republic." Should republicans succeed in their campaign to abolish the constitutional monarchy, the repercussions will be felt far beyond Australia's shores. Indeed, the fate of what used to be called the British race may very well hang on the outcome of this constitutional battle: the abolition of the monarchy in Australia would weaken the institution elsewhere, further fracturing the already fragile sense of kinship between the peoples of Britain and the old settler dominions.

Of course, the recurrent splits in the republican camp may well doom them to yet another defeat. But if republicans believe that popular support for the monarchy is minimal, limited to a minority of spoilers, they will never rest content until they achieve their objective — and who could blame them? Unless and until the British monarchy, understood and accepted as such, captures the hearts and minds of the Australian people, it will be living on borrowed time. Our rulers no longer conceive Australia as a *country*, the homeland of a particular people sharing a language, a religion, and their own distinctive folkways. Instead, Australia has been reduced to an *economy*, open to the free flow of capital, technology, and labour in a global system of production, distribution, and exchange. Swamped by "the rising tide of color"[1] washing in from every overcrowded corner of the Third World, the old Australian dream of a new Britannia in the Southern Ocean is now little more than a faded memory. Only a miracle can save us now. Australia desperately needs a Patriot King to spark new life into the ancient British constitution, rekindling the ancestral spirit of Anglo-Saxon liberty in an ever more rootless, deracinated, and fragmented population.

As things stand now, the hard core of support for the monarchy is to be found in a parochial party of the past possessing few friends among opinion leaders in the state or the corporate sector, or the universities, or the media. Many ordinary Australians do still revere the monarchy as an essential feature of our constitutional heritage. Their loyalty to the Crown reflects the historical experience of a distinctive people rooted in a particular place, sharing a collective memory of their genesis in the epic history of the British Empire. Republicans often assert that they have a lock on the younger generation; still, not all Australian monarchists are only a few steps away from the grave. Generations of republican ideologues have themselves grown old satirizing the hidebound conservatism of Australian monarchists, forever ridiculing the British monarchy as an anachronistic and obsolescent relic of the colonial era. During the 1999 referendum campaign, members of the Australian Republican Movement (ARM) cast themselves as the progressive party of the future. But the future they proposed — a cosmopolitan, inclusive, multicultural regime open to the world with

---

1 See the prophetic book of the same title by Lothrop Stoddard, *The Rising Tide of Color* (New York: Charles Scribners' Sons, 1920).

a resident for president — ran head on into the "parochial" traditions of Anglo-Australian patriotism.²

Far from throwing in the towel, republican leaders will now pursue a more subtle strategy. Having foreshadowed one or more "indicative" plebiscites leading up to a second referendum campaign, their aim is to wear down the opposition, stripping the constitutional monarchy of its legitimacy before committing themselves to any particular model of the republic. This war of attrition will be supplied and directed from the commanding heights of political, corporate, and cultural power. Indeed, the final push for a republic might even produce an unprecedented revolution from the top down. Relying on the best kept, dirty little secret of Australian constitutional law, republicans could break a deadlock by proceeding under s15 of the Australia Act 1986 (UK), permitting a phalanx of Labor-controlled Commonwealth and state parliaments, acting jointly, to proclaim a new republican constitution (thereby bypassing the referendum procedure requiring a majority of the popular vote in a majority of the states).³

Republicans are already accustomed to rule from above, being massively overrepresented among the managerial and professional classes. Republicans attract significant support from non-European migrant communities, but their most important constituency is found in prosperous inner-city electorates within easy reach of an international airport. Priding themselves on their cosmopolitan sophistication, republicans are more likely than those who voted No in 1999 to deny that Australia is a much better country than most other countries. Similarly, republicans are less inclined to agree that they would rather be a citizen of Australia than of any other country.⁴

---

2   On the running battle since the 1960s between "cosmopolitans" and "pa- rochials," see Katharine Betts, *The Great Divide* (Sydney: Duffy & Snellgrove, 1999).

3   B. O'Brien, "The Australia Acts," in M. P. Ellinghaus, et al., *The Emergence of Australian Law* (Sydney: Butterworths, 1989).

4   Bob Birrell, *Federation: The Secret Story* (Sydney: Duffy & Snellgrove, 2001).

The typical, well-educated republican regards himself as a citizen of the world. Although republicans loudly proclaim their national pride, in the end their loyalty is to a state, or more accurately, the transnational state system, not to a particular people. When republicans refer to the sovereign people, they do not mean a pre-political community defined by historic ties of language, religion, and blood, but rather the random collection of individuals who find themselves resident, for the time being, in Australia.

Republicans believe that time is on their side, that the republic is inevitable. They hope that the parochial party of the past will simply fade away, overwhelmed and demoralized by the relentless onrush of replacement migration from the Third World. Should patriotic sentiment continue its steady decline in Australia, as it has elsewhere in the West, they may turn out to be right.

Anglo-Australian Patriotism and the Future of the Anglosphere

Patriotism is a tie that binds members of a particular community together through time. It is a sentiment that acknowledges the obligation on those of us now living to respect the interests of both the dead and the unborn. "In the Greek the word *patriotism* goes back to love of one's fathers," according to Robert Nisbet, "and to this day is quite evidently strongest where a political nation is overwhelmingly composed of citizens who can be thought to be of common ethnic descent."[5] Patriotism presupposes a durable community of memory and for that reason a hereditary monarchy provides a natural focus for patriotic sentiment. But no successful patriotism can be anchored solely in the past. Patriotism must also generate the energy and commitment to carry a people forward into the future. Patriotic triumphs are never inevitable — they are the fruit of will, courage, and determination.

---

5   Robert Nisbet, *Twilight of Authority* (New York: Oxford University Press, 1975): 65.

If it occurs, the advent of an Australian republic will replace the traditionalist patriotism spontaneously generated within a free society with a narcissistic transnationalism manufactured by the interlocking ideological media of state and corporate power. Cosmopolitan elites with no loyalty to the constitutional monarchy already manage almost every aspect of organized social life. Even the private realm has been invaded by highly refined techniques of media manipulation, therapeutic intervention, and disciplinary normalization. Accustomed to being in the driver's seat, members of the managerial overclass remain confident that, sooner or later, they will re-educate the hybrid population of a rootless mass society to accept one of their own as head of their own self-legitimating state.

Make no mistake about it. The republic is a constitutional device to expand managerial control over everyone within the territorial jurisdiction of the Commonwealth government. By getting rid of a British monarch and removing the Union Jack from the flag, republicans aim to detach the federal constitution from its original, or core, ethnocultural identity. Once the supranational authority of the British Crown has been nationalized, citizenship will become the exclusive property of the Commonwealth government. At that point, the corporate welfare state will be free to reconstitute the original Anglo-Australian nation in its own disembodied image. The ideological mullahs of the managerial regime aim to purge the Australian people of their historic Anglo-Celtic, or British, identity.[6]

Australian elites were once ashamed of their convict origins. Nowadays the great and the good are embarrassed by any mention of their "English" King in the presence of visiting foreign potentates. In fact, of course, the Australian nation-state was created by a proudly

---

6   On the managerial revolution generally, see James Burnham, *The Managerial Revolution: What Is Happening in the World* (New York: John Day Company, 1941); also, Paul Edward Gottfried, *After Liberalism: Mass Democracy in the Managerial State* (Princeton, NJ: Princeton University Press, 1999); and Samuel Francis, "Power Trip," *The Occidental Quarterly* 3(2) (Summer 2003): 69–78.

British people for whom it was a matter of historical record that the English Crown — in and out of Parliament — was the original source for the fountain of law and justice. They understood that the term "British" is not simply an ethnic category; its widespread modern usage grew out of a major constitutional achievement, the rise of the United Kingdom of Great Britain and Ireland. Ironically, historians tell us that British patriotism flowered within the neo-classical traditions of eighteenth-century Anglo-American or Atlantic civic republicanism.[7]

Even though the English, the Welsh, the Scots, and the Irish were separate and distinct, albeit closely related ethnic groups, they had all taken on a common, or British, civic identity by the end of the eighteenth century. In the settler colonies ethnic differences were even more readily submerged in a shared civic identity so that colonial Americans and, later, Australians, Canadians, and New Zealanders became more British than the British.[8] Throughout the Empire, increasing numbers of French-Canadians, Jews, Afrikaners, Germans, and Indians, to name but a few, were steadily incorporated into a global community of British subjects owing allegiance to the Crown.

Nevertheless, it must be acknowledged that "Britishness," understood as a civic identity, could never have arisen, nor could it survive, apart from the core ethnocultural identity provided by the English people. Indeed, the greater the genetic distance between any given ethny and the English people, the more likely they are to resent and resist their full assimilation into a British society.[9] Throughout the

---

7 J. G. A. Pocock, *The Machiavellian Moment: Florentine Political Thought and the Atlantic Republican Tradition* (Princeton, NJ: Princeton University Press, 1975); Andrew Fraser, *The Spirit of the Laws: Republicanism and the Unfinished Project of Modernity* (Toronto: University of Toronto Press, 1990).

8 Donald Harman Akenson, "The Historiography of English-Speaking Canada and the Concept of Diaspora: A Skeptical Appreciation," *Canadian Historical Review* 76 (1995): 377.

9 On computing "genetic distance" between different races and ethnic groups, see Frank Salter, *On Genetic Interests: Family, Ethny and Humanity in an Age of Mass Migration* (Frankfurt am Main: Peter Lang, 2004).

old white Commonwealth, even ethnies phenotypically similar to the English, such as the Irish, the Quebecois, and Jews (whether Orthodox separatists or secular humanist advocates of mass immigration and multiculturalism) have worked, each in their own way, to sever the civic significance of British identity from its ethnic roots.

Today, Australia's still predominantly Anglo-Celtic political class also rejects as "racist" any suggestion that the nation possesses a core, specifically British, ethnocultural identity. Contemporary Australian citizenship is grounded, not in ethnicity, but in bureaucratic paperwork. Our rulers are dissolving the old Anglo-Australian nation to put a newly disaggregated, polyethnic, and multiracial people in its place.

The Australian nation-state will cease to exist if republicans have their way. It will become a state without a nation. Patriotism will be displaced by new forms of statist idolatry. "Constitutional patriotism," as the new state religion is called, disapproves of the love of fathers. Instead, we are to transfer our loyalty to an impersonal state liberated from the bonds of history and law. Lest the managerial regime be confined within the old superstitious rituals of "ancestor worship" associated with the common law jurisprudence of liberty, progressive judges have already transformed the meaning of constitutionalism itself. The constitution is no longer a set of fixed rules and principles intended to *limit* the potentially despotic reach of governments. On the contrary, in well-managed, modern republics, constitutions are heavily watered "living trees."[10] Open to perpetual innovation from the top down, their function is to *enhance* the power of the state. Tradition, authority, and the common law spirit of liberty: All will be sacrificed on the multiculturalist altar of equality.[11]

---

10 The Hon. Justice Michael Kirby AC CMG, "Constitutional Interpretation and Original Intent: A Form of Ancestor Worship," *Melbourne University Law Review* 24 (2002): 1.

11 Andrew Fraser, "A Marx for the Managerial Revolution: Habermas on Law and Democracy," *Journal of Law and Society* 28 (2001): 361.

Patriotic resistance could still derail the "inevitable" victory of the managerial republic. However, such a struggle must be waged in the name of the Australian nation, understood as part of a particular ethny. "An ethny," according to Frank Salter, "is analogous to a population of cousins." Anglo-Australians share myths of common ancestry, historical memories, and many elements of a common culture with their ethnocultural "cousins" in the various polities created out of the historic British diaspora emanating from the ancestral homeland in Britain.[12] That Australians can never be an island unto themselves is something that was well understood by our forefathers. They valued their special relationship with other British-derived nations, especially but not exclusively those which still owe allegiance to the King, such as Canada, New Zealand, and the UK itself.

Together with the USA, those nations inhabit a common English-speaking world, the Anglosphere, with its own distinctive language, history, and civic culture.[13] Strong traditions of English individualism dating back to the Middle Ages, if not to prehistoric times, lent dynamism to the British diaspora and provided the cultural basis for the most successful liberal democracies and free market economies.[14] In the future, as in the past, the fate of the Australian nation, no less than that of the British monarchy, will depend upon the capacity of the English-speaking peoples to preserve the vitality while enhancing the strength of their common civilization.

For tactical political reasons, even the organization that led the No campaign in the 1999 referendum, Australians for Constitutional Monarchy (ACM), was loath to acknowledge openly the British

---

12 Salter, 47, 30.

13 Robert Conquest, "Bonds and Bureaucratism," *American Outlook* (Spring 2001); http://americanoutlook.org/index.cfm?fuseaction=article_ detail&id=1130.

14 Alan Macfarlane, *The Origins of English Individualism: The Family, Property and the Social Transition* (Oxford: Basil Blackwell, 1978); Kevin MacDonald, "What Makes Western Culture Unique?" *The Occidental Quarterly* 2(2) (2002); http://theoccidentalquarterly.com/vol2no2/km-unique.html.

character of the Crown. Australian patriots may love the forefathers who framed the Australian Constitution, but they often forget their kinship with the Anglo-Canadians who campaigned for the *British North America Act* of 1867. Even the rebellious Anglo-American colonists who produced a rough facsimile of the eighteenth-century English constitution at the Philadelphia convention of 1787 have slipped from their rightful place in the pantheon of British liberty. Tracing our constitutional ancestry still further back, to the Anglo-Saxon patriots who resisted the imposition of the Norman yoke, is no longer done in polite society, much less the classroom.

By inducing the constitutional amnesia causing us to forget who we are and where we came from, governments in every British dominion, including Britain itself, have effectively corrupted "their" respective peoples. Having transformed British subjects throughout the Commonwealth into Australian, Canadian, New Zealand, and British (now on the road to becoming European) citizens, the managerial state now asserts its own control over questions of national identity.

We have forgotten what it means to be freeborn British subjects. At the same time, Australian citizenship amounts to little more than a legal formality. Citizens may be entitled to an Australian passport or compelled to vote and serve on juries. But we can no longer take it for granted that voters or potential jurors speak the same language. Citizenship is now a vertical relationship between individuals and the state; it does not imply membership in a community of memory. By contrast, old-fashioned British patriotism gathered the far-flung subjects of the Crown together in a common world that would outlive them all. That was then. For decades now, Australian governments have been busy hollowing out the social and cultural significance of the same statutory citizenship they were so eager to substitute for our common law status as British subjects.

All our connections to the ancient British constitution have been severed, save one. That one is the hereditary monarchy. The authority vested in the monarchy has waned, at times precipitously. But the King still serves as the only available polestar of constitutional legitimacy for subjects cut adrift from a durable past by creeping republican governments brazenly acting in the name of the Crown. Could it be that only a Patriot King can now save a people that have grown terminally corrupt?

The Idea of a Patriot King in an Age of Mass Migration

Only the hereditary monarchy can call both despotic governments and corrupted peoples back to the original principles of liberty owing their genesis to the ancient British constitution. At any rate, that is what the eighteenth-century opposition leader Viscount Bolingbroke tells us. Fearful that the rise of a vast, impersonal system of finance capital would transform government into a sort of self-imposed Norman yoke, Bolingbroke wondered "whether, when the people are grown corrupt, a free government could be maintained, if they enjoy it; or established, if they enjoy it not?"[15] Certainly an elective monarch (whether called a president, a governor-general, or a king) was ill-equipped and unlikely to save a corrupt people from themselves.

Bolingbroke was convinced that such a people might indeed be saved but only "by means of a very different kind." That manner of salvation will not be open to us, Bolingbroke suggests, "without the concurrence and the influence of a Patriot King, the most uncommon of all phenomena in the physical or moral world." For Bolingbroke, it was axiomatic that "[p]atriotism must be founded in great principles and supported by great virtues."[16] Therefore, if the people have fallen away from the spirit of liberty once associated with the ancient British

---

15 Viscount Bolingbroke, "The Idea of a Patriot King," [originally published in 1749] in David Armitage ed., *Political Writings* (Cambridge: Cambridge University Press, 1997), 249.

16 Ibid., 221, 234.

constitution, it is the patriotic duty of their king to call them back to the first principles of free government.

Conventional wisdom has it that the monarch has no role to play in any decision to expunge the Crown from the Commonwealth Constitution. Queen Elizabeth herself said it was a matter for the Australian people and that she would accept whatever decision they made. In that respect, Her Majesty *behaved* in the regular and thoroughly predictable manner expected of her. But no one should doubt that the monarch possesses a prerogative power to *act*, spontaneously and unpredictably, in defence of the constitution. Australia's then governor-general, Sir John Kerr, made that clear on November 11, 1975. Ignoring the convention that the governor-general can act only on the advice of his ministers, Kerr invoked the reserve powers of the Crown to dismiss the Whitlam Labor government.[17] The Labor ministry still commanded a majority in the House of Representatives; nevertheless, it immediately surrendered office to a caretaker government under Liberal Prime Minister Malcolm Fraser. Gough Whitlam's diehard supporters remained in a state of denial for many years afterward, but at the time of his dismissal the Labor leader himself never dared to call into question the authority behind the viceregal decision.[18]

The constitutional efficacy of Kerr's action illustrates the truth of Carl Schmitt's dictum that the "exception in jurisprudence is analogous to the miracle in theology."[19] Rooted in the faculty of freedom, political action always interrupts automatic and petrified processes; it represents a new beginning, breaking into the world as an "infinite improbability." For that reason, Hannah Arendt maintained that "it is not in the least superstitious, it is even a counsel of realism, to look

---

17 Sir John Kerr, *Matters for Judgement* (Melbourne: Macmillan, 1978).
18 See, especially, H. O. Browning, *1975: Crisis* (Sydney: Hale and Ironmonger, 1985).
19 Carl Schmitt, *Political Theology: Four Chapters on the Concept of Sovereignty* (Cambridge, MA: MIT Press, 1985), 36.

for the unforeseeable and the unpredictable, to be prepared for and to expect 'miracles' in the political realm."[20]

It is therefore worth asking whether the reign of a Patriot King in Australia (and the other residually British dominions) could "effectively restore the virtue and public spirit essential to the preservation of liberty and national prosperity."[21] Could the hereditary monarchy, once again, become the hinge upon which the whole constitution moves?

In his day, Bolingbroke knew, such a suggestion would "pass among some for the reveries of a distempered brain."[22] Today, the ability of the monarch to act independently is even more hemmed in by rigid laws and conventions. But both reason and experience confirm that neither a king nor his subjects can be transformed forever into automatons. Certainly, as Bolingbroke knew, the ancient British constitution has always stood upon a dual foundation: the common law gave expression to both the inchoate needs of a self-governing society and the sovereign will of an emergent state.

Without question, the legal forms and political conventions of parliamentary sovereignty are an essential feature of our constitutional order. But the constitution dwells, as well, in the spirit and character of the people. Bolingbroke warned that the preservation of liberty depended upon "the mutual conformity and harmony" of those two elements.[23] Once the spirit of the people is broken or corrupted, the fundamental order of the constitution must be altered, if not destroyed.

Our cosmopolitan elites believe that decades of mass immigration have transformed the character of the Australian nation. Certainly, republican manifestoes regularly assert as established fact the conclusory claim that "We are no longer a British people." True, they do not put

---

20 Hannah Arendt, *Between Past and Future: Six Exercises in Political Thought* (New York: Meridian, 1961), 168-70.

21 Bolingbroke, 222.

22 Ibid., 240.

23 Ibid., 247-48.

the change down to immigration alone. For decades, they complained that the United Kingdom abandoned the dominions to enter Europe. Interestingly, John Hirst attributed some of the blame for that betrayal to the Queen, who went "to Strasbourg to give her sanction to British membership of the European Community." In so doing, Hirst charged, she became "one of the enemies of rural Australia."[24]

Hirst's argument implied, of course, that the Queen owed a duty of protection to all her subjects wherever they may be. Bolingbroke agreed, declaring that when a people establish a free constitution, their kings come "under the most sacred obligations that human law can create, and divine law authorize, to defend and maintain the freedom of such constitutions."[25] The Crown has always been under a positive duty to protect the spirit of British liberty. That obligation became especially compelling once universal suffrage permitted every elected government to identify its own absolutist pretensions with the will of the people. Today, the allegedly enlightened despotism holding sway over the British peoples threatens their very survival. In the name of universal human rights, our historic claim to secure possession of an ethnic homeland has been cast into doubt, both "at home" and in the old white settler dominions.

In Australia, Canada, and New Zealand, and even in the United Kingdom, not to mention the United States, the ultimate genetic interests of the Anglo-Saxon ethny are at risk. Ethnies, like individuals and families, have an interest in securing "the indefinite survival of their own distinctive genes and their copies, whether these be resident in the individual, its descendants, or its collateral relatives."[26] Governments opening their borders to Third World immigration and enforcing policies of official multiculturalism have seriously compromised the genetic interests of the Australian ethny. The Anglo-Australian people

---

24 John Hirst, *A Republican Manifesto* (Melbourne: Oxford University Press, 1994), 4–5.

25 Bolingbroke, 244.

26 Richard Alexander, quoted in Salter, 26.

constitute a large, partly inbred, extended family, within which even distant kin "carry genetic interests for each other." But, because—at any given level of technology—the Australian landmass has a finite carrying capacity, mass immigration must replace Australian children with those of other, unrelated, ethnic extended families. If immigrant groups are genetically distant from the Australian ethny, the damage to its genetic interests will be especially pronounced. If England, for example, received 12.5 million closely related Danish immigrants, Frank Salter has calculated that the genetic loss to the remaining English would be relatively low, amounting to the equivalent of 209,000 children. But the same number of immigrants from India would cause a corresponding loss of 2.6 million children. Bantus are even more genetically remote from the English. An influx of 12.5 million Bantus would displace the equivalent of 13 million English children. If Indians or Bantus displayed higher fertility rates than the host population, the genetic losses incurred by the English would be higher still.[27]

The abolition of the White Australia policy has had similar consequences. Anglo-Australians have been stripped of the ethnic monopoly over their antipodean homeland that the federation of the colonies in 1901 was designed to secure. The resultant damage to their genetic interests can also be understood as an attack on the foundation of their constitutional freedom. The word "freedom" is derived from an Indo-European root meaning "dear" or "beloved."[28] In its primordial sense, then, freedom is the right to belong to a community of dearly beloved people, the family being the first and most important model for every such form of association. (Significantly, slaves were denied the right to marry or to raise a family within the walls of their own household.) Every ethny is an extended family with a genetic interest in its own survival and enhanced vitality. Just as parents have a duty

---

27 Ibid., 42, 59–75.
28 See, e.g., the entry for "free" in the *Shorter Oxford English Dictionary*.

to care for their children, it might be said that every free person has a moral obligation to defend his own ethny.[29]

Unfortunately, over the past half-century, governments throughout the Anglosphere have encouraged us to ignore the genetic interests of our ethnic kin through systematic campaigns of indoctrination and legal coercion. Such policies not only subvert the genetic continuity of the Australian ethny; they also deprive us of the right to belong to a community of free people inhabiting its own homeland. But perhaps we are our own worst enemies. To the extent that the Australian people have been willing to squander the genetic interests of their own ethny by directing scarce territorial, cultural, and economic resources to non-kin, they have been corrupted in a manner and to a degree hardly imaginable to Bolingbroke and his eighteenth-century contemporaries. Whether committed by a single individual or an entire race, suicide is a sin.

The problem Bolingbroke identified so long ago has finally come to a head: What can, or should the reigning monarch do to restore the lost freedoms once enshrined in the ancient British constitution? Governments pursuing policies of forced integration in the name of an unachievable ideal of equality have trampled upon the freedom of association as well as the rights of free expression and private property. Having been denied or downplayed for the last three centuries now, the crisis of the ancient constitution has deepened to the point where the very existence of the British people, at home and in the overseas dominions, is now up for grabs. Consequently, a Patriot King worthy of the name would recognize a moral obligation to defend to the death the genetic interests of his own ethny.

It was once taken for granted that the King would defend his realm personally, by force of arms if need be. But George II was the last British monarch to lead his armies into battle. Nowadays, the greatest threat to the survival interests of the British peoples comes, not from

---

29 Salter, 283–320.

without, but from our "own" governing classes. To save his people today, a Patriot King need not take up arms; he could rely instead upon the power of reasoned speech to rouse his people to the dangers of demographic decline and territorial displacement. A modern patriot prince would defend the genetic kinship between hereditary kings and their historic peoples against managerialist regimes bent on extinguishing the ancestral spirit of the ancient British constitution, not just in Australia but throughout the entire Anglosphere.

Deracinated Statism versus the Ancient British Constitution

For their part, constitutional jurists committed to the preservation of a free society should begin at once to consider how the ethnic patriotism of a reigning monarch could be reconciled with his role and responsibilities within the Australian constitutional order. Analysis of that issue must begin from the premise that the King is *not* the Australian head of *state* — that function is performed by the governor-general.[30] This proposition — a staple item in Australians for Constitutional Monarchy's intellectual armoury — is sound as far as it goes, but it does rather beg the question of what the King *is*. The best answer is that she is the head (or sovereign) of a *society*, one extending far beyond the territorial limits of any single state. The most salient feature of that society is its overwhelmingly British, ethnocultural character. Though governments and, today, even the King, are loath to admit it, the British monarch is the *de facto* and even *de jure* head of a globe-girdling ethnic community. But the ethnic solidarity, much less the constitutional unity, of that community can never be taken for granted. Nor can it be assumed that the continued passivity of the reigning monarch is a permanent feature of the constitutional landscape. Almost by definition,

---

30 David Smith, "The Governor-General Is Our Head of State," *Quadrant* 48(7) (July–August 2004); http://www.quadrant.org.au/php/archive_details_list.php?article_id=871.

the sovereign possesses the power to *decide* and the capacity to *act* in exceptional circumstances to save his people.³¹

The king has always been the *parens patriae*, the father of his country. That kinship metaphor is deeply entrenched in the constitutional and legal history of the British dominions. It implies that the king could be held morally, perhaps even legally, accountable should he fail to defend the interests of his ethnic family against a clear and present danger. Unfortunately, regal breaches of ethnic loyalty are not at all unknown. Indeed, in her 2004 Christmas broadcast, Queen Elizabeth II celebrated the Third World invasion of the British homeland. Lending her authority to the multiracialist dogma that "diversity is indeed a strength and not a threat," Her Majesty even took a swipe at those "extremists at home" who posed the only apparent danger to "peaceful and steady progress in our society of differing cultures and heritage."³²

Clearly, Queen Elizabeth failed to recognize her duty of loyalty to her coethnics. Even so, the people of the British diaspora should retain their historic allegiance to the Crown. Sooner or later, the King or one of his heirs and successors will be forced to recognize that the fate of the hereditary British monarchy is inseparably linked to the ethnic constitution of a particular people. If not, and the managerial classes continue their relentless campaign to detach the British (or the Australian) state from the British (or the Anglo-Australian nation, the monarchy is doomed.

It follows that the British monarch speaks not just for himself or even for his subjects in the here and now; he must also give voice to the needs and interests of the dead and the unborn—but "not *any* dead and unborn: only those who belong" to the cross-generational, pre-political community constituting the British ethny in the United Kingdom and the old white Commonwealth. Not being elected by

---

31 Schmitt, 5.
32 http://www.royal.gov.uk/output/Page3624.asp.

popular vote, the monarch cannot be understood as representing the interests of the present generation. Speaking for absent generations, monarchs "are, in a very real sense, the voice of history." There is a spiritual dimension to the kingly office that cannot be replicated, much less usurped, by modern governments managing mundane and material affairs of state in pursuit of yet another short-term electoral mandate. Indeed, it is precisely because the ancestral authority — literally, the genetic legitimacy — of the British Crown transcends the temporal powers of government that republicans want to rid themselves of it. They know, if the King does not, that the fate of the monarchy is bound up with the history and destiny of the British ethny.[33] Fortunately, that history is not yet a closed book.

So long as the British monarchy survives, the succession of a Patriot King, or even its widely perceived possibility, could set the Australian Republican Movement (and its corporate sponsors) back on their heels. If Bolingbroke was right, "a king can, easily to himself and without violence to his people, renew the spirit of liberty in their minds."[34] Kings can quicken the dead letter of the old constitution. To confirm that proposition one need only imagine how the republicanism debate in Australia would be transformed were the King or Prince William to champion the constitutional unity of the British peoples. No doubt any such breach of convention would be met with a firestorm of outrage. Our political class expects the royal family to conform to a rigid code of personal and political *behaviour*. But, for just that reason, a patriot prince refusing to remain silent in the face of vital threats to the common interests of the monarchy and his people would demonstrate that freedom of *action* is open to any citizen possessing the courage of his convictions.

In seeking to renew the freedoms of the ancient British constitution in a modern Australia, a Patriot King would move beyond a sterile

---

33   Cf. "In Defence of the Nation," in Roger Scruton, *The Philosopher on Dover Beach* (South Bend, Indiana: St Augustine's Press, 1998).

34   Bolingbroke, 251.

and backward-looking defence of the past. Instead, a patriot prince would inspire a forward-looking reconstruction of a British, or, more broadly, Anglo-American, civilization. By helping us to recover our historic identity as British peoples, such a prince would inspire efforts to establish closer ties with our natural allies in the English-speaking world, including the most important British-derived nation, the USA.

At present, the King presides over a Commonwealth that has expanded its membership to the point of absurdity. A British Commonwealth that includes Mozambique but not the USA will be patently irrelevant to the future of Anglo-American civilization. Of course, those hostile to the British ethny don't much care. Managerialist republican visions for the future depend on the deliberate devaluation of our British past. Australia's future, many believe, lies in Asia. Meanwhile, their equally Anglophobic counterparts in the UK long to submerge themselves, once again, in Europe. In any case, history, politics, and culture must be subordinated to geography and economics.

Like Turkey, which cannot decide whether to join Europe or remain part of Islamic civilization, Australia has become a "torn country,"[35] split asunder by the deepening division between cosmopolitans and parochials, the "anywhere" versus the "somewhere" people. But, in a curious twist, it is the cosmopolitan, republican elites who have promoted the most parochial understanding of citizenship, carving up the Anglosphere into sovereign states, whose peoples are deemed to be foreigners to each other, despite their common origin in the British diaspora. A Patriot King would help us to see over the walls that governments have erected around us.

Governments have an obvious interest in ensuring that people owe no allegiance to any authority above and beyond the corporate state. For much of the twentieth century, state-building took the place of empire-building, much less nation-building. The appearance of a Patriot King would restore the true image of the British Commonwealth as

---

35 See Samuel Huntington, *The Clash of Civilizations and the Remaking of World Order* (New York: Simon & Schuster, 1996): 138–54.

an association of free people "united by one common interest and animated by one common spirit." A patriot prince would no longer aid and abet the division of the Anglosphere into separate, mutually indifferent, and increasingly hollow nationalities. Instead, he will "endeavor to unite them, and to be himself the center of their union."[36] It is not at all obvious that Australians, Canadians, and New Zealanders have become freer through the systematic obliteration of their common law status as free-born British subjects.

Both the King and his most loyal subjects must now bend the knee before statist definitions of national identity. ACM is always careful to present the monarchy as an Australian institution. One can, of course, point out that Australia is still British in a formal or at least a residual sense by virtue of its allegiance to the Crown and that most of its people trace their origins back to the United Kingdom. But this cuts no ice with officialdom, not even with His Majesty's judges in the High Court of Australia. In their newly minted vision of an autolegitimating state, the Constitution creates the nation, not the other way round.[37]

Given the current ideological climate, one can hardly fault the monarch for remaining silent in the face of endless insulting references to our "foreign" King. In fact, the King is no more foreign to Australia than the spirit of the ancient British constitution, without which the formal, black-letter text of the Commonwealth of Australia Constitution Act 1901 (Imp) could never have sprung into life. But if even the King is not willing to do battle with the enemies of the ancient constitution, small wonder that ordinary citizens sometimes give up the ghost. Indeed, many now feel like strangers in their own land. To resist the massed wealth and power of the political, economic, and cultural elites railroading us towards a republic is no easy task. Yet there can be no doubt that our future as a free people hangs in the balance.

---

36 Bolingbroke, 258.
37 *Sue v Hill* (1999) 199 CLR 462.

Doubts over our fidelity to the original principles of constitutional liberty became unavoidable once the creation of an Australian republic was touted as the first step towards full membership in a new regional polity. Under the Keating Labor government, it seemed that Australia was ready to defect from the West. Indeed, postmodernist republicanism already assumes that the constitution of our Asian future will not be a liberal democracy on any European or Anglo-American model. Alastair Davidson, for example, admits frankly that we may have to jettison a basic premise of Western constitutionalism, namely, the presence of citizens capable of thinking for themselves. Australians, he says, "will have to come to terms with an ideal of Confucian origin that says that wisdom teaches men and women to fit in and that life is suffering." Alone in Asia, Australians will have to "accept what Montesquieu called despotism."[38]

The Civilizing Mission of a Patriot King

Neither the republic nor the Asianization of Australia is inevitable. Moreover, Australian republican rhetoric is fixated on an obsolescent model of sovereign statehood and national independence. International politics is in fact no longer dominated by power struggles between independent nation-states exercising sovereign control over territory, resources, and populations. Even the ideological struggles of the Cold War era have given way to deeper cultural cleavages between civilizations.

According to Samuel Huntington, Australia sits near the intersection of several geopolitical fault lines. Asia is not a homogeneous entity. It is divided between Sinic, Buddhist, Hindu, and Japanese civilizations, not to mention the Islamic and Orthodox countries also to be found there. The "strange multiplicity" of Asia offers new opportunities for trade, commerce, and intercourse but it also poses a

---

38 Alastair Davidson, *From Subject to Citizen: Australian Citizenship in the Twentieth Century* (Cambridge: Cambridge University Press, 1997): 286.

perennial danger to Anglo-Australian civilization. Whatever else they may be, Asian peoples are overwhelmingly non-Western and, not infrequently, anti-Western to boot. Australia, by contrast, is part of the globe-girdling Anglosphere, still the most dynamic and powerful element within Western civilization. It would be an unmistakable sign of Western weakness were Australia to drift away from its ancient constitutional mooring into the vortex of inter-Asian rivalries. A patriot prince will challenge the ideological hegemony enjoyed by deracinated Australian republicans eager to "bandwagon with rising non-Western civilizations."[39]

In a new world order marked by pervasive conflict between cultures and civilizations, it makes little strategic sense for the Australian people to renounce their (distinctively Anglo-American) Western identity. Australia is not alone in the world. The Crown can act to reinvigorate the ethnocultural community uniting us with English Canada, New Zealand, the United Kingdom and above all, the Anglo-American core nation of the USA. Indeed, a patriot prince would crown his reign with everlasting glory by reawakening American citizens to the British roots of their own proudly independent, if increasingly incoherent, sense of nationhood.

A modern patriot prince, Bolingbroke reminds us, would "deem the union of his subjects his greatest advantage." Now, the fissiparous forces of disunity are in the ascendancy. That is why a Patriot King would be today, as in the eighteenth century: "the most powerful of all reformers; for he is himself a sort of standing miracle, so rarely seen and so little understood that the sure effect of his appearance will be admiration and love in every honest breast, confusion and terror to every guilty conscience, but submission and resignation in all."[40]

To a Patriot King, the governments of the dominions would appear as so many factions inhabiting a common civilization. Bolingbroke

---

39 Huntington, 151–54.
40 Bolingbroke, 259, 251.

maintained that: "In whatever light we view the divided state of a people, there is none in which these divisions will appear incurable, nor a union of the members of a great community with one another, and with their head, unattainable."[41]

Precisely because nothing can be more uncommon than a Patriot King, he may be able to accomplish what common sense tells us is improbable or even impossible. Once he succeeds to the throne, nothing less than the hearts of his far-flung people "will content such a prince; nor will he think his throne established, till it is established there." Nowadays Australia is a country whose "people is divided about submission to their prince."[42] Unity can be restored only when a patriot prince demonstrates that allegiance to the British Crown enhances, rather than diminishes the dignity of Australian citizenship.

One hopes that Bolingbroke figures prominently in the education of Prince William, his young heirs and their successors. But all of us should heed Bolingbroke's advice to do everything we can to become the sort of people worthy of a Patriot King. We must prepare ourselves for great changes in the world and in ourselves. Bolingbroke predicted that, after the succession of a Patriot King, the people would remain outwardly the same but "the difference of their sentiments will almost persuade them that they are changed into different beings."[43]

Conclusion

The appearance of a patriot prince would be a miracle indeed. But those who pray for such a deliverance must not neglect such means as are in their own power "to keep the cause of reason, of virtue and of liberty alive." The blessing of a patriot prince might indeed "be withheld from

---

41 Ibid., 269–70.
42 Ibid., 264–65.
43 Ibid., 251.

us" but to "deserve at least that it be granted to us, let us prepare to receive it, to improve it, and to co-operate with it."[44]

Were a patriot prince to campaign in defence of the monarchy, he would be subjected to a raging torrent of criticism and abuse. Yet when a good prince is seen "to suffer with the people, and in some measure for them...many advantages would accrue to him." For one thing, the cause of the British peoples generally "and his own cause would be made the same by their common enemies."[45]

What is the nature of that cause? In short, a patriot prince will call forth a spirit of resistance to both managerial statism and the abstract universalism of the capitalist marketplace. He will do everything in his power to civilize those too often wild and amoral forces. But, unlike the long-awaited Australian republic, the appearance of a Patriot King is not inevitable. Indeed, only a people whose lost liberties are restored to memory will recognize his coming as an opportunity to reshape their allegedly preordained future.

The tables must be turned on statist republicans everywhere in the Anglosphere. They aim to corner the market on both cosmopolitan tolerance and national pride. All defenders of the monarchy must therefore cast the republican movement in a new light. Behind the progressive face of official republicanism lie the sordid realities of worldly ambition, class privilege, and the pursuit of power. Considered in the cold light of class analysis, a republican victory would enthrone the overbearing self-importance and ideological zeal of shortsighted provincial elites willing to sacrifice the genetic interests of their own people in return for a mess of postmodernist pottage.

Sociologically speaking, republicans represent the local branch plant managers and bureaucratic nodes of a transnational corporate state system ever more dependent upon the inscrutable workings of the divine economy. Having embraced the materialist religion of

---

44 Ibid., 222.

45 Ibid., 239.

humanity, republicans rush to renounce their historical roots and traditional allegiances, thereby subverting the constitutionalist culture of mixed monarchy. Playing an important supporting role in the managerial revolution of our time, an all-pervasive, creeping republicanism is steadily deconstructing the fabric of British civilization.

We no longer publicly call upon God to save the King. The ritual absence of the monarch from everyday life is but one more sign that we are no longer a serious people. Forswearing the faith of our fathers, we surrender our bodies to the state and our souls to the gospel of wealth. In the end, a Patriot King may have to save *us*. Remember, though: a king is, indeed, like unto God; he cannot save those who will not save themselves.[46]

---

46 Cf. "James I on monarchy: speech to Parliament, 21 March 1610," in J. P. Kenyon, *The Stuart Constitution: Documents and Commentary* (Cambridge: Cambridge University Press, 1966): 12–14.

OTHER BOOKS PUBLISHED BY ARKTOS

Virginia Abernethy	Born Abroad
Sri Dharma Pravartaka Acharya	The Dharma Manifesto
Joakim Andersen	Rising from the Ruins
Winston C. Banks	Excessive Immigration
Stephen Baskerville	Who Lost America?
Alfred Baeumler	Nietzsche: Philosopher and Politician
Alain de Benoist	Beyond Human Rights
	Carl Schmitt Today
	The Ideology of Sameness
	The Indo-Europeans
	Manifesto for a European Renaissance
	On the Brink of the Abyss
	The Problem of Democracy
	Runes and the Origins of Writing
	View from the Right (vol. 1–3)
Armand Berger	Tolkien, Europe, and Tradition
Arthur Moeller van den Bruck	Germany's Third Empire
Matt Battaglioli	The Consequences of Equality
Kerry Bolton	The Perversion of Normality
	Revolution from Above
	Yockey: A Fascist Odyssey
Isac Boman	Money Power
Charles William Dailey	The Serpent Symbol in Tradition
Ricardo Duchesne	Faustian Man in a Multicultural Age
Alexander Dugin	Ethnos and Society
	Ethnosociology
	Eurasian Mission
	The Fourth Political Theory
	The Great Awakening vs the Great Reset
	Last War of the World-Island
	Politica Aeterna
	Political Platonism
	Putin vs Putin
	The Rise of the Fourth Political Theory
	Templars of the Proletariat
	The Theory of a Multipolar World
Daria Dugina	A Theory of Europe
Edward Dutton	Race Differences in Ethnocentrism
Mark Dyal	Hated and Proud
Clare Ellis	The Blackening of Europe
Koenraad Elst	Return of the Swastika
Julius Evola	The Bow and the Club
	Fascism Viewed from the Right
	A Handbook for Right-Wing Youth
	Metaphysics of Power
	Metaphysics of War
	The Myth of the Blood
	Notes on the Third Reich

OTHER BOOKS PUBLISHED BY ARKTOS

	Pagan Imperialism
	Recognitions
	A Traditionalist Confronts Fascism
GUILLAUME FAYE	*Archeofuturism*
	Archeofuturism 2.0
	The Colonisation of Europe
	Convergence of Catastrophes
	Ethnic Apocalypse
	A Global Coup
	Prelude to War
	Sex and Deviance
	Understanding Islam
	Why We Fight
DANIEL S. FORREST	*Suprahumanism*
ANDREW FRASER	*Dissident Dispatches*
	Reinventing Aristocracy in the Age of Woke Capital
	The WASP Question
GÉNÉRATION IDENTITAIRE	*We are Generation Identity*
PETER GOODCHILD	*The Taxi Driver from Baghdad*
	The Western Path
PAUL GOTTFRIED	*War and Democracy*
PETR HAMPL	*Breached Enclosure*
PORUS HOMI HAVEWALA	*The Saga of the Aryan Race*
LARS HOLGER HOLM	*Hiding in Broad Daylight*
	Homo Maximus
	Incidents of Travel in Latin America
	The Owls of Afrasiab
RICHARD HOUCK	*Liberalism Unmasked*
A. J. ILLINGWORTH	*Political Justice*
INSTITUT ILIADE	*For a European Awakening*
	Guardians of Heritage
ALEXANDER JACOB	*De Naturae Natura*
JASON REZA JORJANI	*Artemis Unveiled*
	Closer Encounters
	Erosophia
	Faustian Futurist
	Iranian Leviathan
	Lovers of Sophia
	Novel Folklore
	Philosophy of the Future
	Prometheism
	Promethean Pirate
	Prometheus and Atlas
	Psychotron
	Uber Man
	World State of Emergency
HENRIK JONASSON	*Sigmund*
EDGAR JULIUS JUNG	*The Significance of the German Revolution*

OTHER BOOKS PUBLISHED BY ARKTOS

Ruuben Kaalep & August Meister	Rebirth of Europe
Roderick Kaine	Smart and SeXy
Peter King	Here and Now
	Keeping Things Close
	On Modern Manners
James Kirkpatrick	Conservatism Inc.
Ludwig Klages	The Biocentric Worldview
	Cosmogonic Reflections
	The Science of Character
Andrew Korybko	Hybrid Wars
Pierre Krebs	Guillaume Faye: Truths & Tributes
	Fighting for the Essence
Julien Langella	Catholic and Identitarian
John Bruce Leonard	The New Prometheans
Diana Panchenko	The Inevitable
Stephen Pax Leonard	The Ideology of Failure
	Travels in Cultural Nihilism
William S. Lind	Reforging Excalibur
	Retroculture
Pentti Linkola	Can Life Prevail?
Giorgio Locchi	Definitions
H. P. Lovecraft	The Conservative
Norman Lowell	Imperium Europa
Richard Lynn	Sex Differences in Intelligence
	A Tribute to Helmut Nyborg (ed.)
John MacLugash	The Return of the Solar King
Charles Maurras	The Future of the Intelligentsia &
	For a French Awakening
John Harmon McElroy	Agitprop in America
Michael O'Meara	Guillaume Faye and the Battle of Europe
	New Culture, New Right
Michael Millerman	Beginning with Heidegger
Dmitry Moiseev	The Philosophy of Italian Fascism
Maurice Muret	The Greatness of Elites
Brian Anse Patrick	The NRA and the Media
	Rise of the Anti-Media
	The Ten Commandments of Propaganda
	Zombology
Tito Perdue	The Bent Pyramid
	Journey to a Location
	Lee
	Morning Crafts
	Philip
	The Sweet-Scented Manuscript
	William's House (vol. 1–4)
John K. Press	The True West vs the Zombie Apocalypse
Raido	A Handbook of Traditional Living (vol. 1–2)

OTHER BOOKS PUBLISHED BY ARKTOS

P R Reddall	*Towards Awakening*
Claire Rae Randall	*The War on Gender*
Steven J. Rosen	*The Agni and the Ecstasy*
	The Jedi in the Lotus
Nicholas Rooney	*Talking to the Wolf*
Richard Rudgley	*Barbarians*
	Essential Substances
	Wildest Dreams
Ernst von Salomon	*It Cannot Be Stormed*
	The Outlaws
Werner Sombart	*Traders and Heroes*
Piero San Giorgio	*Giuseppe*
	Survive the Economic Collapse
	Surviving the Next Catastrophe
Sri Sri Ravi Shankar	*Celebrating Silence*
	Know Your Child
	Management Mantras
	Patanjali Yoga Sutras
	Secrets of Relationships
George T. Shaw (ed.)	*A Fair Hearing*
Fenek Solère	*Kraal*
	Reconquista
Oswald Spengler	*The Decline of the West*
	Man and Technics
Richard Storey	*The Uniqueness of Western Law*
Tomislav Sunic	*Against Democracy and Equality*
	Homo Americanus
	Postmortem Report
	Titans are in Town
Askr Svarte	*Gods in the Abyss*
Hans-Jürgen Syberberg	*On the Fortunes and Misfortunes of Art in Post-War Germany*
Abir Taha	*Defining Terrorism*
	The Epic of Arya (2nd ed.)
	Nietzsche is Coming God, or the Redemption of the Divine
	Verses of Light
Jean Thiriart	*Europe: An Empire of 400 Million*
Bal Gangadhar Tilak	*The Arctic Home in the Vedas*
Dominique Venner	*Ernst Jünger: A Different European Destiny*
	For a Positive Critique
	The Shock of History
Hans Vogel	*How Europe Became American*
Markus Willinger	*A Europe of Nations*
	Generation Identity
Alexander Wolfheze	*Alba Rosa*
	Globus Horribilis
	Rupes Nigra